PN 6112 .B4 Vol. 1
Bentley, Eric Russell
From the Modern Repertoire.

from the

MODERN REPERTOIRE

Series One

EDITED BY ERIC BENTLEY

From the MODERN REPERTOIRE

Series One

INDIANA UNIVERSITY PRESS

BLOOMINGTON

Manufactured in the United States of America

FIFTH PRINTING 1965

For William Carlos Williams

who has promised me he will
write more plays

Contents

Preface

An anthology, these days, is something that needs apologizing for, especially an anthology of modern drama. So many exist already: does not every college sophomore know the bulky double-columned tome containing *Hedda Gabler, The Lower Depths,* Galsworthy, Maxwell Anderson, complete with bibliographies and dates? Nothing is put into these collections that might corrupt the young; sex must not be candid and politics must not be revolutionary. Nor must the secret leak out that anything has happened to dramatic art since 1920. The test of a play's reality is whether or not it reaches Broadway and stays there. Expressionism, Epic Theatre, Poetic Drama? Highbrow fads.

Sophomores are not the only people to whom modern drama remains almost entirely unknown. Professional theatre people are equally ignorant. Gradually, in the course of decades, serious playwrights have built up a remarkable repertoire; but it is not in use. Even the oldest of the moderns are known in the theatre by two or three pieces rather arbitrarily selected from the corpus of their works. The commercially active repertoire is small and stereotyped. Theatre people are interested, on the one hand, in the ephemeral scripts of the moment and, on the other, in a few fixed standbys like *Hamlet* and *The School for Scandal.* In such circumstances even the standbys are only museum pieces.

Wherever possible, the repertoire must be broadened. This anthology is a small contribution to such a broadening. It is a sampling of that remarkable modern repertoire which lies buried in libraries. To most theatregoers most of the plays here reprinted will be unfamiliar. Yet every play in the collection is considered as something written for the stage. Every play in the collection has, in fact, at some time or other been staged. I reprint each play in the hope that someone will be inspired to stage it again. This is not to say that the volume is not meant for the reader. Every good play is at home both on the stage and in the study.

Naturally, playwrights vary in the degree to which they utilize stage effects and in the degree to which they depend on them. But I know of no play which depends mainly on non-verbal effects and which is considered great either by myself or by consensus of critical opinion. Even the degree to which an artist uses the resources of his medium is no index of merit—contrary to an assumption pretty common in all fields since Lessing's *Laoköon.* Strindberg was not a better playwright when he used many extraordinary stage resources in his dream plays than when he used "mere dialogue" in his naturalistic pieces. For economy is just as much an aesthetic principle as variety.

Not that there is anything to be said *against* the use of non-verbal theatre arts. Some of the plays in this book exemplify their most rich and wonderful use. The merit of a play is in neither direct or inverse ratio to such use. It is quite independent of it. All one complains of is that the argument for "theatre arts" in our time has too often been a rationalization of commercialism, a strategy by which you can make mere theatricality seem important.

The plays in this book were chosen above all as good plays, as interesting pieces of dramatic art, independent of all commercial and academic considerations. They are not chosen for their established or probable saleability (the commercial criterion), and they are not specimens of anything (the academic criterion). Of course, I shall be pleased if they sell. And if anyone wants me to, I can pretend that they are specimens. This collection, when you come to think of it, happens to be just as "representative" as those which are intended to be so: it "represents" a number of generations and countries, a number of genres (tragedy, comedy, etc.), a number of styles (realism, fantasy, etc.), a number of preoccupations (politics, sex, religion, history, etc.), at least two media (verse and prose), and the philosophies of as many schools as there are plays.

But the book is representative by accident—or at best only secondarily. Primarily and on purpose it is a group of plays that are interesting in themselves, interesting to readers, playgoers, actors, and directors. Interesting, above all perhaps, to such young writers as are interested in dramatic form. It might be asked if such writers exist any more. The colleges kill the writer's interest in drama by teaching him how to write Broadway plays. He may begin with an interest in expressing something about life in the dramatic mode. He ends, if the schools have their way, as the master of the tricks of a trade. If the schools do *not* have their way, he may become a serious writer, but, in that event, he writes poems and novels on the grounds that "the theatre is dead." Well, there is always plenty of deadness in the theatre, but a young writer should no more decline to write plays because they won't be done on Broadway than he should decline to write novels because they won't be accepted by the Book-of-the-Month Club. To be sure, we have got all our dramatic novels and dramatic poems out of the deflection of dramatic talent from the theatre. But why not a dramatic drama?

The theatre page of *The New York Times* is no more a history of modern drama than *The Publishers' Weekly* is a history of modern literature. Behind the swift succession of noisy successes there is a real history of literature, drama, and all the arts, there is a real—if not always a rich—tradition. The commercial theatre may subsist for some time on the clichés of the 19th century—there is still money in it—but the dramatic artist has known for years that certain forms are now exhausted. They have to be broken down, and new ones built up. The more highbrow commercial playwrights often ridicule all interest in dramatic form, and words like *aestheticism* and *formalism* come in very handy. Nevertheless, the study of form and the technique by which it is achieved does bring us very close to the essence of an art. One should view technique, in Mr. Mark Schorer's phrase, as discovery. An artist starts with raw material. Technique is the way in which he finds the shape and contour which will define the material and make it a work of art. Now shapes and contours in art have to be both fluid and firm. At one period, then, the artist will be struggling for firmness amid prevailing formlessness and flux. At another the forms have become rigid and he struggles for fluidity. Thus the forms are always changing, and the history of form is the history of an art.

It is hoped that the plays in this collection will help some writers to find their places in dramatic tradition. An anthology of modern drama should come down to the most recent work so that the young writer may work alongside his colleagues and learn from them. We live in an age when a young playwright may lose more than he gains by contact with the big theatrical institutions of London and New York. But no writer can live outside the creative tradition of writing. A serious playwright today can do without Broadway. He cannot do without the masters of drama. And for every writer, two sorts of masters are important: the supremely great of all periods and, second, the more original craftsmen of the years immediately preceding his own performance. This anthology has something to do with the second category.

The reasons why each play was chosen should become clear as the reader proceeds with the text and the notes. Obviously the choice could not be without arbitrariness; there are many other good plays. The great omission, of course, is that of the principal playwrights of the modern era: Ibsen, Strindberg, Chekhov, Shaw, and Pirandello. These, I submit, need not be anthologized. Anyone interested in modern drama at all will read them in the separate volumes of their work[1] that are more or less cheaply purchasable. An anthology of modern drama should be supplementary to such volumes.

This book, it will be noted, contains work by playwrights who live by one or two plays or whose work is not easily come by in separate volumes. It is at best a beginning; if it is well received, other volumes will follow.

---

[1]I have in mind *Eleven Plays of Ibsen* (Modern Library), *Plays of Strindberg*, 3 volumes (Luce), *Plays of Anton Chekhov* (Modern Library), *Nine Plays of Shaw* (Dodd, Mead), *Three Plays of Pirandello* (Dutton).

Acknowledgments

The preparation of this volume was made possible by a grant from the Graduate School of the University of Minnesota.

I have also to thank publishers, agents, and authors for their permission to reprint copyright materials.

The editor has made some changes in the English script of *Round Dance* (which the translator called *Hands Around*) and *The Threepenny Opera* (which Mr. Vesey called *A Penny for the Poor*).

E. B.

Fantasio

BY ALFRED DE MUSSET

Translated by MAURICE BARING

CHARACTERS

The King of Bavaria
The Prince of Mantua
Marinoni, *His Aide-de-camp*
Rutton, *The King's Secretary*
Fantasio, Spark, Facio, Hartman — *Young men of the town*
Officers, Pages, etc.
Elsbeth, *Daughter of the King of Bavaria*
An Attendant Lady, *Her Governess*

The Place: Munich

ACT I

SCENE I

(*The Court. The* KING, *surrounded by his Courtiers;* RUTTEN.)

THE KING. My friends, I announced to you some time ago the betrothal of my beloved daughter Elsbeth and the Prince of Mantua. The Prince is due to-day; this afternoon perhaps, at the latest to-morrow, he will be with us at the palace. I proclaim a general holiday; the prisons shall be opened, and the people shall pass the night in feasting. Rutten, where is my daughter?

(*The Courtiers withdraw.*)

RUTTEN. Your Majesty, she is in the park with her lady-in-waiting.

THE KING. Why have I not seen her already to-day? Has her approaching marriage saddened or gladdened her?

RUTTEN. I thought a certain sadness veiled the Princess' face, but where is the young girl who is not wistful on the eve of her wedding? The death of St. Jean distressed her.

THE KING. Do you think so? The death of my Fool! A hunchbacked droll who was half blind!

RUTTEN. The Princess loved him.

THE KING. Tell me, Rutten, you have seen the Prince; what manner of man is he? Alas! I am giving him what I hold dearest in the world, and I do not know him.

RUTTEN. I spent but a little time at Mantua.

THE KING. Be frank. Who can tell me the truth if not you?

RUTTEN. To speak frankly, your Majesty, I have nothing to tell about the character or the mind of the illustrious Prince.

THE KING. Is that true? You hesitate,—you, a courtier? If the Prince who is to be my son-in-law to-morrow had seemed to you to be worthy of the name, I can but think that this room would have resounded with flattering metaphors and extravagant praise. Have I made a mistake, my friend? Have I chosen wrongly?

RUTTEN. Your Majesty, they say the Prince is an exemplary monarch.

THE KING. Politics are like a spider's web, in which many wretched broken flies struggle; I will not dream of sacrificing my daughter's happiness to the interests of state.

(*They go out.*)

ACT I

SCENE II

(*A Street.* SPARK, HARTMAN, *and* FACIO, *drinking around a table.*)

HARTMAN. To-day is the wedding day of the Princess, let us therefore drink and smoke and make a noise.

FACIO. Let us mix with the crowds in the streets and put out torches on the heads of the citizens.

SPARK. No, let us smoke quietly.

HARTMAN. I will do nothing quietly; even if I have to be a clapper and to hang in the great bell of the Church, I must ring on such a holiday. Where the devil is Fantasio?

SPARK. Let us wait for him; let us do nothing without him.

FACIO. He is sure to find us. He belike is drinking in some haunt in the underworld. One last toast! (*He lifts his glass.*)

(*Enter an* OFFICER.)

OFFICER. Sirs, I beg you to withdraw a little, if you do not wish to be disturbed in your feasting.

HARTMAN. Why, sir?

THE OFFICER. The Princess is at this moment on the terrace, before you, and you will understand that it is unseemly that she should witness your roystering.

FACIO. This is intolerable!

SPARK. What does it matter if we laugh here or elsewhere? Who knows they may forbid us even to laugh? Be sure that comic persons dressed in green will spring up in every street of the town and beg us begone to the moon with our laughter.

(*Enter* MARINONI, *draped in a cloak.*)

SPARK. The Princess has never committed a despotic act in her life. God bless her! If she is angered at our laughter, it means that she must be sad, or that she is singing. Let us leave her in peace.

FACIO. Look, there is a man in a tattered cloak who is sniffing out for news. The gull wishes to talk to us.

MARINONI (*drawing near*). I am a stranger, gentlemen; can you tell me in whose honor is this feast?

SPARK. The feast is in honor of the marriage of the Princess Elsbeth.

MARINONI. Ah! She is a beautiful woman, I presume?

HARTMAN. As beautiful as you are handsome.

MARINONI. Beloved by her people, if I may say so, for methinks the city is illuminated?

HARTMAN. You are right, good stranger; all those lights which you see, as you have wisely remarked, are there for no other purpose than illumination.

MARINONI. I wished to ask if the Princess were the cause of all these manifestations.

HARTMAN. The sole cause, eloquent sir. We might all of us marry and then there would be not one sign of rejoicing in this ungrateful city.

MARINONI. Happy is the Princess who can win her people's love!

HARTMAN. Illuminations do not make people happy, dear simpleton. And yet the aforesaid Princess is as wayward as a shepherdess.

MARINONI. Really! Wayward, you say?

HARTMAN. I said it, dear stranger, I used the word, wayward.

(MARINONI *bows and retires.*)

FACIO. What on earth is this fellow driving at, with his Italian jargon? He is now drawing near the others. I would put him down as a spy a mile off.

HARTMAN. He is not a spy, he is a fool.

SPARK. Here is Fantasio.

HARTMAN. What is the matter with him? He is strutting about like a Big Whig on the Bench. If I am not much mistaken some mad idea is simmering in his head.

FACIO. Well, friend, how shall we spend this auspicious night?

FANTASIO (*entering*): We will spend it anywise, except in a new adventure.

FACIO. I was saying that we ought to mingle with the populace there and snatch some fun.

FANTASIO. We should have false noses and crackers.

HARTMAN. And kiss the girls, and pull the citizens by their coat tails, and break the lamps. Let us be off! That's settled.

FANTASIO. Once upon a time there was a King of Persia. . . .

HARTMAN. Come, Fantasio.

FANTASIO. No, not I.

HARTMAN. Why not?

FANTASIO. Give me a glass of wine. (*He drinks.*)

HARTMAN. The month of May is on your cheeks.

FANTASIO. Yes; and the month of January is in my heart. My head is like an old fireless hearth; there is nothing in it but wind and ashes. Oh! (*He sits down.*) how it saddens me to see all the world making merry. I could wish that that great heavy sky were an immense nightcap which could be pulled down to the ears over this absurd city and all its foolish inhabitants. Please tell me some old jest—something thoroughly stale.

HARTMAN. Why?

FANTASIO. To make me laugh. Nothing that people invent can raise a smile from me. Perhaps something which I know by heart might amuse me.

HARTMAN. You seem to me a shade misanthrophic, slightly inclined to melancholy.

FANTASIO. Not at all: the truth is that I have just left my mistress.

FACIO. Will you be one of us: yes or no?

FANTASIO. I will join your party if you will join mine; let us stay here a little and talk of one thing and another, and gaze at our new clothes.

FACIO. Certainly not. If you are tired of standing up I am tired of sitting down. I must have some exercise in the fresh air.

FANTASIO. I feel incapable of effort. I am going to smoke under the chestnut trees with my good friend Spark; he will keep me company. Am I not right, Spark?

SPARK. As you please.

HARTMAN. In that case, good-bye. We are going to see the festivities.

(HARTMAN *and* FACIO *go out.* FANTASIO *sits down with* SPARK.)

FANTASIO. Look at that sunset—what a failure! Nature is beneath contempt to-night. Just look at that valley down there, at those four or five pitiable clouds scaling the mountain. I could paint water-colors like that when I was twelve years old in the covers of my school books.

SPARK. What good tobacco! What excellent beer!

FANTASIO. I must be wearying you, Spark?

SPARK. No, why?

FANTASIO. Well, judging by the way you are wearying me. Do you mind not seeing the same face every day? What on earth will Hartman and Facio do at that merry-making?

SPARK. They are both of them full of life, and they could not sit still.

FANTASIO. The *Arabian Nights*! How wonderful! How magnificent! Oh, Spark, dear Spark! If you could but waft me to China! If only I could escape from my skin for an hour or two! If I could be that man over there who is passing by!

SPARK. I think that would be a little difficult.

FANTASIO. That man who is passing by is enchanting; look at him! What beautiful silk breeches he is wearing. Look at the beautiful red flowers on his waistcoat! The trinkets on his watch chain are dangling on his belly to show off the tails of his coat, which are flapping over his calves. I am sure that in that man's head there are a thousand ideas that are quite alien to me; that he has an especial flavor. Alas! Men always say the same things to one another; they all of them almost always express the same ideas; but inside each of these isolated machines there are many secret windings and recesses! Every man carries a whole world within him! A world which no one knows, it is born and it dies in silence! What a loneliness there is in all these human bodies!

SPARK. Drink, idle one, instead of brooding!

FANTASIO. There is only one thing that has given me pleasure during the last three days; my creditors have a writ against me, and if I set foot in my house four bailiffs will come and seize me by the scruff of the neck.

SPARK. That indeed is a good joke! Where will you sleep to-night?

FANTASIO. In the house of the first damsel I shall encounter. Do you know that my furniture is to be sold to-morrow morning? We will buy some of it, won't we?

SPARK. Are you hard up for money, Henry? Do you need my purse?

FANTASIO. Idiot! If I had not any money I would not be in debt. I have a mind to take a ballet-dancer as a mistress.

SPARK. That would weary you to death.

FANTASIO. Not at all: my mind would be filled with pirouettes and white satin shoes; there would be a glove for me on the balustrade of the balcony from the first of January to St. Sylvester, and I would hum clarinet solos in my dreams, until I died from overeating strawberries in the arms of my beloved. Have you noticed one thing, Spark: that we have no status, we have no profession?

SPARK. Is that saddening you?

FANTASIO. There is not such a thing as a melancholy fencing-master.

SPARK. I think you are sated with everything.

FANTASIO. To be satiated, my friend, one must have tasted much.

SPARK. Well?

FANTASIO. Where do you wish me to go? Look at this old smoky city. There are in it no squares, streets or alleys which I have not trodden over and over again. There are no paving stones which I have not worn out with my broken down heels, no houses where I do not know who is the girl or the old woman whose foolish face is always at the window; I cannot go a step without retracing yesterday's steps. Well, my dear friend, this town is as nothing to my mind. Every corner in *that* is still more familiar to me; all the streets and windings of my imagination are a hundred times more footworn, I have wandered there in a many hundred more directions; in this dilapidated mind, I, the only inhabitant! I have got drunk in all its inns; I have driven through it as a King in his gilded coach; I have trotted through it as an honest citizen on a quiet mule; and I do not dare now even enter it as a thief with a dark lantern.

SPARK. I cannot understand this perpetual introspection; for instance, when I smoke, my thoughts become like tobacco smoke; when I drink my thoughts turn into Spanish wine or Flemish beer; when I kiss my mistress's hand, she steals through the ends of her delicate fingers and thrills my whole being with an electric fire; the scent of a flower is enough to divert me, and the slightest of Nature's works enough to turn me into a bee, and to set me ahovering here and there with an ever fresh delight.

FANTASIO. Let us face the truth: Can you fish, Spark?

SPARK. I can do anything, if it amuses me.

FANTASIO. Even catch the moon with your teeth?

SPARK. That would not amuse me.

FANTASIO. How do you know? To catch the moon with one's teeth is no mean sport. Let us go and play at *trente et quarante.*

SPARK. No, really.

FANTASIO. Why not?

SPARK. Because we should lose our money.

FANTASIO. Good gracious! What are you thinking of? You are never tired of inventing some new torture for the mind! Must you see everything in the darkest colors, wretch? Lose your money! Have you then neither faith nor hope in God in your heart? You are a horrible atheist, capable of drying up my heart and of shattering all my illusions—I, who am full of sap and youth!

(*He begins to dance.*)

SPARK. It is true, there are moments when I would not swear that you are sane.

FANTASIO (*still dancing*). Give me a bell—a crystal bell!

SPARK. Why a bell?

FANTASIO. Because Jean Paul said that a man absorbed by a great thought was like a diver in his diving bell in the midst of the boundless ocean. I have no diving bell, Spark, no bell, and I am walking like Jesus Christ on the waters.

SPARK. You had better be a journalist or a man of letters, Henry; it is still the best way of defeating misanthropy, and deadening the imagination.

FANTASIO. Ah, I would like to have a passion for a lobster, for a grisette, Spark! Let us try to build a house for us two.

SPARK. Why don't you write down all your dreams; they would make a pretty collection.

FANTASIO. A sonnet is better than a long poem, and a glass of wine is better than a sonnet. (*He drinks.*)

SPARK. Why do you not travel? Go to Italy?

FANTASIO. I have been there.

SPARK. Well, do you not think it is a beautiful country?

FANTASIO. It is full of flies, as big as cock-chafers; and they sting you all night long.

SPARK. Go to France.

FANTASIO. There is no Rhine-wine in Paris.

SPARK. Go to England.

FANTASIO. I am there already. Do the Englishmen possess a country of their own? I would just as soon see them here as in their own home.

SPARK. Go to the devil, then!

FANTASIO. Ah, if there were a devil in heaven! If only there were a hell!

I would blow out my brains to go and see all that: What a miserable thing is man! He cannot jump out of the window without breaking his legs! To be obliged to play the violin for ten years before he can become a passable musician! Always having to learn! To learn to be a painter, to learn to be a groom, to learn to make an omelet! Do you know, Spark, I sometimes would like to stand on the parapet and watch the river flowing and to count one, two, three, four, five, six, seven, and so on, until the day of my death!

SPARK. What you are saying would make many people laugh; it fills me with horror; it is the whole history of our century. Eternity is like a great eyrie, from which the centuries like young eagles have flown away, one after another, and soared through the heavens and disappeared; ours in its turn came to the edge of the nest, but they clipped its wings, and it is waiting for death, as it gazes on to the abyss into which it no longer dares to dive.

FANTASIO (*singing*). 'You call me your life; only call me your soul.
For the soul is immortal, and life but a day.'

Do you know a more heavenly ballad than that? It is Portuguese. I have never thought of it without wishing to fall in love with some one.

SPARK. Who, for instance?

FANTASIO. I don't know. Some girl as beautiful, as luscious, as all the women of Mieris; something as soft as the west wind, as pale as the beams of the moon; something pensive like those little servant girls in the inns of Flemish pictures, who hand the stirrup-cup to a traveler in top boots straight as a staff on a great white horse. What a beautiful thing is the stirrup-cup! A young woman at the door, the fire just visible at the end of the room, supper laid on the table, the children asleep; all the quiet, the peace, the contemplation of life, in the corner of the picture! And there, the man still panting, but upright in his saddle; he has just ridden twenty leagues; he has still thirty more leagues to go; a gulp of brandy and then good-bye! Beyond is the dark night; the ominous sky, the perilous forest; the good woman follows him with her eyes for a moment, and then, as she goes back to the fireside, she bestows on him the sublime alms of the poor: 'May God protect him!'

SPARK. If you were in love, Henry, you would be the happiest of men.

FANTASIO. There is no such thing now as Love, my friend. Religion, the nurse of love, is as dry as an old purse that holds but a battered penny. Love is a Host which must be broken by twain at the foot of an altar, and swallowed by them in a single kiss. There is no longer an altar, and there is no more love; long live Nature! There still is wine. (*He drinks.*)

SPARK. You will get drunk.

FANTASIO. I mean to get drunk! You have said it!

SPARK. Is it not a little late?

FANTASIO. What do you call late? Is noon-tide late? Is mid-night early? How do you reckon the day? Let us stay here, Spark, I beg of you. Let us drink; let us talk; let us talk philosophy, let us talk nonsense; let us talk politics; let us invent moves on the political chess-board; let us catch the cock-chafers that are buzzing round this candle, and pocket them. Do you know philosophically-speaking that steam-cannons are important?

SPARK. What do you mean?

FANTASIO. There was once upon a time a King who was so wise, so wise, so happy . . . so happy . . . .

SPARK. And then?

FANTASIO. He lacked only one thing, children. He had prayers said in all the mosques . . . .

SPARK. What are you driving at?

FANTASIO. I am thinking of my beloved *Arabian Nights.* That is how they all of them begin. Spark, I am drunk! I must do something mad! Tra-la, tra-la! Come, let us go. (*A funeral passes.*) Hullo, good people! Whom are you burying there? This is not the proper hour for a burial.

THE CARRIERS. We are burying St. Jean.

FANTASIO. Is St. Jean dead? The King's Fool is dead? Who has taken his place? The Minister of Justice?

THE CARRIERS. His place is vacant. You can take it, if you wish.

(*They go out.*)

SPARK. That is a rude remark which you have brought on yourself. What in the world made you stop those people?

FANTASIO. There was nothing insolent in what they said. That man gave me good advice and I mean to take it instantly.

SPARK. Do you mean to become the new Court Fool?

FANTASIO. To-night, if they will take me. As I cannot sleep at home I mean to treat myself to the royal comedy which will be played to-morrow, and to watch it from the royal box.

SPARK. Clever man! They will recognize you and throw you out. Are you not the late Queen's godson?

FANTASIO. How silly you are! I will put on a hump and a red wig, just as St. Jean used to wear, and no one will recognize me, even if I had a score of godfathers at my heels. (*He knocks at the door of a shop.*) Hullo, good fellow! Open the door if you are at home, you and your wife and your little dogs.

THE TAILOR (*opening the door of the shop*). What does your Lordship desire?

FANTASIO. Are you not the Court Tailor?

THE TAILOR. At your service.

FANTASIO. Is it you who used to make St. Jean's clothes?

THE TAILOR. Yes, sir.

FANTASIO. You knew him? You know whether his hump grew on his right or left shoulder? How he wore his clothes and his moustache, and the cut and color of his wig?

THE TAILOR. You are making fun of me, sir.

FANTASIO. I am not joking. Come into your shop, and if you do not wish to find poison to-morrow in your coffee be careful to be as a deaf-mute on everything that is about to come to pass.

(*He goes out with* THE TAILOR. SPARK *follows him.*)

ACT I

SCENE III

(*A tavern on the road to Munich.* THE PRINCE OF MANTUA, *and* MARINONI.)

THE PRINCE. Well, Colonel?

MARINONI. Your Highness?

THE PRINCE. Well, Marinoni?

MARINONI. She is melancholy, wayward, madly gay, an obedient daughter, and very fond of green peas.

THE PRINCE. Write that all down. I can only understand what I see in writing.

MARINONI (*writing*). mel-an-chol . . .

THE PRINCE. Do not write aloud; I have been brooding over an important scheme ever since we had dinner.

MARINONI. Here, your Highness, is what you have asked for.

THE PRINCE. Very well, I dub you my intimate friend; I know of no one in all my kingdom who has a better handwriting. Sit down a little way off. You think then, my friend, that you have some secret knowledge of the character of the Princess, my future wife?

MARINONI. Yes, your Highness. I have frequented the denizens of the palace, and in these tablets you will find the principal points of various conversations in which I took part.

THE PRINCE (*looking at himself in a hand mirror*). It seems to me that I am powdered like a base fellow.

MARINONI. The suit is magnificent.

THE PRINCE. What would you say, Marinoni, if your master were to don a simple olive-colored coat?

MARINONI. Your Highness is laughing at me.

THE PRINCE. No, Colonel, you must learn that your master is the most romantic of men.

MARINONI. Romantic, your Highness?

THE PRINCE. Yes, my friend—I have given you that title. The important scheme which has been simmering in my mind is a thing unheard of in my family. I mean to arrive at the Court of the King, my father-in-law, dressed as a simple aide-de-camp. Public rumor about the future Princess of Mantua, culled by a man of my household (and that man, Marinoni, yourself), is not enough. I wish to collect evidence myself.

MARINONI. Is that true, your Highness?

THE PRINCE. Do not be astonished. A man such as myself should have for an intimate friend none save a spirit of vast enterprise.

MARINONI. There seems to me to be but one objection to your Highness' plan.

THE PRINCE. What is it?

MARINONI. No one but the illustrious Prince, our Governor, could have imagined such a disguise. But if my gracious sovereign mingles with the staff, to whom will the King of Bavaria offer the splendid banquet which is to take place in the great hall?

THE PRINCE. You are right; if I disguise myself, someone would have to take my place. That is impossible, Marinoni; I had not thought of that.

MARINONI. Why impossible, your Highness?

THE PRINCE. I can abase the princely dignity so far as to the rank of a Colonel, but you cannot think I could ever consent to raise an ordinary *man* to my rank? Besides, do you think my future father-in-law would forgive me?

MARINONI. They say that the King is a man of sense and wit, and has a pleasant fancy.

THE PRINCE. Ah, I confess I abandon my scheme with regret. It would be tempting to come to the new Court without pomp and ceremony, to observe everything, to be presented to the Princess under a false name, and perhaps to win her heart! But my mind wanders. All that is impossible. Marinoni, my friend, try on my Court coat—I shall not be able to resist it.

MARINONI (*bowing*). Your Highness!

THE PRINCE. You think that future centuries will ever forget such doings?

MARINONI. Never, gracious Prince!

THE PRINCE. Come and try on my coat.

(*They go out.*)

ACT II

SCENE I

(*Enter* ELSBETH *and her* ATTENDANT LADY.)

THE LADY. My poor eyes have wept all day—have wept torrents.

ELSBETH. You have such a kind heart! I too loved St. Jean; he was so witty! He was no ordinary Court Fool!

THE LADY. To think that the poor man should go to heaven on the eve of your betrothal! The man who talked of nothing but you at dinner and supper, and all day long! He was so gay, so droll, that one came to love his very ugliness, and you couldn't help looking at him.

ELSBETH. Do not speak to me of my marriage! That is a still greater misfortune.

THE LADY. Do you not know that the Prince of Mantua arrives to-day? They say he is a very Amadis.

ELSBETH. What are you telling me, my dear? He is horrible and idiotic; everybody here is aware of that.

THE LADY. Is that true? They told me he was an Amadis.

ELSBETH. I never asked for an Amadis, my dear; but it is cruel at times to be a king's daughter. My father is the best of men; the marriage which he is arranging assures the peace of his kingdom; in return for it he will receive the people's blessing; but I, alas! will have his blessing, and nothing beside.

THE LADY. What sad things you are saying!

ELSBETH. If I were to refuse the prince, war would break out again; what a misfortune it is that treaties of peace are always signed with tears! Would that I were strong-minded, and could resign myself to marry the first comer at the need of the political situation! To be the mother of a people is a consolation for great hearts, but not for feeble minds. I am only a poor dreamer; perhaps your love stories are to blame—your pockets are always stuffed with them.

THE LADY. Gracious Heaven! Do not talk of it!

ELSBETH. I have known life little, and have dreamed much.

THE LADY. If the Prince of Mantua is what you say, God will not allow this event to come to pass, I am sure.

ELSBETH. You think so? God lets men act as they wish, my poor friend. And he takes no more notice of our complaints than of the bleating of a sheep.

THE LADY. I am sure that if you refuse the Prince, your father will not compel you to marry him.

ELSBETH. Most certainly he will not force me; and that is the reason why

I am sacrificing myself. Do you wish me to go to my father and tell him to cancel his plighted word, and with the stroke of a pen strike out his honored name on the contract which will make the happiness of thousands? What does it matter if he makes one woman unhappy? I allow my good father to be a good king.

(THE LADY *bursts into tears.*)

Do not weep for me, my dear! You would end by making me cry myself; and a royal betrothed must not have red eyes. Do not grieve about all this. After all, I shall be a Queen, and that is perhaps amusing; I shall enjoy my clothes, who knows? my coaches; my new court. Happily for princesses marriage means something more than a husband. Perhaps my wedding gifts will bring me happiness.

THE LADY. You are truly a sacrificial victim.

ELSBETH. Dear heart, let us be laughing at it now; we can cry when the time comes. They tell me that the Prince of Mantua is the most ridiculous creature on earth.

THE LADY. If St. Jean were here . . .

ELSBETH. Ah, St. Jean! St. Jean!

THE LADY. You loved him dearly, my child?

ELSBETH. It is curious; his soul was bound to mine by invisible threads which seemed to proceed from my own heart; I delighted in the fun he would make of my romantic ideas, while it is hard for me to endure many people who agree with me all too well; I do not know what there was about him, in his eyes, in his gestures, in the way he took snuff. He was a strange man; while he spoke to me I used to conjure up enchanting visions; his words gave life as by magic to the most strange things.

THE LADY. He was a real Triboulet.

ELSBETH. I do not know; but his wit shone like a diamond.

THE LADY. Here are some pages bustling about; I think that the Prince will appear before long; you must go back to the palace and dress.

ELSBETH. I beg of you, let me stay a little longer; go and get ready for me what I shall need; alas! my dear, I have not much time left for dreams!

THE LADY. Marvelous providence! Is it possible that this marriage must be, if it displeases you! Must a father sacrifice his daughter! The king will be another Jephtha if he allows it!

ELSBETH. Do not speak ill of my father; but go, my dear, and get ready what I need.

(THE LADY *goes out.*)

ELSBETH (*alone*). It seems to me that there is someone behind those thickets. Is it the ghost of my poor fool whom I see among those corn flowers sitting in the field? Answer me. Who are you? What are you doing there, picking flowers?

(*She walks towards a knoll.* FANTASIO *is sitting down, dressed as a jester with a hump and a wig.*)

FANTASIO. I am one who knows how to pick flowers, and I bid good-morrow to your beautiful eyes.

ELSBETH. What is the meaning of this dress? Who are you? Why are you counterfeiting with that large wig a man whom I was fond of? Are you a student in buffoonery?

FANTASIO. May it please your serene Highness, I am the King's new Fool; the major-domo has received me favorably; I have been introduced to the Groom of the Chambers; the scullions patronize me, ever since last night; and I am here humbly picking flowers until I pick up some wit.

ELSBETH. I do not think you will ever cull that flower.

FANTASIO. Why? Wit may come to an old man as well as to a young girl. It is sometimes so difficult to distinguish between wit and folly. The important thing is to talk a great deal; the worst pistol shot may hit a fly if he fires off seven hundred and eighty shots a minute; just as well as the most skilful shot who will only fire once or twice accurately. All I ask for is enough food to stay my stomach, and I shall watch my shadow in the sun to see if my wig grows.

ELSBETH. So you are clothed in the cast-off clothes of St. Jean? You are right to speak of your shadow; as long as you wear that costume, it will resemble him, I think, more than you.

FANTASIO. I am at this moment composing an elegy which will settle my fate.

ELSBETH. In what way?

FANTASIO. Either it will prove that I am the first man in the world, or it will be worth nothing. I am turning the universe topsy-turvy to set it into an acrostic; the moon, the sun and the stars, are fighting to get into my rhymes, like school-boys at the door of a theatre of blood and thunder plays.

ELSBETH. Poor man! To turn out wit at so much an hour! Have you no arms, no legs? Would you not do better to plow the earth, than your own brain?

FANTASIO. Poor little girl! What a trade you are about to ply. To marry an imbecile whom you have never seen! Have you neither heart nor head, and would you not do better to sell your clothes than your body?

ELSBETH. These are audacious words, Mr. Stranger!

FANTASIO. What is this flower called, please?

ELSBETH. Tulip. What do you wish to prove?

FANTASIO. A red tulip or a blue tulip?

ELSBETH. A blue one, I think.

FANTASIO. Not at all. It is a red tulip.

ELSBETH. Do you wish to dress up an old saw anew? It is not necessary. I know that we must never argue about tastes or colors.

FANTASIO. I am not arguing; I am telling you that this tulip is a red tulip, and yet I agree that it is blue.

ELSBETH. How do you make that fit?

FANTASIO. In the same way as your marriage contract is made to fit. Who is there under the sun who can know whether he is born red or blue? The tulips themselves do not know. Gardeners and lawyers make such extraordinary grafts that apples become pumpkins, and thistles fall from the jaw of an ass, to be bathed in the sauce on the silver plate of a bishop. This tulip which is here thought to be red; but they have given it in marriage; it is astonished at finding itself blue; so is the whole world forever changing in the hands of men; and poor Dame Nature must sometimes have a hearty laugh at herself as she beholds her eternal masquerade mirrored in her lakes and in her seas. Do you think that the garden of Eden was sweet with roses? It smelt but of green hay. The rose is a daughter of civilization; she is a lady of title, like you and me.

ELSBETH. The pale flower of the eglantine may grow into a rose, and a thistle may become an artichoke; but one flower cannot be transformed into another; so what does Nature care? One cannot change Nature; you can make her more beautiful, or kill her. The frailest violet would die sooner than yield if one tried by artificial means to change the shape of one single stamen.

FANTASIO. That is why I care more for a violet than for a king's daughter.

ELSBETH. There are certain things which even fools have no right to laugh at; if you listened to the conversation I had with my lady, mind your ears!

FANTASIO. Not my ears, my tongue. You are making a mistake; there is a flaw in the sense of your words.

ELSBETH. Make me no jests, if you wish to earn your pay, and do not compare me with tulips if you do not wish for a different reward.

FANTASIO. Who knows? A joke is a solace for many sorrows; and playing with words is one way of playing with thoughts, actions and human beings. Everything on earth is a joke, and it is as difficult to understand the look of a four year old child as all the gibberish of three modern dramas.

ELSBETH. It seems to me that you look at the earth through a somewhat shifting prism.

FANTASIO. Everyone has his own spectacles; no one exactly knows what is the color of his glasses. Who can tell me truly if I am happy or unhappy, good or evil, sad or gay, foolish or witty?

ELSBETH. At least you are ugly; that is certain.

FANTASIO. Not more certain than your beauty. Here is your father, here he comes with your future husband. Who can know whether you will marry him.

(*He goes out.*)

ELSBETH. As I cannot avoid the Prince of Mantua, I had better go to meet him.

(*Enter* THE KING. MARINONI *is dressed as* THE PRINCE *and* THE PRINCE *is dressed as an aide-de-camp.*)

THE KING. Prince, here is my daughter. Forgive her simple apparel. You are here in the home of a citizen who governs other citizens, and our etiquette is as lenient towards ourselves as it is towards them.

MARINONI. Allow me to kiss that lovely hand, my Lady, if it be not too great a boon for my lips.

ELSBETH. Your Highness will excuse me if I go back to the palace. I will meet your Highness in a more suitable manner at the presentation this evening.

(*She goes out.*)

THE PRINCE. The Princess is right. She is divinely bashful.

THE KING (*to* MARINONI). Who is that aide-de-camp? He follows you like a shadow. I find it intolerable to hear him cap everything we say with a foolish remark. Send him away, I beg of you.

(MARINONI *whispers something to* THE PRINCE.)

THE PRINCE (*aside, to* MARINONI). It is very clever of you to have persuaded him to send me away; I shall endeavor to join the Princess and to touch her heart with a few delicate words, as though by chance.

(*He goes out.*)

THE KING. What an idiot that aide-de-camp is, my friend. How can you put up with such a man?

MARINONI. H'm! H'm! Let us walk on a little, if your Majesty will allow it. I think I saw a charming summer-house in that grove.

(*They go out.*)

ACT II

SCENE II

(*Another part of the Garden. Enter* THE PRINCE.)

THE PRINCE. My disguise is a great success. I see everything, and I am becoming popular. So far everything has gone well: the father seems to me a great king, although a little too easy-going; and I shall be astonished if I do not instantly make a favorable impression. I see the Princess, on her way to the palace. Chance is befriending me.

(*Enter* ELSBETH. THE PRINCE *goes up to her.*)

THE PRINCE. Your Highness, allow one of the faithful servants of your future husband to offer you his sincere congratulations, which his humble and devoted heart cannot contain on beholding you. Happy are the great! They may wed you; I cannot; for me it is quite impossible; I am too lowly born. I have no worldly goods save a name feared by the enemy, and a pure and stainless heart which beats under this modest uniform; I am a poor soldier covered with scars from head to foot; I do not possess a ducat; I am lonely and exiled from my native land, as well as from my heavenly home; that is to say, the paradise of my dreams; I have no woman's heart to press to mine; I am accursed and silent.

ELSBETH. What do you want of me, my dear sir? Are you mad, or are you seeking alms?

THE PRINCE. How difficult it would be to find words to express what I am feeling! I thought it was my duty to fall at your feet and to offer you my company as far as the palace gate.

ELSBETH. I am obliged to you; please do me the service of leaving me alone.

(*She goes out.*)

THE PRINCE (*alone*). Did I do wrong to address her? Yet it was necessary, since I mean to win her in my disguise. Yes, I did well to address her. Yet she answered me curtly. Perhaps I should not have spoken so eagerly. But the answer was not agreeable. Can it be that she has a false and hard heart? It would be a good thing to investigate the matter cleverly.

(*He goes out.*)

ACT II

SCENE III

(*An ante-chamber.* FANTASIO *lying on a sofa.*)

FANTASIO. What a delightful trade is that of a fool. I think I was drunk last night when I put on this costume and went to the palace in it; but never did sane Reason inspire me with anything so profitable as this act of folly. I came, I was received, made much of, enrolled. I walk about in this palace as though I had lived here all my life. Just now I met the King; he did not even have the curiosity to look at me; as his fool was dead they said to him, 'Your Majesty, here is another one.' It is perfect. Thank heaven: My mind is now at ease. I can commit any folly I please and none can hinder me. I am one of the King of Bavaria's tame pets and if I wish, as long as I keep my hump and my wig, they will let me live here until I die, side by side with a spaniel and a tame guinea fowl. In the meantime my creditors can batter at my doors as much as they please. I am safe here under this wig as in the furthest Indies.

Is not that the Princess whom I see in the next room through this glass? She is arranging her wedding veil. Two large tears are rolling down her cheeks, and there is another one which has fallen like a pearl on to her breast. Poor little girl! I overheard her this morning talking with her lady-in-waiting; and truly it was by chance; I was sitting on the grass with no other thought than to sleep. Now she is weeping, and she has no idea that I am looking at her a second time. Ah! If I were a student in rhetoric, what profound platitudes I would pour out on this regal unhappiness, on this poor lamb round whose neck they have tied a pink ribband to lead her to the slaughter-house! This little girl is doubtless romantic; it will be cruel for her to wed a man she does not know; yet she has accepted the sacrifice in silence. How capricious is Fortune! I must needs get drunk, meet the funeral of St. Jean, take his costume and his place, perpetrate an act of preposterous folly, in order to see through this glass the only two tears that this child will perhaps shed on her sad bridal veil!

(*He goes out.*)

ACT II

SCENE IV

(*An avenue in the Garden.* THE PRINCE *and* MARINONI.)

THE PRINCE. You are nothing but a fool, Colonel!

MARINONI. Your Highness is making the most painful mistake with regard to me.

THE PRINCE. You are a master-fool. Can you not help that! Can you not help this happening? I entrust you with the greatest scheme that has been devised for an incalculable number of years, and you—my best friend, my most faithful servant!—you commit folly upon folly. No, no! Whatever you may say, it is unpardonable.

MARINONI. How can I shield your Highness from the unpleasantnesses which are the necessary consequence of the part your Highness is playing? You order me to take your name, and to behave as the real Prince of Mantua. How, then, can I prevent the King of Bavaria from affronting my aide-de-camp? You had no business to mix yourself up in our affairs.

THE PRINCE. I should like to see a knave like yourself daring to give me orders!

MARINONI. But consider, your Highness, I must either be a Prince or an aide-de-camp. I am carrying out your orders!

THE PRINCE. But to tell me that I am impertinent, before all the Court, because I wish to kiss the Princess' hand! I am ready to declare war against the King, and to return to my own country to put myself at the head of my armies!

MARINONI. But consider, your Highness, that the snub was administered to the aide-de-camp, not to the Prince. Do you expect people to respect you in that disguise?

THE PRINCE. That is enough! Give me back my coat!

MARINONI (*taking off the coat*). If my sovereign demands it, I am ready to die for him!

THE PRINCE. To be truthful, I do not know what course to take. On the one hand, I am furious at what is happening; and on the other hand, I am more than loath to abandon my scheme. The Princess appears not to heed the two-edged compliments with which I ceaselessly load her. I have already whispered to her more than one astounding thing. Come! Let us think this over.

MARINONI (*holding the coat*). What shall I do, your Highness?

THE PRINCE. Put it on again! Put it on, and we will go back to the palace.

ACT II

SCENE V

(THE PRINCESS ELSBETH, THE KING.)

THE KING. My daughter, you must answer frankly what I am going to ask you; does this marriage displease you, Elsbeth?

ELSBETH. It is for you, your Majesty, to answer. It pleases me if it pleases you. If it displeases you, it displeases me.

THE KING. The Prince seems to me an ordinary fellow, it is difficult to say anything definite about him. The foolishness of his aide-de-camp is the only thing I have against him. As to himself, he is perhaps a good Prince, but he is not a man of refinement; there is nothing in him which attracts or which repels me. What can I say to you about it? The heart of a woman has secrets which are hidden from me; sometimes they make heroes of such strange people; they snatch in so curious a fashion at one of two sides of a man whom they encounter, that it is impossible to judge for them, as long as one is without some particular sensitive spot for a guide. Tell me plainly what you think of your betrothed.

ELSBETH. I think that he is Prince of Mantua, and that war would break out again to-morrow between you and him if I do not marry him.

THE KING. That is certain, my child.

ELSBETH. I think, then, that I will marry him, and that there will be no war.

THE KING. May the blessings of my people thank you on behalf of your father. Ah, my dearest daughter, this alliance will make me happy! But I would not like to see any sadness belie the resignation in those beautiful blue eyes. Think over the matter for a few more days.

(*He goes out. Enter* FANTASIO.)

ELSBETH. There you are, poor boy! How do you like being here?

FANTASIO. As a bird which is at large.

ELSBETH. You would have spoken more truly if you had said, like a bird in a cage. This palace is a somewhat beautiful cage, but a cage it is nevertheless.

FANTASIO. Man is not more or less free for the size of a palace or a room. A body moves where it can; sometimes the imagination spreads wings as wide as the sky, in a dungeon no larger than a nutshell.

ELSBETH. So you are happy, Fool?

FANTASIO. Very happy. I converse with the pet dogs and the scullions. There is in the kitchen a little pug-dog no higher than that, which has said delightful things to me.

ELSBETH. In what language?

FANTASIO. In the chastest style. He has not made a single fault in grammar during a whole year.

ELSBETH. Could I hear some words of that language?

FANTASIO. I should not like you to; it is a special language; it is only spoken by pug-dogs; even the trees and the ears of the wheat understand it, but not the daughters of kings. When is your wedding?

ELSBETH. In a few days it will all be over.

FANTASIO. That is to say, it will have just begun. I mean to give you a wedding present.

ELSBETH. What present? I shall be curious to see it.

FANTASIO. I intend to give you a pretty little stuffed canary which will sing like a nightingale.

ELSBETH. How can it sing if it is stuffed?

FANTASIO. It sings perfectly well.

ELSBETH. It is curious how you persist in mocking me.

FANTASIO. Not at all. My canary has a little mechanism inside it. You touch gently a little spring under its left foot, and it sings all the new operas just like Mademoiselle Grisi.

ELSBETH. It is a canary of your invention, no doubt?

FANTASIO. By no means, it is a Court canary; there are many little girls extremely well brought up who behave just like that. They have a little spring under the left arm; a pretty little spring made of diamonds, like a dandy's watch; the tutor or the governess touches the spring, and you at once see her lips opening into the most gracious smile; a charming little cascade of honeyed words falls with the softest sound, and all the social conventions like delicate nymphs pirouette on their toes round the marvelous fountain; the suitor opens wondering eyes; the on-lookers whisper indulgently, and the king, filled with secret satisfaction, looks down with pride at the golden buckles of his shoes.

ELSBETH. You take delight in returning to the same subjects. Tell me, Fool, what have poor young girls done to you, that you should take so much joy in making them your butt? Cannot respect for any duty find favor in your eyes?

FANTASIO. I respect ugliness; that is why I have so profound a respect for myself.

ELSBETH. You seem sometimes to know more than you say. Where do you come from, and who are you? You who in one day can guess the mysteries which princes themselves will perhaps never dream of. Are you saying all these mad things to me, or are you speaking at random?

FANTASIO. At random. I constantly speak at random. Random is my confidential friend.

ELSBETH. He seems to have taught you what you have no right to know. I am inclined to believe that you have been spying on my actions and my words.

FANTASIO. God knows! What can that matter to you?

ELSBETH. More than you know. Just now, when I was putting on my veil, I heard steps behind me in the arras. I should not be surprised if it were not you.

FANTASIO. Be sure that the secret would remain between your handkerchief and myself. I am as little indiscreet as I am inquisitive. What pleasure could I take in your sorrows? What sorrow could I take in your pleasures? You are this, and I am that. You are young, and I am old; you are beautiful and I am ugly; you are rich, and I am poor. You see, there is nothing between you and me. What does it matter to you that Chance has bade cross on its great road-way two wheels which were not following in the same rut and which could not press the same dust? Is it my fault if one of your tears fell upon me as I slept?

ELSBETH. You speak to me in the guise of a man whom I love. That is why I listen in spite of myself. My eyes think that they are seeing St. Jean, but perhaps you are only a spy.

FANTASIO. What good would that do me? Even if it were true that your marriage caused you a few tears and even if I by chance knew this, what would I gain by telling? The knowledge would not be worthy a silver piece, nor on that account would you be immured in a dungeon. I understand that it must be irksome to wed the Prince of Mantua, but, after all, it is not I who am responsible. To-morrow, or the day after, you will have left for Mantua in your bridal garments, and I shall still be on this stool in my shabby clothes. Why do you think that I have anything against you? I have no reason to desire death, and you have never lent me any money.

ELSBETH. But if by chance you saw what I did not wish anyone to see, ought not I turn you out of the house for fear of another such accident.

FANTASIO. Do you wish to compare me to a confidant in a tragedy, and are you afraid that I will follow your shadow spouting verses? Do not turn me away, I pray you. I like being here so much. See, here is your governess, who is arriving with a bag full of mysteries. To prove to you that I shall not listen, I am going off to the pantry to eat the wing of a plover which the major-domo has set aside for his wife.

THE LADY ATTENDANT (*entering*). Have you heard this terrible thing, my dear Elsbeth?

ELSBETH. What are you saying? You are all of a tremble.

THE LADY. The Prince is not the Prince, nor the aide-de-camp the aide-de-camp. It is a real fairy tale!

ELSBETH. What are you telling me?

THE LADY. Hush, hush! It is one of the officers of the Prince who has just told me. The Prince of Mantua is a Count Almaviva; he is disguised and concealed among his aide-de-camps; he wished, no doubt, to try and see you and make your acquaintance in a romantic manner. He is disguised. The worthy Prince is disguised just as Lindor. The man who was presented to you as your husband is only an aide-de-camp called Marinoni.

ELSBETH. It is not possible!

THE LADY. It is true; perfectly true. The worthy man is disguised; it is impossible to recognize him. It is the most extraordinary thing.

ELSBETH. You say an officer told you?

THE LADY. One of the Prince's officers. You can ask him yourself.

ELSBETH. And he did not point out to you the true Prince of Mantua among the aide-de-camps?

THE LADY. He was trembling himself, the poor man! From his news. He only betrayed his secret because he wished to be agreeable to you, and he knew that I would tell you. As for Marinoni, it is true; but as to the true Prince, he did not show me him.

ELSBETH. That would give me something to think about if it were true. Bring me that officer.

(*Enter* PAGE.)

THE LADY. What is the matter, Flamel? You seem to be out of breath.

THE PAGE. Oh, my lady, it is enough to die of laughing. I dare not mention it before your Highness.

ELSBETH. Speak. What new thing has happened?

THE PAGE. Just as the Prince was riding on horseback into the courtyard, at the head of his staff, his wig was carried off in the air and suddenly disappeared.

ELSBETH. Why, how foolish!

THE PAGE. My Lady, I will die if this is not the truth. The wig was carried off in the air on the end of a hook. We found it downstairs in the servants' room, near a broken bottle; nobody knows who perpetrated this joke. But the Duke is all the more angry, and he has sworn that if the culprit is not punished by death, he will declare war on your father and put the whole country to fire and sword.

ELSBETH. Come, listen to this story, my dear; or else I shall not be able to help laughing.

(*Enter another* PAGE.)

Well, what is the news now?

SECOND PAGE. My Lady, the King's Fool has been locked up in gaol; it was he who caught the Prince's wig.

ELSBETH. The Fool in prison! And by order of the Prince?

SECOND PAGE. Yes, your Highness.

ELSBETH. Come, my dear, I must speak.

ACT II

SCENE VI

(THE PRINCE, MARINONI.)

THE PRINCE. No, no; let me take off my disguise! I shall burst! Things cannot go on like this! Blood and fire! The Royal wig at the end of a fish hook! Are we among barbarians in the deserts of Sahara! Is there still something civilized and decent left under the sun? I am foaming with rage, and my eyes are starting from my head!

MARINONI. You spoil everything by your violence.

THE PRINCE. And the father, this King of Bavaria, this monarch praised in all the Almanacs of the past year! This man who has so correct a deportment, who expresses himself in such measured terms, actually bursts out laughing when he see his son-in-law's wig dangling in the air! For I know, Marinoni, that it was *your* wig that was taken off, but still, is it not still the Prince of Mantua's wig, since it is he they thought they were seeing in you? When I think that if it had been myself in flesh and blood, *my* wig had perhaps been . . . Oh! there is a Providence; when God suddenly sent me the idea of disguising myself, when the words 'I must disguise myself' flashed through my mind, Fate had forseen this fatal event. It was Fate that preserved the head that governs my people from the most intolerable of insults: but by heaven! All shall be known. I have slighted my dignity too long. Since divine and human majesty have been pitilessly violated, and outraged, since there is no longer any notion of good or evil among men, since the King who rules over thousands of men bursts out laughing like a groom at the sight of a wig . . . Marinoni,—give me back my coat!

MARINONI (*taking off his coat*). If my sovereign commands, I am ready to endure a thousand tortures for him!

THE PRINCE. I am aware of your devotion. Come, let us tell the King what I think of him!

MARINONI. And refuse the hand of the Princess? Yet she looked at you with interest throughout the banquet.

THE PRINCE. Do you think so? I am lost in an abyss of perplexity. Come, we'll go to the King.

MARINONI (*holding the coat*). What must I do, your Highness?

THE PRINCE. Put it on again for the moment. You shall give it back to me presently. They will be more dumb-struck when they hear me speak as I intend to speak, in the clothes that I am wearing at present.

(*They go out.*)

ACT II

SCENE VII

(*The Prison.* FANTASIO, *alone.*)

FANTASIO. I do not know if there is a Providence, but it is agreeable to believe that there is. However, here was the poor little Princess who was about to wed, willy-nilly, a bestial fellow, a loutish bumpkin, on whose head Fortune dropped a crown, as the eagle dropped the tortoise on the bald pate of Aeschylus. All was ready; the poor little bride had made her confession. She had wiped away the two lovely tears which I saw her shed this morning. There was nothing wanting but a few words murmured by a friar, for the misfortune of her life to be consummated. In all this the fortunes of two kingdoms, the peace of two peoples, were at stake; and I must needs disguise myself as a humpback and then get drunk in our good King's kitchen, and angle with a line and catch the wig of his dear Ally! I verily believe that when I am drunk I have something superhuman about me! Now the marriage is broken off and everything is at sixes and sevens. The Prince of Mantua has asked for my head, in exchange for his wig. The King of Bavaria thought the punishment a little severe, and would sentence me to no more than imprisonment. The Prince of Mantua, thank God! is so stupid that he would rather be cut in pieces than abate his claim. Thus the Princess remains unmarried, this time at least. I swear that here is stuff for an epic in twelve cantos. Pope and Boileau composed admirable poems on far slighter themes. If I were but a poet! How I would depict the scene of the wig flying through the air! But the man who can do such actions deigns not to write about them. So posterity will have to forego my epic. (*He goes to sleep. Enter* ELSBETH *and her* LADY ATTENDANT *carrying a lamp.*)

ELSBETH. He is asleep. Shut the door gently.

THE LADY. So, there was no doubt about it. He has shed his wig, and with it his deformity. That is how he is, as his people see him in his triumphal chariot. It is the noble Prince of Mantua!

ELSBETH. Yes; it is he! My curiosity is satisfied. I wanted to see his face; nothing more. Let me lean over him!

(*She takes the lamp.*)

Psyche, mind the drop of oil.

THE LADY. He is as beautiful as a holy Image!

ELSBETH. Why did you give me so many romances and fairy tales to read? Why have you sowed so many strange and mysterious flowers in my poor brain?

THE LADY. How agitated you are, standing there on tiptoe!

ELSBETH. He is about to wake! Let us go.

FANTASIO (*waking up*). Is it a dream? I am holding the end of a white gown!

ELSBETH. Leave go! Let me go!

FANTASIO. It is you, Princess. If it is the reprieve of the King's Fool that you are bringing me in so celestial a fashion, let me put on my hump, and my wig, once more; it shall be done in a moment.

THE LADY. Ah, Prince, it is wicked of you to deceive us like this. Do not put on that costume again. We know all.

FANTASIO. Prince? Where is the Prince?

THE LADY. What is the use of dissembling?

FANTASIO. I am not dissembling in the least. What makes you call me Prince?

THE LADY. I know my duties towards your Highness.

FANTASIO. My lady, I beg of you to explain to me what this good lady is saying? Has there really been a fantastic bungle, or am I the butt of a joke?

ELSBETH. Why ask this, when it is you yourself who are joking?

FANTASIO. Am I then by chance a Prince? Do they harbor suspicions about my mother's honor?

ELSBETH. Who are you, if you are not the Prince of Mantua?

FANTASIO. My name is Fantasio; I am a citizen of Munich.

(*He shows her a letter.*)

ELSBETH. A citizen of Munich! Then why are you disguised? What are you doing here?

FANTASIO. My lady, I beg of you to forgive me. . . .

ELSBETH. What does this mean. Get up, man, and leave us. I will let you off the punishment which you perhaps deserve. Who made you do this?

FANTASIO. I cannot tell you the motive which led me here.

ELSBETH. You cannot tell me! And yet I wish to know!

FANTASIO. Forgive me, I dare not confess it.

THE LADY. Let us go, Elsbeth; do not expose yourself to words which ill beseem you. The man is a thief, or an insolent fellow. He is about to speak to you of love.

ELSBETH. I want to know the reason which made you use this disguise.

FANTASIO. I beg of you, spare me!

ELSBETH. No, no, speak, or I will have this door closed on you for ten years!

FANTASIO. My lady, I am up to my neck in debts; my creditors have a writ against me; at this very moment my furniture has been sold and if I were not in this prison I should be in another. They must have come to arrest me last night; I did not know where to spend the night, nor how to dodge the bailiffs, so I thought of taking refuge in this costume, at the feet of the King; if you give me back my liberty, I shall be seized by the neck; my uncle is a miser, who lives on potatoes and radishes, and allows me to die of hunger in all the inns of the Country. If you wish to know —I owe twenty thousand crowns.

ELSBETH. Is all this true?

FANTASIO. If I am lying, I will pay them back.

(*The noise of horses is heard.*)

THE LADY. There are horses passing by. It is the King himself. If I could only catch the page's eye!

(*She calls through the window.*)

Flamel, where are you going?

THE PAGE (*from outside*). The Prince of Mantua is leaving.

THE LADY. The Prince of Mantua?

THE PAGE. Yes; war has been declared. There was a fierce altercation between him and King in front of the whole court, and the marriage of the Princess has been broken off.

ELSBETH. Do you hear that, Sir Fantasio? Owing to you, my marriage has been broken off.

THE LADY. Gracious Heavens! The Prince of Mantua has gone and I have not even set eyes on him!

ELSBETH. What a disaster, if war has broken out!

FANTASIO. You call that a disaster, your Highness? Would you prefer a husband who goes to war for his wig? Ah, my lady, if war is declared, we shall know what to do with our arms; the idlers of our streets will put on their uniforms; I myself will take a fowling piece, if it has not yet been sold. We will travel for a while in Italy, and if you ever go to Mantua, you shall enter the city as a queen, and for tapers you shall have nothing but our swords!

ELSBETH. Fantasio, will you still be my father's fool? I will give you twenty thousand crowns.

FANTASIO. I would willingly do so; but truly, if I were obliged to, one of these days I should jump out of the window and escape.

ELSBETH. Why? You know that St. Jean is dead. We must have a fool.

FANTASIO. I prefer the profession to any other, but I can follow no trade. If you think it was worth twenty thousand crowns to be saved from the Prince of Mantua, give them to me, and do not pay my debts. A gentleman without debts would be at his wits' ends. I have never dreamed of being free from debt.

ELSBETH. Well! I give them to you; but take the key of my garden; the day when you are weary of being pursued by your creditors, come and hide among the corn-flowers where I found you this morning; be careful to bring your wig and your motley; never appear before me save in this counterfeit, and with those silver bells; for it is thus that you pleased me once; you shall once more be my fool for as long as it pleases you, and then you will go back to your own affairs.

Now you can go away; the door is open.

THE LADY. To think that the Prince of Mantua has gone and that I never set eyes on him!

Danton's Death

By GEORG BÜCHNER

Translated by STEPHEN SPENDER *and* GORONWY REES

CHARACTERS

Georges Danton Legendre Camille Desmoulins Hérault-Séchelles Lacroix Philippeau Fabre d'Eglantine Mercier Thomas Payne	*Deputies*
Robespierre Saint-Just Barère Collot d'Herbois Billaud-Varennes	*Members of the Committee of Public Safety*
Chaumette,	*Procureur of the Paris Commune*
Dillon,	*a General*
Fouquier-Tinville,	*Public Prosecutor*
Amar Vouland	*Members of the Committee of Security*
Herman Dumas	*Presidents of the Revolutionary Tribunal*
Paris,	*friend to Danton*
Simon,	*a Prompter*
Laflotte,	
Julie,	*Danton's wife*
Lucile,	*wife of Camille Desmoulins*
Adelaide Marion Rosalie	*Prostitutes*

Men and Women of the People, Prostitutes, Executioners, *etc.*

ACT I

SCENE I

(HÉRAULT-SÉCHELLES, *ladies (at a card table)*. DANTON, JULIE, *a little apart*, DANTON *on a stool at* JULIE'S *feet.*)

DANTON. See the pretty lady, how cleverly she shuffles the cards! Yes, really, she understands! They say she deals hearts to her husband and diamonds to everyone else. She has clumsy legs and she's apt to fall; her husband carries the bumps on his forehead, he thinks they're bumps of humor and laughs them off. You could make a man fall in love with lies.

JULIE. Do you believe in me?

DANTON. How do I know? We know little of one another. We are thick-skinned, our hands reach out to each other but it's waste of time, leather rubs against leather—we are very lonely.

JULIE. You know me, Danton.

DANTON. Yes, what one calls knowing. You have dark eyes and curly hair and a delicate complexion and always call me 'Dear George.' But there, there! (*Touching her eyes and her forehead.*) What lies behind them? Look, our senses are gross. Know each other! We'd have to break open our skulls and pick out the thoughts from our brain-boxes.

A LADY (*to* HÉRAULT). What are you doing with your fingers?

HÉRAULT. Nothing.

LADY. Don't stick your thumbs in like that, it's unbearable.

HÉRAULT. You see, it has a peculiar significance.

DANTON. No, Julie, I love you like the grave.

JULIE (*turning away*). Oh!

DANTON. No, listen. They say that in the grave there is peace, and that the grave and peace are one. If that is so, then lying in your lap I am already under the earth. Sweet grave, your lips are funeral bells, your voice my death knell, your breast the mound above me, and your heart my coffin.

LADY (*to* HÉRAULT). You've lost.

HÉRAULT. It was a lover's adventure, that cost money like all the others.

LADY. Then you declared your love like a deaf mute—with your fingers.

HÉRAULT. And why not? People even say that they are easiest to understand. I had an affair with a queen, my fingers were princes bewitched into spiders, and you, madam, were the fairy; but it went badly, the queen was always pregnant, and every minute gave birth to a knave. I wouldn't let my daughter play such games; kings and queens lie on top of each other so shamelessly, and the knaves come close behind.

(*Enter* CAMILLE DESMOULINS *and* PHILIPPEAU.)

HÉRAULT. What sad eyes, Philippeau! Have you torn a hole in your red cap? Has St. Jacob frowned on you? Did it rain during the executions? Or did you get a bad place and see nothing?

CAMILLE. You parody Socrates. Do you know what the divine philosopher asked Alcibiades, when he found him sad and depressed? 'Have you lost your shield on the battle-field? Have you been beaten in a race or a duel? Has someone sung better or struck the lyre better than you?' What classical Republicans! Take some of our guillotine romanticism against it!

PHILIPPEAU. To-day another twenty victims have fallen. We made a mistake, the Hébertists were only sent to the guillotine because they weren't systematic enough, and perhaps because the Decemvirs thought they were lost, if for over a week men existed who were even more feared than they.

HÉRAULT. They'd like to send us back to the stone age. Saint-Just wouldn't mind if we crawled on all fours, so that the lawyer from Arras could give us school-caps and benches and a God Almighty after the mechanism of the Geneva watchmaker.

PHILIPPEAU. They wouldn't shrink from hanging on a few noughts to Marat's figures for the proscriptions. How long must we remain dirty and bloody like new-born children, have coffins for cradles and heads for dolls? We must advance. The Committee of Clemency must be set up, the expelled deputies must be reinstated.

HÉRAULT. The Revolution has entered the period of reorganization.—The Revolution must end, and the Republic must begin.—In our Constitution right must take the place of duty, happiness the place of virtue, protection the place of punishment. Every individual must count, and be able to assert his own nature. He may be reasonable or unreasonable, educated or uneducated, good or bad—it's no concern of the State's. We are all fools and no one has the right to impose his own particular folly on any one else.—Every one must be allowed to enjoy himself in his own way, so long as he does not enjoy himself at the expense of others and does not interfere with their pleasure. The individuality of the majority must be revealed in the form of the State.

CAMILLE. The Constitution should be a transparent veil, clinging closely to the body of the People. It must answer to every throb of their veins, every tension of the muscles, every pulse of desire. The body may be fair or foul, it has the right to be what it is, and we have no right to cut its clothes to our measure.—We will rap over the knuckles those who wish to throw a nun's hood over the naked shoulders of France, loveliest of sinners. —We want naked Gods, Bacchantes, Olympic games, roses in our hair, sparkling wine, heaving breasts and singing lips; oh, wicked, limb-loosening Love!—We don't want to prevent the Romans from sitting in the corner and cooking roots; but we'll have no more gladiatorial games. The divine Epicurus and Venus with the lovely buttocks shall be the door-keepers of the Republic, instead of St. Marat and St. Chalier. Danton, you will make the attack in the Convention!

DANTON. I shall, thou wilt, he will. If we live till then, as the old women say. After an hour sixty minutes will have passed, isn't that so, my boy?

CAMILLE. What do you mean? that goes without saying.

DANTON. Oh, it all goes without saying. And who is to put all these fine things into action?

PHILIPPEAU. We, and all honest men.

DANTON. That 'and' in between is a long word, it holds us rather far apart; there's a long distance to cover and Honesty will be out of breath before we meet. And when we do!—you can lend money to honest men, you can be godfather to their children and marry them to your daughters, but that's all.

CAMILLE. If you know that, why did you begin the struggle?

DANTON. Those people annoyed me. I couldn't look at those swaggering Catos, without giving them a kick. That is my nature.

(*Rises.*)

JULIE. You're going?

DANTON (*to* JULIE). I must get out of here, they rub me up the wrong way again with their politics. (*On his way out.*) Between the door and the door-post I will prophesy unto you; the Statue of Liberty has not yet been cast, the furnace is glowing, and we can still all burn our fingers.

(*Exit* DANTON.)

CAMILLE. Leave him alone! Do you think he can keep his hands off if it comes to action?

HÉRAULT. No, but only to kill time, as one plays chess.

ACT I

SCENE II

(*A Street.* SIMON. HIS WIFE.)

SIMON (*beats his wife*). You old pimp, you wrinkled pill, you maggotty apple of sin.

WIFE. Help, help!

PEOPLE *run in:* Pull them apart, pull them apart!

SIMON. Unhand me, Romans! I'll batter these bones to bits! You vestal virgin!

WIFE. Me a vestal virgin? I'll say I am.

SIMON. Thus from thy shoulders I tear off thy robe, and naked in the sun display thine arse. You whore's bed, lust breeds in every wrinkle of your body.

(*They are separated.*)

FIRST CITIZEN. What's the matter?

SIMON. Where is the virgin? Speak! No, I can't say virgin. The maiden? No, nor that either. The woman, the wife! Oh, not even that! There's only one other name; oh, it chokes me! I've no breath to say it.

SECOND CITIZEN. Lucky you haven't, or it would stink of brandy.

SIMON. Aged Virginius, veil your hoary head—the raven shame sits upon it and pecks at your eyes. Give me a knife, Romans!

(*He sinks to the ground.*)

WIFE. Ah, usually he's a good man, but he can't carry much drink; brandy gives him an extra leg.

SECOND CITIZEN. Then he must walk on three.

WIFE. No, he falls down.

SECOND CITIZEN. Quite right, first he walks on three legs, then falls over the third until the third itself falls down again.

SIMON. You're the vampire's tongue that sucks my warmest heart's blood.

WIFE. Just leave him alone; now's the time he always gets sentimental; it'll soon be over.

FIRST CITIZEN. But what's up?

WIFE. Well, it was like this, you see. I was sitting on a stone in the sun, warming myself, you see—we've got no firewood, you see—

SECOND CITIZEN. Use your husband's nose—

WIFE. —and my daughter had gone down to the corner—she's a fine girl and supports her parents.

SIMON. There, she confesses!

WIFE. You Judas, would you have a pair of trousers to put on if the young gentlemen didn't take theirs off with her? You brandy cask, do you want to thirst when the fountain ceases to flow?—We work with all our limbs, why not with that one? Her mother did, when she brought her into the world, and it gave her pain; can't she get something for her mother with it, eh? and does it give her pain, eh? You idiot!

SIMON. Ha, Lucretia! A knife, give me a knife, Romans! Ha, Appius Claudius!

FIRST CITIZEN. Yes, a knife, but not for the poor whore! What has she done? Nothing! Her hunger whores and begs. A knife for the people who buy the flesh of our wives and daughters! Woe to those who whore with the daughters of the people! Your stomachs are empty, theirs are filled to bursting; you have holes in your coats, they have warm clothes; you have horny hands, theirs are soft as silk. *Ergo,* you toil and they do nothing; *ergo,* you earn your bread and they have stolen it; *ergo,* when you want a few coppers of your stolen property you must whore and beg; *ergo,* they are thieves, and we must cut off their heads.

THIRD CITIZEN. They have no blood in their veins but what they have sucked out of ours. They told us: kill the aristocrats, they are wolves! We hanged the aristocrats from the lantern. They said to us: the veto devours your bread. We killed the veto. They said to us: the Girondins are starving you. We sent the Girondins to the guillotine. But they have taken the dead men's clothes and we go naked and freeze as before. We will peel the skin from their bones to make trousers for ourselves, we will melt down their fat and make soup out of it. Forward! Death to all who have no holes in their clothes!

FIRST CITIZEN. Death to all who can read and write!

SECOND CITIZEN. Death to all who go abroad!

ALL. Death, death!

(A YOUNG MAN *is dragged on.*)

VOICES. He's got a handkerchief! An aristocrat! To the lantern! to the lantern!

SECOND CITIZEN. What? He doesn't wipe his nose with his fingers? To the lantern!

(*A lantern is let down.*)

YOUNG MAN. Gentlemen!

SECOND CITIZEN. There are no gentlemen here! To the lantern!

SOME (*sing*). Who lie in the earth
Are eaten by worms,
Better hang in the air
Than rot in the grave.

YOUNG MAN. Mercy!

THIRD CITIZEN. Only a game with a hempen noose round your neck! It only takes a minute, we're kinder-hearted than you. Our life is murder by hard labor; for sixty years we hang by the rope and struggle, but we'll cut ourselves loose.—To the lantern!

YOUNG MAN. I don't care, it won't help you to see any clearer.

CROWD. Bravo, bravo!

SOME VOICES. Let him go!

(*He disappears.*)

(*Enter* ROBESPIERRE, *followed by* WOMEN *and* SANSCULOTTES.)

ROBESPIERRE. What's wrong, citizens?

THIRD CITIZEN. What's wrong? The few drops of blood shed in August and September have not made the cheeks of the people red. The guillotine is too slow. We need a hailstorm.

FIRST CITIZEN. Our wives and children cry for bread, we want to feed them with the flesh of aristocrats. Death to all with no holes in their clothes!

ALL. Death, death!

ROBESPIERRE. In the name of the law!

FIRST CITIZEN. What is the law?

ROBESPIERRE. The will of the people.

FIRST CITIZEN. We are the people, and our will is there should be no law; *ergo,* our will is the law, *ergo,* in the name of the law there is no law, *ergo,* death!

VOICES. Silence for Aristides! silence for the Incorruptible!

A WOMAN. Hear the Messiah, who is sent to elect and to judge; he will strike the wicked with the edge of the sword. His eyes are the eyes of election, his hands are the hands of judgment.

ROBESPIERRE. Poor, virtuous People! You do your duty, you sacrifice your enemies. People, thou art great! In flashes of lightning and in thunder thou art revealed. But, my people, your blows must not wound your own body; you murder yourself in your fury. You can fall only through your own strength; your enemies know it well. Your legislators watch over you, they will guide your hands; their eyes are unerring, your hands are inescapable. Come with me to the Jacobin Club! Your brothers will open their arms to you, we will hold a bloody assize on our enemies.

MANY VOICES. To the Jacobins! Long live Robespierre!

(*All off.*)

SIMON. Alas, abandoned!

(*He tries to rise.*)

WIFE. There! (*Supports him.*)

SIMON. Ah, my Baucis, you heap coals of fire on my head.

WIFE. Now stand up.

SIMON. You turn away? Can you forgive me, Portia? Did I strike you? It was not my hand, it was not my arm, my madness did it.

His madness is poor Hamlet's enemy.
Then Hamlet did it not; Hamlet denies it.

Where is our daughter, where is my Susie?

WIFE. There, on the corner!

SIMON. Let us go to her! Come, my virtuous spouse!

(*Exeunt.*)

ACT I

SCENE III

(*The Jacobin Club.*)

A CITIZEN FROM LYONS. Our brothers in Lyons have sent us to pour out their bitter anger on your breast. We do not know if the tumbril that carried Ronsin to the guillotine was the hearse of Liberty; but we do know that since that day Chalier's murderers have trod the earth as safely as if no grave were waiting for them. Have you forgotten that Lyons is a stain upon the earth of France which must be covered by the limbs of traitors? Have you forgotten that this whore of kings has only the waters of the Rhone in which to wash her scabs? Have you forgotten that the flood tide of the Revolution must wash Pitt's Mediterranean fleet aground on the corpses of aristocrats? Your compassion is murdering the Revolution. The breath of an aristocrat is the death rattle of Freedom. Only a coward dies for the Republic; a Jacobin kills for her. I warn you; if we no longer find in you the energy of the men of the 10th of August, of September, and the 31st of May, there remains for us, as for the patriot Gaillard, only the dagger of Cato.

(*Applause and confused cries.*)

A JACOBIN. We will drink the cup of Socrates with you!

LEGENDRE (*springs to the tribune*). We have no need to turn our eyes to Lyons. In the last few days the people who wear silken clothes, who ride in carriages, who sit in boxes at the theatre and speak like the dictionary of the Academy have carried their heads firmly on their shoulders. They are witty and say Marat and Chalier should be given a second martyrdom and be guillotined in effigy.

(*Sensation throughout the assembly.*)

SOME VOICES. They are dead men, their tongues have guillotined them.

LEGENDRE. The blood of these saints be upon them! I ask the members of the Committee of Public Safety here present, since when have their ears become so deaf—

COLLOT D'HERBOIS (*interrupting*). And I ask you, Legendre, whose voice gives breath to such thoughts, so that they come to life and dare to speak? The time has come to tear off the mask. Listen to me! The cause is accusing its effect, the voice its echo, the premise its conclusion. The Committee of Public Safety is more logical than that, Legendre. Be calm! The busts of these saints will remain undisturbed and like heads of Medusa they will turn the traitors to stone.

ROBESPIERRE. I demand the tribune!

THE JACOBINS. Silence, silence for the Incorruptible!

ROBESPIERRE. We waited only for the cries of dissatisfaction which resounded on every side before we spoke. Our eyes were open, we saw the enemy arm and rise, but we did not sound the alarm; we let the people watch over itself, and the people has not slumbered, the people has rushed to arms. We allowed the enemy to come out of hiding, we allowed him to advance; now he stands free and unconcealed in the light of day, and every stroke will find its mark; he is dead as soon as you have seen him.

I have said it to you before; the internal enemies of the Republic have fallen into two groups, like two armies. Under different flags and by different ways they march towards the same goal. One of these factions is no more. In its affectation and madness it tried to set aside as worn-out weaklings the most proven patriots, so as to deprive the Republic of its strongest arms. They declared war on God and on Property, to create a diversion in favor of the Kings. They parodied the sublime drama of the Revolution, so as to discredit it by calculated excesses. The triumph of Hébert would have transformed the Republic into chaos, and despotism would have been satisfied. The sword of the law has struck down the traitor. But what do the foreigners care, so long as they have criminals of another brand through whom to achieve the same end? We have accomplished nothing, so long as a second faction remains to be destroyed.

That faction is the opposite of the first. They force us to be weak, their battle-cry is: Mercy! They wish to rob the People of its weapons, and the strength to use these weapons, so as to hand the people over naked and enfeebled to the Kings.

The weapon of the Republic is the Terror, the strength of the Republic is Virtue—Virtue because without it the Terror is pernicious, the Terror because without it Virtue is powerless. The Terror is the consequence of Virtue, the Terror is nothing else than swift, strong, and unswerving Justice. They say that the Terror is an instrument of dictatorship and that our Government therefore resembles a dictatorship. Granted! but only as the sword in the hand of Freedom's heroes resembles the sabre with which the satellites of tyrants are armed. If a tyrant rules his brutish subjects through terror he is, as a tyrant, justified; destroy the enemies of freedom through terror and as the founders of the Republic you are no less justified. The Revolutionary Government is the dictatorship of freedom against tyranny.

Certain people shout 'Mercy on the Royalists!' Mercy for criminals? No! Mercy for the innocent, mercy for the weak, mercy for the unfortunate, mercy for Mankind! Only the law-abiding citizen deserves protection by society.

In a republic only republicans are citizens, royalists and foreigners are enemies. To punish the oppressors of mankind is mercy; to pardon them is barbarism. Every display of false sensibility seems to me a sigh that flies to England or to Austria.

But they are not content to disarm the People; they even try to poison the purest sources of its strength by Vice. Of all attacks on Freedom, that is the subtlest, the most dangerous, the most loathsome. Only the most hellish Machiavellianism—but no! I will not say that such a plan could be misbegotten in a human mind! It may not be intentional, but the intention is beside the point, the effect is the same, the danger equally great. Vice is the brand of Cain on the forehead of Aristocracy. In a republic it is not merely a moral but a political offence. The libertine is the political opponent of freedom, and is the more dangerous the greater the services he seems to perform. The most dangerous citizen is he who finds it easier to wear out a dozen red caps than to do a single good action.

You will find it easy to understand me, if you think of people who once lived in attics and now ride in carriages and fornicate with ci-devant countesses and duchesses. We may well ask: have they plundered the People or have they pressed the golden hands of the Kings, when we see the People's law-givers parading with all the vices and luxury of the former courtiers, when we see these counts and marquesses of the Revolution marrying rich wives, giving magnificent banquets, gambling, keeping servants, and wearing costly clothes? We may well be astonished when we hear of their wit, their culture, and their good taste. A short time ago one of them gave a shameful parody of Tacitus, I could answer out of Sallust and travesty Catiline; but I imagine there is nothing more for me to add, the portrait is complete.

No compromise, no truce with men who thought only of exploiting the people, who hope to carry out their plans with impunity, to whom the Republic is a speculation and the Revolution a trade! Terrified by the mounting tide of examples, they now softly seek to mitigate our justice. One might think that each of them said to himself: 'We are not virtuous enough to employ such terror. Philosophic law-givers, have pity on our weakness! I dare not say to you that I am vicious; so I say to you rather: be not pitiless!'

Be calm, virtuous People, be calm, you patriots! Tell your comrades in Lyons: the sword of the law does not rust in the hands to which you have entrusted it!—We shall set the Republic a great example.

(*General applause.*)

MANY VOICES. Long live the Republic! Long live Robespierre!

PRESIDENT. The session is closed.

ACT I

SCENE IV

(*A street.*)

LACROIX. What have you done, Legendre? Do you realize whose head you've thrown down with those busts of yours?

LEGENDRE. A few dandies, and some elegant women, that's all.

LACROIX. You're a suicide, a shadow who murders his original and with it himself.

LEGENDRE. I don't understand.

LACROIX. I thought Collot spoke clearly enough.

LEGENDRE. What does that matter? It was as if a champagne bottle burst. He was drunk again.

LACROIX. Fools, babes, and—well?—drunkards tell the truth. Whom do you think Robespierre meant by Catiline?

LEGENDRE. Well?

LACROIX. The thing's simple. The atheists and the extremists have been sent to the guillotine; but the people are no better off, they go barefoot in the streets and want to make shoes out of the skins of aristocrats. The thermometer of the guillotine must not fall; a few degrees lower and the Committee of Public Safety can make its bed on the Place de la Révolution.

LEGENDRE. What has all this to do with my busts?

LACROIX. Still don't you see? You have made the counter-revolution known officially, you've forced the Committee to take energetic measures, you've directed their hands. The people is a Minotaur that must be fed with corpses every week if it is not to eat the Committee alive.

LEGENDRE. Where is Danton?

LACROIX. How should I know? He's trying to discover the Venus de Medici piecemeal in all the tarts in the Palais Royal; he's making mosaics, as he says. God knows what limb he's got to now. What a pity that Nature cuts up beauty into so many pieces, like Medea with her brothers, and deposits it in fragments in people's bodies.—Let's go to the Palais Royal.

ACT I

SCENE V

(*A Room.* DANTON, MARION.)

MARION. No, don't touch me! At your feet like this. I'll tell you a story.

DANTON. Your lips have better uses.

MARION. No, let me alone for once.—I came of a good family. My mother was a clever woman and brought me up carefully. She always told me that modesty is a great virtue. When people came to the house and began to speak of certain things she sent me out of the room; if I asked what they meant she said I ought to be ashamed of myself; if she gave me a book to read, there were almost always some pages I had to leave out. But I could read as much as I liked of the Bible; every page of it was holy. There were some things in it I couldn't understand. I couldn't ask any one; I brooded over myself. Then the Spring came, and all around me something was happening, something I had no share in. A strange atmosphere surrounded me; it almost stifled me. I looked at my own body; sometimes I felt as if there were two of me, and then again I melted into one. In those days a young man came to visit us; he was handsome and often said silly things to me; I didn't quite know what they meant, but I couldn't help laughing. My mother made him come often; it suited us both. In the end we couldn't see why we shouldn't just as well lie beside each other between the sheets as sit beside each other on two chairs. It gave me more pleasure than his conversation and I didn't see why I should be allowed the smaller and denied the greater. We did it secretly. That went on. But I was like a sea that swallowed everything up and sank deeper and deeper into itself. For me only my opposite existed, all men melted into one body. It was my nature, who can get beyond that? In the end he noticed. One morning he came and kissed me as if he was going to suffocate me; his arms closed tightly round my neck, I was in terrible fear. Then he released me, laughed and said he had nearly done a very stupid thing. He said I need only keep my dress and use it, it would soon wear out by itself; he didn't want to spoil my fun for me too soon, and after all it was the only thing I had. Then he went away; I still didn't know what he meant. In the evening I was sitting at the window; I am very sensitive and my only hold on everything around me is through feeling; I sank into the waves of the sunset. Then a crowd came down the street, children ran ahead, women watched from the windows. I looked down; they carried him past in a basket, the moon shone on his pale forehead, his curls were wet—he had drowned himself. I had to cry. It was the one break in my whole being.

Other people have Sundays and weekdays, they work for six days and pray on the seventh, once a year they have a birthday and feel sentimental, and every year they look forward to New Year. All that means nothing to me; for me there are no dates, no changes. I am always one thing only, an unbroken longing and desire, a flame, a stream. My mother died of grief; people point their fingers at me. That is stupid. Only one thing matters, what people enjoy, whether it's the body, or holy images, wine, flowers, or toys; the feeling is the same; those who enjoy most, pray most.

DANTON. Why can't I gather your beauty into myself, embrace it completely?

MARION. Danton, your lips have eyes.

DANTON. I wish I were part of the air, to bathe you in my flood and break myself on every wave of your beautiful body.

(*Enter* LACROIX, ADELAIDE, ROSALIE.)

LACROIX (*remains in the doorway*). I must laugh, I must laugh.

DANTON (*suspiciously*). Well?

LACROIX. I was thinking about the street.

DANTON. And?

LACROIX. In the street two dogs—a mastiff and an Italian poodle—were having a go at each other.

DANTON. What does that matter?

LACROIX. It just occurred to me and I couldn't help laughing. It was so edifying. The girls were watching from the windows; people ought to be more careful and not let them sit in the sun. The flies tickle their hands and that puts ideas into their heads.—Legendre and I have visited nearly every cell here, and the nuns of the Revelation through the Flesh clung to our coat tails and demanded a blessing. Legendre is administering penance to one of them, but he'll have to fast a month for it himself. Here are two priestesses of the body I've brought with me.

MARION. Good day, Mlle Adelaide, good day, Mlle Rosalie.

ROSALIE. It's a long time since we had the pleasure.

MARION. I was sorry not to see you.

ADELAIDE. Oh God, we're busy night and day.

DANTON (*to* ROSALIE). What slender hips you've acquired, little one.

ROSALIE. Oh, one improves every day.

LACROIX. What's the difference between an ancient and a modern Adonis?

DANTON. And Adelaide's become spiritually suggestive; it's a piquant change. Her face looks like a fig leaf which she holds before her whole body. Such a fig-tree gives a refreshing shade in so crowded a street.

ADELAIDE. I'd be a cattle track, if Monsieur—

DANTON. I understand; only don't be angry, my girl.

LACROIX. Listen! A modern Adonis is torn not by a boar but by sows.

He receives his wound not in the thigh but the parts, and from his blood no roses blossom but buds of mercury shoot up.

DANTON. Mlle Rosalie is a restored torso, of which only the hips and feet are antique. She's a magnetic needle, and what the pole of the head repels the pole of the feet attracts; the center is an equator where every one crossing the line for the first time needs to be ducked in mercury.

LACROIX. Two sisters of mercy; each works in a hospital, that is, in her own body.

ROSALIE. Aren't you ashamed of yourselves? Our ears are burning.

ADELAIDE. You ought to have more manners!

(*Exeunt* ROSALIE *and* ADELAIDE.)

DANTON. Good night, pretty children.

LACROIX. Good night, mercury mines.

DANTON. I'm sorry for them, they've lost their supper.

LACROIX. Listen, Danton, I've come from the Jacobins.

DANTON. Is that all?

LACROIX. The delegation from Lyons read a proclamation, as if there was nothing left for them but to wrap themselves in a toga. Every one made a face as if to say to his neighbor: 'Paetus, it doesn't hurt.' Legendre cried that there were some who wished to destroy the busts of Marat and Chalier. I think he wants to paint himself red again. He's come through the Terror with a whole skin and the children tug at his coat in the streets.

DANTON. And Robespierre?

LACROIX. Tapped his fingers on the tribune and said: Virtue must rule through Terror. The phrase gives me a pain in the neck.

DANTON. It saws the planks for the guillotine.

LACROIX. And Collot cried as if possessed that the masks must be torn off.

DANTON. The faces will come away with them.

(*Enter* PARIS.)

LACROIX. What is it, Fabricius?

PARIS. From the Jacobins I went to Robespierre; I demanded an explanation. He tried to look like Brutus sacrificing his children, generalized about duty and said that in the defence of freedom he had no scruples and would make every sacrifice—himself, his brothers, his friends.

DANTON. That's perfectly clear; one has only to reverse the order and he comes underneath and holds out the ladder for his friends. We ought to thank Legendre, he has made them speak out.

LACROIX. The Hébertists aren't dead yet, and the people are starving; that is a terrible lever. The scale of blood must not grow lighter or it will lift the Committee of Public Safety to the lantern. They need ballast, they need one heavy head.

DANTON. I know, I know—the Revolution is like Saturn and devours her own children. (*After a pause.*) And yet, they will not dare.

LACROIX. Danton, you're a dead saint; but the Revolution has no use for relics, it threw the limbs of kings into the gutter and all the holy images out of the churches. Do you think they'd leave you standing as a monument?

DANTON. My name! The People!

LACROIX. Your name! You're a moderate, and so am I and so are Camille, Philippeau, Hérault. To the people moderation is the same as weakness; they kill every one who lags behind. The tailors in the Section of Red Caps would feel all Roman history in their needles if the Man of September had become a moderate compared with them.

DANTON. Perfectly true; and besides—the People is a child who smashes everything to see what's inside.

LACROIX. And in any case, Danton, as Robespierre says, we are vicious; that is, we enjoy ourselves. The People are virtuous, that is, they do not enjoy themselves, because work dulls their organs of pleasure; they don't drink because they have no money, and they don't go to brothels because their breath stinks of cheese and herrings and the girls are disgusted by it.

DANTON. They hate the pleasure-loving, as eunuchs hate men.

LACROIX. They call us rogues, and (*In* DANTON'S *ear.*) between ourselves there's something in what they say. Robespierre and the masses will be virtuous, Saint-Just will write a novel, Barère will cut a Carmagnole and wrap the Convention in a mantle of blood and—I see it all.

DANTON. You're dreaming. They had no courage without me, they'll have none against me. The Revolution is not yet ended, they may still need me; they'll hang me up in the Arsenal.

LACROIX. We must act.

DANTON. A way will be found.

LACROIX. A way will be found when we are lost.

MARION (*to* DANTON). Your lips have grown cold, your words have choked your kisses.

DANTON (*to* MARION). So much time wasted! It's not worth the trouble! —(*To* LACROIX.) To-morrow I'll go to Robespierre; I'll make him angry, he can't keep his mouth shut then. So to-morrow! Good night, my friends, good night! Many thanks!

LACROIX. Get out, my good friends, get out! Good night, Danton! A girl's legs will be your guillotine, the Mound of Venus your Tarpeian Rock. (*Exit with* PARIS.)

ACT I

SCENE VI

(*A Room.* ROBESPIERRE, DANTON, PARIS.)

ROBESPIERRE. I tell you, any one who falls on my arm when I draw the sword is my enemy—his motive's beside the point; a man who hinders me from defending myself kills me just as much as if he attacked me.

DANTON. Where self-defence ends, murder begins; I see no reason that forces us to go on killing.

ROBESPIERRE. The social revolution is not yet ended; to carry out a revolution by halves is to dig your own grave. Aristocracy is not yet dead; the healthy forces of the people must take the place of this completely degenerate class. Vice must be punished, Virtue must rule through the Terror.

DANTON. I do not understand the word punishment.—You and your virtue, Robespierre! You have not taken money, you have no debts, you haven't slept with women, you've always worn a respectable suit and have never been drunk. Robespierre, you're appallingly righteous. I'd be ashamed to walk between heaven and earth for thirty days with the same moral expression, merely for the miserable pleasure of finding others less virtuous than myself.—Isn't there something within you which sometimes whispers, softly, secretly: you lie, you lie?

ROBESPIERRE. My conscience is clear.

DANTON. Conscience is a mirror before which a monkey torments himself; every one gets himself up as best he can and goes out to take his pleasure in his own way. It's not worth the trouble to make a fuss about it. Every one has the right to protect himself if some one else spoils his fun. Have you the right to turn the guillotine into a washtub for other people's dirty linen and use their heads as cakes of soap for washing their dirty clothes, merely because your coat has always been brushed and clean? Yes, you can defend yourself if they spit on it and want to tear it to rags; but so long as they leave you in peace, what business is it of yours? If they don't trouble about the way they carry on, does that give you the right to lock them up in the tomb? Are you God's policeman? And if you're not able to look on, like your good God Himself, then hold your handkerchief before your eyes.

ROBESPIERRE. You deny Virtue?

DANTON. And Vice. All men are hedonists, some crude and some sensitive; Christ was the most sensitive of all; that is the only difference between men I've been able to discover. Every one acts according to his nature, that is, he does what does him good.—It's a shame, isn't it, Incorruptible, to tread on your corns like this?

ROBESPIERRE. Danton, at certain moments Vice is High Treason.

DANTON. But you mustn't suppress it, for God's sake don't, it would be ungrateful; you owe it too much, by contrast I mean.—But to speak in your terms, our blows must be of service to the Republic, we mustn't strike innocent and guilty alike.

ROBESPIERRE. Who says that an innocent man has been struck?

DANTON. Did you hear that, Fabricius? Not one innocent man dead! (*He goes; on his way out, to* PARIS.) There's not a moment to lose, we must show ourselves to the people.

(*Exeunt* DANTON *and* PARIS.)

ROBESPIERRE (*alone*). Let him go! He wants to halt the wild horses of the Revolution at a brothel, like a coachman with his tame hacks. They'll have enough strength to drag him to the guillotine.

To tread on my corns!—To speak in my terms!—Stop! Stop! Is that it?—They will say his gigantic figure threw me so much into the shade that I had to get him out of the sun.—What if they're right?—Is it so necessary? Yes, yes, the Republic! He must go. It's laughable, how my thoughts suspect each other.—He must go. A man who stands still in a crowd that presses forward is as much of an obstacle as if he opposed it; he'll be trampled under foot.

We will not allow the ship of the Revolution to run aground on the shallow scruples and mudbanks of these people; we must cut off the hand which dares to hold it back—yes, and even if he tries to hang on by his teeth!

Away with a clique that has stolen the clothes of the dead aristocrats and inherited their sores!

No Virtue! Virtue one of my corns! In my terms!—How that always comes back to me!—Why can't I get away from the thought? Always he points a bloody finger there, there! I may wrap as many bandages as I like around it, but the blood still pulses through.—(*After a pause.*) I don't know what it is in me that denies the pretence.

(*He goes to the window.*)

Night snores over the earth and tosses in wild dreams. Thoughts, desires, hardly conscious, confused and formless, that timidly hide away from the light of day, now take form and raiment and steal into the silent house of dreams. They open the doors, look out of the windows, they half become flesh, limbs stretch themselves in sleep, the lips murmur.—And is not our waking a clearer dream? Are we not sleep-walkers? Are not our actions those of our dreams, only more precise, defined and brought to completion? Who will blame us for that? In one hour the mind performs more acts of thought than the sluggish organism of our body can carry out in years. The sin is in our thoughts. Whether the thought becomes action, whether the body carries it out, is mere chance.

(*Enter* SAINT-JUST.)

ROBESPIERRE. Help, who's there in the dark? Help, lights, lights!

SAINT-JUST. Do you know my voice?

ROBESPIERRE. Oh, you Saint-Just!

(A MAID *brings lights.*)

SAINT-JUST. Were you alone?

ROBESPIERRE. Danton had just left.

SAINT-JUST. I met him on the way in the Palais Royal. He was making his revolutionary face, speaking in epigrams, and fraternizing with the *sans-culottes;* the whores clustered around his legs and the crowd stood still and whispered to each other what he had said.—We shall lose the benefit of the attack. Must you delay any longer? We shall act without you; our minds are made up.

ROBESPIERRE. What do you want to do?

SAINT-JUST. Summon the Legislative Committee, the Committee of Security, and the Committee of Public Safety to a solemn session.

ROBESPIERRE. Very formal.

SAINT-JUST. We must bury the great corpse decently, like priests, not murderers. It mustn't be torn to pieces, all the limbs must be there.

ROBESPIERRE. Speak more clearly.

SAINT-JUST. We must bury him in full armor, and sacrifice his horses and slaves on the tomb. Lacroix—

ROBESPIERRE. An absolute scoundrel, formerly barrister's clerk, now Lieutenant-General of France. Go on.

SAINT-JUST. Hérault-Séchelles.

ROBESPIERRE. A lovely head.

SAINT-JUST. He was the finely engraved capital letter of the Constitution; we've no need of such ornaments any more, he shall be obliterated.—Philippeau.—Camille.

ROBESPIERRE. Him too?

SAINT-JUST (*gives him a paper*). I thought as much. Read that.

ROBESPIERRE. Oh, 'Le Vieux Cordelier'. Is that all? He's a child, he laughs at you.

SAINT-JUST (*points to a passage*). Read that; read that!

ROBESPIERRE (*reads*). 'This bloody Messiah, Robespierre, on his calvary between the two thieves, Couthon and Collot, to whom he sacrifices and himself is not sacrificed. The holy sisters of the guillotine stand at his feet like Mary and Magdalene. Saint-Just lies in his bosom like John the Beloved Apostle and imparts to the Convention the apocalyptic revelations of the Master; he carries his head like a monstrance.'

SAINT-JUST. I'll make him carry his like Saint-Denis.

ROBESPIERRE (*reads on*). 'Must we believe that the Messiah's neat frock coat is France's winding-sheet, that his thin fingers twitching on the tribune are the knives of the guillotine?—And you, Barère—who once said money would be minted on the Place de la Révolution! But enough —I will not delve into that old sack. He is a widow, who already has had six husbands and helped to bury them all. But what can be done? That is his talent—to see death in people's faces, like Hippocrates, six months before they die. Who wants to sit with corpses and smell their decay?' You too then, Camille?—Away with them! Quickly! Only dead men never return. Have you the indictment ready?

SAINT-JUST. It's not difficult. You gave the hints in the Jacobins.

ROBESPIERRE. I wanted to frighten them.

SAINT-JUST. I need only carry out your threats. Forgers shall give them meat and foreigners drink—they'll die of their meal, I give you my word.

ROBESPIERRE. Quickly then, to-morrow! No long death struggle! I've grown sensitive in the last few days.—Only be quick.

(*Exit* SAINT-JUST.)

(*Alone.*) Yes, a bloody Messiah, who sacrifices and is not sacrificed.—He redeemed men with His blood, and I redeem them with their own. He made them sin against Him and I take the sin upon myself. He had the pleasure of suffering and I have the torments of the hangman. Who denied himself most, He or I?—And yet there's something of folly in that thought—Why must we always look towards Him? Truly the Son of Man is crucified in each of us, and we all wrestle in bloody sweat in the Garden of Gethsemane, but not one of us redeems the others by his wounds.

My Camille!—They are all leaving me—all is waste and empty—I am alone.

ACT II

SCENE I

(*A Room.* DANTON, LACROIX, PHILIPPEAU, PARIS, CAMILLE DESMOULINS.)

CAMILLE. Quickly, Danton, we have no time to lose!

DANTON (*dressing*). But time loses us. How tedious drawing on the shirt first and then the trousers over it, and evening for bed and then creaking out again in the morning, and always setting one foot in front of the other; there's no prospect at all of its ever being any different. That's very sad, and that millions have already done so, and that millions will do again, and that over and above all, we consist of two halves which both do the same thing, so that everything happens double—that is very sad.

CAMILLE. You speak absolutely like a child.

DANTON. The dying often become childish.

LACROIX. You fall into ruin by your delay and you drag all your friends with you. Inform the cowards that it's time for them to rally around you, summon them from the valleys as well as from the hills; shriek over the tyranny of the Committee, speak of daggers, invoke Brutus, then you'll terrify the spectators and collect round you even those who were threatened as accomplices of Hébert's. You must give yourself over to your anger. At least don't let us die disarmed and thrown in the mud, like the shameful Hébert.

DANTON. You have a bad memory, you called me a dead saint. You were more in the right than you yourself thought. I have been to the Sections, they were respectful but like undertakers. I am a relic, and relics are thrown into the gutter; you were right.

LACROIX. Why have you let things come to this?

DANTON. To this? Yes, indeed, finally it bored me, always going round in the same coat and knitting my brow into the same wrinkles! It's so pitiful! To be such a miserable instrument, on which one string always gives out one note! It's not to be borne. I wanted to make myself comfortable. I've succeeded; the Revolution sets me at rest, but in a different way from what I thought.

What else can one rely on? Our whores might take it up with the nuns of the guillotine. I can think of nothing else. You can figure it all out on your fingers. The Jacobins have declared that virtue is on the agenda; the Cordeliers call me Hébert's hangman; the Commune does penance. The Convention—that might still have been a way!—but there was a 31st of May, they wouldn't soften willingly. Robespierre is the dogma of the Revolution which can't be struck out. In any case it wouldn't work. We haven't made the Revolution, the Revolution made us.

And even if it worked—I'd rather be guillotined than guillotine. I've had enough of it, why should we men fight with each other? We should sit down side by side and have peace. A mistake was made in the creating of us; something's lacking in us, I don't know the name for it, but we won't be able to burrow it out of each other's entrails, so why break our bodies over it? Enough, we're sick alchemists.

CAMILLE. Said with more pathos, it would run: how long will humanity in everlasting hunger devour its own limbs? Or how long shall we shipwrecked being on a wreck suck the blood from each other's veins in unquenchable thirst? Or how long must we algebraists in flesh, in our search for the unknown, ever-witheld *x*, write our sums with mutilated limbs?

DANTON. You are a powerful echo.

CAMILLE. You think so?—A pistol shot resounds just like a thunderclap. So much the better for you, you should have me always by you.

PHILIPPEAU. And France remains with her hangmen?

DANTON. What of it? The people enjoy themselves just the same. They are unhappy; can a man ask more to make him compassionate, noble, virtuous, witty, or never bored?—Does it matter whether they die on the guillotine or from fever or from old age? The first is even preferable; they tread with supple limbs behind the scenes, and are able to gesticulate prettily as they go off, and hear the spectators clap. It's very proper and suits us who always stand on the stage, even though finally we're stabbed in earnest.

It's quite right that the length of life should be reduced a little; the coat was too long, our limbs couldn't fill it out. Life becomes an epigram, that's good; for who has breath and spirit enough for an epic in fifty or sixty cantos? It's time one started drinking one's little elixir out of tubs not out of liqueur glasses, so long as one still fills one's mouth full; otherwise one could scarcely make the few drops run together in the clumsy vessel.

But finally I have to cry out that the effort is too great for me, life is not worth the trouble one takes to hold on to it.

PARIS. Then fly, Danton!

DANTON. Can you take your country with you on the soles of your shoes? And finally—and that's the chief thing: they won't dare. (*To* CAMILLE.) Come, my boy, I tell you, they won't dare. Adieu, adieu!

(*Exeunt* DANTON *and* CAMILLE.)

PHILIPPEAU. There he goes.

LACROIX. And doesn't believe a word of what he said. Nothing but laziness! He'd sooner be guillotined than make a speech.

PARIS. What's to be done?

LACROIX. Go home and like Lucretia study some honest matter.

ACT II

SCENE II

(*A Promenade. Passers by.*)

A CITIZEN. My good Jacqueline—I mean to say Korn . . . I meant . . . Cor. . . .

SIMON. Cornelia, citizen, Cornelia.

CITIZEN. My good Cornelia has blessed me with a little boy.

SIMON. Has borne a son to the Republic.

CITIZEN. The Republic? That sounds too universal: one might say. . . .

SIMON. That's exactly it; the particular and the universal must. . . .

CITIZEN. Ah yes, that's what my wife says too.

BALLAD-SINGER (*sings*).

What is then, what is then
A joy and pleasure for all men?

CITIZEN. Ah, but the names; I can't get them right.

SIMON. Christen him Pike, Marat!

BALLAD-SINGER.

In spite of care, in spite of sorrow
Toil and sweat from early morrow
Till the day is past again.

CITIZEN. I should like three; there's something about the number three, something useful and something right; now I have it: Plough, Robespierre. And then the third?

SIMON. Pike.

CITIZEN. Thank you, neighbor; Pike, Plough, Robespierre, three pretty names, that sounds well.

SIMON. I tell you, the breast of your Cornelia will, like the udder of the Roman she-wolf—no, that's no good. Romulus was a tyrant, that's no good.

(CITIZEN *and* SIMON *walk aside.*)

A BEGGAR (*sings*). 'A handful of earth and a little moss!' Dear sirs, lovely ladies!

FIRST GENTLEMAN. Work, you lout, you look quite well-nourished.

SECOND GENTLEMAN (*gives him money*). There, he has a hand like silk. Shameless.

BEGGAR. Sir, where did you get your coat from?

SECOND GENTLEMAN. Work, work! You can have the same; I will give you work, come with me, I live. . . .

BEGGAR. Sir, why did you work?

SECOND GENTLEMAN. Fool, in order to have the coat.

BEGGAR. You've tortured yourself, in order to have a pleasure; for a coat like that's a pleasure, a tramp does that as well.

SECOND GENTLEMAN. Certainly. It's the only way.

BEGGAR. If only I were a fool then. It cancels itself out. The sun shines warm on the corner, and things go easily. (*He sings.*) 'A handful of earth and a little moss.'

ROSALIE (*to* ADELAIDE). Hurry along, there come the soldiers! We haven't had anything warm in our bodies since yesterday.

BEGGAR. 'Is once upon this earth my final lot!' Ladies and Gentlemen!

SOLDIER. Halt! Where are you going, my children? (*To* ROSALIE.) How old are you?

ROSALIE. Just as old as my little finger.

SOLDIER. You're very sharp.

ROSALIE. And you're very blunt.

SOLDIER. Then I'd better sharpen myself on you. (*He sings.*)

Christina, my Christina,
Does the pain hurt you sore,
Hurt you sore, hurt you sore, hurt you sore?

ROSALIE (*sings*).

Oh no, Mister Soldier,
I'd gladly have some more,
Have some more, have some more, have some more.

(*Enter* DANTON *and* CAMILLE.)

DANTON. Isn't it a merry scene?—I scent something in the atmosphere, it's as though the sun hatched out lechery. Wouldn't one like to spring into the middle of it, tear off one's trousers and take them from behind like dogs in the street?

(*Both walk aside.*)

YOUNG GENTLEMAN. Ah, Madame, the sound of a bell, the evening light on the trees, the twinkling of a star. . . .

MADAME. The scent of a flower, the natural pleasures, this pure enjoyment of nature! (*To her daughter.*) See, Eugénie, only virtue has eyes for this!

EUGÉNIE (*kisses her mother's hand*). Ah, Mamma, I see only you!

MADAME. Good child.

YOUNG GENTLEMAN (*whispers in Eugénie's ear*). Do you see the pretty lady with the old gentleman over there?

EUGÉNIE. I know her.

YOUNG GENTLEMAN. They say her barber has done her hair *à l'enfant.*

EUGÉNIE (*laughing*). Naughty gossip!

YOUNG GENTLEMAN. The old gentleman walks beside her, he sees the bud swell and carries it into the sun and thinks that he is the thundery shower which has made it grow.

EUGÉNIE. How improper! I feel like going red!

YOUNG GENTLEMAN. That could make me go white.

DANTON (*to* CAMILLE). Only don't expect me to be serious. I fail to understand why the people don't stand still in the street and laugh in each other's faces. I mean they must laugh up to the windows and out of the graves, and Heaven must burst, and Earth must waltz round with laughter.

(*Exeunt* DANTON *and* CAMILLE.)

FIRST GENTLEMAN. I assure you, an extraordinary discovery. Through it, all the technical arts assume an altogether different physiognomy. Humanity hurries with giant strides towards its high destiny.

SECOND GENTLEMAN. Have you seen the new play? A Babylonian tower, a maze of arches, steps, gangways, and all blown up so light and brave into the air. One grows dizzy at every step. A bizarre head! (*He stands thoughtful.*)

FIRST GENTLEMAN. What is it?

SECOND GENTLEMAN. Oh nothing! Your hand, sir. The puddles, look! Thank you, thank you, I can hardly get past: that might be very dangerous.

FIRST GENTLEMAN. Surely you weren't afraid?

SECOND GENTLEMAN. Yes, the earth is a thin crust; I mean I might fall through, where there's a hole like that.

One must go carefully, one might fall through. But go to the Theatre, that's what I advise.

ACT II

SCENE III

(*A room.* DANTON, CAMILLE, LUCILE.)

CAMILLE. I tell you, if they don't have wooden copies of everything scattered in theatres, concert halls, and art exhibitions, people have neither eyes nor ears for it. Let some one cut out a marionette, so that you see the string which it's tugged by hanging down, and with its joints cracking out a five-foot blank verse at every step—what a character, what consistency! Let him take a little feeling, a sentence, an idea, and dress it in jacket and trousers, give it hands and feet, paint its face and let the thing moan its way through three acts until finally it's married or shoots itself dead—an ideal! Let him fiddle out an opera which reproduces the floating and sinking of human life as a bird warbler does the nightingale—behold art!

Turn the people out of the theatre on to the street—behold pitiful reality! They forget their Lord God Almighty on account of his bad imitators. Of creation, the glowing, roaring, lightening, newly born in them each moment, they hear and see nothing. They go into the theatre, read poems and novels, and make grimaces like the faces they find in them, and say to God's creations, 'How commonplace!' The Greeks knew what they were saying when they told how Pygmalion's statue came to life but bore no children.

DANTON. And the artists treat nature like David, who, when the murdered bodies were thrown out of La Force on to the streets in September, cold-bloodedly drew them and said: I snatch the last spasms of life from these scoundrels.

(*He is called outside.*)

CAMILLE. What have you to say, Lucile?

LUCILE. Nothing, I so like watching you talk.

CAMILLE. Do you listen as well?

LUCILE. Why, certainly!

CAMILLE. Am I in the right? Did you know what I was saying?

LUCILE. No, really not.

(DANTON *comes back.*)

CAMILLE. What's the matter?

DANTON. The Committee of Public Safety has decided on my arrest. I've been warned and offered a place where I can take refuge.

They want my head; they can have it, for all I care. I'm sick of these vexations. Let them take it, what does it matter? I'll know how to die with courage: it's easier than living.

CAMILLE. Danton, there's still time!

DANTON. Impossible—but I shouldn't have thought . . .

CAMILLE. Your laziness!

DANTON. I'm not lazy, but tired; the soles of my feet burn me.

CAMILLE. Where will you go?

DANTON. Yes, who knows where?

CAMILLE. Seriously, where?

DANTON. For a walk, my boy, for a walk.

(*Exit.*)

LUCILE. Camille—

CAMILLE. Quiet, dear child!

LUCILE. When I think that they . . . this head . . .! Camille, dear, it's nonsense, I'm crazy, aren't I?

CAMILLE. Quiet, Danton and I are not one person!

LUCILE. The earth is broad and there are many things on it—then why always this one thing? Who would take it from me? It would be outrageous. And what do they want it for?

CAMILLE. I tell you again: you need not be disturbed! I spoke yesterday with Robespierre: he was friendly. We're a little on edge, that's true; different points of view, nothing else.

LUCILE. Go to see him.

CAMILLE. We sat together on the same school bench. He was always sombre and lonely. I alone sought him out and made him laugh sometimes. He has always shown a great affection for me. I'll go.

LUCILE. So swiftly, my friend? Go! Come! Only this (*She kisses him.*) and this! Go! Go!

(*Exit* CAMILLE.)

These are wicked times. Sometimes things happen like that. Who knows the way out? One must restrain oneself. (*Sings.*)

Oh, parting, parting, parting,
Who of parting had thought?

Why does that, of all things, run through my head? It's bad that it should come of its own like that.—When he went out it seemed to me as though he could never come back again and must always go further away from me, ever further.

How empty this room is! The windows are open, as though a corpse had lain in here. I can't stand being up here any longer.

(*Exit.*)

ACT II

SCENE IV

(*A field.* DANTON.)

DANTON. I can go no further. In this silence, I will make no noise with the chattering of my footsteps and the panting of my breath. (*He sits down. After a pause.*) I've been told of an illness which makes one lose one's memory. There is something of that in death. Then sometimes the hope comes to me that it is still more powerful and makes one lose everything.—Oh, if that were so!—Then I'd run like a Christian to rescue an enemy, that is, my memory.—This place should be safe, yes, for my memory but not for me: the grave gives me more safety, it gives me at least forgetting. It would kill my memory. But here my memory lives and kills me. I or it? The answer is easy. (*He gets up and turns round.*) I flirt with death, it is very pleasant to make eyes at her through lorgnettes from a distance.

Actually, I have to laugh at the whole business. There's a sense of permanence in me which says: to-morrow and the day after to-morrow and so on and on, and everything will be as it is now. This is just a false alarm to frighten me; they'd never dare!

(*Exit.*)

ACT II

SCENE V

(*A room. Night.*)

DANTON (*at a window*). Will it never stop? Will the light never cease glowing and the echoes never be up to date? Will it never be still and dark, so that we no longer listen to and watch each other's filthy sins?—September!

JULIE (*calls from within*). Danton! Danton!

DANTON. Eh!

JULIE (*enters*). What did you call out?

DANTON. Did I call?

JULIE. You spoke of filthy sins and then you groaned: September!

DANTON. I, I? No, I didn't speak, I hardly thought anything—they were only quite gentle, secret thoughts.

JULIE. You are trembling, Danton.

DANTON. And have I no cause for trembling, when the walls chatter so? If my body is so jarred that my fitful thoughts speak madly with lips of stone? That's strange.

JULIE. George, my own George.

DANTON. Yes, Julie, it's very strange. I'd better not think any more, if my thoughts immediately speak. Julie, there are thoughts for which there should be no ears. It's bad that they should cry out like children at their birth; it's bad.

JULIE. God preserve your reason, George. George, do you recognize me?

DANTON. Yes, why not? You're a human being and then a woman and finally my wife, and the earth has five continents, Europe, Asia, Africa, America, Australia, and twice two makes four. You see, I'm in my senses. . . . Didn't I cry out September? Didn't you say something of the sort?

JULIE. Yes, Danton, I heard it through all the rooms.

DANTON. When I went to the window—(*He looks out.*) the town is quiet, all the lights out.

JULIE. A child is crying near by.

DANTON. When I went to the window—through all the streets it cried out and shrieked: September!

JULIE. You were dreaming, Danton: pull yourself together!

DANTON. Dreaming? Yes, I dreamed; but that was different. I'll tell you quickly what—my poor head is weak—quickly. Good, now I have it. Under me the globe panted in its rotation; I had laid hold of it like a wild horse, with giant limbs I clutched into its mane and gripped its flanks, my head bent backwards, my hair streaming over the abyss; so I was dragged along. Then I called out in terror and I awoke. I sprang to the window—and there I heard it, Julie.

What is it that the word wants? Why that of all words? What have I to do with it? Why does it stretch out its bloody hands to me? I never struck it.—Oh, help me, Julie, my brain is numb. Wasn't it in September, Julie?

JULIE. The kings were within forty hours of Paris . . .

DANTON. The fortresses had fallen, the aristocrats were in the city . . .

JULIE. The Republic was lost.

DANTON. Yes, lost. We couldn't let our enemies stab us in the back, we should have been fools, two enemies on a single plank; we or they, the stronger would push the weaker under, isn't that right?

JULIE. Yes, yes.

DANTON. We killed them, that was no murder, it was civil war.

JULIE. You saved the fatherland.

DANTON. Yes, I did, it was self-defence, we did what we had to do. The Man on the Cross made it so easy for himself: 'It must needs be that offences come; but woe to that man by whom the offence cometh.'—It must; that was this must! Who will curse the hand on which the curse of 'must' has fallen? Who spoke that 'must', who? What is it in us that whores, lies, steals, and murders?

We're puppets drawn by unknown powers on wire; nothing, nothing in ourselves—the swords with which spirits fight—only one doesn't see the hands, as in fairy tales.—Now I'm quiet.

JULIE. Perfectly quiet, dear heart?

DANTON. Yes, Julie, come to bed!

ACT II

SCENE VI

(*A street before* DANTON'S *House.* SIMON. CITIZENS *armed as soldiers.*)

SIMON. How late is it in the night?

FIRST CITIZEN. What in the night?

SIMON. How late is the night?

FIRST CITIZEN. As late as between sunset and sunrise.

SIMON. Rogue, what time is it?

FIRST CITIZEN. Look at your watch-dial, it's the time when the pendulum swings to and fro between the sheets.

SIMON. We must up! Forward, citizens! We answer with our heads for it! Dead or living! He has strong limbs! I will go first, citizens. Clear the way for freedom.—Take care of my wife! I will bequeath a crown of acorns to her!

FIRST CITIZEN. A crown of acorns! Enough acorns must fall in her lap every day without that.

SIMON. Onward, citizens, you will have deserved well of the fatherland!

SECOND CITIZEN. I wish the fatherland would deserve well of us. For all the holes we've made in other people's bodies not a single one has yet closed up in our trousers.

FIRST CITIZEN. Do you want your fly-buttons closed up? Ha, ha, ha!

THE OTHERS. Ha, ha, ha!

SIMON. Forward, forward.

(*They crowd into* DANTON'S *house.*)

ACT II

SCENE VII

(*The National Convention. A group of* DEPUTIES.)

LEGENDRE. Will the execution of deputies never cease? Who is safe if Danton falls?

A DEPUTY. What's to be done?

ANOTHER. He must be heard before the bar of the Convention. The success of this method is certain. What could they oppose to his voice?

ANOTHER. Impossible. A decree prevents us.

LEGENDRE. It must either be withdrawn or an exception allowed. I will propose the motion; I count on your support.

THE PRESIDENT. The session is opened.

LEGENDRE (*ascends the tribune*). Four members of the National Convention were arrested during the past night. I know that Danton is one of them, the names of the remainder I do not know. Nevertheless, whoever they are, I demand that they be heard before the bar.

Citizens, I make this declaration: I hold Danton to be as innocent as myself, and I don't believe that any accusation can be made against me. I will attack no member of the Committee of Security or of the Committee of Public Safety, but well-founded reasons leave me afraid lest private hatred and private passions may deprive Liberty of men who have done her the greatest services. The man who through his energy saved France in the year 1792 deserves to be heard; he should be allowed to clear himself, if he is charged with high treason.

(*Great excitement.*)

SOME VOICES. We support Legendre's motion.

A DEPUTY. We are here in the name of the people; without the will of those who voted for us, no one can deprive us of our places.

ANOTHER. Your words stink of corpses; you have taken them out of the mouths of the Girondists. Do you want privilege? The knife of the law sweeps over all heads.

ANOTHER. We cannot allow our committees to send our lawgivers from the sanctuary of the law to the guillotine.

ANOTHER. Crime has no sanctuary, only crowned criminals find one on the throne.

ANOTHER. Only thieves appeal to their right of sanctuary.

ANOTHER. Only murderers fail to recognize it.

ROBESPIERRE. Such disorder, unknown for so long in this assembly, shows that great matters are under discussion. To-day will decide whether a few men will benefit by it to win a victory over their country.—How can you so far deny your fundamental principles as to grant a few individuals to-day that which yesterday you refused Chabot, Delaunai, and Fabre? What is the meaning of this discrimination in favor of a few men? Why should I concern myself with the complimentary speeches which people pay to themselves and their friends? Only too many experiences have shown us how much they are worth. We do not ask whether a man has brought to completion this or that task of patriotism; we ask after his whole political career.—Legendre appears to be ignorant of the names of the arrested men; the whole Convention knows them. His friend Lacroix is one of them. Why does Legendre seem ignorant of this? Because he knows that only shamelessness could defend Lacroix. Danton alone he named, because he thinks that a privilege has attached itself to this name. No, we want no privileges, we want no idols.

(*Applause.*)

What is there in Danton that places him before Lafayette, before Dumouriez, before Brissot, Fabre, Chabot, Hébert? What does one say of these that one cannot also say of him? And did you spare them? Through what service has he earned precedence over his fellow citizens? Perhaps because certain betrayed individuals, and others who had not let themselves be betrayed, had ranged themselves behind him, so that in his train they might run into the arms of power and fortune? The more he has betrayed those patriots who put trust in him, the more energetic must he find the strength of the friends of liberty.

They wish to inspire you with fear at the misuse of a power which you yourselves have exercised. They whine over the despotism of the

Committees, as though the trust which the people have placed in you, and which you have handed over to these committees, were not a sure guarantee of your patriotism. They pretend that everybody is trembling. But I tell you that whoever at this moment trembles is guilty, because innocence never trembles before public vigilance.

(*General applause.*)

They've tried to frighten me too; they gave me to understand that the danger, if it neared Danton, could also reach as far as me. They wrote to me that Danton's friends held me besieged, believing that the memory of an old association, a blind faith in a simulated virtue could induce me to restrain my ardor and my passion for liberty.—So I declare that nothing will stop me, not even should Danton's danger become my own. We all need a certain courage and a certain grandeur of soul. Only criminals and vulgar spirits fear to see those who resemble them fall at their side, because if a troop of accomplices no longer stuck to them, they would see themselves exposed in the light of truth. But if there are spirits such as these in this assembly, so also are there those who are heroic. The number of scoundrels is not great; we have only to lop off a few heads and the country is saved. (*Applause.*)

I demand that Legendre's motion be rejected.

(*The delegates rise together as a sign of general approbation.*)

SAINT-JUST. There seem to be in this assembly a few sensitive ears which cannot hear the word 'blood' with equanimity. A few general observations on the relations between nature and history should convince them that we are not crueller than Nature or than Time. Nature follows quietly and irresistibly her laws; Man is destroyed, wherever he comes in conflict with them. An alteration in the ingredients of the air, a flaring up of the tellurian fires, a vacillation in the balance of masses of water, and an epidemic, a volcanic eruption, a flood bury thousands. What is the result? A meaningless, on the whole, scarcely noticeable alteration of physical nature, which would have passed by scarcely leaving a trace, if corpses did not lie in its path.

I ask you: shall moral nature be more considerate than physics in making her revolutions? Shall not an idea, just as well as a law of physics, annihilate that which opposes it? Above all, shall an experience which alters the whole configuration of moral nature, which means humanity, not dare to wade through blood? The spirit of the world uses our arms in the spiritual sphere just as in the physical it uses volcanoes and floods. What difference does it make whether one dies now through an epidemic or through the Revolution?

The strides of humanity are slow; one can only count them by centuries; behind each one rise the graves of generations. To arrive at the simplest invention and fundamental truth has cost the lives of millions who died on the way. Is it not then simply that in a time where the space of history is faster, more men lose their breath?

We conclude quickly and simply: since all men were created in the same circumstances, all are equal, apart from those differences which Nature herself has made. Therefore every one has merits but none has privileges, either as individuals or as a smaller or larger class of individuals.—Every link in this argument translated into reality has killed its men. The 14th of July, the 10th of August, the 31st of May are its punctuation marks. It required four years to be carried out in the physical world, and under ordinary conditions it would have required centuries and been punctuated by generations. Is it so miraculous that the stream of the Revolution at every stop, at every new bend, discharges its corpses?

We still have a few inferences to add to our proposition; shall a few hundred corpses prevent us from making them? Moses led his people through the Red Sea and into the desert, till the old corrupted generation had been annihilated, before he founded the new state. Legislators! We have neither Red Sea nor desert, but we have war and the guillotine.

The Revolution is like the daughter of Pelias; she dismembers humanity to make it young. Humanity comes out of the cauldron of blood, like earth out of the waters of the deluge, to raise itself with primordial limbs, as though it were first created. (*Long-sustained applause, some deputies rise in enthusiasm.*) We call upon all the secret enemies of tyranny, who in Europe and the whole globe carry under their cloaks the dagger of Brutus, to share with us this exalted moment.

(*The spectators and the deputies join in singing the 'Marseillaise.'*)

ACT III

SCENE I

(*The Luxembourg. A hall with prisoners.* CHAUMETTE, PAYNE, MERCIER, HÉRAULT-DE-SÉCHELLES *and other prisoners.*)

CHAUMETTE (*takes* PAYNE'S *arm*). Listen, Payne, that might be it. Before it came over me so clearly, to-day I have a headache; help me a little with your arguments, it seems to me quite uncannily difficult.

PAYNE. Come, come, philosopher Anaxagoras, I will catechize thee.—There is no God, for either God made the world, or he did not. If he did not create it, then the world contained its origins in itself, and there is no

God, since God is only God through the fact that he contains the origins of all being. Now God cannot have created the world; for creation must either be eternal like God, or it must have a beginning. If it had a beginning, God must have created it at a certain point in time. Thus God, having rested for an eternity, must once suddenly have become active, and must therefore have undergone an alteration in himself, which made him apply the conception of time, both of which conflict with the nature of God's being. Thus it is impossible for God to have created the world. Now since we know very clearly that we exist or at least that our own ego exists and that, in accordance with what I have just told you, it also must have origins in itself or in something not itself which is not God, then it follows that there is no God .*Quod erat demonstrandum.*

CHAUMETTE. Yes, indeed, that gives me light again. I thank you, I thank you.

MERCIER. Wait, Payne! Supposing though that creation were eternal?

PAYNE. Then it ceases to be creation any more, it becomes one with God or an attribute of him, as Spinoza said, then God is present in everything, in thee, my worthiest philosopher Anaxagoras, and in me. That wouldn't be so bad, but you must admit that it's not saying much for the heavenly majesty if the Lord God Almighty gets a headache in each one of us, or leprosy, or is buried alive, or at least experiences a very unpleasant impression of these things.

MERCIER. But surely there must be a first cause?

PAYNE. Who denies it? But who insists that this first cause must be that which we think of as God—that is to say, as perfection? Do you hold that the world is perfect?

MERCIER. No.

PAYNE. Then how do you arrive at an imperfect effect from a perfect cause?—Voltaire dared displease Gods as little as kings, and for that reason he did. He who has nothing except his reasoning, yet who does not know how or does not dare to use it consistently, is a blunderer.

MERCIER. Against that, I ask can a perfect cause have a perfect effect, which means—can something perfect create something perfect? Is it not impossible, because the created thing can never contain its origin within itself, which indeed, as you say, appertains to perfection?

CHAUMETTE. Be quiet! Be quiet!

PAYNE. Calm yourself, philosopher! You are quite right; but if God once starts creating, then if he can only create imperfect things he would have done better to leave well alone. Isn't it very human of us that we can only think of God as creating? Since we must always stir and shake ourselves, only in order that we may ever be saying to ourselves that we exist! But must we ascribe to God as well this sickening need?—Must we, if our spirit is sunk in a being harmoniously at rest with itself in eternal blessedness, at once assume that it stretches out a finger over the table and kneads homunculi of bread—through immeasurable need for love, as we secretly whisper in each other's ears? Must we do all this merely to make ourselves the sons of God? I prefer a lesser father, at least I will not be able to say afterwards that he let me be educated beneath his rank in the manger or amongst the slaves.

Do away with imperfection: then alone can you demonstrate God—Spinoza tried it. One can deny evil but not pain, only the understanding can accept God, the feeling rebels against him. Mark well, Anaxagoras, why do I suffer? That is the rock of atheism. The least twinge of pain, stir it only an atom, rends your creation from top to bottom.

MERCIER. And morality?

PAYNE. First you prove God from morality and then morality from God. A nice vicious circle that licks its own hindquarters. What do you want with your morality? I don't know whether there is an intrinsic good or evil and have no need to alter my way of life on that account. I act according to my nature; what suits it is good for me and I do it, and what is bad for it is bad for me and I don't do it and take sides against it when it lies in my way. You can be virtuous, as they call it, and arm yourself against so-called vice, without being obliged on that account to despise your opponents, which is a very sad feeling to have!

CHAUMETTE. True, very true!

HÉRAULT. O, philosopher Anaxagoras, one can also say since God is everything, he must also be his own opposite, that's to say perfect and imperfect, evil and good, blessed and suffering; the result would admittedly then be nil, it would cancel itself out, we should end with nothing.—Rejoice, you emerge victorious, you can pray undisturbed to Madame Momoro as nature's masterpiece; at least she's left you a crown of roses in the groin.

CHAUMETTE. Gentlemen, I give you my heartiest thanks.

(*Exit.*)

PAYNE. He still has no trust, he'll still give himself extreme unction, set his feet towards Mecca, and have himself circumcised, in order to lose no opportunity.

(DANTON, LACROIX, CAMILLE, PHILIPPEAU *are brought in.*)

HÉRAULT (*runs to* DANTON *and embraces him*). Good morning! No—I should say—Good night! I can't ask how you slept? How will you sleep?

DANTON. Well, well. One must go laughing to bed.

MERCIER (*to* PAYNE). These mastiffs with wings of doves! He's the evil genius of the Revolution, he defied his mother but she was stronger than he.

PAYNE. His life and his death are equal misfortunes.

LACROIX (*to* DANTON). I hadn't thought that you'd be here so soon.

DANTON. I knew, I was warned.

LACROIX. And you said nothing?

DANTON. To what? An apoplexy is the best death. Would you care to be ill first? And I thought they'd never dare. (*To* HÉRAULT.) It's better to lie down in the earth than to walk on it with corns. I'd rather have her as a cushion than as a footstool.

HÉRAULT. At least we won't have warts on our fingers when we stroke the cheeks of the pretty lady putrefaction.

CAMILLE. Only don't trouble yourself, you can hang your tongue out as far as your neck, but still you can't lick the death-sweat from your brow. O Lucile! That is a great affliction.

(*The prisoners crowd around the newcomers.*)

DANTON (*to* PAYNE). What you did for the good of your country, I have tried to do for mine. I was less fortunate; they send me to the scaffold; for my own part, I won't trip.

MERCIER (*to* DANTON). The blood of the twenty-two drowns you.

A PRISONER (*to* HÉRAULT). The power of the people and the power of reason are one.

ANOTHER (*to* CAMILLE). Well, General Procurator of the Lanterns, your improvements in the lighting of the streets have not made France any lighter.

ANOTHER. Leave him alone. His are the lips which spoke the word pity.

(*He embraces* CAMILLE, *several other prisoners follow his example.*)

PHILIPPEAU. We are priests who have prayed with the dying. We have been infected and die of the same epidemic.

A FEW VOICES. The blow that falls on you, kills us all.

CAMILLE. Gentlemen, I grieve deeply that our efforts were so fruitless; I go to the scaffold, because my eyes were wet at the fate of a few unfortunate ones.

ACT III

SCENE II

(*A room.* FOUQUIER-TINVILLE, HERMAN.)

FOUQUIER. All prepared?

HERMAN. It will be difficult; if Danton weren't amongst them it would be easy.

FOUQUIER. He must open the ball.

HERMAN. He will frighten the jury, he's the scarecrow of the revolution.

FOUQUIER. The jury must will it.

HERMAN. I thought of a way, but it would violate the letter of the law.

FOUQUIER. Only say it!

HERMAN. We don't draw by lot, but pick out our stalwarts.

FOUQUIER. That must be done—that will provide a good bonfire. There are nineteen of them. They're cleverly mixed together. The four forgers, then a few bankers and foreigners. That's a piquant tribunal. The people need such. Good then, let's have reliable people. Who, for example?

HERMAN. Leroi, he is deaf, so he hears nothing the accused say. With him there, Danton can scream himself hoarse.

FOUQUIER. Very good. Go on.

HERMAN. Vilatte and Lumière, the one sits in the pub all day, and the other's always asleep. Both only open their mouths to say the word 'Guilty!' Girard makes it a principle that no one can clear himself once he's been put before the Tribunal. Renaudin. . . .

FOUQUIER. He too? He once helped get some parsons off.

HERMAN. Don't worry, a few days ago he came to me and demanded that all the condemned should be bled before their execution to make them a little pale; the defiant look of most of them annoys him.

FOUQUIER. Very good. Then I shall rely on you.

HERMAN. Leave it to me!

ACT III

SCENE III

(*The Luxembourg. A Corridor.* LACROIX, DANTON, MERCIER, *and other prisoners pacing to and fro.*)

LACROIX (*to a prisoner*). What, so many unfortunates, and in such a wretched situation?

PRISONER. Have the guillotine carts never told you that Paris is a slaughterhouse?

MERCIER. Isn't it so, Lacroix? Equality swings its sickle over all heads, the lava of revolution flows; the guillotine makes Republicans. The gallery clap and the Romans rub their hands; but they don't hear in every one of these words the death rattle of a victim. Follow your slogans to the point at which they become incarnate. Stare around you, you have said it all, it is a mimic translation of your words. These grief-stricken people, their hangmen and their guillotines are your speeches turned to life. You build your system, as Bajazet his pyramids, from the heads of men.

DANTON. You're right! To-day one works out everything in human flesh. That is the curse of our time. My body also will be used now.

It's exactly a year since I established the Revolutionary Tribunal. I pray forgiveness of God and humanity for it; I wished to anticipate a new September massacre, I hoped to save the innocent, but this slow murder with its formalities is more cruel and just as inescapable. Gentlemen, I hoped to have you all out of this place.

MERCIER. Oh, we shall all get out of it!

DANTON. Now I am with you; Heaven knows how it will end!

ACT III

SCENE IV

(*The Revolutionary Tribunal.*)

HERMAN (*to* DANTON). Your name, citizen?

DANTON. The Revolution names my name. My dwelling will soon be in nothing and my name in the Pantheon of history.

HERMAN. Danton, the Convention accuses you of having conspired with Mirabeau, with Dumouriez, with Orleans, with the Girondists, with the foreigners, and with the factions of Louis XVII.

DANTON. My voice, which I have so often raised for the people's cause, will easily refute this calumny. The wretches who accuse me should appear here, and I will cover them with shame. The Committee should present themselves here, I shall only answer in front of them. I need them as prosecutors and as witnesses. They ought to show themselves.

Apart from all this, what concern have I with you and your accusations? I have told you already: the void will soon be my sanctuary. To me life is a load, they may tear it away from me, I long to shake it off.

HERMAN. Danton, audacity is the mark of crime, calm the mark of innocence.

DANTON. Private audacity is doubtless blameworthy, but that national audacity which I have so often shown, with which I have so often fought for freedom, is the most meritorious of all the virtues. That is my audacity, that is what, for the good of the Republic, I use here against my miserable accusers. Can I control myself when I see myself calumniated in so shameful a manner? No one can expect cool pleading from a revolutionary like me. Men of my stamp are inestimable in revolutions, the genius of freedom hovers on their brows.

(*Signs of applause amongst the audience.*)

I am accused of having conspired with Mirabeau, with Dumouriez, with Orleans, of having sat at the feet of sick despots; I am called upon to make my answer before inescapable, unbending justice! You, cowering Saint-Just, will be responsible to posterity for this blasphemy.

HERMAN. I call upon you to answer calmly; think of Marat, he came before his judges with awe.

DANTON. You have laid hands on my whole life; for that reason it rises and faces you. I will bury you under the weight of each one of my deeds.

I am not proud of this. Fate controlled our arms, but only powerful natures are her instruments.—On the field of Mars I declared war on the monarchy, I struck it on the 10th of August, on the 21st of January I killed it and threw the head of a king as a gauntlet to kings. (*Repeated signs of applause; he becomes the accuser.*) When I throw a glance at this shameful document, I feel my whole being quiver. Who then are those who had to force Danton to show himself on that memorable 10th of August? Who are the privileged beings from whom he borrowed his energy?—My accusers should appear! I am quite in my senses when I make this demand! I will expose these worthless scoundrels and cast them back into the nothing out of which they have crawled.

HERMAN (*rings a bell*). Don't you hear the bell?

DANTON. The voice of a man who defends his honor and his life must cry louder than your bell.

In September I fed the young brood of the Revolution with the dismembered bodies of the aristocrats. My voice has forged weapons for the People from the gold of the aristocrats and the rich. My voice was the hurricane which drowned the satellites of despotism under waves of bayonets. (*Loud applause.*)

HERMAN. Danton, your voice is exhausted. You are too violently moved. You will conclude your defence next time. You need rest.—The session is ended.

DANTON. Now you still know Danton—a few hours more and he will slumber in the arms of fame.

ACT III

SCENE V

(*The Luxembourg. A cell.* DILLON, LAFLOTTE, *a* GAOLER.)

DILLON. Fool, don't shine your nose in my face like that. Ha, ha, ha!

LAFLOTTE. Keep your mouth shut, your sickle moon has a stinking halo! Ha, ha, ha, ha!

GAOLER. Ha, ha, ha! Do you think, sir, that you could read by your light?

(*He shows the writing on a paper which he holds in his hand.*)

DILLON. Give it to me!

GAOLER. Sir, my sickle moon has ebbed.

LAFLOTTE. Your trousers look as if it were the flood.

GAOLER. No, they draw water. (*To* DILLON.) She has waned at your sun, sir; you must give me that which makes you fiery again, if you wish to see.

DILLON. There, knave! Clear out!

(*Gives him money. Exit* GAOLER.)

DILLON (*reads*). Danton has terrified the tribunal, the jury hesitated, the audience muttered. The crowd was extraordinary. The people pressed round the Palace of Justice and stood right up to the benches. A handful of gold, an arm to strike—hm! hm! (*He walks to and fro and drinks from time to time from a glass.*) If only I had one foot on the pavement, I wouldn't allow myself to be struck down like this. Yes, only one foot on the pavement.

LAFLOTTE. And one in the tumbrils.

DILLON. You think so? A couple of strides still lie between, long enough to cover with the corpses of the Committee. The time has come at last when right-thinking people should lift their heads.

LAFLOTTE (*to himself*). So that it's easier to cut them off. Go on, old man, only a few glasses more and I'll be floating.

DILLON. The rascals, the fools, in the end they'll guillotine themselves.

(*He paces to and fro.*)

LAFLOTTE (*aside*). One could love life again properly, like a child, if one gave it to oneself. But that doesn't often happen, to commit incest with chance and become one's own father. Father and child at the same time. A crazy Oedipus!

DILLON. You don't fodder the people with corpses. Let the wives of Danton and Camille throw banknotes among the people, that's better than heads.

LAFLOTTE (*aside*). Unlike Oedipus, I won't tear my eyes out, I may need them to weep for the good general.

DILLON. Hands on Danton! Who's safe after that? Fear will unite them.

LAFLOTTE (*aside*). Yes, he's lost. What does it matter then if I tread on a corpse in order to clamber out of the grave?

DILLON. Only a foot on the pavement. I will find enough people, old soldiers, Girondists, çi-devants; we'll break open the prisons, we must come to terms with the prisoners.

LAFLOTTE. Certainly it smells a little of treachery. What does it matter? I should like to try that myself, until now I've been too one-sided. One gets remorse, that too is a change; it isn't so unpleasant to smell one's own stink. The prospect of the guillotine has begun to bore me; to wait so long for the thing! I have been through it at least twenty times in my mind. There's nothing spicy about it any longer. It's become quite vulgar.

DILLON. A letter must be got through to Danton's wife.

LAFLOTTE (*aside*). And then—it isn't death I fear but the pain. It might hurt, who can guarantee it doesn't? True they say it only lasts a moment; but pain has a finer measure for time; it splits up a fraction of a second. No, pain's the only sin, and suffering the only burden; I will stay virtuous.

DILLON. Listen, Laflotte, where is that fellow gone to? I have money, it must succeed. We must strike while the iron is hot; my plan is ready.

LAFLOTTE. At once, at once! I know the turnkey, I'll speak to him; you can count on me, general. We'll get out of this hole (*To himself, going out.*) to go into another: I into the broadest, the world—he into the narrowest, the grave.

ACT III

SCENE VI

(*The Committee of Public Safety.* SAINT-JUST, BARÈRE, COLLOT D'HERBOIS, BILLAUD-VARENNES.)

BARÈRE. What does Fouquier write?

SAINT-JUST. The second hearing is over. The prisoners demand the appearance of several members of the Convention and the Committee of Public Safety; they appeal to the people against the silencing of witnesses. The excitement seems to be indescribable. Danton parodied Jupiter and shook his locks.

COLLOT. The easier for Samson to shear them.

BARÈRE. We mustn't show ourselves, the fishwives and rag-collectors might find us less imposing.

BILLAUD. The people have an instinct for letting themselves be trodden on, even if it's only with glances: these insolent physiognomies please them. Such expressions are more awe-inspiring than a nobleman's coat of arms; the fine aristocracy of those who despise humanity sits on them. Every one whom it disgusts to be looked at up and down, should help to smash them in.

BARÈRE. He is like the horned Siegfried. The blood of the Septembrists has made him invulnerable.—What does Robespierre say?

SAINT-JUST. He behaves as though he had something to say. The jury must declare themselves sufficiently instructed and close the debate.

BARÈRE. Impossible—that would never do.

SAINT-JUST. They must be done away with—at any price—even if we have to throttle them with our hands. 'Dare!' Danton mustn't have taught us that word in vain. The Revolution won't stumble over their bodies; but if Danton stays alive—he will seize her by the skirt and he has something in his face as though he might rape liberty. (*He is called away.*)

(*The* GAOLER *enters.*)

GAOLER. Some prisoners in St. Pelagie lie dying, they are asking for a doctor.

BILLAUD. Unnecessary; so much the less trouble for the executioner.

GAOLER. There are pregnant women amongst them—

BILLAUD. So much the better. Their children will need no coffins.

BARÈRE. The consumption of an aristocrat spares the Tribunal a session. Any medicine would be counter-revolutionary.

COLLOT (*taking up a paper*). A petition! A woman's name!

BARÈRE. Yes, from one of those who are compelled to choose between the plank of a guillotine and the bed of a Jacobin. Those who, like Lucretia, die at the loss of their honor, but somewhat later than the Roman . . . in childbirth or of old age. Perhaps it may not be so unpleasant to drive a Tarquin out of the virtuous Republic of a virgin.

COLLOT. She is too old. Madame desires death, she knows how to express herself, prison lies on her like the lid of a coffin. She's been there four weeks. The answer's easy. (*He writes and reads out.*) 'Citizeness, you have not yet wished long enough for death.'

BARÈRE. Well said! But Collot, it's not good that the guillotine begins to laugh; the people aren't afraid of it any more; one mustn't make oneself so familiar.

(SAINT-JUST *returns.*)

SAINT-JUST. I have just received a denunciation. There is a conspiracy in the prison; a young man called Laflotte has discovered all. He was in the same cell as Dillon. Dillon got drunk and blabbed.

BARÈRE. He cuts his own neck off with his bottle; that's happened often enough before.

SAINT-JUST. Danton's and Camille's wives must scatter money amongst the people; Dillon will break out; the prisoners will be freed; the Convention will be blown up.

BARÈRE. Fairy stories!

SAINT-JUST. We'll send them to sleep with these fairy tales. I hold the proofs in my hands; add to them the impudence of the accused, the muttering of the people, the dismay of the jury; I'll make a report.

BARÈRE. Yes, go, Saint-Just, and spin your periods, where every comma is the stroke of a sword and every period a head struck off.

SAINT-JUST. The Convention must decree that the Tribunal carry through the session without interruption and that it exclude from the proceedings any witness who shows contempt for the judges or who creates a scene causing disturbance.

BARÈRE. You have the revolutionary instinct; that sounds quite moderate and yet it will achieve its purpose. They cannot be silent, Danton is bound to cry out.

SAINT-JUST. I count on your support. In the Convention there are people as ill as Danton who fear the same cure. They've gained courage, they'll scream about the irregular procedure . . .

BARÈRE (*interrupting him*). I'll say to them: in Rome the consul who discovered the Catiline conspiracy and punished the criminals with instant death was accused of irregular procedure. Who were his accusers?

COLLOT (*with pathos*). Go, Saint-Just, the lava of revolution flows! Liberty will suffocate in her embrace those weaklings who wished to fertilize her mighty womb; the majesty of the people will appear in thunder and lightning, as Jupiter to Semele, and change them into ashes. Go, Saint-Just, we will help you; the thunderbolt must strike on the heads of cowards.

(SAINT-JUST *exit.*)

BARÈRE. Did you hear the word 'Cure'? They'll end by making the guillotine a specific against syphilis. They don't fight the moderates, they fight vice.

BILLAUD. Until now our ways have gone together.

BARÈRE. Robespierre will make the Revolution a hall for preaching moral sermons and use the guillotine as a pulpit.

BILLAUD. Or as a hassock.

COLLOT. On which finally he'll not stand but lie.

BARÈRE. That will happen easily enough. The world would be topsy turvy if the so-called wrong-doers were hanged by the so-called righteous folk.

COLLOT (*to* BARÈRE). When do you return to Clichy?

BARÈRE. When the doctor stops visiting me.

COLLOT. Doesn't a star stand over the place, under whose beams the marrow of your spine will be quite dried up?

BILLAUD. Soon the pretty fingers of that charming Demaly will tear it out of its sheath, and make it hang down over his back as a pigtail.

BARÈRE (*shrugs his shoulders*). Pooh! Virtue should know nothing of those things.

BILLAUD. He's an impotent free-mason.

(BILLAUD *and* COLLOT *exeunt.*)

BARÈRE. The monster! 'You have not yet wished long enough for death!' These words should have withered the tongue that spoke them.

And I? When the Septembrists broke into the prisons, a prisoner seized his knife, joined with the assassins, and plunged it into the breast of a priest; he was saved! Who could object to that? Shall I now go join with the murderers or sit on the Committee of Public Safety? Shall I use the guillotine or a pocket knife? It's the same situation only under rather more complex circumstances; the fundamentals are the same.—And dare he murder one, two, or three or even more of us? Where does it end? There come the barleycorns, do two make a heap, or three, or four, or how many? Come, my conscience, come, my chicken, cluck, cluck, cluck, here's your fodder.

Yet—if I also were a prisoner? If I were suspected, it would be the same thing, my death would be certain. Come, my conscience, you and I still carry on all right!

(*Exit.*)

ACT III

SCENE VII

(*The Conciergerie.* LACROIX, DANTON, PHILIPPEAU, CAMILLE.)

LACROIX. You have shrieked well, Danton; had you taken such pains earlier with your life, things would be different now. You realize now, don't you, when death comes so shamelessly close to one, and has such stinking breath, and becomes more and more importunate?

CAMILLE. If only she'd ravish one, and tear her prize from the hot limbs with fighting and struggle! But with such formality, like a marriage with an old woman, with the contracts set out, with the witnesses called, with the amens said, and then with the counterpane lifted up when, with her cold limbs, she creaks slowly into bed.

DANTON. Would it were a fight so that arms and teeth clutched at each other! But I feel as though I'd fallen into a mill-shaft and that my limbs were slowly and systematically being wrenched off by the cold physical power. To be killed so mechanically!

CAMILLE. And then to lie there, alone, cold, stiff, in the damp vapor of putrefaction. Perhaps death slowly torments the life out of one's fibres, with the knowledge, perhaps, that one's falling to pieces.

PHILIPPEAU. Quiet, my friend. We are like the meadow saffron which first bears seed after the winter. We only distinguish ourselves from flowers which are transplanted because in the attempt we stink a little. Is that so bad?

DANTON. An edifying prospect! From one manure heap to another. Isn't that the theistic theory of classes? From first to second, second to third and so on? I've had enough of the school bench, I've got piles on my seat like an ape from sitting on it.

PHILIPPEAU. Then what would you like?

DANTON. Rest.

PHILIPPEAU. Rest is in God.

DANTON. In nothingness. What can you sink back in which is more restful than nothingness, and if the highest peace is God, isn't nothingness God? But I'm an atheist; that accursed phrase! Something cannot become nothing! And I am something, that is the trouble! Creation has made itself so broad, nothing is empty. Everything full of multitude. Nothingness has killed itself, creation is its wound, we are the drops of its blood, the world is the grave in which it decomposes. That sounds mad but there's some truth in it.

CAMILLE. The world's the eternal Jew, nothingness is death, but that's impossible. Oh, not to be able to die, as the song goes!

DANTON. We are all buried alive and set aside like kings in threefold or fourfold coffins, under the sky, in our houses, in our coats and shirts. We scratch for fifty years on our coffin lids. If one could believe in annihilation! Yes, that would be a help.—There is no hope in death. It is only a simpler form of laziness, whilst life is one that is more complex, more organized. That's the whole difference! But it's exactly this form of indolence which I've been accustomed to; the devil knows how I'll get used to another.

O, Julie, if I could go alone! If she would leave me in solitude! And if I could fall to pieces utterly, dissolve entirely—then I would be a handful of tormented dust—every one of my atoms could only find peace in her. I cannot die, no, I cannot die. We aren't struck down yet. We must shriek, they must tear every drop of life-blood out of my limbs.

LACROIX. We must stand by our demands. Our accusers and the Committee must appear before the Tribunal.

ACT III

SCENE VIII

(*A room.* FOUQUIER, AMAR, VOULAND.)

FOUQUIER. I no longer know what answer to make: they are demanding a commission.

AMAR. We've got the scoundrels—here you have what you want. (*Hands* FOUQUIER *a paper.*)

VOULAND. That will satisfy them.

FOUQUIER. Certainly. We needed it.

AMAR. Quickly then, so that we rid ourselves of this affair and of them. . . .

ACT III

SCENE IX

(*The Revolutionary Tribunal.*)

DANTON. The Republic is in danger and is not instructed of it. We call upon the people; my voice is still strong enough to speak the funeral oration of the Committee. I repeat—we demand a commission; we have important matters to reveal. I will re-establish myself in the citadel of reason, I will break through with the cannons of truth and pulverize my enemies. (*Signs of applause.*)

(*Enter* FOUQUIER, AMAR, *and* VOULAND.)

FOUQUIER. Silence in the name of the Republic and in the name of the law! The Convention decrees: in view of the fact that signs of mutiny have been shown in the prisons; in view of the fact that the wives of Danton and Camille distribute money amongst the people and that General Dillon has plotted to escape and put himself at the head of an insurrection to free the accused; lastly, in view of the fact that they themselves have endeavored to provoke disturbances and to insult the Tribunal: the Tribunal will be empowered to carry out its inquiry without interruption and to exclude any of the accused who shall ignore the respect due to the law.

DANTON. I ask all here whether we have derided the Tribunal, the People or the Convention?

VOICES. No! No!

CAMILLE. Miserable wretches, they wish to murder my Lucile!

DANTON. One day the truth will be known. I see a great misfortune overwhelming France. It is dictatorship; it has torn off its veils, it carries its head high, it strides over our bodies. (*Pointing at* AMAR *and* VOULAND.) See there the cowardly murderers, see the ravens of the Committee of Public Safety! I accuse Robespierre, Saint-Just and their hangmen of high treason. They want to suffocate the Republic in blood. The ruts of their guillotine carts are the roads by which the foreign armies will thrust into the heart of the Fatherland.

How long will the footprints of liberty be graves? You need bread and you are thrown heads! You thirst, and they make you lap up the blood from the steps of the guillotine! (*Great emotion amongst the audience, cries of applause.*)

MANY VOICES. Long live Danton! Down with the Committee! (*The prisoners are led away by force.*)

ACT III

SCENE X

(*A square in front of the Palace of Justice. A crowd.*)

VOICES. Down with the Committee! Long live Danton!

FIRST CITIZEN. Yes, that's right. Heads instead of bread, blood instead of wine.

WOMEN. The guillotine is a bad mill and Samson a bad baker. We want bread, bread!

SECOND CITIZEN. Your bread—Danton's devoured it. His head will give bread to all of you. He was right.

FIRST CITIZEN. Danton was with us on the 10th of August. Danton was with us in September. Where were the people who make accusations against him?

SECOND CITIZEN. And Lafayette was with you in Versailles, and was a traitor just the same.

FIRST CITIZEN. Who says that Danton is a traitor?

SECOND CITIZEN. Robespierre.

FIRST CITIZEN. Then Robespierre is a traitor!

SECOND CITIZEN. Who says that?

FIRST CITIZEN. Danton.

SECOND CITIZEN. Danton has beautiful clothes, Danton has a beautiful house, Danton has a beautiful wife, he bathes himself in Burgundy, eats pheasants off silver plates and sleeps with your wives and daughters when he's drunk. Danton was poor like you. Where does it all come from? The king bought it for him, hoping Danton would save his crown for him. The Duke of Orleans made him a present of it, hoping he would *steal* the crown for *him*. The foreigner gave it to him, hoping he would betray you all. What has Robespierre got? The virtuous Robespierre! You all know him.

ALL. Long live Robespierre! Down with Danton! Down with the traitor.

ACT IV

SCENE I

(*A room.* JULIE, A BOY.)

JULIE. It's all over. They trembled before him. They kill him out of fear. Go! I have seen him for the last time; tell him I could not see him as he is now. (*Gives him a lock of hair.*) There, give him this and tell him he will not go alone—he will understand. And come back quickly, I will read his look in your eyes.

ACT IV

SCENE II

(*A street.* DUMAS, A CITIZEN.)

CITIZEN. How can they condemn so many unfortunates to death after such a trial?

DUMAS. Indeed it's extraordinary; but revolutionaries have a sense other men lack, and their instinct never betrays them.

CITIZEN. It's the instinct of the tiger.—You have a wife?

DUMAS. Soon I shall have had one.

CITIZEN. So it's true?

DUMAS. The Revolutionary Tribunal will pronounce our divorce; the guillotine will divide us from bed and board.

CITIZEN. You are a monster!

DUMAS. Idiot! You admire Brutus?

CITIZEN. With all my soul.

DUMAS. Must one be a Roman consul and be able to hide one's head in a toga, to sacrifice one's dearest to the Fatherland? I shall wipe my eyes with the sleeve of my red coat; that's the only difference.

CITIZEN. That is horrible!

DUMAS. Go, you don't understand me.

(*Exeunt.*)

ACT IV

SCENE III

(*The Conciergerie.* LACROIX, HÉRAULT-SÉCHELLES *on one bed,* DANTON, CAMILLE *on another.*)

LACROIX. One's hair grows long, and one's fingernails, really one's ashamed of oneself.

HÉRAULT. Take care what you're doing, you sneeze sand all over my face!

LACROIX. And don't tread on my feet, my dear fellow, I've got corns.

HÉRAULT. You've got lice too.

LACROIX. Ah! If I only were free of the worms.

HÉRAULT. Anyhow, sleep well! We must see how we get on with each other, there's not much room.—Don't scratch me with your nails in your sleep!—So!—Don't pull at the shroud like that, it's cold down there!

DANTON. Yes, Camille, to-morrow we're worn out shoes, thrown into the lap of the beggar woman Earth.

CAMILLE. The cowhide which Plato says the angels make slippers out of, when they grope their way about the earth. But there's more to come hereafter.—My Lucile!

DANTON. Be calm, my boy!

CAMILLE. How can I? What do you think, Danton? Can I? They can't lay their hands on her, it's impossible! The light of beauty that pours from her lovely body can't be put out. Look, the Earth would not dare to bury her; it would arch itself above her, the damp of the grave would sparkle like dew on her eyelashes, crystals would shoot up like flowers about her limbs and bright springs murmur to her in sleep.

DANTON. Sleep, my boy, sleep.

CAMILLE. Listen, Danton, between ourselves, it's so miserable to have to die. And it does no good. I'll still steal from life a last look from her pretty eyes, I will have my eyes open.

DANTON. They will stay open anyhow. Samson does not close one's eyes. Sleep is more merciful. Sleep, my boy, sleep!

CAMILLE. Lucile, your kisses play tricks upon my lips, every kiss becomes a dream, my eyelids drop and close fast upon it.

DANTON. Will the clock not be quiet? With every tick it pushes the walls closer round me, till they're as close as a coffin—I read such a story as a child, my hair stood on end. Yes, as a child! It wasn't worth their trouble to fatten me up and keep me warm. Only work for the grave-diggers!

I feel as if I stank already. My dear body, I will hold my nose and pretend you're a woman sweating and stinking after a dance and pay you compliments. We've often passed the time together in other ways.

To-morrow you're a broken violin; the melody is played out. To-morrow you're an empty bottle; the wine is finished but hasn't made me drunk and I go soberly to bed—lucky people who can still get tight. To-morrow you're a worn-out pair of trousers; you'll be thrown into the wardrobe and the moths will eat you, you may smell as much as you like.

Ugh, it's no good! Yes, it is miserable to have to die. Death mimics birth, and dying we're as helpless and naked as new-born children. Of course, we're given a shroud for swaddling-clothes, but how will that help? In the grave we can whimper just as well as in the cradle.

Camille! He's asleep; (*Bends over him.*) a dream plays between his eyelashes. I will not brush the golden dew of sleep from his eyes.

(*Rises and goes to the window.*) I shall not go alone; I thank you, Julie! And yet I should have liked to die differently, without any effort, as a star falls, as a note expires, kissing itself dead with its own lips, as a ray of light buries itself in the clear stream.—

Like glimmering tears the stars are sprinkled through the night; there must be some great sorrow in the eyes from which they fall.

CAMILLE. Oh!

(*He has sat up and reaches towards the ceiling.*)

DANTON. What is it, Camille?

CAMILLE. Oh, Oh!

DANTON (*shakes him*). Do you want to scratch the roof down.

CAMILLE. Oh you, you, hold me, speak to me!

DANTON. You're trembling in every limb, there's sweat on your forehead.

CAMILLE. It is you, it is me—so! This is my hand! Yes, now I remember. Oh Danton, it was terrible!

DANTON. What was?

CAMILLE. I lay between dream and waking. Then the roof disappeared, and the moon sank into the room, close and thick, my arm took hold of it. The roof of heaven with its lights had sunk lower, I knocked on it, I touched the stars, I reeled like a drunken man under the roof of ice. It was terrible, Danton.

DANTON. The lamp throws a round shadow on the ceiling, that's what you saw.

CAMILLE. As for me, it doesn't need much to make me lose my scrap of reason. Madness grasped me by the hair. (*He rises.*) I won't sleep any more, I don't want to go mad. (*He reaches for a book.*)

DANTON. What are you taking?

CAMILLE. The 'Night Thoughts.'

DANTON. Do you want to die beforehand? I'll take 'La Pucelle.' I'll steal away from life not as from a praying-desk but as from the bed of a sister of mercy. Life is a whore; she fornicates with the whole world.

ACT IV

SCENE IV

(*Before the Conciergerie.* A GAOLER, TWO CARTERS *with tumbrils,* WOMEN.)

GAOLER. Who said you were to come here?

FIRST CARTER. I'm not To-Come-Here, what a curious name.

GAOLER. Fool, who gave you the commission?

FIRST CARTER. I don't get any commission, nothing except ten sous a head.

SECOND CARTER. The villain takes the bread out of my mouth.

FIRST CARTER. What do you call your bread? (*Pointing to the window of the prisoners.*) That's food for worms.

SECOND CARTER. My children are worms too, and they also want their share. Oh, things are going badly with our business and yet we're the best carters.

FIRST CARTER. Why's that?

SECOND CARTER. Who is the best carter?

FIRST CARTER. He who carries furthest and fastest.

SECOND CARTER. Well, donkey, who can carry further than to carry you out of the world, and who can carry faster than one who does it in quarter of an hour! It's exactly a quarter of an hour from here to the Place de la Révolution.

GAOLER. Quickly, you villains! Nearer to the door; make way, my girl!

FIRST CARTER. Don't move! A man doesn't go round a girl, he always goes through her.

SECOND CARTER. I'll bet he does; you can drive your cart and horses through her, you'll find the ruts easy; but you'll have to go into quarantine when you come out.

(*They drive forward.*)

SECOND CARTER (*to the women*). What are you staring at?

A WOMAN. We're waiting for old customers.

SECOND CARTER. Do you mean my cart is going to be turned into a brothel? It's a respectable cart, it carried the King and all the fine gentlemen of Paris to the scaffold.

(LUCILE *enters. She sits on a stone under the prisoners' window.*)

LUCILE. Camille! Camille!

(CAMILLE *appears at the window.*)

LUCILE. Listen, Camille, you make me laugh with that long coat of stone and that iron mask before your face; can't you bend down? Where are your arms?—I'll entice you, sweet bird. (*Sings.*)

Two stars stand in the sky
Shining brighter than the moon,
One shines at my darling's window
The other at her door.

Come, come, my friend! Softly up the steps, they're all asleep. The moon has helped me to wait. But you can't get through the door, your clothes are impossible. The joke's gone too far, give it up. You don't move, why don't you speak to me? You frighten me.

Listen, the people say that you must die, and they make such serious faces over it. Die! I can't help laughing at their faces. Die! What kind of a word is that? Tell me, Camille. Die! I will think it over. There it is, there! I'll run after it, come, sweet friend, help me catch it, come, come!

(*She runs away.*)

CAMILLE (*calls*). Lucile, Lucile!

ACT IV

SCENE V

(*The Conciergerie.* DANTON, *at a window which looks into the next room.* CAMILLE, PHILIPPEAU, LACROIX, HÉRAULT.)

DANTON. You're quiet now, Fabre.

A VOICE (*from within*). As death.

DANTON. Do you know what we are doing now?

A VOICE. Well?

DANTON. What you've done all your life; making verses—*des vers*.

CAMILLE (*to himself*). Madness sat behind her eyes. More people have gone mad already. It's the way of the world. What can we do? We wash our hands of them.—It is better so.

DANTON. I leave everything in terrible confusion. Not one of them knows how to govern. Things might still be managed if I left Robespierre my whores and Couthon my legs.

LACROIX. We'd have turned liberty into a whore!

DANTON. And what else is it? Liberty and whores are the most cosmopolitan things under the sun. Liberty will now prostitute herself decently in the marriage bed of the lawyer from Arras. But I think she will be a Clytemnestra to him; I don't give him more than six months' respite, I drag him with me.

CAMILLE (*to himself*). Heaven help her to some comfortable *idée fixe!* The universal *idée fixe* which is called good sense is intolerably boring. The happiest man would be he who could persuade himself that he was God the Father, the Son, and the Holy Ghost.

LACROIX. The fools will cry 'Long live the Republic!' as we pass by.

DANTON. What does it matter? The deluge of the Revolution may carry our corpses where it likes; with our fossilized bones men can always break the heads of all kings.

HÉRAULT. Yes, so long as there's a Samson to use our jaw-bones.

DANTON. They bear the brand of Cain.

LACROIX. Nothing shows more clearly that Robespierre is a Nero than that he was never so friendly to Camille as two days before his arrest. Isn't it so, Camille?

CAMILLE. What does it matter, so far as I'm concerned?—(*To himself.*) What an attractive thing she has made of madness. Why must I go away now? We'd have laughed over it together, have nursed it and kissed it.

DANTON. If History once opens her vaults, Despotism may still suffocate from the vapors of our corpses.

HÉRAULT. We stank quite sufficiently in our lifetime.—These are phrases for posterity, aren't they, Danton; they have nothing to do with us.

CAMILLE. He makes a face, as if it ought to turn to stone and be dug up by posterity as an antique.

That isn't worth the trouble either, to pull faces and put on red and speak with a good accent; once in a while we should take off the masks, then we should see everywhere, as in a room of mirrors, the one, primeval, toothless, everlasting sheep's head, no more and no less. The differences are not so big, we are all villains and angels, fools and geniuses, and indeed all of them in one; the four find plenty of room in one body, they are not so large as people pretend. Sleep, digest, breed children—every one does that; other things are only variations in different keys on the same theme. And yet men have to walk on tiptoes and make faces, still they have to be embarrassed in front of each other. We have all eaten ourselves sick at the same table and have now got the gripes; why do you hold your napkins before your faces? Scream and cry as the fancy takes you! But don't make such virtuous and such witty and such heroic and such brilliant grimaces. After all, we know each other; spare yourselves the trouble.

HÉRAULT. Yes, Camille, let us sit beside each other and scream; nothing stupider than pressing your lips together if something is hurting you.—Greeks and Gods screamed, Romans and Stoics made heroic grimaces.

DANTON. The second were as good Epicureans as the first. They gave themselves a very comforting self-respect. It's not so bad to drape your toga and look around to see if you throw a long shadow. What should we aim at? To hide our shame with laurel leaves, rose wreaths or vine leaves or to show the ugly thing openly and let it be licked by the dogs?

PHILIPPEAU. My friends, one need not stand very high above the earth to see nothing more of all the confused flux and glimmer and have one's eye filled by a few great godlike outlines. There is an ear for which the clamor and discordance which deafen us are a stream of harmonies.

DANTON. But we are the poor musicians and our bodies the instruments. Do the ugly sounds that are ground out of them only exist so that rising higher and higher and finally softly echoing they expire in a voluptuous sigh in the ear of heaven?

HÉRAULT. Are we sucking-pigs which are whipped to death for princely tables, so that their flesh is tastier?

DANTON. Are we children, roasted in the glowing Moloch arms of this world and tickled with rays of light so that the Gods may enjoy their laugh?

CAMILLE. Is the air with its golden eyes a dish full of golden carp that stands on the table of the blissful Gods, and the blissful Gods laugh eternally, and the fish die eternally, and the Gods rejoice eternally at the play of color in the death struggle.

DANTON. The world is chaos. The Nothing is its too fertile Deity.

(*Enter the* GAOLER.)

GAOLER. Gentlemen, you may go, the carriages wait at the door.

PHILIPPEAU. Good night, my friends! Let us quietly draw over our heads the great coverlet, under which all hearts burn out and all eyes close.

(*They embrace each other.*)

HÉRAULT (*takes* CAMILLE'S *arm*). Rejoice, Camille, we shall have a good night. The clouds hang in the calm evening sky like a burnt-out Olympus with the fading sinking forms of the Gods.

(*They leave.*)

ACT IV

SCENE VI

(*A room.*)

JULIE. The people ran into the street, now all is quiet. I should not like to keep him waiting a moment. (*She takes out a phial.*) Come, dearest priest, whose Amen sends us to bed. (*Goes to the window.*) It is so lovely to say good-bye; now I have only to close the door behind me. (*Drinks.*)

One would like to stand like this forever.—The sun has gone down. The earth's features were so sharp in her light, but now her face is as calm and grave as a dying woman's.—How beautifully the evening light plays about her forehead and her cheeks.—Paler and paler she becomes, like a corpse she drives downwards on the flood of the air. Will no arm seize her by the golden hair and take her from the stream and bury her?

I go softly. I do not kiss her, so that no breath, no sigh may wake her from her slumber.—Sleep, sleep!

(*Dies.*)

ACT IV

SCENE VII

(*Place de la Révolution. The tumbrils are driven on and halt at the guillotine.* MEN *and* WOMEN *sing and dance the Carmagnole. The* PRISONERS *sing the Marseillaise.*)

WOMAN (*with children*). Make room, make room! The children are crying, they're hungry. I must make them watch, so they'll be quiet. Make room!

A WOMAN. Hey, Danton, now you can go to bed with the worms.

ANOTHER. Hérault, I'll get myself a wig made from your lovely hair.

HÉRAULT. I haven't enough bush to cover so denuded a Mound of Venus.

CAMILLE. Damned witches! You shall still cry: may the mountains fall upon us.

A WOMAN. The mountain has fallen on you, or rather you've fallen beneath it.

DANTON (*to* CAMILLE). Quiet, my boy! You've shouted yourself hoarse.

CAMILLE (*gives the driver money*). There, old Charon, your cart is a fine platter!—Gentlemen, I shall serve myself first. This is a classical banquet; we lie in our places and scatter a little blood as a libation. Adieu, Danton!

(*He ascends the scaffold, the* PRISONERS *follow him one by one,* DANTON *last.*)

LACROIX (*to the people*). You kill us on the day when you've lost your reason; you'll kill them on the day you recover it.

SOME VOICES. That's been said before; how tiresome!

LACROIX. The tyrants will break their necks over our graves.

HÉRAULT (*to* DANTON). He thinks his corpse a breeding-ground of Freedom.

PHILIPPEAU (*on the scaffold*). I forgive you; I hope that your hour of death may be no bitterer than mine.

HÉRAULT. I knew it! He has to reach into his bosom once more to show the people down there that he has clean linen.

FABRE. Good luck, Danton! I die twice over.

DANTON. Adieu, my friend! The guillotine is the best doctor.

HÉRAULT (*tries to embrace* DANTON). Ah, Danton, I can't even make a joke. The time has come.

(*An* EXECUTIONER *separates them.*)

DANTON (*to the* EXECUTIONER). Do you wish to be more cruel than death? Can you prevent our heads from kissing at the bottom of the basket?

ACT IV

SCENE VIII

(*A Street.*)

LUCILE. And yet there's something serious in it. I must think about it. I'm beginning to understand a little.

To die—to die!—Yet everything may live, yes, everything, the little fly there, the birds. Why not he? The river of life would cease to flow if but one drop were spilled. The earth would have a wound from such a blow.

Everything moves, the clocks tick, the bells peal, the people run, the water flows, and everything else goes on except there, there—! No, it shall not happen, no, I will sit upon the ground and scream, so that everything will stand still in fear, everything come to a stop, nothing move any more.

(*She sits down, covers her eyes, and gives one cry. Then after a pause she gets up.*)

It doesn't help, everything remains as before; the houses, the street, the wind blows, the clouds pass.—We have to bear it.

(*Some women come down the street.*)

FIRST WOMAN. A handsome man, Hérault!

SECOND WOMAN. When he stood at the triumphal arch at the Feast of the Constitution, I thought to myself, he'd look well on the guillotine, that's what I said. It was a presentiment, as you might say.

THIRD WOMAN. Yes, one must see people under all conditions; it's a good thing dying's become so public.

(*They pass by.*)

LUCILE. My Camille! Where shall I look for you now?

ACT IV

SCENE IX

(*Place de la Révolution. Two* EXECUTIONERS *at work on the guillotine.*)

FIRST EXECUTIONER (*stands on the guillotine and sings*).

And when home go I
The moon shines so shy. . . .

SECOND EXECUTIONER. Hey, hallo! Will you finish soon?

FIRST EXECUTIONER. In a minute! (*Sings.*)

Shines in my old father's window—
Boy, where have you been for so long?

Hey, give us my coat. (*They go singing away.*)

And when home go I
The moon shines so shy. . . .

LUCILE (*enters and sits on the steps of the guillotine*). I lay myself in your lap, quiet angel of death. (*Sings.*)

There is a reaper, his name is Death,
Has power from Almighty God. . . .

Dear cradle, who lulled my Camille to sleep, who stifled him beneath your roses. You bells of death, whose sweet tongue sang him to the grave. (*Sings.*)

Hundreds of thousands without number
Fall beneath the sickle only.

(*Enter a* PATROL.)

A CITIZEN. Hey, who goes there?
LUCILE. Long live the King!
CITIZEN. In the name of the Republic!

(*She is surrounded by the watch and taken away.*)

La Parisienne

BY HENRY BECQUE

Translated by JACQUES BARZUN

CHARACTERS

Clotilde
Lafont
Du Mesnil
Simpson
Adèle

The Time: The eighteen-eighties
The Place: Paris

TRANSLATOR'S NOTE: In the reading aloud or stage production of Becque's play in English, it is advisable that no attempt be made to give the proper names their French pronunciation—if for no other reason than that two of the persons referred to are named Simpson and yet are not foreigners. The names of the other principals may be anglicized as follows: Doomeny (accent on first syllable) and Lafont (accent on second syllable, sounded like "font"). As for Beaulieu, it is pronounced Bolio in Canada and the example is worth following; Mercier becomes Mur-cyay; and the two women's Christian names are most readily intelligible if vowels and consonants are allowed their usual English pronunciation.

ACT I

(*A fashionably furnished drawing-room. At center, double folding doors. To the left, a second pair of doors. Right, a window. On each side, additional doors—a double door on the right, a single on the left, which is also farther downstage. Against the wall, right, a secretary desk; left, a small table with a blotting-pad. Other furniture, chairs, mirrors, flowers, etc.*

When the curtain rises, the stage is empty. Clotilde, *dressed to go out, with hat and gloves on, enters center, hurriedly, with a letter in her hand. She goes to the table and conceals it beneath a writing case, at the same time drawing a bunch of keys from her pocket and going to the secretary desk. At that point,* Lafont *appears. She pretends to lock the desk.* Lafont *puts down his hat, goes towards her, upset and controlling himself with difficulty.*)

Lafont. Open the desk and give me that letter.
Clotilde. No. (*Pause.*)
Lafont. Open the desk and give me that letter.
Clotilde. I shan't. (*Longer pause.*)
Lafont. Where have you been?
Clotilde. Ah! Something else, now.
Lafont. Yes, it is something else. I'm asking you where you've been.
Clotilde. I shall tell you. I wish you could see yourself now, with the face you're making. You don't look handsome, my dear. I like you better with your usual face. Heavens! What are we coming to if you lose your head over a wretched little note that anybody at all may have written me.
Lafont. Open the desk and give me that letter.
Clotilde. You shall have it. . . . But you can see that scenes like these, if often repeated, would soon alienate me from you. I warn you, I won't stand a cross-examination every time I set foot outside the house.
Lafont. Where have you been?
Clotilde. Try to be logical, at least. Is it likely that I'm leaving someone and find a note from him when I get home?
Lafont. Open the desk and give me that letter.
Clotilde. You're joking, aren't you?
Lafont. Do I look like it?
Clotilde. You suspect me, then?

LAFONT. That's more likely. (*He points to the desk.*)

CLOTILDE. You really want it? You demand it? You issue orders? Very well. (*Slowly, with affectation, she draws out of her pocket first a handkerchief, next a small engagement book, then the keys. She replaces the handkerchief and the book, and throws the keys across the room.*) Open it yourself. (*She turns her back. He stands motionless, undecided.*) Go on, pick them up and open it. You've begun, go through with it. Be a man at least. (*He makes up his mind, goes to the keys, stoops down.*) Be careful! Consider what you're going to do. If you touch those keys with so much as your fingertips—your fingertips—I shan't be the one to regret it: you will.

LAFONT (*picks up the keys*). Take back your keys. (*Pause; she takes off her hat and gloves.*)

CLOTILDE. It's getting worse, you know.

LAFONT. What is getting worse?

CLOTILDE. The disease is gaining.

LAFONT. What disease?

CLOTILDE. I had already noticed that you were watching my comings and goings and I laughed at the trouble you were taking—so fruitlessly. I couldn't say anything, then. It was jealousy, but a pleasant sort of jealousy, which flatters the vanity of a woman, which amuses her. Now you've come to that other, stupid, crude, brutal, jealousy which wounds us deeply and which we never forgive twice. Will you ever do this again?

LAFONT. Clotilde!

CLOTILDE. Will you?

LAFONT. No.

CLOTILDE. Good.

LAFONT. Clotilde!

CLOTILDE. What is it, my dear?

LAFONT. You love me?

CLOTILDE. Less than yesterday.

LAFONT. You want me to be happy?

CLOTILDE. I think I have proved it often enough.

LAFONT. I'm worried about all these young men you meet, who hang about you.

CLOTILDE. You're silly to worry. I talk with this one and that, and once gone I don't even know which I was talking to.

LAFONT. You don't recall anyone you might have encouraged—inadvertently—who might have felt entitled to address you?

CLOTILDE. No one.

LAFONT (*piteously*). Open the desk and give me that letter.

CLOTILDE. Again! That letter is from my friend, Mme Doyen Beaulieu, (LAFONT *starts.*) the most virtuous of women—under her flighty appearance. I know what Pauline says in it and I shall tell you as soon as you've stopped asking me.

LAFONT. Clotilde!

CLOTILDE. What now?

LAFONT. Do you feel sensible?

CLOTILDE. More than ever.

LAFONT. Your head is cool?

CLOTILDE. My head is cool—and my heart also.

LAFONT. Think of me, Clotilde, and think of yourself. Reflect that a mistake is easily made and can never be mended. Don't give in to that taste for adventures which makes so many victims nowadays. Resist it, Clotilde, resist it. As long as you stay faithful to me, you remain worthy and respectable. If you should deceive me. . . . (*She stops him by getting up and going towards the center door.*)

CLOTILDE. Careful! Here comes my husband!

(*Enter* DU MESNIL.)

DU MESNIL. I thought I heard Lafont's voice! My! But you do talk and gossip and argue when you're together! An earthquake wouldn't stop you!

CLOTILDE (*to* DU MESNIL *alone*). So, you were back?

DU MESNIL. Yes, I was back.

CLOTILDE. You've been home a good while?

DU MESNIL. A little while.

CLOTILDE. It seems to me that when one of your friends is here you could at least show yourself and entertain him.

DU MESNIL. I was finishing a piece of work.

CLOTILDE. What did your uncle say?

DU MESNIL. I didn't find him in.

CLOTILDE. He's not easily found.

DU MESNIL. He left word that I should drop in later today.

CLOTILDE. Do you want me to go with you?

DU MESNIL. You'd only be in the way.

CLOTILDE. Thanks.

DU MESNIL (*going to* LAFONT). How are things with you?

LAFONT. Fairly well. What about you?

DU MESNIL. Well, I don't feel very lively right now.

LAFONT. What's the matter?

DU MESNIL. I work a great deal and my health suffers.

LAFONT. Take a rest.

DU MESNIL. That takes time—and money.

LAFONT. Money—yes, but you're earning a good deal.

DU MESNIL. I get it with one hand and spend it with the other.

LAFONT. That'd be fun, I should think.

DU MESNIL. Fun—when one's a bachelor.

CLOTILDE. Aren't you done complaining? Do you suppose you're entertaining Mr. Lafont or pleasing me? Why the lamentation? Your appetite is good, you sleep well; I don't know of any husband more pampered than you are. You work! Of course you do! Everybody does. If I were you, I'd work four times as much and say forty times as little about it.

DU MESNIL. She's a wonder, my wife! You don't know, my dear fellow, what a household like this is like, with expenses going up every year and tastes getting more expensive every day.

CLOTILDE. You keep on?

DU MESNIL. Let me talk a little. I didn't stop the two of you a while ago. Why don't you sit down and do your sewing since you are so industrious. Take a look at the children's pants, it won't do any harm; the poor things are always exposed to the air.

CLOTILDE. I spoil them too much.

DU MESNIL. But you don't mend them enough.

CLOTILDE. That's the maid's job.

DU MESNIL. We lodge as modestly as possible. I pay a great deal to live in a prison. Servants are no longer contented with wages, they want salaries. We dine out often, it's true, almost every day; but my wife, naturally, wants to dress like all the other women, and what's saved on the one hand is spent with the other. . . . The only advantage is that one gets better meals.

CLOTILDE. Well, you enjoy that.

DU MESNIL. I don't deny it. I'd rather have a good dinner outside than a bad one at home.

CLOTILDE. That's enough now, let's talk of more entertaining things.

DU MESNIL. You're a bachelor, my dear Lafont; well, take my advice and stay one.

LAFONT. Do you agree with that, Mrs. Du Mesnil?

CLOTILDE. Marry or not, as you please. (*She moves away.*)

DU MESNIL. Will you be more agreeable than my wife and listen to me?

LAFONT. With pleasure—

DU MESNIL. Some people just now are making efforts in my behalf, efforts worth the trouble.

LAFONT. Tell me the whole story.

DU MESNIL. It's my uncle, my uncle John, who's a member of the Institute and who has long been dissatisfied with my position. He wants me in the Finance Ministry. He has friends there, most of them know me. They have made up their minds to find me a certain post.

LAFONT. That would be just the thing for you. You could do your own work and you wouldn't depend on anybody.

DU MESNIL. At the same time, my work is going pretty well, now. The learned societies think well of me. Not an appropriation that I don't pass on. I'm very much in demand by the "Monitor of Agricultural Interests" in the pages of which I explode a bombshell once in a while. It spreads my name. I take on everything that comes my way. But my uncle does not approve. He thinks at my age, with wife and children, my place should be secure.

LAFONT. He's right.

DU MESNIL. Perhaps he is right. I'm not a statistician, I'm not an economist, I'm a . . . something apart. Let me tell you, between ourselves, that my little work called "Moral Considerations on the Budget" has been widely noticed. Such books are only for the few and don't sell like novels; but nevertheless, to date, one hundred and nineteen copies have been sold—or one hundred and eighteen—there's one copy missing; it may have been stolen. I see ahead of me a grand opening for my activities, a field of specialization to exploit.

LAFONT. Try to get your Finance job first: it's a surer thing; afterwards you can do what you want. I'll try, by the way, to help the thing along; I know someone . . .

DU MESNIL. Please don't. My uncle has taken the lead and he wants to be the one to push it through. It seems to me that when a member of the Institute of Political Science consents to ask a favor, when he asks that favor for his nephew—when that nephew happens to be somebody, the government can only grant it, don't you agree?

LAFONT. Positions are not always open.

DU MESNIL. I happen to know of one that will be very soon.

LAFONT. Tell me, is it certain that the post you've been promised is in Paris?

DU MESNIL. In Paris, of course. My wife couldn't stand it in the country. (CLOTILDE, *during these last words, has been sitting at the small table from which she has picked up her letter to show it behind her husband's back to* LAFONT, *with a taunting look and gesture. The end of the business should coincide with* DU MESNIL'S *last speech.*)

CLOTILDE (*getting up*). Adolph, read this letter.

DU MESNIL (*turning around*). What does it say?

CLOTILDE. Open it and you'll see. (*Gives him the letter.*) It's from Pauline.

DU MESNIL. "My dearest, you will receive, if you have not already done so, an invitation to Mrs. Simpson's ball for the 25th. Your request was in good hands, and your self-respect in no wise suffered. I mentioned your name; it was taken up with many agreeable comments; you were said to be extremely pretty, and that it would be charming to have you. You are now among the intimates of the house. I feel sure you will like Mrs. Simpson immensely. You shall tell me how old you think her; I shall tell you how old she is. Which does not prevent her, in decolleté and with all her jewels on, from getting away with it; the ex-beauty Mrs. Simpson still creates an illusion. What shoulders and eyes, and a way of smiling like no one else! And what kindliness! Nothing shocks her; she understands every weakness; there is no indiscretion, however great, which does not seem to her either interesting or excusable. She is a true aristocrat."

DU MESNIL (*exchanging with* LAFONT *a look of displeasure; both nod disapproval*). "What kindliness!" "Nothing shocks her!" "She understands every weakness." "There is no indiscretion, however great. . . ." I don't think I care very much for Pauline's letter.

LAFONT. Your friend, Mrs. Du Mesnil, seems a rather—irresponsible person.

DU MESNIL. You see, you see! I've heard of Mrs. Simpson. There are rather shady stories about her.

LAFONT. Mrs. Simpson has a deplorable reputation.

DU MESNIL. You hear that, don't you? I'll not take you into such a house.

LAFONT. I assure you it's not at all your set, you don't belong with women of dubious reputation.

DU MESNIL. Well, aren't you struck by the fact that Lafont and I are of the same mind?

CLOTILDE. Very well, we'll do as you wish. If we don't go to Mrs. Simpson's we'll go elsewhere, that's all. But in the future, I wish that before you discuss certain things you'd wait until we are alone. I'm not in the habit of taking advice from strangers. (*She turns from them abruptly.*)

DU MESNIL. What are you talking about? Lafont a stranger! (*To* LAFONT.) So you two have had a tiff?

LAFONT. It's you, ever since you've been here, who have got on her nerves for no reason.

DU MESNIL (*to* CLOTILDE). I'm going.

CLOTILDE (*drily*). Good luck to you.

DU MESNIL. What are you doing today?

CLOTILDE. What I please.

DU MESNIL. Where are we dining tonight?

CLOTILDE. I haven't the slightest idea.

DU MESNIL. Lord! What answers.

CLOTILDE. As if I should put myself out for a man who is quarrelsome and disagreeable.

DU MESNIL. So you want very much to go to this ball?

CLOTILDE. The ball has nothing to do with it. I'd already forgotten it. I'm no longer in my 'teens to worry about a dance more or less. But you—you complain, you lecture, you abuse your wife without the least consideration for her. If someone overheard you he would have a very false idea of our home-life.

DU MESNIL. You mustn't take me seriously, stupid! Do you suppose there are many husbands like me? I growl for a second, but when you've made up your mind, I do things your way after all. Who is master here? (*She smiles.*) I'm very intent about this appointment, which would be a big thing for us, and which ought to interest you more than a ball. Seriously, Clotilde, do you think I'll get it?

CLOTILDE. We shall see.

DU MESNIL. I have good claims and plenty of merit on my side, haven't I?

CLOTILDE. Merit—what good is that?

DU MESNIL. I'm backed by able men.

CLOTILDE. What if they have no influence?

DU MESNIL. But don't you think the support of the Institute will swing it?

CLOTILDE. You don't want me to take a hand in it—I think you're wrong.

DU MESNIL. What could you do?

CLOTILDE. Oh, a thousand things that are no trouble to a woman, which she can do as she goes her usual rounds. I'd put all my friends on the war-path; Pauline first, she admires you so much. She wishes her husband were like you. Pauline, who is very close to Mrs. Simpson, would have interested her in our affairs. You make me smile when you don't want to go to Mrs. Simpson's. A lot she cares about our company. Every day, everyone in Paris who counts is at her house. She always has two or three cabinet members at her table; and you could have dined with them. You would have expounded your ideas to them, quietly, on a footing of equality, while you smoked those large cigars you are so fond of. And the day that your able men at the Institute come to tell you "We're very sorry; the appointment was given to someone else," you'll say, "I know it, I have it in my pocket." That's how business is done!

DU MESNIL. You may be right. Listen, let's not do anything rash. If later things don't go right for my uncle and his friends, then we'll try your method.

CLOTILDE. Whenever you like—you know that's my motto with you. (*They laugh.*)

DU MESNIL. I'm going to see Uncle. Shall I take Lafont with me or are you keeping him?

CLOTILDE. I'll keep him. He irritates me but he amuses me. His nose always makes me laugh. (*They laugh.*)

DU MESNIL. You don't treat him right, you know. He is always so kind and obliging.

CLOTILDE (*whispering*). I wouldn't want a man with a nose like that to kiss me. (*They laugh.*)

DU MESNIL. Well, goodbye. (*To* LAFONT.) You'd better stay here if I'm as disagreeable as my wife says. You don't know what it is to have wife and children. You love them a great deal, you don't find time to think of anything else, and you couldn't get along without them—but just the same, every once in a while, you wish them all to the devil. (*Exit.*)

CLOTILDE. Don't you see, now, how careful you must be? If my husband had come in one minute sooner, I was lost.

LAFONT. You made a fool of me.

CLOTILDE. How so?

LAFONT. With that letter. It would have been so easy to show it to me in the beginning.

CLOTILDE. I thought you wouldn't like it and I was right. Besides, it was a trap I set for you. I wanted to find out just how far you would go.

LAFONT. For the next time?

CLOTILDE. For the next time, precisely. My! how stupid you are, my dear, how unlucky in your suppositions! Look here, I'm going to set your mind at ease, though you hardly deserve it: my husband opens all my letters—all, without exception. I have always preferred it so. Now let's sit down and talk a while, and, please, let's talk without getting angry. My husband on one side, then you—it's a bit too much in one day. Can you give me any reason for acting the way you do? What does this absurd jealousy mean and what is it coming to? It took you all of a sudden—without warning—around January 15. (*He looks at her; she smiles.*) I have a reason for remembering that date.

LAFONT. What reason?

CLOTILDE. I have one, that's enough. Are you going to take me up on every word now? Go ahead, talk, I'm listening.

LAFONT. Where have you been?

CLOTILDE (*laughing*). That's right. I beg your pardon, my dear. I forgot you had asked me that question several times and I hadn't answered. I had an appointment—don't start—with my modiste, where one meets very few gentlemen, I assure you. You allow me to go to my modiste once in a while, don't you? Now do what I ask and tell me just what you reproach me with. I always find it difficult to discover anything wrong in the way I treat you.

LAFONT. I hardly see you any more.

CLOTILDE. Boo! What are you doing now? Aren't I here? It's your own fault if you waste the time quarreling when we might spend it more agreeably.

LAFONT. I waited for you all this week—last week too—and the week before that also.

CLOTILDE. Nonsense!—why not say all last year? And even if it were true, even if I hadn't kept my promises, not once, but a hundred times, is that any reason to imagine all sorts of horrible things? Am I always free to do what I want? Don't I depend on everyone here? (*Touching his arm.*) I'm married, you know, you don't seem to realize it. . . . But there's something else on your mind. I want to hear about it.

LAFONT. It seems to me that our relation no longer interests you . . . that you want novelty . . . and may have found it . . . that we're at the inevitable stage where . . .prevarication enters in, and the shabby tricks and little indignities.

CLOTILDE. I don't quite know when all those pretty things begin. You doubtless know more about them than I do, I'm asking you for facts—something clear and positive that I can refute with one word. As for what goes on in your imagination, what can I possibly say? It doesn't strike me as very jolly, your imagination, nor filled with very rosy memories.

LAFONT. That date—January 15—that you remember so well.

CLOTILDE (*more attentive*). Well, what about that date?

LAFONT. It struck me too.

CLOTILDE. Tell the truth—it didn't strike you. I'm sorry I bothered you with it. It means something to me and can mean nothing whatever to you.

LAFONT. I've observed a number of things since.

CLOTILDE. What?

LAFONT. I've taken note.

CLOTILDE. Of what?

LAFONT. Oh, nothing. They're just nuances. But, after all, nuances . . . You mustn't trifle with nuances.

CLOTILDE. Let's have a look at these nuances.

LAFONT. You've changed a good deal, my dear Clotilde, without noticing it. You make fun of me, for one thing, which is not nice. I find you absent-minded, very often, and then also very much embarrassed. I see you're hiding something from me and I'm afraid to ask you questions. Sometimes you contradict yourself.

CLOTILDE. You amaze me.

LAFONT. You tell me about people of an altogether different set from yours, whom you've come to know overnight. How do you do it? Nowadays it's you who tell me all the scandals—hitherto I've had the pleasure of telling them to you. Even your politics have changed.

CLOTILDE. What a child you are! And here I am, listening to you solemnly. My politics! You mean I'm reactionary? I haven't changed. Yes, as to that, you're quite right, I'm a good, staunch, reactionary. I love order, quiet, well-established principles. I want the churches to be open if I feel like going into one. I want the shops also open and full of pretty things, so that I may look at them even if I can't buy. But even if my politics were changed, it seems to me that you should be the last to complain. *You* have changed with the times, you are a liberal; it's the fashion today; it doesn't commit you, every party is full of liberals. You're a free-thinker, too. I do believe you could get along with a mistress who had no religion. Horrors!—What did my husband talk to you about?

LAFONT. About a position he would like to get and that he may get.

CLOTILDE. Were you interested?

LAFONT. Very much.

CLOTILDE. You say "very much" just as you would say "not at all." How did you find my husband?

LAFONT. Pretty well.

CLOTILDE. Doesn't he seem to you worried and worn out?

LAFONT. No.

CLOTILDE. Enough of that. I don't know why I should talk to you about Adolph—for all the affection you bear him! No matter. This is my point—you know my husband's expecting a position, expecting it from the government. No matter what government is in power, when one wants something, one must apply to it. Do you suppose then that I would go around criticizing the present order just when we're expecting favors! A man would do that. Men are such chatterboxes, they're so clumsy and ungrateful. Women, never! Shall I tell you, my friend, you've acted on a very low scheme. You thought that if you voiced suspicion at random you might find out something—but you won't . . . because there is nothing to find out. I shan't forget it, though. Meanwhile you must be good, patient, trusting. You must be content with what you get and not try for the impossible. You must realize I'm not free, that I have a house to manage, friends to entertain—. Pleasure comes after. Keep in mind also that the slightest outburst might compromise me, and if my husband heard of it, destroy me entirely. I do not want—do you hear?—I do not want ever again to find you, as I found you today, planted in front of my door, gesticulating and ready to eat up everything when I'm peacefully returning from my dressmaker's. (*He raises his head sharply.*) Well, what's biting you now?

LAFONT. Where have you been?

CLOTILDE. I've just told you.

LAFONT. Is it your milliner or your dressmaker?

CLOTILDE. Why?

LAFONT. Answer me. Is it your milliner or your dressmaker?

CLOTILDE. I went to both, are you satisfied? Now it's time for you to get up and go.

LAFONT. No.

CLOTILDE. Yes.

Lafont. Later.
Clotilde. Right now.
Lafont. Are you busy, or in a hurry?
Clotilde. I've nothing to do, I'm in no hurry.
Lafont. Let me stay then.
Clotilde. I can't. If my husband came back and found you still here he might be annoyed. Be reasonable and say good-bye. You'll talk less next time.
Lafont. Clotilde?
Clotilde. What now?
Lafont. I'm going home.
Clotilde. Go ahead, I'm not keeping you.
Lafont. You know what time it is?
Clotilde. Approximately.
Lafont. The day's not over.
Clotilde. It isn't dawn either.
Lafont. All you have to do is put on your hat.
Clotilde. I thought we were coming to that. I should have been surprised if all your fussing had ended up otherwise.
Lafont. Put on your hat, won't you?
Clotilde. All right. It's the one good idea you've had. It's only fair I should take advantage of it. Go on first.
Lafont. You're coming after.
Clotilde. Right after.
Lafont. In a minute?
Clotilde. One minute. But go on, go.
Lafont. Till then.
Clotilde. Till then.

(*Exit* Lafont, Clotilde *rings.*)

Adèle. Did you ring, madam?
Clotilde. Adèle, please bring me my wrapper and slippers. I'm not going out again.

ACT II

(*Same as* Act I.)

Clotilde (*dressed, ready to go out, looking at herself in a mirror*). Do I look all right, Adèle?
Adèle. Yes, madam.
Clotilde. Do I look quite right?
Adèle. Quite, madam.

CLOTILDE. What time is it?

ADÈLE. Almost three, madam.

CLOTILDE. Is everything on the table?

ADÈLE. Everything that madam usually takes—keys, address book, powder box. . . .

CLOTILDE. Let me have them.

ADÈLE (*knowingly*). Madam will not return today.

CLOTILDE. Possibly not.

ADÈLE. Probably not.

CLOTILDE. How so?

ADÈLE. I believe the master dines with the economists. He wouldn't miss it for the world.

CLOTILDE. Well?

ADÈLE. I've noticed madam always spends the day with a schoolmate whom the master never sees.

CLOTILDE. So you've been eavesdropping.

ADÈLE. No, I haven't, madam; I've just caught a word here and there—I told madam that my brother—

CLOTILDE. I know all about your brother! You want to go out; all right, go!

ADÈLE. Thank you, madam. (*Going out.*) Madam wishes for nothing else?

CLOTILDE. No. Don't let the cook leave. Mr. Du Mesnil might want something when he comes in to dress.

ADÈLE. Yes, madam. Does madam not want me to call a cab for her?

CLOTILDE. No thanks. I'll find one on my way.

ADÈLE. Good-bye, madam, pleasant time, ma'am. (*Following* CLOTILDE *out.*)

(*Bell rings.*)

Someone rang, madam.

CLOTILDE. Yes, I heard it. (*Coming back.*) Three o'clock! He hasn't seen me for quite a while. He knows today is the economists' dinner. I should have expected some such performance. (*Second ring.*)

ADÈLE. What is madam going to do?

CLOTILDE. Go to the door, Adèle. I am at home to no one.

ADÈLE. If it were Mr. Lafont, madam?

CLOTILDE. I said "to no one." I make no exception for Mr. Lafont or anyone else.

ADÈLE. Very good, madam.

CLOTILDE. Leave the door open so I can hear what it is. If it should be business for my husband, ask the person to sit down and I'll come out.

ADÈLE. I understand, madam. (*Third ring.*) My! What impatience, and how useless! (*Exit.*)

CLOTILDE. I should have hurried. I'd be gone by now and wouldn't have been bothered. (*Goes to center door which she holds ajar.*) It's he all right. He couldn't miss such a fine opportunity. . . . Talk on, my friend, talk. . . . That's right, question the servant. He's asking Adèle where I am. He insists. What's this, she's letting him in? He's walking in, as I live, he's walking in! (*Coming back.*) Is he going to take a siesta here? Ah, these men! How they hang on to us when we no longer care for them! (CLOTILDE *hides behind door at right.*)

LAFONT. All right, my girl, all right.

ADÈLE. But why don't you believe me, sir? You can see that no one's home.

LAFONT. I shall wait.

ADÈLE. Wait for whom? Both the master and the mistress have just gone out.

LAFONT (*hesitating*). Together?

ADÈLE. No, sir, not together. Mr. Du Mesnil went his way, madam hers.

LAFONT. Did he say when he would be back?

ADÈLE. I know only that madam will not be home for dinner. She's dining out.

LAFONT (*hesitating*). With Mr. Du Mesnil?

ADÈLE. No, sir they are dining separately.

LAFONT. Well, you can go back to your work. I'm going to write a note here at the desk.

ADÈLE. As you wish, sir, this isn't my house. I can't show you the door. (*Exit.*)

LAFONT. I came in and I don't know why I came in; it's just another blunder on my part, that's what it is. I must take hold of myself, make up my mind to a necessary break. In Paris, you can't keep a mistress who is half-way respectable. Damn it, it can't be done! The more respectable she is, the less chance you have of keeping her. I'll have an explanation with Clotilde, and a bloody one! It'll be kinder on my part, then I'll leave her for good. I fret, run, pursue, look for her this way when she's gadding the other way, what's the use? What more can I find out? She's the mistress of that fellow Mercier, it's as clear as day. Since when? What good will it do me to know? Yes, why fuss? Ah, why—I don't know. Perhaps she doesn't love him—that's one consolation. But what am I going to do? If Adolph were here, at least we could have spent the rest of the day together. Really, when I'm blue and Clotilde has upset me, there's nobody like her husband to set me up again. I feel less lonely. Adolph's position cheers me a lot. It's not so good as mine. It certainly is not. Clotilde, after all, doesn't owe me anything, but she's certainly cheating him atrociously. I can judge her conduct pretty severely when I put myself in her husband's shoes—what a mess! Here I am, suddenly alone, without a friend, sick at heart about an unconscionably vulgar situation into which I am sinking deeper and deeper. What a life we men lead! Either bachelors or cuckolds—what a choice!

CLOTILDE. Here goes. I'll come out and at least find out what he wants.

LAFONT. What? You here!

CLOTILDE. What's so strange about my being here? The queer thing is *your* being here, especially when I'm not at home and you are told so in unmistakable language. That's how grateful you are for my kindness. You can't think of enough things to do to make yourself unpleasant, and every time, I'm weak enough to forgive you.

LAFONT. It's your own fault.

CLOTILDE. Oh, let's not start all over again, please! No scenes today, not today. I shan't *let* you make any, by the way. Had you any reason, may I ask, for coming, any pretext—some dreadful discovery that you couldn't keep to yourself any longer?

LAFONT. I confess I feared you were ill.

CLOTILDE. How charming of you! You've seen me, you're reassured—now (*Showing him the door, with a flip of her hands.*) take wing.

LAFONT. You're going out?

CLOTILDE. Don't I look as if I were going out? I'm not in the habit of going about the house with my hat on.

LAFONT. In a hurry?

CLOTILDE. I'm late.

LAFONT. Shall we make up our minds?

CLOTILDE. What does that mean?

LAFONT. I thought we might dine out—if I'm still your old schoolmate.

CLOTILDE. There isn't any schoolmate any more—neither you nor anyone else. I've come to the conclusion that these escapades in restaurants were full of danger. They involve me in lies that are revolting. I don't want to go on. Don't you think I am right?

LAFONT. Don't ask me what I think.

CLOTILDE. You resent what I've just said?

LAFONT. I'm ready for anything now.

CLOTILDE. That's a good way to be. Then you'll never be disappointed. (*Pause.*)

LAFONT. Please sit down and let's have a friendly chat.

CLOTILDE. I can't spare the time—to chat. Some other time, tomorrow, if you wish.

LAFONT. Tomorrow I'll expect you and something else will prevent—at the last minute—

CLOTILDE. Tomorrow won't do? Very well, that suits me. I'm never in a hurry to find myself with discontented and disagreeable people.

LAFONT. It's loving you that makes me so.

CLOTILDE (*disgusted*). Then love is a nuisance.

LAFONT. That's right—complain now! It's easy to see you're not in my place. I despair and mope while you're gadding about.

CLOTILDE. Gadding about! What sort of language is that! Admitting just for argument that I've grown a little cooler toward you, do you suppose a woman is won back by behaving as you do and by nagging her all the time? You accomplish just the opposite—you annoy her, bore her, and put notions into her head that she would never have thought of. (*Going near him with a show of tenderness.*) Take a little trip. Yes, take a little trip. Go away for—six months. It isn't long. Separation just now would do you worlds of good, and you'd come back all the more attractive. Don't be afraid about me. I'm not a woman who forgets easily. You'll find me just the same as ever. Will you go? No, you won't go. You can't go away for six months when your mistress asks you to—even though she'd regard it as a real proof of your attachment.

LAFONT. Where are you going?

CLOTILDE. That's all you can find to say to me?

LAFONT. Where are you going?

CLOTILDE. I was sure you'd ask me that question. I've been waiting for it ever since you came in.

LAFONT. Does it embarrass you?

CLOTILDE. Not in the least. You'll be a great deal wiser, of course, when I tell you where I'm going. What is to prevent my saying "I'm going there," and then going somewhere else?

LAFONT. I'll follow you.

CLOTILDE. Go ahead: follow me! Much good it's done you so far. But take care. I have a weakness for you, a great weakness. I make allowances for everything—the state you get into and the moments we've spent together, but don't feel free to abuse the privilege. (*Emphatically.*) I do whatever I like and it's nobody's business but my husband's.

LAFONT. You're deceiving me.

CLOTILDE. Me? Who with? Tell me who—who—who? You know, vague suspicions aren't enough. To accuse a woman you must have proofs. And when proofs exist and the woman is guilty, a man of the world knows what he's supposed to do—he leaves her or shuts up.

LAFONT. Clotilde!

CLOTILDE. Who! Tell me his name, if you're so sure of him. I'd be glad to know this Don Juan. Perhaps I pester him with my attentions, or he doesn't suspect his own good luck. You're forcing me to tell you something I'd always wanted to keep from you, I've made a sad mistake. I had a husband, children, a charming home. I wanted something more. I wanted everything. I dreamed like all other women of an ideal existence, in which I could fulfill my duties without sacrificing my heart. I wanted heaven and earth! And you've managed to demonstrate to me that it was impossible. I don't know what might have happened with someone else, certainly nothing worse. What's done is done. I don't blame you for it; but it's been the first and last time. (*She puts her handkerchief to her eyes.*)

LAFONT. You are unhappy?

CLOTILDE (*going to a chair*). It's nothing. It will pass.

LAFONT. I've been horrible!

CLOTILDE. Quite.

LAFONT. I'm going.

CLOTILDE. It's the best thing you could do. (*He goes away and comes back.*)

LAFONT. Please forget that one word I said beyond what I meant. I don't believe that you're deceiving me. You are too good and too sincere; at heart you appreciate the fondness I feel for you. I thought our usual little celebration still held; I was beside myself when you said No. Where are you going? Paying calls, visiting a friend? Is it such fun or so absolutely necessary? Why don't you call it off? Write that your husband is ill and that you must stay with him. It's so easy; do as I say. Give me back my evening, which has been mine for so long and which you always kept free for me.

CLOTILDE. Even if I would I couldn't.

LAFONT. Why not?

CLOTILDE. I am being called for in a carriage to take me to the Park.

LAFONT. But you were going out.

CLOTILDE. No, I wasn't. I was waiting.

LAFONT. Mrs. Simpson?

CLOTILDE. Mrs. Simpson, precisely. I'm dining with her. What a strange man you are. You take everything the wrong way, even what ought to reassure you.

LAFONT. Mrs. Simpson!

CLOTILDE. That's right. I was forgetting that Mrs. Simpson is not on your calling list, and that you wanted to forbid me her house. A charming house, beautifully appointed, and irreproachable. There may be trifling love affairs going on—I don't know—but that's like everywhere else.

LAFONT. Mrs. Simpson, as you very well know, has the worst of reputations.

CLOTILDE. So much the worse for those who made it so. When a man has been intimate with a woman she ought to be sacred for him—yes, sacred! Remember that principle and let it be your guide on occasion. I am very much perturbed, I assure you. I wonder what we're headed for and what you still have in mind. The gravest offence a man may do to a woman, you committed today toward me. What next? What else is there you can do? Violence, I suppose. I trust you will keep your self-control and stop short of blows. Think it over, my friend. It would be better to break off right now than wait and come to blows. Come now, I'm dismissing you in earnest this time; your mind is at rest, isn't it? Whatever loathing Mrs. Simpson may arouse in you, you'd rather have me be with her than. . . . We'll talk over the idea of your trip again; and I may bring you around to my point of view.

LAFONT. Tomorrow?

CLOTILDE. Ah, tomorrow. You've come back to that. You're willing to wait for me tomorrow? Well and good. I'll keep my word. But do watch yourself. You're calm enough now, don't go upsetting yourself when you're on the other side of the door. You have no luck with stairways. I promise you, if before tomorrow I run into you—at the Park or elsewhere—if I catch sight of the tip of your classic nose anywhere—you'll never see me again!

LAFONT. Till tomorrow, then?

CLOTILDE. Yes, tomorrow. (*He goes out quickly.*) Well, he wasn't so bad. Fairly sensible. When he gets angry, it's amusing enough, but I couldn't stand his tears. (*At the window.*) Better make sure before I go down that he won't follow me. He looks pretty sad, with his head hanging, poor fellow! I'll surely drop in to see him tomorrow. What! He's coming back! Hoho, into the house opposite. The devil! He's going to lie in wait and keep me here till he drops from sheer fatigue! I must show him he's been seen, or I'll never get rid of him. (DU MESNIL *enters from rear, with a look of ill humor and discouragement; throws his hat on the table angrily.*) Now the other one! Adolph! Adolph! What are you doing? Adolph, please answer me!

DU MESNIL. Let me alone for a bit, please!

CLOTILDE. What's the matter? What sort of face is this to come home with? I'd never seen that one before.

DU MESNIL. Don't annoy me more than I am already, will you, I'm not in a mood to trifle or listen to your nonsense. (*Pause.*)

CLOTILDE (*in a new tone*). What is the matter?

DU MESNIL. You'll find out soon enough.

CLOTILDE. So it's serious?

DU MESNIL. Very serious.

CLOTILDE. You're cross?

DU MESNIL. I have good reason to be.

CLOTILDE. You're cross—with me?

DU MESNIL. It has nothing to do with you. You were leaving—well, run along. Where are you going, anyway?

CLOTILDE. Shopping.

DU MESNIL. Yes, do. Buy yourself trinkets and things. It's most appropriate.

CLOTILDE. I'm getting tired of this. I shan't budge a step until you've told me what it is. (*Bruskly takes off her hat.*) I don't go out when my husband is worrying and I don't know what he's worrying about. (*Sits down.*) If he makes me wait to tell me, I wait.

DU MESNIL (*getting up and going to her*). You're a dear.

CLOTILDE. Speak up, you goose.

DU MESNIL. We're done for.

CLOTILDE. What about? — How?

DU MESNIL. What about?—About the position.

CLOTILDE. Is that it? You, a man, get into such a state and upset me about a little thing that didn't come through. It didn't, that's all. That's the definition of business, something goes through, something else doesn't. Make use of one, forget the other. Perhaps you thought I was going to complain and reproach you. Never, dear, never in the world. Come now, brace up; drop that hangdog look. What would you do, if you ran into a real calamity? If you lost me, for example? And now, tell me who was right? A fine sponsor, your uncle! Nothing suits him. Your position, your writings, your wife—nothing. And when he goes out for something you can be sure it'll be a fizzle. How did he ever get into the Institute, I wonder? If he were married, I could guess, but . . . Tell me just what happened. You've told me everything and I don't know a thing as yet.

DU MESNIL. I don't know any more than you do.

CLOTILDE. Well, but is the thing settled?

DU MESNIL. Almost.

CLOTILDE. Only almost? What do you mean, almost? Has the appointment been made or not?

DU MESNIL. Not yet.

CLOTILDE. Then nothing is settled?

DU MESNIL. The appointment is going to be made and I've been given to understand that I shan't get it.

CLOTILDE. That's better. Now we're getting to the point. Who's getting it?

DU MESNIL. A very—ordinary fellow!

CLOTILDE. Of course!—Married?

DU MESNIL. What has it got to do with it?

CLOTILDE. Tell me anyway.

DU MESNIL. Yes, married.

CLOTILDE. Young wife?

DU MESNIL. About your age.

CLOTILDE. Pretty?

DU MESNIL. Attractive.

CLOTILDE. Easy-going?

DU MESNIL. So they say.

CLOTILDE. The hussy!

DU MESNIL. I get you.

CLOTILDE. It's about time.

DU MESNIL. But you're wrong. They don't do things that way in the Treasury Department.

CLOTILDE. At any rate, nobody's been appointed—neither you nor anyone else—and you lost heart too soon, as usual.

DU MESNIL. All right, have it your way. But what are we to do?

CLOTILDE (*reflecting*). Get out of the way. (*She sits at the table and writes.*)

DU MESNIL. But tell me—

CLOTILDE. Don't bother me.

DU MESNIL. But let's consult first.

CLOTILDE. No need. I'm writing to Lulu, asking her for an appointment; she'll know it's something important.

DU MESNIL. Lulu? Who the devil's Lulu?

CLOTILDE. Lulu is Mrs. Simpson. We call her Lulu ever since she played that part in a comedy, and she likes it.

DU MESNIL. Go to it—write to Lulu, but if she succeeds where a member of the Institute has failed, I'll be delighted personally but I shall be sorry for France.

CLOTILDE. Never mind about that. France doesn't worry about you, don't you worry about France. (*Getting up.*) What are you doing in the next few minutes?

DU MESNIL. I want to lock myself in for a week and see nobody.

CLOTILDE. I won't have it. I don't want you to make yourself sick over something that may still come out all right. Take this letter to Mrs. Simpson's, it'll get you out into the fresh air. And from there you can go and see your uncle.

DU MESNIL. Why should I? A perfectly useless old fogy—you said so yourself. I'll write to him and tell him I'm fed up on his advice and that he may bestow his influence elsewhere.

CLOTILDE. I won't have that, either. Everyone knows your uncle has been behind this affair. Now, whoever makes it succeed, we shall owe the position to your uncle, do you understand? I don't suppose you want it said that we get favors through Mrs. Simpson and her friends.

DU MESNIL. Right again. I'll take your letter and see the uncle. But the economists will have to do without me tonight.

CLOTILDE. I won't have it. Why change your habits? That dinner is no chore for you. You generally come back late, quite gay, and with stories that give me an insight into the nature of your conversation. You're among men, and you say a lot of silly things, but you have a good time and you're right. Don't pass it up, there's little enough to be had in this world. You'll be with people you like, and I'll drop in on my little friend who'd miss me awfully if I didn't.

DU MESNIL. All right. I won't insist. But I feel pretty low and I would rather stay with you.

CLOTILDE. Thanks, but you'll have plenty of opportunities again.

DU MESNIL. Good-bye; where's the letter?

CLOTILDE. Here. (*He goes, sheepishly.*) And brace up a bit, a little cheerfulness in your face if you can manage it. Let's not take others into our confidence when we have trouble: it never helps.

DU MESNIL (*coming back*). What shall I say to uncle?

CLOTILDE. Whatever you wish.

DU MESNIL. So really you're packing me off to this dinner? I'm going there in the worst of moods.

CLOTILDE. The mood will change when you get some food.

DU MESNIL. Yes. I'm going to gorge. (*Exit.*)

CLOTILDE. Talk of Madame Bovary! Bring up women to be quiet and respectable! Let a woman stay at home and her house will prosper—not so I can notice it! What would he have done if I hadn't been here? Not to mention the fact that decent folk have all the luck and are welcome everywhere. Yes, yes! Every time there's something to be given out—a position, a favor, a medal—anything, important or unimportant, and there are two applicants, one a modest and deserving fellow, not very strong on pull; the other a clever humbug with nothing to recommend him but his social graces, it's the humbug who gets it and the good fellow who gets—left . . . Now perhaps I'll get out before nightfall. I hope Mr. Lafont will have tired waiting. He won't complain, anyway, if I get the start of him. I'm off. (*She goes rapidly to the back door, which opens slowly in.* LAFONT *appears hesitantly.*) This is too much! (*She comes back, furious.*)

LAFONT. You're angry with me for coming back? This is what happened. I was leaving, I swear to you. I didn't want to think of you until tomorrow. I saw your husband coming home. What was I to do? I should have liked to shake his hand; but perhaps you did not want him to know of my visit. You always say that I care nothing and disregard everything, though really I spend my life saving appearances with Adolph. In fact, I quickly retraced my steps and hid in a doorway to let him go by. He did come home, didn't he? I'm not making up anything? Afterwards, it is true, I was weak. I shouldn't have stayed. I told myself: Clotilde has been expecting Mrs. Simpson but she doesn't seem to be calling for her very promptly. What if her plans had changed? Clotilde might be glad to see me. You can't reproach me for so—so humble and tender a thought? Your husband came out again, which left things—as they were. So I looked once more to see if Mrs. Simpson was coming, I didn't see her, I came up. Oh, I came trembling, I assure you; I might have gone down again (*Laughing.*) if it had not been for one of those little coincidences that are so funny: your husband had left the front door open. I say, Clotilde, it's all quite simple and natural; you mustn't be angry for so slight a thing. Say something. You won't answer? One word? Only one? (*Going away.*) All right, I'm leaving you. You still want to have the evening to yourself? Till tomorrow. (*Coming back.*) Till tomorrow? (*Impatiently.*) You won't say one word? (*Going away.*) You won't say one word? I am very much hurt, if you must know. You've been treating me for some time past with too little consideration. (*Coming back.*) You're resolved not to answer me? (*Going away.*) As you wish. Let it be over and done with. You don't love me any more; I'm in your way; I have no joy of your friendship and I could be happy elsewhere. Let us part. (*Coming back and holding out his hand.*) But let's part like sensible people. Shall I tell you? You're not waiting for anybody. You're going to see your lover; it's with him you're dining. You can't deny it: I know. I did not want to mention it before. It's Ernest Mercier.

CLOTILDE. Alfred.

LAFONT. Alfred?

CLOTILDE. Alfred Mercier.

LAFONT. 28 Madeleine Street?

CLOTILDE. 28 Madeleine Boulevard.

LAFONT (*upset*). Clotilde! Is this a joke or is it the truth you're confessing?—It's the truth, isn't it? Ah! Clotilde! Clotilde! What have you done! (*Sobbing.*) You should have deceived me without telling me, delicately, so that I might not notice it. This time it is the end. Good-bye. (*Stopping.*) Good-bye? Good-bye! (*Exit.*)

CLOTILDE. That's about enough. I've been indulgent and always ready to explain—or at least once in a while; but every day, twice a day, no! It surely would be pleasant, wouldn't it, living with a passion like that, which doesn't give you time to breathe. And what's more, always hovering on the brink of scandal! It's come to the point where I'm never safe from him except when my husband's at home.

ACT III

(*Same as* ACTS I *and* II. *The double door, right, is wide open. Coffee is being served to* CLOTILDE *and* SIMPSON, *who are alone.*)

CLOTILDE (*near the table*). Mr. Simpson.

SIMPSON (*sipping coffee*). Yes, Mrs. Du Mesnil?

CLOTILDE. Please make yourself at home, as you would at your mother's. Just help yourself.

SIMPSON. Yes, Mrs. Du Mesnil.

CLOTILDE (*to Adèle*). Give this cup to Mr. Du Mesnil. Then you may go.

ADÈLE. Madam will not need me any more?

CLOTILDE. No.

ADÈLE. I had told madam that my brother—

CLOTILDE. Please go; you may talk of that later.

ADÈLE (*sourly*). Very well, madam. (*Exit with cup.*)

CLOTILDE (*half aloud, going to him*). So it's true, you're leaving Paris for good?

SIMPSON. Yes, it's true.

CLOTILDE. This very day?

SIMPSON. I'm taking the seven o'clock train, which will drop me at home about midnight.

CLOTILDE. Your trunks are packed?

SIMPSON. My man is putting in the last things now.

CLOTILDE. There's nothing you would like to have me do?

SIMPSON. I have so little time left I should be afraid to put you to any trouble.

CLOTILDE. As you wish. (*She turns away from him. He rises to put his cup on the table.*) What does your mother think of this sudden resolution?

SIMPSON. My mother's delighted to see me go. It's partly on her account that I'm leaving earlier than usual. She wants me to overhaul her old place and supervise the repairs. I want to do it so that she won't be able to recognize Gingerbread—that's the name of it—when she comes down.

CLOTILDE. If your mother approves, I have nothing more to say.

SIMPSON. You like Paris too well; you won't admit that one can be bored in Paris or that one can live somewhere else.

CLOTILDE. I don't think any such thing. Only I think that a man of your age and in your position does not quit the capital so easily, especially if he is held back by any the slightest attachment. The season is not nearly over; the weather's atrocious; no one dreams of leaving except you. You must have some reason.

SIMPSON. If I had one it would be rather a reason for staying.

Clotilde. Then why are you leaving?

Simpson. I'm bored. I'm annoyed and humiliated. I feel like a pauper in your capital. What does that wretched flat of mine look like? I'm ashamed to live in it. It's even worse when people call on me. My mother has always refused to set me up decently. She'd rather have me travel. I spend a lot of money without getting either pleasure or happiness from it. Down there, at Gingerbread, the scene is different. I lead a great life. I'm somebody in the country. People take off their hats when I go by, I have everything I miss here—my horses, my dogs, my guns. You know I have a magnificent collection of shotguns that I'm always eager to go back to and see properly cared for. Paris is fun, to be sure, and perhaps I'd like it as much as anybody else, if I could live in it so as to satisfy my self-respect.

Clotilde. It's my fault. I haven't known how to console and keep you. To part as we're doing, as if with a light heart, after only four months—well, I hope it won't have seemed too long for you.

Simpson. It's five months.

Clotilde. Are you sure?

Simpson. Let's see: January 15, February 15, March 15—

Clotilde. You are right. Let's call it five months and say no more about it. (*Pause.*)

Simpson (*going to her*). You should come down to Gingerbread later on, when my mother will be there with some of her friends.

Clotilde. Don't count on me. My husband cannot easily get away.

Simpson. You could come by yourself.

Clotilde. He wouldn't like that.

Simpson. Your friend Mrs. Beaulieu will be there. Those considerations don't seem to bother her.

Clotilde. Oh, it's different with Pauline. She has an independent income, in the first place; it enables her to do what she wants. Then her husband has wronged her dreadfully and she takes advantage of it; she's right!

Simpson. She has a good time of it, hasn't she?

Clotilde. That I don't know. We're very close, Pauline and I, but we don't discuss everything.

Simpson. But it's through her that you came to know my mother?

Clotilde. Yet Pauline never knew why I wanted to know your mother. What made you think Mrs. Beaulieu didn't behave altogether—regularly? Have you heard anything about her?

Simpson. I happen to know of her infatuation for one of my friends.

Clotilde. What's his name?

Simpson. Hector de Godefroy.

Clotilde. It's a lie.

SIMPSON. You mean it's not quite a secret.

CLOTILDE. You should know that Mrs. Beaulieu has been living for years with a charming young man who adores her and never leaves her side.

SIMPSON. What's his name?

CLOTILDE (*hesitating, then smiling*). Alfred Mercier.

SIMPSON. Yes, but Mrs. Beaulieu has suddenly gone crazy, I don't know why, about my friend Hector, and she doesn't spend a day without seeing him.

CLOTILDE. Who told you that?

SIMPSON. Mrs. Beaulieu herself. She's not at all shy about such things.

CLOTILDE. What a child Pauline is! Why couldn't she keep it to herself!

SIMPSON (*going away from her*). That's another thing I like about leaving Paris. One buries a deal of stories that aren't very pretty.

CLOTILDE. Is it about my friend you're saying this?

SIMPSON. Well, she can take her share of it.

CLOTILDE. Pauline has suffered a great deal, you know.

SIMPSON. She doesn't show many traces of it now.

CLOTILDE. Perhaps you made love to her?

SIMPSON. It never occurred to me.

CLOTILDE. But Mrs. Beaulieu is simply adorable.

SIMPSON. I don't like to be merged in with the common herd.

CLOTILDE. Still, it's bound to happen to you more or less.

SIMPSON. The ladies wouldn't like to hear you admit it.

CLOTILDE. What did I give away? That we're weak, fickle, guilty, if you like; that we always let ourselves be led astray; that we meet oafs who don't love us as they should, or, worse, ungrateful wretches who have respect and affection only for themselves . . . You may be right after all. The best thing would be to have nothing to do with either kind; to blind one's eyes and stop one's ears, to upbraid oneself and say, "Here is your place, stick to it." Perhaps life wouldn't be very thrilling or amusing, but one would avoid many worries, many disillusions, many regrets.

SIMPSON. What is the matter?

CLOTILDE. Don't—!

SIMPSON. You're in tears!

CLOTILDE. Real ones, I may say.

SIMPSON. Why do you weep, my dear?

CLOTILDE. Who knows? There is a bit of everything in a woman's tears.

SIMPSON. I should be sorry if my leaving—

CLOTILDE. No; don't make yourself out worse than you are. We met, grew fond, separate—it's something that happens every day. But you men, who are so accommodating when you want to obtain our good graces, are terribly harsh when we have granted them. Come! I must call my husband. He'd leave us here together until tomorrow, with his trusting faith and sublime ignorance of all our follies. (*Holding out her hand.*) Say farewell, now. Keep a happy memory of these five months, that's all I ask. Keep it to yourself, though—you must; and I know you will. It is thanks to you that we succeeded in obtaining what we desired, but your help came after my wrong-doing, and was not strictly needed. If some time you want to drop in and say how do you do, you know the house; you've done everything you should to be a welcome guest here.

SIMPSON. You are charming.

CLOTILDE. I know it. (*Going to the door on the right.*) I say, Adolph, haven't you smoked your fill? You can finish your paper later, Adolph, do you hear? Mr. Simpson is getting his hat, hurry up if you want to go down with him. (*Coming back.*) My husband will be in immediately. (*Enter* DU MESNIL.)

DU MESNIL. I'm behaving like a boor, leaving you alone like this.

SIMPSON. It's perfectly all right.

DU MESNIL. I've got into the habit of napping for an instant after lunch. That's the only time I really feel at home.

SIMPSON. Are you ready?

DU MESNIL. At your service.

SIMPSON. Let's go then.

DU MESNIL. Excuse my saying a word to my wife?

SIMPSON. Certainly.

DU MESNIL (*whispers to* CLOTILDE). Should I thank this young man?

CLOTILDE. No, we had him to lunch, that's enough.

DU MESNIL. We're greatly obliged to his friend in the Government.

CLOTILDE. His mother did everything—after I wrote to her, you remember, in your presence.

DU MESNIL. I didn't know Mrs. Simpson had a son that old; what do you think of him?

CLOTILDE. He's distinguished looking.

DU MESNIL. Grand airs about him, eh?

CLOTILDE. I don't dislike it.

DU MESNIL. What was he saying to you?

CLOTILDE. That I was perfect.

DU MESNIL. Morally?

CLOTILDE. Personally, too.

DU MESNIL. I suppose I'm a trusting soul to have left you together.

CLOTILDE. He's leaving tonight.

DU MESNIL. Yes, but he can come back.

CLOTILDE. He's still not the one to make me forget my duty. (*She turns away.*)

SIMPSON (*joining her*). You'll forgive me, Mrs. Du Mesnil, for running off so hurriedly.

CLOTILDE. I know your time is short; you said so, and I wouldn't dare keep you.

SIMPSON. I seem already to regret Paris, even before I leave it.

CLOTILDE. Oh, you'll forget it quite easily.

SIMPSON. My mother will doubtless see you soon and give me news of you.

CLOTILDE. We shall also inquire about you.

SIMPSON. Remember that you are expected at Gingerbread.

CLOTILDE. It's not likely that you'll see me there.

SIMPSON. Oh, I won't give up so easily. If any occasion brings me to Paris—if need be, I shall make one—I'll try again to persuade you.

CLOTILDE. Don't come to invite me, come to see me.

SIMPSON. Good-bye, then, until the near future.

CLOTILDE. Good-bye, until then.

DU MESNIL. What was I telling you?

CLOTILDE. And what did I tell you? Never mind him and attend to your business. (*He goes out.*)

A silly episode! None of the young men today is worth the trouble one takes about them. They are dry, full of pretensions, believe in nothing. They love to pose and that's about all. I had thought that Mr. Simpson, having been educated by his mother, could become seriously attached to a woman. I shouldn't complain about him anyway, I suppose. He's always been very well-bred and obliging—he's a bit dull on the subject of his shotguns—but it serves me right: I had what I needed, an excellent friend, a second husband, you might say; I mistreated him in every possible way, and he got tired of it, that's natural enough. Who knows? He may think me angrier than I really am; men know so little about us. We're very weak, it is true, for those who charm us, but we always come back to those who love us. (*Bell rings.*)

ADÈLE. Mr. Lafont, madam.

CLOTILDE. Well, why do you take that astonished air to announce Mr. Lafont.

ADÈLE. Is madam going to receive him?

CLOTILDE. Why certainly.

ADÈLE. Very well, madam.

CLOTILDE. You can go out, if you wish to.

ADÈLE. Thank you, ma'am.

LAFONT (*much moved, enters slowly*). How do you do.

CLOTILDE (*with a calculated inflection*). How do you do, dear friend.

LAFONT. How are you?

CLOTILDE. Quiet, very quiet, and you?

LAFONT. Pretty bad—very bad. Am I in your way?

CLOTILDE. Not in the least.

LAFONT. You were perhaps going out?

CLOTILDE. No. I scarcely go out nowadays. Where should I go?

LAFONT. You had guests for lunch?

CLOTILDE. Guests? No—a guest.

LAFONT. A friend?

CLOTILDE. An acquaintance.

LAFONT. Do I know him?

CLOTILDE (*puzzling*). My husband told me his name, but I've mislaid it!

LAFONT. I just saw them leave together.

CLOTILDE. Really? You were there under my window? Had I known I would have shown myself for an instant. It was very sweet of you. At least you didn't forget me right away.

LAFONT. Who was that gentleman?

CLOTILDE. A stranger, I tell you, a very casual acquaintance. You can't possibly take umbrage at his being here. My husband introduced him this morning and tonight he will have left town.

LAFONT. You're speaking the truth?

CLOTILDE. Why should I lie to you? You, at least, don't change. That's one thing I must say in your favor. Come here and sit in the easy chair and try to stay there if you can. Don't let me see you move, pace or jump about as formerly. I have memories of you that are so much pleasanter.

LAFONT. Clotilde!

CLOTILDE. There is no longer any such person.

LAFONT. My dear!

CLOTILDE. Let's be calm, please; don't let us wander off so soon.

LAFONT. I do regret, you may be sure, that ridiculous scene which you could so easily have prevented. Look at me: Alfred Mercier! (*She laughs.*) Ah, but you know, I had been jealous of that fellow Mercier for so long. All my suspicions pointed to him. Mrs. Beaulieu will be grateful for your discretion.

CLOTILDE. That may be. What have you been doing since I saw you last?

LAFONT. I've thought about you.

CLOTILDE. That's easily said. What else?

LAFONT. What else? I've lived as usual.

CLOTILDE. You didn't go on a trip?

LAFONT. I had the opportunity, but I didn't have the heart.

CLOTILDE. Have the ladies been kind to you? Have you been well looked after?

LAFONT. I refuse to answer that.

CLOTILDE. Why? It may be that previously an infidelity on your part would have wounded me—deeply; but what was forbidden to you then is allowed now. As if I didn't know you, and as if you were the sort of man to deny yourself consolations. You weren't always very lovable, you know, nor very jolly, nor very trusting, but still—

LAFONT. Still?

CLOTILDE. Let us not talk of those things.

LAFONT. I am much too miserable, I assure you, to be thinking of consolations. And besides, if it is fated that I should lose you forever, I shall never try to replace you from a circle I no longer frequent.

CLOTILDE. That's wrong. You should frequent at least the ladies of that circle. They enjoy freedom. You don't have to handle them with kid gloves. They love scenes, tears, and battles. Which you won't find with us. We can only give a peaceful, quiet affection, sincere and . . . disinterested.

LAFONT. That is what I want. That is what we all want.

CLOTILDE. Then, my friend, you should have taken care and not risked losing what you had, merely for the pleasure of being headstrong.

LAFONT. Clotilde?

CLOTILDE. What is it, my dear?

LAFONT. Give me your hand.

CLOTILDE. No.

LAFONT. Can't you give me your hand?

CLOTILDE. We'll see. And don't put on that look or I shall send you home.

LAFONT. Give me your hand.

CLOTILDE. Well, there it is. Now you want the other, I suppose.

LAFONT. You're so—frigid.

CLOTILDE. What do you mean, frigid? I let you sit down near me, I let you kiss my hand—you didn't think I was going to fall on your neck as soon as you entered, did you?

LAFONT. I am here as a culprit. I agree with all your reproaches but I think you deserve some yourself.

CLOTILDE. None.

LAFONT. Was it my fault or yours that our relations suddenly changed? No man was happier than I until the day you turned your own life topsy-turvy.

CLOTILDE. What do you mean—I turned my life topsy-turvy? Only you could have done that—would have done it, if I hadn't stopped you in time.

LAFONT. You may be right. I don't know why I harp on what happened. Let bygones be bygones.

CLOTILDE. Bygones! You're incorrigible. I receive you, I listen to you, I believe that you sincerely regret your inexplicable behavior. I tell myself that later, if you reform sincerely, it might not be impossible for me to forgive you—and you begin again, baiting me with that evil streak in you that I detest and have never been able to eradicate. Nothing happened, do you hear—nothing, nothing, nothing—absolutely nothing. Please move away.

Lafont. Why?

Clotilde. Please move. I want to get up.

Lafont. No.

Clotilde. Yes.

Lafont. Let us stay as we are.

Clotilde. Let me get up for a moment. You're not leaving yet.

Lafont. Let us be.

Clotilde. How stubborn you are!

Lafont. You're not upset?

Clotilde. I'm nervous and agitated.

Lafont. All the more reason.

Clotilde. I beg your pardon?

Lafont. I'm trying hard to keep cool.

Clotilde. Don't lose your temper. I'll stay put.

Lafont. So you were thinking of forgiving me a little.

Clotilde. I said so and I was wrong.

Lafont. Let's go back to our good old ways.

Clotilde. What's the use? You'll never be happy with me, and I'll never have a quiet moment with you. You refuse to understand my position.

Lafont. What position?

Clotilde. My position. Haven't I a husband on whom I am wholly dependent and who must find me at home whenever he wishes? It's the least I can do for him, you must admit. And that's another fault of yours which you would correct if you really understood me.

Lafont. What have I done now?

Clotilde. You don't like my husband.

Lafont. Of course I do, I do!

Clotilde. But you don't, I tell you. You don't like Adolph. I can see it in many ways. Perhaps your temperaments don't jibe, or perhaps it's due to the situation.

Lafont. That is very unfair to me. Your husband—why, your husband never had but two friends in the world.

Clotilde. Two?

Lafont. Yes, two.

Clotilde. Who?

Lafont. You and me. (*They laugh.*) Let's leave the others out. Come, Clotilde, be honest! Don't you think that you suited me?

Clotilde. As for that, yes. I do believe I suit your taste.

Lafont. Now, a devotion like mine is not met with every day. Do you ever think of that?

CLOTILDE. Certainly. It is precisely because I valued it that I was considerate and used to put up with all your storming.

LAFONT. I am very gentle, usually, very tender.

CLOTILDE. I don't deny it. You know extremely well how to please when you want to, and you find very pretty things to say that are very agreeable to hear . . . *you're* not the one to talk to a woman about shotguns.

LAFONT. What does that mean?

CLOTILDE. Nothing. A story I was told, not worth repeating.

LAFONT (*coming nearer*). Tell me you forgive me.

CLOTILDE (*softly*). Yes. Now be good.

LAFONT. You forgive me—altogether?

CLOTILDE. Altogether—don't pester me, I'll go and see you.

LAFONT. Soon?

CLOTILDE. Whenever you wish. Only take care. I'm not my own mistress here.

LAFONT. Clotilde!

CLOTILDE. You love me?

LAFONT. I adore you.

CLOTILDE (*getting up*). Dear me! How many wasted words to get to where we were before.

LAFONT (*joining her*). Do you regret it?

CLOTILDE. Not yet.

LAFONT. I was feeling rather blue when I came here. I shall leave in a better mood.

CLOTILDE. Well, I hope you've learned a lesson! Namely, no more scenes, and no more of those appalling suspicions that disgust a woman and that are so useless. When something goes wrong or annoys you, tell me; I'm always ready to listen to reason. Now, I'm going to tell you something that will rather please you.

LAFONT. I'm all ears.

CLOTILDE. I think my friendship with Mrs. Simpson is about over.

LAFONT. Nonsense!

CLOTILDE. I mean it!

LAFONT. She has offended you?

CLOTILDE. On the contrary, I feel nothing but gratitude for her. It is not so much that I don't want to see Mrs. Simpson, it's her house that I think it wiser to avoid.

LAFONT. What did I tell you in the first place?

CLOTILDE. You're cleverer than I, that's all.

LAFONT. I know another person whose company is not good for you, and whom you ought to drop.

CLOTILDE. You're going to say something stupid, I can see it coming. That person is . . ?

LAFONT. Mrs. Beaulieu.

CLOTILDE. Pauline? I, drop Pauline? I should indeed like to know why, tell me why?

LAFONT. It seems to me—

CLOTILDE. It seems to you—what?

LAFONT. Mr. Mercier!

CLOTILDE. What about Mr. Mercier?

LAFONT. Well, I know all about him and you doubtless know it too.

CLOTILDE. Yes, I do know; what of it?

LAFONT. You don't defend Mrs. Beaulieu, I trust?

CLOTILDE. I say, do you know what you're saying? Are you going to blame Pauline for doing for Mr. Mercier what I am doing for you?

LAFONT. It isn't the same thing.

CLOTILDE. Are you sure? Where is the difference?

LAFONT. I can see one.

CLOTILDE. What is it? Let's hear it. Oh, you're all alike, you men. For your sake, we can allow ourselves everything, but you object when others benefit. Rather than meddle in Pauline's business, you should be thinking of my husband who has complained every day that you didn't come around any more, and who'll ask you for an account of yourself.

LAFONT (*pointing to the door*). Is it Adolph we just heard?

CLOTILDE. Yes, it's Adolph. Have you thought of what you're going to tell him?

LAFONT. No.

CLOTILDE. The idea makes you laugh? So much the worse for you, my dear. You'll have to extricate yourself as best you can.

(*Enter* DU MESNIL.)

DU MESNIL. What, is that you?

LAFONT (*embarrassed*). Hello, old man.

DU MESNIL. Hello. Why haven't we seen you these many—

LAFONT (*again*). How are you?

DU MESNIL. Splendid. You don't answer my question. What happened to you that you dropped out of sight like a plummet?

CLOTILDE. Don't torment him. He's had great troubles. Isn't that so, Mr. Lafont?

LAFONT. Yes, Mrs. Du Mesnil.

DU MESNIL. What sort of troubles?

CLOTILDE. Shall I tell my husband?

LAFONT. Just as you wish.

DU MESNIL. Come, out with it.

CLOTILDE. He was jealous.

DU MESNIL. Jealous! What? You still jealous at your age? (*To* CLOTILDE.) And who the devil was he jealous about? About some woman who doesn't belong to him, I suppose! These bachelors, they never deny themselves anything, and they're jealous into the bargain. Shall I tell you the opinion of a famous economist on jealousy? Jealousy is just the fact of being deprived. Nothing more. If you were married you wouldn't feel deprived and you wouldn't be jealous. Isn't that true, Clotilde?

CLOTILDE. Come, now, that's enough.

DU MESNIL. Jealous! Have you told him?

CLOTILDE. Told him what?

DU MESNIL. That I'd been appointed.

CLOTILDE. Mr. Lafont was the first to congratulate you by letter.

DU MESNIL. Of course, I'd forgotten. He wrote to me! Instead of coming to see me. (*To* LAFONT, *but looking at* CLOTILDE.) It's my uncle, my good old uncle, who swung the thing.

CLOTILDE. Everybody knows it's your uncle, you don't need to shout it from the housetops.

DU MESNIL. Well, it's better to be a government official than to be jealous, eh? (*To* CLOTILDE.) Poor fellow, he's not completely recovered. His nose doesn't look right. By the bye, did she or did she not deceive you?

LAFONT. Why don't you leave me alone?

DU MESNIL. Surely you can tell that much to an old friend.

CLOTILDE. My husband's asking you a question, why don't you answer it?

LAFONT. What do you expect me to say? Is there any man, any one man, who could swear that his mistress never deceived him? Mine says she hasn't. She couldn't very well say she had. We've had a reconciliation. No doubt that's what we both wanted.

CLOTILDE. Indeed! It's too bad the lady is not present to hear you; she would know what opinion you have of her and of all other women. Trust us, Mr. Lafont, trust us—that's the only system that works with us.

DU MESNIL. It's always been mine, hasn't it, dear?

Round Dance

TEN DIALOGUES

BY ARTHUR SCHNITZLER

Translated by KEENE WALLIS

CHARACTERS

The Prostitute
The Soldier
The Housemaid
The Young Man
The Young Wife
The Husband
The Little Darling
The Poet
The Actress
The Count

The Time: The eighteen-nineties
The Place: Vienna

THE DIALOGUES

I. THE PROSTITUTE AND THE SOLDIER
II. THE SOLDIER AND THE HOUSEMAID
III. THE HOUSEMAID AND THE YOUNG GENTLEMAN
IV. THE YOUNG GENTLEMAN AND THE YOUNG WIFE
V. THE YOUNG WIFE AND THE HUSBAND
VI. THE HUSBAND AND THE LITTLE DARLING
VII. THE LITTLE DARLING AND THE POET
VIII. THE POET AND THE ACTRESS
IX. THE ACTRESS AND THE COUNT
X. THE COUNT AND THE PROSTITUTE

I

THE PROSTITUTE AND THE SOLDIER

(*Late evening on the Augarten Bridge.* THE SOLDIER, *whistling, on his way home.*)

THE PROSTITUTE. Hello, good lookin'!

(THE SOLDIER *turns and goes on.*)

What's your hurry?

THE SOLDIER. Me, good-lookin'?

THE PROSTITUTE. Sure, who do you think? Say, come on. My place is right around the corner.

THE SOLDIER. I haven't got time. I got to get back to the barracks.

THE PROSTITUTE. You've got plenty of time to get back to your barracks. It's nicer here with me.

THE SOLDIER (*close to her*). Yeah?

THE PROSTITUTE. Ps-st! Look out for the cops.

THE SOLDIER. Cops! Say, I've got a night stick, myself.

THE PROSTITUTE. Come on.

THE SOLDIER. Let me alone. I'm broke anyway.

THE PROSTITUTE. I don't want your money.

THE SOLDIER (*stopping. They are under a street-lamp*). You don't want money? What kind of a dame are you?

THE PROSTITUTE. Civilians pay me for it but a guy like you doesn't have to pay for things.

THE SOLDIER. Maybe you're the girl my buddy told me about.

THE PROSTITUTE. I don't know any buddy of yours.

THE SOLDIER. You're the one, all right! You know—the cafe down the street. He went home with you.

THE PROSTITUTE. I've taken lots of 'em home with me from that place . . . lots of 'em!

THE SOLDIER. All right. Let's go!

THE PROSTITUTE. In a hurry now, huh?

THE SOLDIER. Well, what are you waiting for? Say, gal, I've got to be back at the barracks by ten.

THE PROSTITUTE. Been in the service long?

THE SOLDIER. What do you care how long I've been in? Is it far?

THE PROSTITUTE. Make it in ten minutes.

THE SOLDIER. Too far for me. Give's a kiss.

THE PROSTITUTE (*kissing him*). That's what I like best—when I love 'em.

THE SOLDIER. I don't. No. Can't go with you. It's too far.

THE PROSTITUTE. Say, how about to-morrow afternoon?

THE SOLDIER. Fine. Let's have your address.

THE PROSTITUTE. But maybe you won't come.

THE SOLDIER. Me! I will, if I say I will.

THE PROSTITUTE. Look here—if my place is too far—over there . . . to-night.

(*She points toward the Danube.*)

THE SOLDIER. What's there?

THE PROSTITUTE. It's nice and quiet there . . . no one around.

THE SOLDIER. Say, that's no good.

THE PROSTITUTE. It's always good with me. Come on. Who knows? We may be dead to-morrow.

THE SOLDIER. All right, let's go—but make it snappy.

THE PROSTITUTE. Oh, it's so dark. Look out! You'll fall in the river.

THE SOLDIER. Good thing if I did, I guess.

THE PROSTITUTE. Sh-h. Wait, we're coming to a bench.

THE SOLDIER. You seem to know all about this place.

THE PROSTITUTE. I'd like to have a guy like you for a boy friend.

THE SOLDIER. I'd make you jealous all the time.

THE PROSTITUTE. I'll fix that, all right.

THE SOLDIER. Is zat so?

THE PROSTITUTE. Don't make such a racket. There's cops around. We're right in the middle of Vienna.

THE SOLDIER. Come on. Come over here.

THE PROSTITUTE. Crazy! We'll fall in the river.

THE SOLDIER (*has grabbed her*). Oh you—

THE PROSTITUTE. Hold me tight.

THE SOLDIER. Don't be afraid.

* * * * *

THE PROSTITUTE. It'd have been nicer on the bench.

THE SOLDIER. It's all the same to me . . . Well, get up.

THE PROSTITUTE. What's your hurry—?

THE SOLDIER. Got to get to the barracks. I'm late already.

THE PROSTITUTE. Say, what's your name?

THE SOLDIER. What do you care what's my name?

THE PROSTITUTE. My name's Leocadia.

THE SOLDIER. What a name!

THE PROSTITUTE. Say!

THE SOLDIER. Well, what do you want?

THE PROSTITUTE. Give's two-bits for the janitor.

THE SOLDIER. Huh! . . . What do you think I am? A meal-ticket? Good-bye, Leocadia . . .

THE PROSTITUTE. Rat! Heel! (*He has disappeared.*)

II

THE SOLDIER AND THE HOUSEMAID

(*Prater Gardens. Sunday evening. A path leading away from the amusement park. Trees. Darkness. The wild medley from the amusement park can still be heard; also strains of music from the cheap dancehall, a vulgar polka, played by a brass band.* THE SOLDIER. THE HOUSEMAID.)

THE HOUSEMAID. Now tell me why you wanted to leave.

(THE SOLDIER *grins sheepishly.*)

It was so nice, and I love to dance.

(THE SOLDIER *puts his arm around her waist. She submits.*)

But we aren't dancing. Why do you hold me so tight?

THE SOLDIER. What's your name? Katy?

THE HOUSEMAID. You've got a "Katy" on your brain.

THE SOLDIER. I know—I know . . . Marie.

THE HOUSEMAID. Goodness, it's dark here. I'm afraid.

THE SOLDIER. You needn't be afraid when I'm with you. I know how to run things.

THE HOUSEMAID. But where are we going? And nobody around. Come, let's go back! . . . It's so dark!

THE SOLDIER (*pulling at his Virginia cigar until it glows brightly*). There . . . it's lighter already. Ha—ha! Oh, you little treasure!

THE HOUSEMAID. Oh! What are you doing? If I had thought this was what you—

THE SOLDIER. I'll be a son-of-a-gun if there was any one around here who felt softer and rounder than you, Fraülein Marie.

THE HOUSEMAID. How do you know? Have you felt all of them?

THE SOLDIER. A guy notices things dancing. Lots of things!

THE HOUSEMAID. But you danced with that sourpuss blonde a lot more than you did with me.

THE SOLDIER. She's an old friend of my buddy's.

THE HOUSEMAID. That corporal with the turned-up mustache?

THE SOLDIER. No, I mean the civilian. You know, the one who was talking with me at the table before we started dancing. The one who talks so hoarse.

THE HOUSEMAID. Oh, I know. He's pretty fresh.

THE SOLDIER. Did he do anything to you? I'll show him! What did he do to you?

THE HOUSEMAID. Oh, nothing . . . I noticed what he did with the others.

THE SOLDIER. Say, Fraülein Marie . . .

THE HOUSEMAID. You'll burn me with your cigar.

THE SOLDIER. Pardon me! Fraülein Marie—or may I say Marie?

THE HOUSEMAID. We're not such good friends yet . . .

THE SOLDIER. Lots of people that don't like each other don't say Herr and Fraülein.

THE HOUSEMAID. Next time, if we . . . But, Franz!

THE SOLDIER. Oh, you got my name?

THE HOUSEMAID. But Franz . . .

THE SOLDIER. That's right, call me Franz, Fraülein Marie.

THE HOUSEMAID. Don't get fresh—but, sh-h, suppose some one should come!

THE SOLDIER. What if they did? They couldn't see a thing. Even a foot away.

THE HOUSEMAID. For goodness' sake, where are we going?

THE SOLDIER. Look! There's two just like us.

THE HOUSEMAID. Where? I can't see anything.

THE SOLDIER. There . . . straight ahead.

THE HOUSEMAID. Why do you say: "two like us"?

THE SOLDIER. Well, I mean, they like each other, too.

THE HOUSEMAID. Look out! What's that there? I nearly fell.

THE SOLDIER. Oh, that's the gate. There's a meadow on the other side.

THE HOUSEMAID. Don't shove me. I'll fall.

THE SOLDIER. Sh-h, not so loud.

THE HOUSEMAID. Stop! I'm going to scream — What are you doing? But—

THE SOLDIER. There's no one around.

THE HOUSEMAID. Then, let's go back where there's people.

THE SOLDIER. We don't want people. Why Marie, what . . . we want . . . Ho! Ho!

THE HOUSEMAID. Herr Franz, please, for heaven's sake! Listen to me. If I had . . . known . . . oh . . . do . . .

* * * * *

THE SOLDIER (*blissfully*). Well, I'm damned . . . Oh . . .

THE HOUSEMAID. I can't see your face . . .

THE SOLDIER. Face? — Hell!

* * * * *

THE SOLDIER. Well, Fraülein Marie, you can't stay here all night.

THE HOUSEMAID. Please, Franz, help me.

THE SOLDIER. Oh, get up.

THE HOUSEMAID. Oh, good heavens, Franz!

THE SOLDIER. Well, what do you want?

THE HOUSEMAID. You're a wicked man, Franz.

THE SOLDIER. Uhum . . . Say, wait a minute.

THE HOUSEMAID. Why are you leaving me?

THE SOLDIER. Can't you let me light my cigar?

THE HOUSEMAID. It's so dark.

THE SOLDIER. It'll be light again to-morrow morning.

THE HOUSEMAID. Tell me you love me, anyways.

THE SOLDIER. Well, you must have felt that, Fraülein Marie—

THE HOUSEMAID. Where are we going now?

THE SOLDIER. Back, of course.

THE HOUSEMAID. Please don't walk so fast.

THE SOLDIER. Well, what's the matter? I don't like to hang around in the dark.

THE HOUSEMAID. Tell me, Franz . . . do you love me?

THE SOLDIER. I just told you I loved you!

THE HOUSEMAID. Won't you give me a little kiss?

THE SOLDIER (*condescendingly*). There . . . Listen . . . The music again.

THE HOUSEMAID. Do you really want to go back and dance?

THE SOLDIER. Sure, why not?

THE HOUSEMAID. But, Franz, I have to get home. Madame will scold me anyways, she's cranky . . . she'd rather I never went out at all.

THE SOLDIER. You can go home.

THE HOUSEMAID. But I thought you'd take me home.

THE SOLDIER. Take you home? Huh!

THE HOUSEMAID. Please, it's kind of lonely going home alone.

THE SOLDIER. Where do you live?

THE HOUSEMAID. Not very far—in Porzellanstrasse.

THE SOLDIER. Sure enough! Then we go the same way . . . but it's too early for me . . . I want to dance . . . I won't have to be back at the barracks before twelve o'clock. I'm going to dance.

THE HOUSEMAID. Oh, I see, now it's that sourpuss blonde's chance.

THE SOLDIER. Humph! She isn't such a sourpuss.

THE HOUSEMAID. Oh Lord, how wicked men are! I bet you do the same to every girl.

THE SOLDIER. That'd be a big job for one man!

THE HOUSEMAID. Please, Franz, no more to-night—but don't leave me, you see—

THE SOLDIER. Okay, okay. But I suppose you'll let me dance.

THE HOUSEMAID. To-day I'm not going to dance with any one but you.

THE SOLDIER. There it is.

THE HOUSEMAID. What?

THE SOLDIER. The hall! How quick we got back. They're playing the same thing . . . that tatata-tum tatata-tum. (*He hums with the band.*)

. . . Well, I'll take you home, if you'll wait for me . . . if not . . . good-bye.

THE HOUSEMAID. Yes, I'll wait.

(They enter the dancehall.)

THE SOLDIER. Say, Fraülein Marie, get yourself a glass of beer. (*Turning to a blonde who is just dancing past with a young man. Very formally.*) May I have the next dance, Fraülein?

III

THE HOUSEMAID AND THE YOUNG GENTLEMAN

(*Sultry summer afternoon. The parents of* THE YOUNG GENTLEMAN *are away in the country. The cook is out.* THE HOUSEMAID *is in the kitchen writing a letter to the soldier who is now her sweetheart.* THE YOUNG GENTLEMAN'S *bell rings. She gets up and goes to his room.* THE YOUNG GENTLEMAN *is lying on a couch, smoking a cigarette and reading a French novel.*)

THE HOUSEMAID. Sir?

THE YOUNG GENTLEMAN. Oh, yes, Marie, yes, I rang, yes . . . I only wanted . . . of course . . . Oh, yes, of course, let the blinds down, Marie . . . It's cooler with the blinds down . . . yes . . .

(THE HOUSEMAID *goes to the window and pulls down the blinds.*)

THE YOUNG GENTLEMAN (*continues reading*). What are you doing, Marie? Oh, yes. But now I can't read.

THE HOUSEMAID. You always study so hard, sir.

THE YOUNG GENTLEMAN (*ignoring the remark*). There, that's better.

(THE HOUSEMAID *goes out.* THE YOUNG GENTLEMAN *tries to go on with his reading, lets the book fall, and rings again.* THE HOUSEMAID *enters.*)

THE YOUNG GENTLEMAN. I say, Marie . . . let's see, what was it I wanted to say? Oh, yes . . . Is there any cognac in the house?

THE HOUSEMAID. Yes, but it's locked up.

THE YOUNG GENTLEMAN. Who has the key?

THE HOUSEMAID. Lini has.

THE YOUNG GENTLEMAN. Who is Lini?

THE HOUSEMAID. The cook, Herr Alfred.

THE YOUNG GENTLEMAN. Ask Lini for it.

THE HOUSEMAID. Sure, but it's Lini's day out.

THE YOUNG GENTLEMAN. Oh . . .

THE HOUSEMAID. Can't I get anything for you from the cafe, sir?

THE YOUNG GENTLEMAN. Thank you, no . . . It's hot enough as it is. I don't need any cognac. Listen, Marie, bring me a glass of water. Wait, Marie—let it run, till it gets quite cold.

(*Exit* HOUSEMAID. THE YOUNG GENTLEMAN *gazes after her. At the door the maid looks back at him and* THE YOUNG GENTLEMAN *looks into space.* THE HOUSEMAID *turns on the water and lets it run. Meanwhile she goes into her room, washes her hands, and arranges her curls before the mirror. Then she brings the glass of water to* THE YOUNG GENTLEMAN. THE YOUNG GENTLEMAN *raises himself a bit, leaning on his elbow.* THE HOUSEMAID *gives him the glass of water and their fingers touch.*)

THE YOUNG GENTLEMAN. Thank you—Why what is the matter?—Careful. Put the glass back on the tray. (*He leans back, and stretches himself.*) What time is it?

THE HOUSEMAID. Five o'clock, sir.

THE YOUNG GENTLEMAN. Ah, five o'clock. That's fine.

(THE HOUSEMAID *goes. At the door she turns around.* THE YOUNG GENTLEMAN *has followed her with his eyes; she notices it, and smiles.* THE YOUNG GENTLEMAN *remains stretched out awhile; then, suddenly, he gets up. He walks to the door, back again, and lies down on the couch. He again tries to read. After a few moments, he rings once more.* THE HOUSEMAID *appears with a smile which she does not try to hide.*)

THE YOUNG GENTLEMAN. Listen, Marie, there was something I wanted to ask you. Didn't Dr. Schueller call this morning?

THE HOUSEMAID. No, sir. Nobody called.

THE YOUNG GENTLEMAN. That is strange. So Dr. Schueller didn't call? Do you know Dr. Schueller by sight?

THE HOUSEMAID. Of course. He's the big gentleman with the black beard.

THE YOUNG GENTLEMAN. Yes. Perhaps he called after all?

THE HOUSEMAID. No, sir. Nobody called.

THE YOUNG GENTLEMAN (*resolutely*). Come here, Marie.

THE HOUSEMAID (*coming a little nearer*). Yes, sir.

THE YOUNG GENTLEMAN. Closer . . . so . . . ah . . . I only thought . . .

THE HOUSEMAID. Do you want anything, sir?

THE YOUNG GENTLEMAN. I thought . . . Well, I thought—only about your blouse. What kind of a blouse is it? Can't you come closer? I won't bite you.

THE HOUSEMAID (*comes close to him*). What is the matter with my blouse? Don't you like it, sir?

THE YOUNG GENTLEMAN (*takes hold of her blouse, and draws her down to him*). Blue? It is a nice blue. (*Simply.*) You are prettily dressed, Marie.

THE HOUSEMAID. But, sir . . .

THE YOUNG GENTLEMAN. Ah . . . What is the matter? . . . (*He has *opened her blouse. In a matter of fact tone.)* You have a beautiful white skin, Marie.

THE HOUSEMAID. You flatter me, sir.

THE YOUNG GENTLEMAN (*kissing her on the breast*). That won't hurt you.

THE HOUSEMAID. Oh, no.

THE YOUNG GENTLEMAN. But you sigh. Why are you sighing?

THE HOUSEMAID. Oh, Herr Alfred . . .

THE YOUNG GENTLEMAN. And what charming little slippers you have . . .

THE HOUSEMAID. But . . . sir . . . if the doorbell rings—

THE YOUNG GENTLEMAN. Who would ring now?

THE HOUSEMAID. But, sir . . . look . . . it is so light . . .

THE YOUNG GENTLEMAN. You needn't feel shy with me. You needn't feel shy with anybody . . . a girl as pretty as you. Yes, really, you are, Marie . . . Do you know your hair smells sweet?

THE HOUSEMAID. Herr Alfred . . .

THE YOUNG GENTLEMAN. Don't make such a fuss, Marie . . . Anyway, I've already seen you different. When I came home the other night and went to get some water, the door to your room was open . . . and . . .

THE HOUSEMAID (*covering her face*). Oh, my, I didn't think Herr Alfred could be so naughty.

THE YOUNG GENTLEMAN. I saw lots then . . . this . . . and this . . . this . . . and—

THE HOUSEMAID. Oh, Herr Alfred!

THE YOUNG GENTLEMAN. Come, come . . . here . . . yes, like that . . .

THE HOUSEMAID. But if the doorbell rings now—

THE YOUNG GENTLEMAN. Forget it . . . We simply wouldn't open the door.

* * * * *

THE YOUNG GENTLEMAN (*the bell rings*). Damn it . . . What a racket that man makes—Perhaps he rang before, and we didn't hear.

THE HOUSEMAID. Oh, no. I was listening all the time.

THE YOUNG GENTLEMAN. Well, see what's the matter. Look through the peephole.

THE HOUSEMAID. Herr Alfred . . . you are . . . No . . . you're such a bad man.

THE YOUNG GENTLEMAN. Please go and see . . .

(THE HOUSEMAID *goes.* THE YOUNG GENTLEMAN *quickly puts up the blinds.*)

THE HOUSEMAID (*returns*). He must have gone away. Anyway, no one is there now. Maybe it was Dr. Schueller.

THE YOUNG GENTLEMAN (*annoyed*). Thank you.

(THE HOUSEMAID *drawing close to him.*)

THE YOUNG GENTLEMAN (*evading her*). Listen, Marie—I'm going to the cafe now.

THE HOUSEMAID (*tenderly*). So soon—Herr Alfred?

THE YOUNG GENTLEMAN *(formally)*. I am going to the cafe now . . . If Dr. Schueller should call—

THE HOUSEMAID. He won't come any more to-day.

THE YOUNG GENTLEMAN (*severely*). If Dr. Schueller should come, I . . . I'm in the cafe.

(*He goes to the adjoining room.* THE HOUSEMAID *takes a cigar from the smoking-stand, puts it in her blouse and goes out.*)

IV

THE YOUNG GENTLEMAN AND THE YOUNG WIFE

(*Evening—A drawing-room furnished with cheap elegance in a house in Schwind Street.* THE YOUNG GENTLEMAN *has just come in and still has his hat and overcoat on. He lights the gas. Then he opens the door to a side-room and looks in. The light from the drawing-room shines across the inlaid floor as far as the Louis Quinze bed, which stands against the opposite wall. A reddish light plays from the fireplace in the corner of the bedroom upon the hangings of the bed.* THE YOUNG GENTLEMAN *now inspects the bedroom. He takes an atomizer from the dressing-table, and sprays the bed-pillows with essence of violet. Then he goes with the atomizer through both rooms, constantly pressing upon the bulb, so that soon the scent pervades the apartment. He then takes off his hat and coat. He sits down in a blue velvet armchair, lights a cigarette, and smokes. After a short pause he rises again, and makes sure that the green shutters are closed. Suddenly, he goes into the bedroom, and opens a drawer in the dressing-table. He feels around in the drawer and finds a tortoise-shell hair-pin. He looks for a place to hide it, and finally puts it into a pocket of his overcoat. He opens the buffet in the drawing-room; takes a silver tray, with a bottle and two liqueur glasses, and puts them on the table. He goes back to his overcoat, and takes from it a small white package. Opening this, he places it beside the cognac. He goes to the buffet again and takes two small plates and knives and forks. He takes a marron glacé from the package and eats it. Then he pours himself a glass of cognac, and drinks it quickly. He then looks at his watch. He walks up and down the room. He stops awhile before a large mirror, combing his hair and tiny mustache with a pocket-comb. He next goes to the door of the vestibule and listens. Nothing there. Then he pulls together the blue portieres, which hang in front of the bedroom. The bell rings. He starts slightly. Then he sits down in the armchair, and does not rise until the door has been opened and* THE YOUNG WIFE *enters.* THE YOUNG WIFE, *heavily veiled, closes the door behind her, pausing a moment with her left hand over her heart, as though mastering a strong emotion.* THE YOUNG GENTLEMAN *goes toward her, takes her left hand, and presses a kiss on the white glove.)*

THE YOUNG GENTLEMAN (*softly*). Thank you.

THE YOUNG WIFE. Alfred—Alfred!

THE YOUNG GENTLEMAN. Come, gnädige Frau . . . Come, Emma . . .

THE YOUNG WIFE. Let me alone for a minute—please . . . Oh, please, please, Alfred!

(*She is still standing at the door.* THE YOUNG GENTLEMAN *standing before her, holding her hand.*)

THE YOUNG WIFE. Where am I, really?

THE YOUNG GENTLEMAN. With me.

THE YOUNG WIFE. This place is terrible, Alfred.

THE YOUNG GENTLEMAN. Why? It is a very proper house.

THE YOUNG WIFE. But I met two gentlemen on the stairs.

THE YOUNG GENTLEMAN. Acquaintances of yours?

THE YOUNG WIFE. I don't know. They might be.

THE YOUNG GENTLEMAN. But gnädige Frau—you surely know your friends!

THE YOUNG WIFE. I couldn't see their faces.

THE YOUNG GENTLEMAN. But even if they were your best friends—they couldn't possibly recognize you . . . I, myself . . . if I didn't know it was you . . . this veil—

THE YOUNG WIFE. I am wearing two veils.

THE YOUNG GENTLEMAN. Won't you come in? . . . And at least take off your hat?

THE YOUNG WIFE. What are you thinking of, Alfred? I promised five minutes . . . Not a second more . . . I swear, no more—

THE YOUNG GENTLEMAN. Well, your veil—

THE YOUNG WIFE. There are two of them.

THE YOUNG GENTLEMAN. All right, both . . . you will at least let me see your face.

THE YOUNG WIFE. Do you really love me, Alfred?

THE YOUNG GENTLEMAN (*deeply hurt*). Emma! Can you ask?

THE YOUNG WIFE. It's so warm here.

THE YOUNG GENTLEMAN. You've still got your coat on. Really, you will catch cold.

THE YOUNG WIFE (*finally enters the room, and throws herself into the armchair*). I'm tired, so tired.

THE YOUNG GENTLEMAN. Permit me.

(*He takes off her veils, removes her hatpin, and puts hat, pin and veils aside.* THE YOUNG WIFE *permits.* THE YOUNG GENTLEMAN *stands before her, shaking his head.*)

THE YOUNG WIFE. Why, what's the matter?

THE YOUNG GENTLEMAN. You've never been so beautiful.

THE YOUNG WIFE. How is that?

THE YOUNG GENTLEMAN. Alone . . . alone with you, Emma! (*He kneels beside her chair, takes both her hands and covers them with kisses.*)

THE YOUNG WIFE. And now . . . now let me go. I have done what you asked me.

(THE YOUNG GENTLEMAN *lets his head sink into her lap.*)

You promised to be good.

THE YOUNG GENTLEMAN. Yes.

THE YOUNG WIFE. It is stifling in this room.

THE YOUNG GENTLEMAN (*gets up*). You still have your coat on.

THE YOUNG WIFE. Put it with my hat.

(THE YOUNG GENTLEMAN *takes off her coat, and puts it on the sofa.*)

THE YOUNG WIFE. And now . . . good-bye—

THE YOUNG GENTLEMAN. Emma! Emma!

THE YOUNG WIFE. The five minutes were up long, long ago.

THE YOUNG GENTLEMAN. It isn't a minute!

THE YOUNG WIFE. Alfred, tell me truly now, what time is it?

THE YOUNG GENTLEMAN. It is exactly a quarter past six.

THE YOUNG WIFE. I should have been at my sister's long ago.

THE YOUNG GENTLEMAN. You can see your sister any time . . .

THE YOUNG WIFE. Oh, good God, Alfred, why did you lure me here?

THE YOUNG GENTLEMAN. Because . . . I adore you, Emma!

THE YOUNG WIFE. How many women have you said that to?

THE YOUNG GENTLEMAN. Not one, since I met you.

THE YOUNG WIFE. What a weak woman I am! If anybody had predicted . . . a week ago . . . or even yesterday.

THE YOUNG GENTLEMAN. But you had already promised me day before yesterday.

THE YOUNG WIFE. You kept after me so. But I didn't want to . . . God is my witness—I didn't want to . . . Yesterday, I was firmly decided . . . Do you know I wrote you a long letter last night?

THE YOUNG GENTLEMAN. I didn't receive any.

THE YOUNG WIFE. I tore it up. Oh, if only I had sent it!

THE YOUNG GENTLEMAN. It is better as it is.

THE YOUNG WIFE. Oh, no, it's awful . . . awful of me. I don't understand myself. Good-bye, Alfred, let me go.

(THE YOUNG GENTLEMAN *seizes her, and covers her face with burning kisses.*)

So . . . is that the way you keep your promise?

THE YOUNG GENTLEMAN. One more kiss . . . just one more.

THE YOUNG WIFE. The last. (*He kisses her, and she returns the kiss; their lips remain joined for a long time.*)

THE YOUNG GENTLEMAN. Shall I tell you something, Emma? Now for the first time I know what happiness is.

(THE YOUNG WIFE *sinks back into the armchair.* THE YOUNG GENTLEMAN *sits on the arm of the chair, and puts one arm lightly about her neck.*)

Rather, I know now what happiness might be.

(THE YOUNG WIFE *sighs deeply.* THE YOUNG GENTLEMAN *kisses her again.*)

THE YOUNG WIFE. Alfred, Alfred, what are you doing!

THE YOUNG GENTLEMAN. Wasn't I right? It isn't so awfully uncomfortable here. And we are safe here. It's a thousand times better than those meetings in public.

THE YOUNG WIFE. Oh, don't remind me of them.

THE YOUNG GENTLEMAN. I shall always recall them with a thousand delights. Every minute you let me spend with you is a sweet memory.

THE YOUNG WIFE. Do you remember the ball at the Manufacturers' Club?

THE YOUNG GENTLEMAN. Do I remember it? . . . I sat beside you through the whole supper . . . close to you. Your husband had champagne . . .

(THE YOUNG WIFE *looks at him with a hurt expression.*)

Oh, I just meant to speak of the champagne. Emma, would you like a glass of cognac?

THE YOUNG WIFE. Only a drop, but first give me a glass of water.

THE YOUNG GENTLEMAN. Surely . . . but where is . . . oh, yes. I remember . . .

(*He opens the portieres, and goes out into the bedroom.* THE YOUNG WIFE *follows him with her eyes.* THE YOUNG GENTLEMAN *comes back with a decanter and two glasses.*)

THE YOUNG WIFE. Where have you been?

THE YOUNG GENTLEMAN. In the . . . next room. (*Pours her a glass of water.*)

THE YOUNG WIFE. Now I'm going to ask you something, Alfred, and you must swear you will tell me the truth.

THE YOUNG GENTLEMAN. I swear—

THE YOUNG WIFE. Has there ever been any other woman in these rooms?

THE YOUNG GENTLEMAN. But, Emma, this house was built twenty years ago!

THE YOUNG WIFE. You know what I mean, Alfred . . . in these rooms, with you!

THE YOUNG GENTLEMAN. With me . . . here . . . Emma! It's mean of you even to imagine such a thing.

THE YOUNG WIFE. Then there was . . . how shall I . . . But, no, I'd rather not ask. It is better that I shouldn't ask. It's my own fault. And I must suffer for it.

THE YOUNG GENTLEMAN. But what is wrong? What's the matter with you? Why?

THE YOUNG WIFE. No, no, no, I mustn't let myself think . . . If I did I should sink through the floor with shame.

THE YOUNG GENTLEMAN (*with the decanter in his hand. Shakes his head sadly*). Emma, if you only knew how you hurt me.

(THE YOUNG WIFE *pours a glass of cognac.*)

I want to tell you something, Emma. If you're ashamed, if you don't care for me, if you don't feel you are all the happiness in the world for me, then you'd better go.

THE YOUNG WIFE. Yes, I will go.

THE YOUNG GENTLEMAN (*taking hold of her hand*). But if you feel that I cannot live without you, that a kiss upon your hand means more to me than all the caresses of all the women in the whole world . . . Emma, I'm not like the other young men, who are experienced in love-making . . . perhaps, I am too naive . . . I . . .

THE YOUNG WIFE. But suppose you were like other young men?

THE YOUNG GENTLEMAN. Then you wouldn't be here to-night . . . because you are not like other women.

THE YOUNG WIFE. How do you know that?

THE YOUNG GENTLEMAN (*drawing her close beside him on the sofa*). I have thought a lot about you. I know you are unhappy.

THE YOUNG WIFE (*pleased*). Yes.

THE YOUNG GENTLEMAN. Life is so dreary, so empty, so futile, and so short, so frightfully short! There is only one happiness, to find some one who loves you.

(THE YOUNG WIFE *takes a candied pear from the table, and puts it into her mouth.*)

Give me half!

(*She offers it to him with her lips.*)

THE YOUNG WIFE (*catches* THE YOUNG GENTLEMAN'S *hands as they threaten to stray*). What are you doing, Alfred? . . . Is this the way you keep your promise?

THE YOUNG GENTLEMAN (*swallows the pear, then, more daringly*). Life is so short.

THE YOUNG WIFE (*weakly*). But that's no reason—

THE YOUNG GENTLEMAN (*mechanically*). Oh, yes.

THE YOUNG WIFE (*still more weakly*). Alfred, you promised to be good . . . and it's so light . . .

THE YOUNG GENTLEMAN. Come, come, you only, only . . . (*He lifts her from the sofa.*)

THE YOUNG WIFE. What are you doing?

THE YOUNG GENTLEMAN. It isn't light in the other room.

THE YOUNG WIFE. Is there another room?

THE YOUNG GENTLEMAN (*drawing her with him*). A beautiful one . . . and quite dark.

THE YOUNG WIFE. We'd better stay here.

(THE YOUNG GENTLEMAN *already past the bedroom portieres with her, loosening her waist.*)

You are so . . . Merciful heaven, what are you doing to me? Alfred!

THE YOUNG GENTLEMAN. I adore you, Emma!

THE YOUNG WIFE. Then wait, wait a little . . . (*Weakly.*) Go . . . I'll call you.

THE YOUNG GENTLEMAN. Let you help me . . . let help. (*Confused.*) Let . . . me help you.

THE YOUNG WIFE. You'll tear everything.

THE YOUNG GENTLEMAN. You have no corset on?

THE YOUNG WIFE. I never wear a corset. Stylish women don't wear them any more. But you may unbutton my shoes.

(THE YOUNG GENTLEMAN *unbuttons her shoes and kisses her feet.*)

THE YOUNG WIFE (*slips into bed*). Oh, how cold it is.

THE YOUNG GENTLEMAN. It'll be warm in a minute.

THE YOUNG WIFE (*laughing softly*). Do you think so?

THE YOUNG GENTLEMAN (*slightly hurt, to himself*). She oughtn't to have said that. (*He undresses in the dark.*)

THE YOUNG WIFE (*tenderly*). Come, quick, come!

THE YOUNG GENTLEMAN (*mollified*). Just a minute, dear—

THE YOUNG WIFE. It smells like violets here.

THE YOUNG GENTLEMAN. That's you . . . Yes. (*To her.*) You, yourself.

THE YOUNG WIFE. Alfred . . . Alfred . . .

THE YOUNG GENTLEMAN. Emma . . .

* * * * *

THE YOUNG GENTLEMAN. Apparently I love you too much . . . yes . . . I feel as if I were out of my mind.

THE YOUNG WIFE. . . . . . .

THE YOUNG GENTLEMAN. I have been crazy for you all these days. I was afraid of this.

THE YOUNG WIFE. Don't mind it.

THE YOUNG GENTLEMAN. Oh, certainly not. It's perfectly natural, if one . . .

THE YOUNG WIFE. No . . . don't . . . You are nervous. Calm yourself first.

THE YOUNG GENTLEMAN. Do you know Stendhal?

THE YOUNG WIFE. Stendhal?

THE YOUNG GENTLEMAN. His book on psychology "De l'amour."

THE YOUNG WIFE. No. Why do you ask me?

THE YOUNG GENTLEMAN. There's a story in that book which is very much to the point.

THE YOUNG WIFE. What kind of a story?

THE YOUNG GENTLEMAN. A bunch of cavalry officers get together.

THE YOUNG WIFE. Yes.

THE YOUNG GENTLEMAN. And they tell each other about their love affairs. And every one of them relates that with the woman he loved best . . . most passionately, you know . . . that his, that he . . . well, in short, that the same thing happened that happened to me just now.

THE YOUNG WIFE. Yes.

THE YOUNG GENTLEMAN. That is very significant.

THE YOUNG WIFE. Yes.

THE YOUNG GENTLEMAN. The story isn't over. One of them claimed . . . that this thing had never happened to him, but, adds Stendhal . . . he was a notorious liar.

THE YOUNG WIFE. I see—

THE YOUNG GENTLEMAN. And, yet, it makes a man feel bad . . . that's the stupid part of it, because it really doesn't mean a thing.

THE YOUNG WIFE. Of course not. Anyway, you know . . . you promised to be good.

THE YOUNG GENTLEMAN. Oh! Don't make fun of me. That doesn't help a bit.

THE YOUNG WIFE. But, I'm not. That story of Stendhal's is really interesting. I have always thought that only older people or people who . . . you know, people who have been pretty fast.

THE YOUNG GENTLEMAN. The idea! That has nothing to do with it. By the way, I had completely forgotten the best of Stendhal's stories. One of the officers went so far as to say that he stayed for three or even six nights . . . I don't remember now—that is, he stayed with a woman he had wanted for weeks—*désiré*—you understand, and nothing happened all those nights except that they wept for happiness . . . both . . .

THE YOUNG WIFE. Both?

THE YOUNG GENTLEMAN. Yes. Does that surprise you? I can understand it very well . . . especially when two people love each other.

THE YOUNG WIFE. But surely there are a good many who don't weep.

THE YOUNG GENTLEMAN (*nervously*). Certainly . . . this is an exceptional case.

THE YOUNG WIFE. Oh, I thought Stendhal said all cavalry officers weep on such occasions.

THE YOUNG GENTLEMAN. Now you are laughing at me again.

THE YOUNG WIFE. What an idea! Don't be childish, Alfred.

THE YOUNG GENTLEMAN. Well, it makes me nervous anyway . . . Besides I have the feeling that you are thinking about it all the time. That's what really hurts.

THE YOUNG WIFE. I'm not thinking of it at all.

THE YOUNG GENTLEMAN. If I were only sure you love me.

THE YOUNG WIFE. Do you want more proofs?

THE YOUNG GENTLEMAN. Didn't I tell you . . . you are always laughing at me.

THE YOUNG WIFE. Why do you think so? Come, let me hold your sweet little head.

THE YOUNG GENTLEMAN. Oh, that feels good.

THE YOUNG WIFE. Do you love me?

THE YOUNG GENTLEMAN. Oh, I'm so happy.

THE YOUNG WIFE. And you needn't cry about it.

THE YOUNG GENTLEMAN (*moving away from her, highly irritated*). There! Again! I begged you not to . . .

THE YOUNG WIFE. To tell you that you shouldn't cry . . .

THE YOUNG GENTLEMAN. You said: "You needn't cry about it."

THE YOUNG WIFE. You are nervous, sweetheart.

THE YOUNG GENTLEMAN. I know.

THE YOUNG WIFE. But you ought not to be. I even like our being together like good comrades.

THE YOUNG GENTLEMAN. Now you are beginning again.

THE YOUNG WIFE. Don't you remember! That was one of the first things we said to each other. We wanted to be comrades, nothing more. Oh, how nice that was . . . at my sister's ball in January, during the quadrille . . . For heaven's sake, I should have gone long ago . . My sister expects me . . . What shall I tell her . . . Good-bye, Alfred—

THE YOUNG GENTLEMAN. Emma! Can you leave me this way?

THE YOUNG WIFE. Yes, I can!

THE YOUNG GENTLEMAN. Five minutes more . . .

THE YOUNG WIFE. All right. Five minutes more. But if you promise me not to move? . . . Yes? . . . I want to give you a good-bye kiss . . . Psst . . . be still . . . don't move, I told you, or I'll get up at once, my sweetheart, you sweet . . .

THE YOUNG GENTLEMAN. Emma . . . my ador . . . . . .

* * * * *

THE YOUNG WIFE. My Alfred!

THE YOUNG GENTLEMAN. Oh, it is heaven to be with you.

THE YOUNG WIFE. But now I've really got to go.

THE YOUNG GENTLEMAN. Oh, let your sister wait.

THE YOUNG WIFE. I must go home. It is too late to see my sister. What time is it, anyway?

THE YOUNG GENTLEMAN. How should I know?

THE YOUNG WIFE. You might look at your watch.

THE YOUNG GENTLEMAN. My watch is in my vest.

THE YOUNG WIFE. Get it.

THE YOUNG GENTLEMAN (*gets up with a jump*). Eight o'clock.

THE YOUNG WIFE (*jumps up quickly*). For heaven's sake . . . Quick,

Alfred, give me my stockings. What shall I say? They must be waiting for me at home . . . eight o'clock.

THE YOUNG GENTLEMAN. When shall I see you again?

THE YOUNG WIFE. Never.

THE YOUNG GENTLEMAN. Emma! Don't you love me any more?

THE YOUNG WIFE. It's because I do. Give me my shoes.

THE YOUNG GENTLEMAN. Never again? Here are your shoes.

THE YOUNG WIFE. My button-hook is in my bag. Please, be quick . . .

THE YOUNG GENTLEMAN. Here is the button-hook.

THE YOUNG WIFE. Alfred, this may cost us our lives.

THE YOUNG GENTLEMAN (*affected very unpleasantly*). How so?

THE YOUNG WIFE. What shall I say, if he asks me where I've been?

THE YOUNG GENTLEMAN. At your sister's.

THE YOUNG WIFE. If I could only lie.

THE YOUNG GENTLEMAN. You'll have to.

THE YOUNG WIFE. Anything for a man like you. Oh, come here . . . let me give you a last kiss. (*She embraces him.*) And now, leave me to myself, go in the other room. I can't dress with you around.

(THE YOUNG GENTLEMAN *goes into the drawing-room, where he dresses. He eats some pastry and drinks a glass of cognac.*)

THE YOUNG WIFE (*calls after a while*). Alfred!

THE YOUNG GENTLEMAN. Yes, sweetheart.

THE YOUNG WIFE. Isn't it better that we didn't weep?

THE YOUNG GENTLEMAN (*smiling, not without pride*). How can you talk so flippantly?

THE YOUNG WIFE. How awful it will be now . . . if we should meet by chance in society.

THE YOUNG GENTLEMAN. By chance? . . . Surely you are coming to Lobheimer's to-morrow?

THE YOUNG WIFE. Yes. Are you?

THE YOUNG GENTLEMAN. Of course. May I ask for the cotillion?

THE YOUNG WIFE. Oh, I shan't go. What do you think I am? I'd certainly . . . (*She enters the drawing-room fully dressed, and takes a chocolate pastry.*) sink through the floor with shame.

THE YOUNG GENTLEMAN. To-morrow at Lobheimer's. That's fine.

THE YOUNG WIFE. No, no . . . I shall decline . . . I'll certainly decline—

THE YOUNG GENTLEMAN. Well, the day after to-morrow . . . here.

THE YOUNG WIFE. The idea!

THE YOUNG GENTLEMAN. At six . . .

THE YOUNG WIFE. There are cabs at this corner, aren't there?

THE YOUNG GENTLEMAN. Yes, as many as you want. Well, the day after to-morrow, here at six o'clock. Please say "yes," sweetheart.

THE YOUNG WIFE. We'll discuss that to-morrow night during the cotillion.

THE YOUNG GENTLEMAN (*embracing her*). My angel.

THE YOUNG WIFE. Don't muss my hair again.

THE YOUNG GENTLEMAN. Well then, to-morrow night at Lobheimer's, and the day after to-morrow in my arms.

THE YOUNG WIFE. Good-bye . . .

THE YOUNG GENTLEMAN (*suddenly anxious again*). And what will you tell him to-night?

THE YOUNG WIFE. Don't ask me . . . don't ask me . . . it's too terrible. Why do I love you so? Good-bye. If I meet any one again on the stairway, I shall faint. Ugh!

(THE YOUNG GENTLEMAN *kisses her hand for the last time.* THE YOUNG WIFE *exits.*)

THE YOUNG GENTLEMAN (*remains standing. Then he sits down on the couch. He smiles reflectively, and says to himself*). Well, so I have an affair with a respectable woman. At last.

V

THE YOUNG WIFE AND THE HUSBAND

(*A comfortable bedroom. Half past ten at night.* THE YOUNG WIFE *is in bed, reading. Her* HUSBAND *enters the room in a dressing gown.*)

THE YOUNG WIFE (*without looking up*). Through working?

THE HUSBAND. Yes. I'm tired. And besides . . .

THE YOUNG WIFE. What?

THE HUSBAND. I felt lonely at my desk all at once. I began to long for you.

THE YOUNG WIFE (*looking up*). Really?

THE HUSBAND (*sitting down on the bed beside her*). Don't read any more to-night. You'll surely ruin your eyes.

THE YOUNG WIFE (*closing the book*). What's the matter?

THE HUSBAND. Nothing, dear. I'm in love with you. You know that.

THE YOUNG WIFE. One might forget it sometimes.

THE HUSBAND. One must forget it sometimes.

THE YOUNG WIFE. Why?

THE HUSBAND. Because, if one didn't, marriage would be imperfect. It would . . . how shall I express it? . . . it would lose its sanctity.

THE YOUNG WIFE. Oh . . .

THE HUSBAND. Believe me, it is so . . . If at times we hadn't forgotten that we were in love with each other during the five years we have been married, we might not be in love any more.

THE YOUNG WIFE. That's too deep for me.

THE HUSBAND. It's simply this: we've had about a dozen love-affairs with each other . . . Doesn't it seem so to you, too?

THE YOUNG WIFE. I haven't counted them!

THE HUSBAND. If we'd enjoyed the first one to the limit, if I had abandoned myself completely to my passion for you in the beginning, the same thing would have happened to us that has happened to millions of other lovers. We should be through with each other.

THE YOUNG WIFE. Ah . . . do you mean that?

THE HUSBAND. Believe me, Emma, in the early days of our marriage, I dreaded that that might happen.

THE YOUNG WIFE. So did I.

THE HUSBAND. See? Wasn't I right? That's why it is wise for us, now and then, to be nothing but good friends to each other.

THE YOUNG WIFE. Oh.

THE HUSBAND. That's how it's possible for us to keep on having new honeymoons. I never let our honeymoons . . .

THE YOUNG WIFE. Last too long.

THE HUSBAND. Exactly.

THE YOUNG WIFE. And now . . . another period of friendship is up.

THE HUSBAND (*pressing her tenderly to him*). It ought to be.

THE YOUNG WIFE. But if . . . it isn't up for me?

THE HUSBAND. It is up for you. You are the nicest and most sensible person in the world. I am very lucky to have found you.

THE YOUNG WIFE. It's wonderful, the way you make love. Now and then.

THE HUSBAND (*also gone to bed*). For a man who has seen something of the world—there, lay your head on my shoulder—marriage is much more mysterious than it is for you sheltered girls. You come to us innocent and to a degree, at least, ignorant, and so you really have a clearer perception of the true nature of love.

THE YOUNG WIFE (*laughing*). Oh!

THE HUSBAND. Certainly. For we get confused by all the experiences we went through before marriage. You women, of course, hear a lot of things, you know a lot of things, and of course, read too much, but you can't have any real idea of the things men experience. Actually we men become quite disgusted with what is commonly called love. Creatures who are thrown in our way are a sort of . . .

THE YOUNG WIFE. Of what? Tell me.

THE HUSBAND (*kissing her on the forehead*). You ought to be glad, dear child, that you never had occasion to learn. After all, most of the poor creatures are quite pitiful. Let's not cast any stones.

THE YOUNG WIFE. I can't see for the life of me, why we should pity them.

THE HUSBAND (*with gentle benevolence*). They deserve pity. Whereas you girls with your "good family background" . . . who wait at home under the protection of your parents for an eligible man to come courting! You don't know the poverty that drives most of these poor creatures into the arms of sin.

THE YOUNG WIFE. Are they all so poor that they have to sell themselves?

THE HUSBAND. That's not what I mean. I'm not speaking of material poverty, as much as of a moral misery. A lack of opportunity to know what is right, and, especially, what is noble.

THE YOUNG WIFE. But why pity them? They seem to get along pretty well.

THE HUSBAND. You have strange ideas, my dear. You mustn't forget that such creatures are naturally doomed to fall lower and lower. There is no stopping them.

THE YOUNG WIFE (*cuddling to him*). Apparently falling is quite pleasant.

THE HUSBAND (*hurt*). How can you say such things, Emma? I should think that to a respectable woman like you, no one could be more repulsive than those who have forfeited—

THE YOUNG WIFE. Of course, Karl, of course. I just said that to be saying something. Go on. It's so nice to hear you talk like this. Tell me something.

THE HUSBAND. What?

THE YOUNG WIFE. Why—about these creatures.

THE HUSBAND. What do you want to know?

THE YOUNG WIFE. Remember, when we were first married I was always asking you to tell me about your bachelor life.

THE HUSBAND. Why should that interest you?

THE YOUNG WIFE. Aren't you my husband? Isn't it an injustice for me to know nothing about your past?

THE HUSBAND. You surely don't think I have such bad taste, as . . . No, Emma . . . it would be sacrilege.

THE YOUNG WIFE. And yet you have held heaven knows how many other women in your arms, just as you are holding me now.

THE HUSBAND. Don't say "women." You are *the* woman.

THE YOUNG WIFE. But you positively must answer one question . . . or . . . or . . . there won't be any . . . honeymoon.

THE HUSBAND. That's a fine way to talk . . . remember you are a mother . . . our little girl is sleeping in there . . .

THE YOUNG WIFE (*snuggling against him*). But I want a boy, too.

THE HUSBAND. Emma!

THE YOUNG WIFE. Don't be silly . . . of course, I am your wife . . . but I'd like to be . . . to be your sweetheart, a little, too.

THE HUSBAND. Would you? . . .

THE YOUNG WIFE. First my question.

THE HUSBAND (*wheedled*). All right.

THE YOUNG WIFE. Was there . . . a married woman among them?

THE HUSBAND. Why? What do you mean?

THE YOUNG WIFE. You know what I mean.

THE HUSBAND (*slightly disconcerted*). What makes you think of such a thing?

THE YOUNG WIFE. I'd like to know if . . . I mean—there *are* such women. I know that. But did you? . . .

THE HUSBAND (*earnestly*). Do you know such a woman?

THE YOUNG WIFE. I don't know whether I do or not.

THE HUSBAND. Perhaps, one of your friends is such a person?

THE YOUNG WIFE. How can I make sure—one way or the other?

THE HUSBAND. Did any of your friends—women talk about a lot of things when they get together—did any of them ever confess?

THE YOUNG WIFE (*uncertain*). No.

THE HUSBAND. Do you suspect any friend of yours of . . .

THE YOUNG WIFE. Suspect . . . hummm . . . suspect . . .

THE HUSBAND. You seem to.

THE YOUNG WIFE. No, Karl, of course not. When I think it over, I wouldn't believe it of any of them.

THE HUSBAND. Not one?

THE YOUNG WIFE. Not any friend of mine.

THE HUSBAND. Promise me, Emma . . .

THE YOUNG WIFE. What?

THE HUSBAND. That you will never associate with a woman whom you suspect, ever so little, of not leading a perfectly blameless life.

THE YOUNG WIFE. Do I have to promise that?

THE HUSBAND. I know that you will not deliberately cultivate such women. But it might happen that you . . . in fact it often happens that such women, whose reputations are not of the best, cultivate good women, partly as foils, and partly because they feel . . . how shall I say it . . . because they feel homesick for virtue.

THE YOUNG WIFE. Do they?

THE HUSBAND. Yes. I believe it is quite true what I just said. Homesick for virtue. For all these women are really very unhappy; take my word for that.

THE YOUNG WIFE. Why are they unhappy?

THE HUSBAND. You ask me, Emma? How can you? Just imagine what a life these women lead! A life of lies, trickery, vulgarity, and danger.

THE YOUNG WIFE. Yes, of course. You are quite right.

THE HUSBAND. Truly . . . they pay for their little happiness . . . their little . . .

THE YOUNG WIFE. Pleasure.

THE HUSBAND. Why "pleasure"? What makes you call it "pleasure"?

THE YOUNG WIFE. Well, there must be something in it! Or they wouldn't do it.

THE HUSBAND. It's nothing . . . an intoxication.

THE YOUNG WIFE (*pensively*). Intoxication . . .

THE HUSBAND. It is not even intoxication. Anyway—it is dearly paid for, that much is certain.

THE YOUNG WIFE. Well . . . it has happened to you, hasn't it?

THE HUSBAND. Yes, Emma. It is the thing I most regret.

THE YOUNG WIFE. Who was she? Tell me! Do I know her?

THE HUSBAND. What can you be thinking of?

THE YOUNG WIFE. Was it long ago? Was it long before you married me?

THE HUSBAND. Don't ask me. Please, don't ask.

THE YOUNG WIFE. But, Karl!

THE HUSBAND. She is dead.

THE YOUNG WIFE. Honest?

THE HUSBAND. Yes . . . it may sound ridiculous, but I have the feeling that all these women die young.

THE YOUNG WIFE. Did you love her very much?

THE HUSBAND. One doesn't love women who lie.

THE YOUNG WIFE. Then why . . .

THE HUSBAND. Drink . . .

THE YOUNG WIFE. You see!

THE HUSBAND. Don't talk about it any more, please. It was over and done with long ago. I have loved only one woman: you. A man doesn't fall in love until he finds purity and truth.

THE YOUNG WIFE. Karl!

THE HUSBAND. How secure, how happy I feel in these arms. Why didn't I know you as a child? I am sure I wouldn't have looked at other women.

THE YOUNG WIFE. Karl!

THE HUSBAND. And how beautiful you are! . . . beautiful! Come . . . come . . . (*He puts the light out.*)

* * * * *

THE YOUNG WIFE. Do you know what I am thinking of to-night?

THE HUSBAND. What, sweetheart?

THE YOUNG WIFE. Of . . . of . . . Venice.

THE HUSBAND. The first night . . .

THE YOUNG WIFE. Yes . . .

THE HUSBAND. What else? Tell me!

THE YOUNG WIFE. You love me as much to-day?

THE HUSBAND. Yes, just as much.

THE YOUNG WIFE. Oh . . . if you always would . . .

THE HUSBAND (*in her arms*). Would what?

THE YOUNG WIFE. My Karl!

THE HUSBAND. What do you mean? If I always would? . . .

THE YOUNG WIFE. Mmmmm.

THE HUSBAND. But what? If I would always what?

THE YOUNG WIFE. Then I should always know you love me.

THE HUSBAND. Yes. But you must remember this. One cannot always be a lover, sometimes one has to go out into the hostile world, into the struggle for existence! Don't forget that, my dear. There is a time for everything in marriage—that is the beauty of it. There are not many who can remember their Venice after five years.

THE YOUNG WIFE. There certainly aren't.

THE HUSBAND. And . . . good-night, my dear.

THE YOUNG WIFE. Good-night!

VI

THE HUSBAND AND THE LITTLE DARLING

(*A* chambre séparée *in the Riedhof, comfortably and tastefully furnished. A lighted gasgrate is disclosed. The remains of a meal on the table, cream cakes, fruit, cheese. In the wine-glasses is a Hungarian white wine.* THE HUSBAND *and* THE LITTLE DARLING. THE HUSBAND *smoking a Havana cigar, and lolling at the end of the sofa.* THE LITTLE DARLING *sits near him in a chair at the table eating the cream out of a cake with a spoon, and smacking her lips.*)

THE HUSBAND. Is it good?

THE LITTLE DARLING (*without stopping*). Mmmmm.

THE HUSBAND. Do you want another?

THE LITTLE DARLING. No. I've eaten too much already.

THE HUSBAND. Your wine is all gone. (*He fills her glass.*)

THE LITTLE DARLING. Stop. I wouldn't drink it.

THE HUSBAND. Come and sit here with me.

THE LITTLE DARLING. In a minute, I'm not through yet.

(THE HUSBAND *gets up and stands behind her chair, puts his arms around her, turning her face toward him.*)

What's the idea?

THE HUSBAND. I want a kiss.

THE LITTLE DARLING (*kissing him*). You sure got your nerve.

THE HUSBAND. Just finding that out?

THE LITTLE DARLING. No. I knew it when you stopped me in the street. You must think I'm a nice one.

THE HUSBAND. Why?

THE LITTLE DARLING. Because I came right along when you said "Let's go to a . . . to a *chambre séparée.*"

THE HUSBAND. You didn't rush, at that.

THE LITTLE DARLING. You got such a cute way of asking.

THE HUSBAND. Do you think so?

THE LITTLE DARLING. And, after all, what's the difference—

THE HUSBAND. Exactly.

THE LITTLE DARLING. Whether we go walking or—

THE HUSBAND. It's much too cold for walking.

THE LITTLE DARLING. Of course.

THE HUSBAND. But it's good and warm here, isn't it?

(*He sits down again, puts his arms around the girl, and draws her to his side.*)

THE LITTLE DARLING (*weakly*). Please . . . don't.

THE HUSBAND. Tell me . . . You had noticed me before, hadn't you?

THE LITTLE DARLING. Yes. Several blocks before you spoke to me.

THE HUSBAND. I don't mean to-day. I mean yesterday and the day before, when I was following you.

THE LITTLE DARLING. A lot of men follow me.

THE HUSBAND. I should say so. But did you notice me?

THE LITTLE DARLING. Guess what happened to me not long ago. My cousin's husband followed me in the dark, and didn't know who I was.

THE HUSBAND. Did he speak to you?

THE LITTLE DARLING. What do you think? Think everybody is as fresh as you?

THE HUSBAND. But they sometimes do, don't they?

THE LITTLE DARLING. Of course, they do.

THE HUSBAND. What do you do?

THE LITTLE DARLING. Nothing—I just don't answer.

THE HUSBAND. Hm-m—but you answered me.

THE LITTLE DARLING. Sorry, aren't you?

THE HUSBAND (*kisses her vehemently*). Your lips are as sweet as whipped cream.

THE LITTLE DARLING. They taste that way naturally.

THE HUSBAND. I suppose a good many men have told you that?

THE LITTLE DARLING. A good many! You sure got your imagination.

THE HUSBAND. Now, be honest. How many men have kissed this sweet mouth before?

THE LITTLE DARLING. Why do you ask? You wouldn't believe me if I told you.

THE HUSBAND. Why not?

THE LITTLE DARLING. Guess.

THE HUSBAND. All right, I'll guess—but you mustn't get mad!

THE LITTLE DARLING. Me get mad?

THE HUSBAND. Well, then, I guess . . . twenty.

THE LITTLE DARLING (*disengaging herself*). Why not a hundred?

THE HUSBAND. Come, I was just guessing.

THE LITTLE DARLING. You guessed wrong!

THE HUSBAND. Say—ten.

THE LITTLE DARLING (*offended*). Of course! A girl who lets a man talk to her on the street, and goes with him to a *chambre séparée!*

THE HUSBAND. Don't be childish. Whether we stroll around in the streets or sit in a room . . . we are in a restaurant. The waiter may come in any minute. There's nothing to this.

THE LITTLE DARLING. That's just what I thought.

THE HUSBAND. Have you ever been in a *chambre séparée* before?

THE LITTLE DARLING. To tell the truth—yes.

THE HUSBAND. I am glad you are honest with me.

THE LITTLE DARLING. But it wasn't the way you think. I was in a *chambre séparée* with my girl friend and her fiancé, last carnival.

THE HUSBAND. It wouldn't have been anything terrible, even if you had gone there with your boy friend—

THE LITTLE DARLING. Of course, it wouldn't have been anything terrible. But I haven't any boy friend.

THE HUSBAND. Oh, go on!

THE LITTLE DARLING. I swear, I haven't.

THE HUSBAND. You aren't trying to tell me that I . . .

THE LITTLE DARLING. That you are what? I haven't had one—haven't had one for more than six months.

THE HUSBAND. I see . . . But before then? Who was he?

THE LITTLE DARLING. Why are you so curious?

THE HUSBAND. Because I love you.

THE LITTLE DARLING. Really?

THE HUSBAND. Of course! You must have seen it already. Tell me about him. (*Presses her tightly to him.*)

THE LITTLE DARLING. What do you want me to tell?

THE HUSBAND. Don't keep me asking! Who was he, that's what I want to know.

THE LITTLE DARLING (*laughing*). Just a man.

THE HUSBAND. Well . . . well . . . who?

THE LITTLE DARLING. He looked something like you.

THE HUSBAND. I see.

THE LITTLE DARLING. If you hadn't looked like him—

THE HUSBAND. What then?

THE LITTLE DARLING. Now, don't ask, don't you see that's . . .

THE HUSBAND (*understanding*). That's why you let me speak to you.

THE LITTLE DARLING. Yes, that's it.

THE HUSBAND. I really don't know whether I ought to be tickled or get mad.

THE LITTLE DARLING. If I were you, I'd be tickled.

THE HUSBAND. All right.

THE LITTLE DARLING. You talk like him too. And you have the same way of looking at . . . a person . . .

THE HUSBAND. What did he do for a living?

THE LITTLE DARLING. No, your eyes—

THE HUSBAND. What was his name?

THE LITTLE DARLING. Please, don't look at me that way; please don't.

(THE HUSBAND *embraces her. A long, burning kiss.* THE LITTLE DARLING *shivers, tries to get up.*)

THE HUSBAND. Why do you want to leave?

THE LITTLE DARLING. It's time to go home.

THE HUSBAND. Later.

THE LITTLE DARLING. No, I really have to get home. What will mother say?

THE HUSBAND. You live with your mother?

THE LITTLE DARLING. Of course, I live with my mother. What did you suppose?

THE HUSBAND. So—with your mother. You two alone?

THE LITTLE DARLING. Alone, like fun. There are five of us! Two boys and two more girls.

THE HUSBAND. Don't sit so far away from me. Are you the oldest?

THE LITTLE DARLING. No, I'm next oldest. Kitty is the oldest. She works in a flower store.

THE HUSBAND. Where do you work?

THE LITTLE DARLING. I stay at home.

THE HUSBAND. Always?

THE LITTLE DARLING. One of us has to stay home.

THE HUSBAND. Of course, and what do you tell your mother, when you come home so late?

THE LITTLE DARLING. That hardly ever happens.

THE HUSBAND. Well, to-night, for instance. Your mother will ask you, won't she?

THE LITTLE DARLING. Of course, she'll ask. It doesn't matter how careful I am when I come home, she always wakes up.

THE HUSBAND. And what do you tell her?

THE LITTLE DARLING. Oh—that I've been to the theater.

THE HUSBAND. Does she believe it?

THE LITTLE DARLING. Why shouldn't she believe it? I often go to the theater. Only last Sunday I went to the opera with my girl friend and her fiancé, and my oldest brother.

THE HUSBAND. Where did you get the tickets?

THE LITTLE DARLING. My brother is a hairdresser.

THE HUSBAND. A hairdresser . . . oh, at the theater, I suppose.

THE LITTLE DARLING. Why do you ask so many questions?

THE HUSBAND. Just because I am interested. What does your other brother do?

THE LITTLE DARLING. He's still going to school. He wants to be a teacher. Imagine!

THE HUSBAND. And you have a little sister?

THE LITTLE DARLING. Yes, she is just a child, but you have to keep an eye on her all the time, already. You have no idea how girls are spoiled at school. What do you think? The other day I caught her having a date.

THE HUSBAND. Really?

THE LITTLE DARLING. Yes! She was out walking one evening at half-past seven with a boy from the school across the street. A baby like her!

THE HUSBAND. What did you do?

THE LITTLE DARLING. I gave her a spanking.

THE HUSBAND. Are you as strict as all that?

THE LITTLE DARLING. Who would be if I wasn't? My older sister is working and mother does nothing but grumble . . . it's all up to me.

THE HUSBAND. Heavens, you're nice. (*Kisses her, and grows more tender.*) You remind me of some one, too.

THE LITTLE DARLING. Who?

THE HUSBAND. No one in particular . . . of bygone days . . . of my youth. Come on, drink, little girl.

THE LITTLE DARLING. Say, how old are you? . . . You . . . why . . . I don't even know your name.

THE HUSBAND. Karl.

THE LITTLE DARLING. Is it possible? Your name is Karl?

THE HUSBAND. Was his name Karl, too?

THE LITTLE DARLING. No, that's what's so queer . . . your . . . eyes . . . The way you look at me . . .

THE HUSBAND. What was he? You haven't told me yet.

THE LITTLE DARLING. Oh, he was a bad man . . . he must have been or he wouldn't have left me in the lurch.

THE HUSBAND. Did you love him very much?

THE LITTLE DARLING. Of course, I loved him.

THE HUSBAND. I know what he was—a lieutenant.

THE LITTLE DARLING. No, he wasn't in the army. They wouldn't take him. His father owns a house in . . . but why do you have to know?

THE HUSBAND (*kisses her*). Your eyes are really grey. At first, I thought they were black.

THE LITTLE DARLING. Aren't they pretty enough for you?

(THE HUSBAND *kisses her eyes.*)

Don't please—I won't have it . . . O, please don't! Let me get up . . . only for a minute . . . please.

THE HUSBAND (*more tenderly still*). No, indeed.

THE LITTLE DARLING. But, please, Karl . . .

THE HUSBAND. How old are you? Eighteen, aren't you?

THE LITTLE DARLING. Just past nineteen.

THE HUSBAND. Nineteen . . . and I—

THE LITTLE DARLING. You are thirty . . .

THE HUSBAND. And a little over. Let's not talk about it.

THE LITTLE DARLING. He was thirty-two, when I first met him.

THE HUSBAND. How long ago was that?

THE LITTLE DARLING. I don't remember . . . Say, there must have been something in that wine.

THE HUSBAND. What makes you think so?

THE LITTLE DARLING. I am all . . . see,—everything going round and round.

THE HUSBAND. Then hold tight to me. Like this . . . (*He holds her close to him, and becomes more and more tender. She resists very little.*) I'll tell you something, dear. We might go on . . . go on . . .

THE LITTLE DARLING. Home . . .

THE HUSBAND. Well, not exactly home . . .

THE LITTLE DARLING. What do you mean? Oh, no—no . . . I won't go anywhere else. What do you think I am?

THE HUSBAND. But listen to me, child, the next time we meet, you know, we will arrange it so that . . . (*He has slipped to the floor with his head in her lap.*) This is so nice, so nice!

THE LITTLE DARLING. What are you doing? (*She kisses his hair.*) There must have been something in that wine . . . I'm so sleepy . . . What would happen, if I couldn't get up again? But, but, look, but Karl, if some one should come in . . . please . . . the waiter.

THE HUSBAND. No . . . waiter . . . will ever come in here . . .

* * * * *

(THE LITTLE DARLING *leaning back at the end of the sofa with closed eyes.* THE HUSBAND *pacing up and down the little room, after lighting a cigarette. Long silence.*)

THE HUSBAND (*looking for a long time at the girl; speaking to himself*). Who knows what sort of a person she really is? Damn it! So quick . . . This wasn't very prudent of me . . . hmm . . .

THE LITTLE DARLING (*without opening her eyes*). There must have been something in the wine.

THE HUSBAND. Why do you think so?

THE LITTLE DARLING. If there hadn't been . . .

THE HUSBAND. Why do you blame everything on the wine?

THE LITTLE DARLING. Where are you? Why are you so far away? Come here, to me.

(THE HUSBAND *sits beside her.*)

Now tell me if you really love me.

THE HUSBAND. But you know . . . (*He interrupts himself quickly.*) Of course.

THE LITTLE DARLING. Listen . . . There must have . . . Come, tell me the truth, what was in the wine?

THE HUSBAND. Why, do you think I would drug your wine?

THE LITTLE DARLING. Well, you see, I can't understand it. I'm really not the kind . . . We've just met . . . I swear, I'm not the kind . . . Honestly, I'm not. If you think that of me—

THE HUSBAND. Well, why worry about it? I don't think anything bad of you. I think you love me, that's all.

THE LITTLE DARLING. Hmm . . . hmm . . .

THE HUSBAND. After all, when two young people are alone in a room, and have dinner, and drink wine . . . there doesn't have to be anything in the wine.

THE LITTLE DARLING. I just said so to be saying something.

THE HUSBAND. Really, why?

THE LITTLE DARLING (*almost defiantly*). Because I was ashamed.

THE HUSBAND. How absurd! There is no reason to be ashamed. Especially, since I made you think of your first boy friend.

THE LITTLE DARLING. Yes.

THE HUSBAND. Your first boy friend.

THE LITTLE DARLING. Mmmm.

THE HUSBAND. Now I should like to know who the others were.

THE LITTLE DARLING. There weren't any others.

THE HUSBAND. That isn't true, it can't be true.

THE LITTLE DARLING. Oh, please, don't tease me.

THE HUSBAND. Would you like a cigarette?

THE LITTLE DARLING. No, thanks.

THE HUSBAND. Do you know what time it is?

THE LITTLE DARLING. What?

THE HUSBAND. Half-past eleven.

THE LITTLE DARLING. Really?

THE HUSBAND. Well . . . and your mother? She's used to this, isn't she?

THE LITTLE DARLING. Do you really want me to go home?

THE HUSBAND. Earlier in the evening you asked me yourself—

THE LITTLE DARLING. You're not the same person you were awhile ago. What have I done to make you change so?

THE HUSBAND. What *is* the matter with you, dear? What's on your mind?

THE LITTLE DARLING. And it was only your looks, believe me, or you could have talked yourself blue in the face. All sorts of men have asked me to go to a *chambre séparée* with them.

THE HUSBAND. Well, would you like . . . to come here again with me soon . . . or somewhere else—

THE LITTLE DARLING. I don't know.

THE HUSBAND. What do you mean, "I don't know"?

THE LITTLE DARLING. Oh, don't ask so many questions!

THE HUSBAND. Then when? First of all, I must explain that I don't live in Vienna. I'm only here for a few days at a time, now and then.

THE LITTLE DARLING. Oh, you're not Viennese?

THE HUSBAND. Yes, I am. But I'm living out of town now . . .

THE LITTLE DARLING. Where?

THE HUSBAND. Oh, that doesn't matter.

THE LITTLE DARLING. Don't get scared, I won't come to see you.

THE HUSBAND. If it'd be any fun for you, you can come. I live in Graz.

THE LITTLE DARLING. Honest?

THE HUSBAND. Yes, what's so wonderful about that?

THE LITTLE DARLING. You are married, aren't you?

THE HUSBAND (*very much astonished*). What makes you think so?

THE LITTLE DARLING. I just got a notion you were.

THE HUSBAND. You don't mind?

THE LITTLE DARLING. Well, I would rather you were single. So you are married!

THE HUSBAND. Come on, tell me what made you think I was married.

THE LITTLE DARLING. When a man says he doesn't live in Vienna and doesn't always have time—

THE HUSBAND. After all it's not very unlikely.

THE LITTLE DARLING. I don't believe it.

THE HUSBAND. Does it hurt your conscience to lead a married man astray?

THE LITTLE DARLING. I don't doubt your wife acts just like you.

THE HUSBAND (*very indignant*). That will do. Such remarks—

THE LITTLE DARLING. I thought you didn't have a wife.

THE HUSBAND. Whether I have or not, such remarks are not made in my presence.

(*He has risen.*)

THE LITTLE DARLING. But Karl, Karl, what's the matter? Are you mad at me? Really, I didn't know you were married. I was just talking to hear myself talk. Come, don't be mad.

THE HUSBAND (*comes back to her after a few minutes*). You are strange creatures, you . . . women. (*He becomes tender again.*)

THE LITTLE DARLING. Please . . . don't . . . it's so late.

THE HUSBAND. Well, then, listen to me. Let's talk seriously. I'd like to see you again. I'd like to see you often.

THE LITTLE DARLING. Would you?

THE HUSBAND. But I've got to be absolutely sure I can depend on you. I can't be watching you.

THE LITTLE DARLING. Oh, I can take care of myself.

THE HUSBAND. You are . . . well, I can't say inexperienced . . . but, you are young, and, men in general are pretty thoughtless.

THE LITTLE DARLING. Oh, my!

THE HUSBAND. I'm not talking about morals. You know what I mean—

THE LITTLE DARLING. Tell me, just what do you take me for?

THE HUSBAND. Look here. If you want me, and me only, we can easily arrange it, even if I do generally live in Graz. A place like this where some one may come in any moment is no place for us.

(THE LITTLE DARLING *snuggles up to him.*)

Next time . . . we'll go somewhere else, what do you say?

THE LITTLE DARLING. Yes.

THE HUSBAND. Where we can be entirely alone.

THE LITTLE DARLING. Yes.

THE HUSBAND (*embracing her passionately*). We'll talk it over on the way home. (*He rises, and opens the door.*) Waiter . . . the check!

VII

THE LITTLE DARLING AND THE POET

(*A small room comfortably furnished. Window-drapes which make the room half-dark. Red curtains. A large writing-table covered with books and papers. A baby-grand piano against the wall.* THE LITTLE DARLING *and* THE POET *are just entering.* THE POET *closes the door.*)

THE POET (*kisses her*). My darling!

THE LITTLE DARLING (*has her hat and coat on*). Oh! It's gorgeous here! Only you can't see anything!

THE POET. Your eyes will get used to the soft twilight. Those sweet eyes. (*Kisses her eyes.*)

THE LITTLE DARLING. But these sweet eyes haven't time to do that.

THE POET. Why not?

THE LITTLE DARLING. Because I can only stay a minute.

THE POET. Won't you take off your hat though?

THE LITTLE DARLING. Just for a minute.

THE POET (*takes out the pin and puts the hat aside*). And your coat—

THE LITTLE DARLING. The idea! I have to leave right away.

THE POET. No, you must take a good rest. We've been knocking around for three hours.

THE LITTLE DARLING. We were riding.

THE POET. We rode home, but we ran around, it must have been fully three hours, at the country place. Please sit down, anywhere you like.

Here at the desk—no, that wouldn't do. On the sofa—how's that. (*Forces her to sit down.*) If you're very tired, stretch out—like this. (*She lies down.*) Put your head on the cushion.

THE LITTLE DARLING (*laughing*). But I'm not tired a bit!

THE POET. You just think you're not. There, and if you are sleepy, go to sleep. I will be very quiet. And if you like I'll play you a lullaby . . . one of my own . . . (*He goes to the piano.*)

THE LITTLE DARLING. One of your own?

THE POET. Yes.

THE LITTLE DARLING. Why, Robert, I thought you were a doctor.

THE POET. How so? I told you I was a writer.

THE LITTLE DARLING. Well, all those writers are called doctor, aren't they?

THE POET. Not all of them. I'm not, for instance. Why did you think I was?

THE LITTLE DARLING. Why, you just said the piece you're playing is your own.

THE POET. Perhaps it isn't. But it doesn't matter, does it? It certainly doesn't matter who composed it, as long as it is beautiful. Don't you think so?

THE LITTLE DARLING. Of course it must be beautiful. That's the main thing.

THE POET. Do you know what I mean?

THE LITTLE DARLING. Mean — ?

THE POET. By what I just said.

THE LITTLE DARLING (*sleepily*). Of course I do.

THE POET (*gets up, goes to her, and strokes her hair*). You can't understand a word.

THE LITTLE DARLING. I'm not so dumb.

THE POET. Yes, you are, but that is just why I love you. It is wonderful when girls are dumb. I mean in the way you are.

THE LITTLE DARLING. Say, you're being insulting!

THE POET. Angel! Little one! Isn't it nice to lie on this soft, Persian couch cover?

THE LITTLE DARLING. Oh, yes. Don't you want to play something else on the piano?

THE POET. No, I'd rather be with you. (*Caressing her.*)

THE LITTLE DARLING. Hadn't you better light the light?

THE POET. Oh, no . . . The dusk is so restful. We've been bathing in sunshine all day. Now we've just climbed out of the bath and slipped on . . . a bathrobe of twilight. (*Laughs.*) No—that ought to be expressed differently. Don't you think so?

THE LITTLE DARLING. I don't know.

THE POET (*moves away from her a little*). Divine stupidity! (*He takes out a notebook, and writes a few words in it.*)

THE LITTLE DARLING. What are you doing? (*She turns toward him.*) What are you writing?

THE POET (*softly*). Sun, bath, twilight, cloak . . . yes . . . (*He puts the notebook back. Aloud.*) Nothing . . . Now, tell me, sweetheart, wouldn't you like something to eat or drink?

THE LITTLE DARLING. I'm really not thirsty, but I'm hungry.

THE POET. Hmm . . . I'd rather you were thirsty. I have some cognac here, but I have to go out for food.

THE LITTLE DARLING. Can't you send somebody?

THE POET. Not very easily. The cleaning woman isn't here now—Oh well. I'll go . . . What would you like?

THE LITTLE DARLING. Really it's hardly worth while. I am going right home, anyway.

THE POET. That's out of the question. I'll tell you what—when we leave, let's go somewhere and have supper.

THE LITTLE DARLING. Oh, no. I haven't time for that. And, anyway, where can we go? Somebody we know might see us.

THE POET. Do you know so many people?

THE LITTLE DARLING. It takes only one to make trouble.

THE POET. What sort of trouble?

THE LITTLE DARLING. Well, suppose mother should hear about this . . .

THE POET. We can go where no one can see us. There are plenty of restaurants with *chambres séparées.*

THE LITTLE DARLING (*singing*). "A little cafe. A *chambre séparée* . . ."

THE POET. Have you ever been in a *chambre séparée*?

THE LITTLE DARLING. To tell the truth—yes.

THE POET. Who was the happy man?

THE LITTLE DARLING. Oh, it wasn't that way . . . I went with my girl friend and her fiancé. They took me along.

THE POET. You expect me to believe that?

THE LITTLE DARLING. You needn't believe it!

THE POET (*close to her*). Are you blushing? I can hardly see. I can't even distinguish your features. (*He touches her cheeks with his hands.*) But even so I recognize you.

THE LITTLE DARLING. Well, be careful you don't take me for some one else.

THE POET. It is strange, I can't remember how you look.

THE LITTLE DARLING. Thanks.

THE POET (*seriously*). It is uncanny. I can't visualize your features. In a certain sense I have forgotten you already—Now, if I couldn't remember even the sound of your voice either . . . what would you really be? Something near and far at the same time . . . Eerie.

THE LITTLE DARLING. What are you talking about?

THE POET. Nothing, my angel, nothing. Where are your lips? (*He kisses her.*)

THE LITTLE DARLING. Won't you please put the light on?

THE POET. No . . . (*Becomes very tender.*) Tell me, do you love me?

THE LITTLE DARLING. Very much . . . Oh, so much!

THE POET. Have you ever loved any one as much as me?

THE LITTLE DARLING. I told you already I never truly loved before.

THE POET. But . . .(*He sighs.*)

THE LITTLE DARLING. He was my fiancé.

THE POET. I'd rather you didn't mention him now.

THE LITTLE DARLING. Say . . . what are you doing . . . see here! . . .

THE POET. We might imagine we are in a palace in India.

THE LITTLE DARLING. I'm sure the people there aren't as naughty as you are.

THE POET. How idiotic! Perfectly divine—Ah, if you only could understand what you are to me . . .

THE LITTLE DARLING. What?

THE POET. Don't push me away like this all the time. I'm not doing anything—

THE LITTLE DARLING. But my corset hurts.

THE POET (*simply*). Take it off.

THE LITTLE DARLING. All right. But you mustn't think you can do anything, just because I haven't any corset on.

THE POET. Of course not.

(THE LITTLE DARLING *rises, and takes off her corset in the darkness.*)

THE POET (*sitting, meanwhile, on the sofa*). Tell me, aren't you at all interested in knowing my name?

THE LITTLE DARLING. Yes, what is your name?

THE POET. I'd rather not tell you my real name, but my pseudonym is—

THE LITTLE DARLING. What's a pseudonym?

THE POET. The name I sign to the things I write.

THE LITTLE DARLING. Oh, you don't sign your real name?

(THE POET *close to her.*)

Please . . . Don't . . . Stop.

THE POET. What a fragrance ascends to my nostrils! Ah, how sweet! (*He kisses her breasts.*)

THE LITTLE DARLING. You are tearing my chemise.

THE POET. Off with it . . . Off with it . . . It's in the way.

THE LITTLE DARLING. Oh, Robert.

THE POET. And now let's enter our Indian palace.

THE LITTLE DARLING. Tell me first—do you really love me?

THE POET. I adore you. (*Kisses her passionately.*) I adore you, my sweetheart, my springtime . . . my . . .

THE LITTLE DARLING. Robert . . . Robert . . .

* * * * *

THE POET. That was celestial bliss . . . My pen name is . . .

THE LITTLE DARLING. Robert—oh, my Robert!

THE POET. Biebitz.

THE LITTLE DARLING. Why is your pen name Biebitz?

THE POET. That isn't my real name, my pseudonym . . . Well, don't you recognize it?

THE LITTLE DARLING. No.

THE POET. You don't know the name Biebitz? Divine! Really? You are only pretending you don't know it, aren't you?

THE LITTLE DARLING. I swear, I never heard it.

THE POET. Don't you ever go to the theater?

THE LITTLE DARLING. Oh, yes. I was at the opera only the other night with—you know, with one of my girl friends and her uncle, to hear Cavalleria Rusticana.

THE POET. Hm, you never go to plays.

THE LITTLE DARLING. I never get passes for them.

THE POET. I'll send you one very soon.

THE LITTLE DARLING. Oh, do! And don't forget, for something funny.

THE POET. Oh . . . something funny . . . you don't care to see anything sad?

THE LITTLE DARLING. I'd rather not.

THE POET. Not even if it is a play of mine?

THE LITTLE DARLING. A play of yours? Do you write plays?

THE POET. Excuse me, I just want to light a candle. I haven't seen you since you have become my beloved—Angel!

(*He lights a candle.*)

THE LITTLE DARLING. Don't, I'm ashamed. Give me something to cover myself, please.

THE POET. Later! (*He approaches her with the light, and looks at her a long time.*)

THE LITTLE DARLING (*covering her face with her hands*). Go away, Robert!

THE POET. You are beautiful. You're Beauty. Perhaps you are Nature. You are Holy Simplicity.

THE LITTLE DARLING. Ouch! You're dropping wax on me. Can't you be more careful?

THE POET (*puts the candle away*). You are that which I have long sought. You love me for my own sake. I might be only a clerk, but you would love me. It does my heart good. I must confess I could not help being suspicious until this moment. Tell me, honestly, you didn't think I might be Biebitz?

THE LITTLE DARLING. Gosh, I don't know him. What are you trying to get me to say? I never heard of Biebitz before.

THE POET. Such is fame! No, forget what I have told you. Forget Biebitz. I am Robert and I want to be only Robert to you. I was only joking. (*Lightly.*) I'm no writer at all. I'm a clerk and in the evening I play the piano in a night-club.

THE LITTLE DARLING. But now I'm all mixed up . . . and the way you look at a person. What's the matter with you? What do you mean?

THE POET. Very strange! It's something that has never happened to me, sweetheart; I am on the verge of tears. You move me deeply. Live with me, will you? We shall be very dear to each other.

THE LITTLE DARLING. Is it true about the night-club?

THE POET. Yes, but don't speak about it any more. If you love me, don't ask me any questions at all. Tell me, can you get away for a few weeks?

THE LITTLE DARLING. How do you mean—get away?

THE POET. I mean, leave home?

THE LITTLE DARLING. How can I! What would mother say? And if I wasn't there, the whole house would be upside down in no time.

THE POET. I had a beautiful picture of you and me together, in the solitude of a great forest, living the life of nature for a few weeks . . . Eden. And then, some day, "Good-bye"—going our separate ways, not knowing where . . .

THE LITTLE DARLING. You are already talking about "Good-bye." And I thought you loved me so much.

THE POET. That's just the reason. (*Bends over her, and kisses her on the forehead.*) You sweet thing!

THE LITTLE DARLING. Please, hold me tight. I feel so cold.

THE POET. I suppose it's time you were getting dressed. Wait, I'll light a few more candles for you.

THE LITTLE DARLING (*rising*). Don't look.

THE POET. No. (*At the window.*) Tell me, sweet, are you happy?

THE LITTLE DARLING. How do you mean?

THE POET. I mean are you glad you're alive? Is the world a great old place?

THE LITTLE DARLING. Things could be a lot better.

THE POET. You don't get me. I know you're having a hard time at home. I know you are not a princess. All the same there's such a thing as feeling alive. Do you ever feel alive?

THE LITTLE DARLING. Got a comb?

THE POET (*goes to the dressing-table, hands her a comb, and watches her*). Heavens, how ravishing you look!

THE LITTLE DARLING. Please . . . no more!

THE POET. Please, stay here a while. I'll get something for supper, and . . .

THE LITTLE DARLING. But it is awfully late already.

THE POET. It isn't nine yet.

THE LITTLE DARLING. Gee. I must hurry. Please!

THE POET. When shall I see you again?

THE LITTLE DARLING. When do you want to see me?

THE POET. To-morrow.

THE LITTLE DARLING. What's to-morrow?

THE POET. Saturday.

THE LITTLE DARLING. Oh, I can't. I must take my little sister to see her guardian.

THE POET. Then Sunday . . .hm . . . Sunday . . . on Sunday . . . now I'll have to explain something to you. I'm not Biebitz, but Biebitz is a friend of mine. I'll introduce you sometime. Biebitz's play will be given Sunday. I'll send you a pass, and take you home after the show. You'll tell me how you liked the play. Won't you?

THE LITTLE DARLING. Here you are talking about this Biebitz again. I don't understand what it's all about.

THE POET. I shan't know you really, until I know what the play means to you.

THE LITTLE DARLING. Well . . . I'm ready.

THE POET. Come, sweetheart.

(*They go out.*)

VIII

THE POET AND THE ACTRESS

(*A room in a country inn. It is a spring night. Moonlight over the meadows and hills. The windows are open.* THE POET *and* THE ACTRESS *enter, and as they cross the threshold, the candle* THE POET *carries is blown out.*)

THE POET. Oh . . .

THE ACTRESS. What's the matter?

THE POET. The candle.—But we don't need it. Look how light it is. Wonderful!

(THE ACTRESS *sinks down suddenly before the window with joined hands.*)

What's the matter?

(THE ACTRESS *remains silent.* THE POET *goes to her.*)

What are you doing?

THE ACTRESS (*indignant*). Can't you see? I'm praying—

THE POET. Do you believe in God?

THE ACTRESS. Certainly. Do you take me for a scoundrel?

THE POET. I understand.

THE ACTRESS. Come, kneel down beside me. Really, you may pray just once. It won't take the crease out of your trousers.

(THE POET *kneels beside her, and puts his arm around her waist.*)

Profligate! (*Rises.*) And do you know to whom I prayed?

THE POET. To God, presumably.

THE ACTRESS (*with deep sarcasm*). Oh no, I was praying to you!

THE POET. Then why did you look out the window?

THE ACTRESS. Suppose you tell me first where you have dragged me, seducer.

THE POET. But, darling, it was your idea. You wanted to go to the country—and chose this very place.

THE ACTRESS. Well, isn't it a good place?

THE POET. Certainly. It's charming here. Just think—two hours from Vienna—perfect solitude. And what a landscape!

THE ACTRESS. Yes. You could even write something if you had talent.

THE POET. You've been here before?

THE ACTRESS. Have I been here before? I lived here for years.

THE POET. With whom?

THE ACTRESS. With Fred, of course.

THE POET. Oh!

THE ACTRESS. How I loved that man!

THE POET. You've told me all about it.

THE ACTRESS. I'm sorry. I can go away if I bore you!

THE POET. Bore me? You can't imagine what you mean to me . . . You are a whole world to me . . . You are divine, you are genius . . . You are Holy Simplicity. Yes, you are . . . But you oughtn't to talk about Fred now.

THE ACTRESS. That was a *faux pas*. Well?

THE POET. I'm glad you see it that way.

THE ACTRESS. Come, give me a kiss!

(THE POET *kisses her.*)

But now we had better say good-night. Good-night, darling!

THE POET. What do you mean?

THE ACTRESS. I mean, I am going to lie down and go to sleep.

THE POET. Certainly, do that very thing, but this . . . "good-night" business . . . Where do I stay?

THE ACTRESS. There are lots of other rooms here.

THE POET. The others don't appeal to me. Don't you think I'd better light a candle?

THE ACTRESS. Yes.

THE POET (*lights a candle, which stands upon the dressing-table*). What a charming room . . . and what pious people they must be. Pictures of saints everywhere. It would be interesting to spend some time among people like this . . . quite another world. How little we know of our fellow creatures.

THE ACTRESS. Quit talking nonsense, and reach me the bag from the table.

THE POET. Here, my only beloved!

(THE ACTRESS *takes a small framed picture out of the hand-bag and puts it on the dressing-table.*)

What's that?

THE ACTRESS. That's the Virgin.

THE POET. Do you always carry her around with you?

THE ACTRESS. She is my talisman. And now go, Robert!

THE POET. What kind of a joke is this? Don't you want me to . . .

THE ACTRESS. No, you must go.

THE POET. And when am I to come in?

THE ACTRESS. In ten minutes.

THE POET (*kisses her*). Au revoir!

THE ACTRESS. Where are you going?

THE POET. I shall walk up and down under your window. I love to stroll about in the fresh air at night. My finest inspirations come to me that way. And now, near you, enveloped in the atmosphere of your longing . . . and wafted away by your art . . .

THE ACTRESS. You talk like an idiot . . .

THE POET (*hurt*). There are women who might say . . . like a poet.

THE ACTRESS. All right, but now do go. And don't start an affair with the waitress.

(THE POET *goes.* THE ACTRESS *undresses. She hears* THE POET *going downstairs, and now she hears his steps under her window. As soon as she is undressed, she goes to the window and looks down where he stands waiting. She whispers to him.*)

Come!

(THE POET *comes quickly upstairs and runs toward her. She, meanwhile, has gone to bed and put out the light. He locks the door.*) Now you may sit down beside me, and tell me a story.

THE POET (*sits down on the bed beside her*). Hadn't I better close the window? Isn't it too cold for you?

THE ACTRESS. Oh, no!

THE POET. Now, what shall I tell you?

THE ACTRESS. Tell me to whom you are unfaithful at this moment.

THE POET. Unfortunately, I'm not unfaithful at all yet.

THE ACTRESS. Then take comfort in knowing that I am unfaithful to some one.

THE POET. I can well imagine.

THE ACTRESS. Who do you suppose it is?

THE POET. But, my dear, how do you expect me to know?

THE ACTRESS. Guess, then.

THE POET. Let's see . . . your manager.

THE ACTRESS. My dear man, I'm not a chorus-girl.

THE POET. Well, I just thought . . .

THE ACTRESS. Guess again.

THE POET. Then it's your leading-man . . . Benno.

THE ACTRESS. Stupid! He doesn't care for women . . . didn't you know that? He's having an affair with the postman!

THE POET. You don't say.

THE ACTRESS. Come, kiss me.

(THE POET *embraces her.*)

What are you doing?

THE POET. Don't torment me so!

THE ACTRESS. Listen, Robert, I'll make you a proposition. Come, lie down in bed with me.

THE POET. You bet I will!

THE ACTRESS. Hurry, hurry!

THE POET. Yes . . . if it had been up to me I'd have been there long ago . . . Listen . . .

THE ACTRESS. What to?

THE POET. To the crickets chirping out there.

THE ACTRESS. You are crazy, my dear, there are no crickets in these parts.

THE POET. But you can hear them.

THE ACTRESS. Will you hurry up?

THE POET (*beside her*). Here I am.

THE ACTRESS. Now lie quiet . . . Sh-h . . . don't move . . .

THE POET. But, what's the idea?

THE ACTRESS. You'd like to have an affair with me?

THE POET. That ought to be pretty clear to you by now.

THE ACTRESS. There are a good many men who would like to . . .

THE POET. Yet it can scarcely be gainsaid that at this particular moment my chances seem to be the best.

THE ACTRESS. Then, come, my cricket! I shall call you "cricket" from now on.

THE POET. All right. . . .

THE ACTRESS. Now, tell me, who am I deceiving?

THE POET. Who? . . . Me perhaps . . .

THE ACTRESS. My dear, you have softening of the brain.

THE POET. Or some one . . . whom you have never seen . . . some one, whom you don't . . . some one—who is set apart for you but whom you will never find . . .

THE ACTRESS. Please! Please don't talk extravagant nonsense.

THE POET. Isn't it strange . . . you too, and yet one would think . . . But no, that would take away the best in you. Come—my dear—come.

* * * * *

THE ACTRESS. That's better than acting in idiotic plays. Don't you think so?

THE POET. Well it's good to know that you get to act in an intelligent one occasionally.

THE ACTRESS. You conceited puppy. I suppose you're thinking of that play of yours?

THE POET. Yes, I am.

THE ACTRESS (*seriously*). Undoubtedly it is a masterpiece.

THE POET. Right!

THE ACTRESS. Yes, you are a genius, Robert!

THE POET. I seize the opportunity of asking why you cancelled your performance the night before last. There was absolutely nothing the matter with you.

THE ACTRESS. Well, I wanted to annoy you.

THE POET. But why? What have I done to you?

THE ACTRESS. You were arrogant.

THE POET. How so?

THE ACTRESS. Everybody at the theater thinks you are.

THE POET. Really?

THE ACTRESS. But I told them, "I guess he has a perfect right to be arrogant."

THE POET. And what did they say?

THE ACTRESS. How could they say anything? I don't talk to any of them.

THE POET. Oh, I see.

THE ACTRESS. They would like nothing better than to poison me, every one of them. But they won't get the chance.

THE POET. Don't think now of anybody else. Be glad that you are here with me, and tell me you love me.

THE ACTRESS. What more proof do you want?

THE POET. It can't be proved.

THE ACTRESS. Fine! Then what more do you want?

THE POET. How many other men have . . . had this sort of proof? Did you love them all?

THE ACTRESS. No, I have loved only one.

THE POET (*embraces her*). My . . .

THE ACTRESS. Fred . . .

THE POET. My name is Robert. What do I mean to you, if you are thinking of Fred, now?

THE ACTRESS. You are just a caprice.

THE POET. Thanks for letting me know.

THE ACTRESS. Well, aren't you glad?

THE POET. Glad of being a caprice?

THE ACTRESS. It seems to me that you have a very good reason to be glad.

THE POET. Oh, this—

THE ACTRESS. Yes, this, my pale cricket!—Say, what about that chirping? Are they still chirping?

THE POET. Don't you hear them?

THE ACTRESS. Of course, I hear them. But, my dear, those are frogs.

THE POET. You are mistaken. Frogs croak.

THE ACTRESS. Of course, they croak.

THE POET. Those things aren't croaking, dear, they're chirping.

THE ACTRESS. You are the most obstinate person I have ever run into. Kiss me, Froggie.

THE POET. Please don't call me that. It makes me nervous all over.

THE ACTRESS. Well, what shall I call you?

THE POET. I have a name. Robert.

THE ACTRESS. Oh, but that's too stupid.

THE POET. Please simply call me by my own name.

THE ACTRESS. Well, then, Robert, give me a kiss . . . Ah! (*She kisses him.*) Now, are you satisfied, Froggie? Ha-ha-ha.

THE POET. May I light a cigarette?

THE ACTRESS. Give me one, too. (*He takes his cigarette-case from the dressing-table; takes out two cigarettes, lights both, and gives her one.*) By the way, you haven't said a word about my performance yesterday.

THE POET. What performance?

THE ACTRESS. What performance!

THE POET. Oh, yes. I wasn't at the theater.

THE ACTRESS. You're trying to be funny.

THE POET. Why should I? Since you cancelled your performance only two days ago, I assumed you wouldn't be in full possession of your powers, yesterday, so I decided not to go.

THE ACTRESS. You missed something wonderful.

THE POET. Yes?

THE ACTRESS. It was a sensation. The people actually turned pale.

THE POET. You really could tell?

THE ACTRESS. Benno said, "Dearest, you acted divinely."

THE POET. Hm! . . . And so ill the day before.

THE ACTRESS. Indeed I was. And do you know why? Because of my longing for you.

THE POET. A little while ago you said you stayed away just to hurt me.

THE ACTRESS. What do *you* know about my love for you? You are so cold. I was delirious all night. Had high fever, a hundred and four.

THE POET. Rather a high temperature for a caprice.

THE ACTRESS. You call it a caprice! I am dying for love of you, and you call it a caprice . . .

THE POET. And Fred . . .
THE ACTRESS. Fred? . . . Don't mention that tramp to me!

IX

THE ACTRESS AND THE COUNT

(*The bedroom of* THE ACTRESS, *luxuriously furnished. It is midday. The blinds are still down. A candle is burning on the dressing-table.* THE ACTRESS *is lying in her four-poster bed. On the cover are many newspapers.* THE COUNT, *wearing his uniform of captain in the Dragoons, enters. He stops just inside the door.*)

THE ACTRESS. Ah, Count.

THE COUNT. Your mother said I might, otherwise I wouldn't—

THE ACTRESS. Please, come in.

THE COUNT. I kiss your hand. Pardon me . . . just coming in from the street . . . I can't see a thing yet. Oh, now I find the way. (*At her bedside.*) I kiss your hand.

THE ACTRESS. Please sit down, Count.

THE COUNT. Your mother said, "The young lady isn't well." . . . Nothing serious, I hope.

THE ACTRESS. Nothing serious? I was at the point of death.

THE COUNT. Dear me! Surely not.

THE ACTRESS. You are very kind to bother about me.

THE COUNT. At the point of death! And last night you were still able to give a divine performance.

THE ACTRESS. It seems to have been a great success.

THE COUNT. Tremendous! . . . The audience was carried away. To say nothing of myself.

THE ACTRESS. Thanks for the beautiful flowers.

THE COUNT. Don't mention it, Fraülein.

THE ACTRESS (*looking significantly at a large basket of flowers on a little table near the window*). You see I have them near me.

THE COUNT. You were literally overwhelmed with flowers and wreaths yesterday.

THE ACTRESS. I left them in my dressing-room. All I brought home was your basket.

THE COUNT (*kissing her hand*). That's nice of you.

(THE ACTRESS *suddenly seizes his hand, and kisses it.*)

Fraülein!

THE ACTRESS. Don't be frightened, Count, it doesn't bind you to anything.

THE COUNT. You are a strange being . . . enigmatic, one might almost say. (*Pause.*)

THE ACTRESS. Fraülein Birken, I suppose, is less puzzling.

THE COUNT. Little Birken is no puzzle at all. That is, of course, I really know her only very slightly.

THE ACTRESS. Oh!

THE COUNT. Believe me. But you are a puzzle. And I've always been fascinated by puzzles. I have missed a great deal of enjoyment by not seeing you act until last night.

THE ACTRESS. Oh, had you never? How did that happen?

THE COUNT. It's hard for me to go to the theater. I am used to dining late . . . then by the time I can get there, the best part of the play is over. Don't you see?

THE ACTRESS. From now on, I suppose, you will dine earlier.

THE COUNT. I've thought of that too. Or maybe I won't dine at all. There is really no pleasure in eating.

THE ACTRESS. What pleasure is there of any sort for an elderly man, even if he's as well preserved as you are?

THE COUNT. I often ask that myself. But I am not an old man. There are other reasons why I don't care for certain things.

THE ACTRESS. Do you think so?

THE COUNT. Yes. Louis, for instance, says I am a philosopher. You see he means I am much given to meditation.

THE ACTRESS. Yes . . . Thinking never made anyone happy.

THE COUNT. I have too much time on my hands, that's why. You see, I've often thought it would be better if they would transfer me to Vienna, where there is diversion, excitement. Really, though, it's not much better here than it was over there.

THE ACTRESS. Where is "over there"?

THE COUNT. Down in Hungary, in the ghastly holes where I've been stationed most of the time.

THE ACTRESS. What kept you in Hungary? In ghastly holes?

THE COUNT. The service, as I am telling you.

THE ACTRESS. But why so long in Hungary?

THE COUNT. It just happened that way.

THE ACTRESS. It must be enough to drive one mad.

THE COUNT. I don't know about that. There's a lot more to do there than here. You know, drilling recruits, breaking in mounts . . . and the country really isn't as bad as they say. The lowlands are really quite beautiful . . . and such sunsets. Too bad I'm no painter. I've often thought if I were, I would paint them. We have a young chap in our regiment, Splany, who could do it. But, dear me, what dull stories I'm telling you.

THE ACTRESS. Please go on; I am enjoying myself royally.

THE COUNT. I can just talk and talk with you. Louis said the same. It isn't often one can find a good listener.

THE ACTRESS. In Hungary, anyway.

THE COUNT. Or in Vienna either. People are the same everywhere. Where there are more of them, the crowd's bigger, that's all. Do you really like people?

THE ACTRESS. Like them? I detest them! I can't bear the sight of them. I never see any one. I'm always alone. Nobody ever comes here.

THE COUNT. You know, I sort of thought you were a misanthrope. Artists must often be like that. If one lives on a higher plane . . . Well, you are lucky. You know at least what you live for.

THE ACTRESS. What makes you think so? I haven't the slightest idea what I live for!

THE COUNT. But surely to be famous . . . to be fêted . . .

THE ACTRESS. And you think that is happiness?

THE COUNT. Pardon me. There is no happiness. And it's the same with all that people talk about most . . . For instance, love: there is no such thing.

THE ACTRESS. You are right about that!

THE COUNT. Pleasure . . . intoxication . . . we can have that, all right . . . they are definite things. When I'm having a good time I know I'm having a good time. When I'm drunk I know I'm drunk. All right. We can be sure of things like that. And when they're over, why, they're just over.

THE ACTRESS (*grandly*). Just over.

THE COUNT. But as soon as one—how shall I put it—as soon as one gets away from the present moment, I mean, if one looks ahead or back . . . well, everything is lost. Ahead—darkness. Back—confusion . . . In a word, one gets all mixed up. Am I right?

THE ACTRESS (*wide-eyed, nods*). You seem to have it all down.

THE COUNT. And, you see, my dear lady, once this is clear, it really doesn't matter whether one lives in Vienna or in ghastly Hungarian holes. You see, for instance . . . Where may I put my cap? Yes, thank you . . . What were we talking about?

THE ACTRESS. About living in ghastly holes in Hungary.

THE COUNT. Yes, yes. Well, as I said, there isn't much difference whether I spend the evening at the casino or at the club. It's all the same.

THE ACTRESS. And what has all this to do with love?

THE COUNT. If a person thinks there *is* such a thing, he'll always have somebody who'll love him.

THE ACTRESS. Fraülein Birken, for instance.

THE COUNT. I really don't see why you always have to come back to little Birken.

THE ACTRESS. But she's your mistress, isn't she?

THE COUNT. Who says so?

THE ACTRESS. Everybody knows it.

THE COUNT. Except myself, I would have you observe.

THE ACTRESS. But you fought a duel on her account!

THE COUNT. Maybe I was even killed without knowing it.

THE ACTRESS. Now, Count, you are a man of honor. Won't you sit closer to me?

THE COUNT. I will take the liberty.

THE ACTRESS. Over here. (*She draws him to her, and passes her hand through his hair.*) I knew you would come to-day.

THE COUNT. How did you know?

THE ACTRESS. I knew it last night in the theater.

THE COUNT. Could you see me from the stage?

THE ACTRESS. My dear sir! Didn't you notice I acted for you alone?

THE COUNT. Surely not?

THE ACTRESS. When I saw you in the first row, I felt I could fly.

THE COUNT. Could fly? Because of me? I never even suspected you noticed me!

THE ACTRESS. Your aristocratic reserve is enough to drive one to despair.

THE COUNT. Yes, Fraülein . . .

THE ACTRESS. "Yes, Fraülein"! . . . At least, take your saber off!

THE COUNT. If I may. (*Takes it off and leans it against the bed.*)

THE ACTRESS. And now do give me a kiss.

(THE COUNT *kisses her. She does not release him.*)

It would have been better if I had never seen you.

THE COUNT. No, it's better this way.

THE ACTRESS. Count, you are a poseur!

THE COUNT. I—how so?

THE ACTRESS. Can't you imagine how happy most men would be in your shoes?

THE COUNT. I am very happy.

THE ACTRESS. I thought there *was* no happiness? Why do you look at me that way? I believe I frightened you, Count!

THE COUNT. I told you, you are a puzzle.

THE ACTRESS. Oh, don't bother me with your philosophy . . . come closer . . . and ask me for anything at all . . . you can have whatever you want. You are so handsome.

THE COUNT. Well, then, I ask (*Kissing her hand.*) permission to call again this evening.

THE ACTRESS. This evening . . . but I have to work.

THE COUNT. After the play.

THE ACTRESS. And you ask for nothing else?

THE COUNT. I shall ask for everything else after the play.

THE ACTRESS (*hurt*). You can go right on asking, you abominable poseur.

THE COUNT. But, look, we've been perfectly frank with each other so far . . . it seems to me it would be much nicer after the play . . . much cozier than now, when . . . I have a sort of feeling the door might fly open any moment . . .

THE ACTRESS. It doesn't open from the outside.

THE COUNT. Well, you see, I have an idea one shouldn't lightly spoil in advance something which may be very beautiful.

THE ACTRESS. Which may be . . .

THE COUNT. To be frank, love in the morning seems horrible to me.

THE ACTRESS. Well, you are about the craziest I ever—

THE COUNT. I am not talking about women in general . . . because in general it doesn't make any difference anyway. But women like you . . . no, you may call me crazy as often as you want to. But women like you . . . one doesn't take them before breakfast. That way . . . you know . . . that way . . .

THE ACTRESS. Oh, you are a darling!

THE COUNT. You understand what I mean, don't you? Now that is what I am looking forward to . . .

THE ACTRESS. How do you want it to be?

THE COUNT. Like this . . . I wait for you in a carriage after the play, then we drive somewhere for supper . . .

THE ACTRESS. I am not Fraülein Birken.

THE COUNT. I didn't say you were. Only, it seems to me, one has to be in the right mood for everything. I don't get into the right mood until supper. The best part of it will be when we drive home, and then . . .

THE ACTRESS. And then?

THE COUNT. Well, that depends on circumstances.

THE ACTRESS. Do sit closer. Closer.

THE COUNT (*sitting down on the bed*). It seems to me the pillows are scented . . . Mignonette—isn't it?

THE ACTRESS. It's very warm in here, don't you think so?

(THE COUNT *bends down, and kisses her neck.*)

Oh, Count, this is contrary to your program.

THE COUNT. Who said anything about a "program"? I have none.

(THE ACTRESS *drawing him close to her.*)

It really is very warm.

THE ACTRESS. Do you think so? And so dark, just as if it were evening . . . (*Draws him toward her.*) It is evening . . . it is night . . . Close your eyes, if it's too light for you. Come! . . . Come! . . .

(THE COUNT *offers no further resistance.*)

* * * * *

THE ACTRESS. And what about moods now, you poseur?

THE COUNT. You are a little devil.

THE ACTRESS. What a thing to say!

THE COUNT. Well, then, an angel.

THE ACTRESS. You should have been an actor. Really! You understand women. And do you know what I am going to do now?

THE COUNT. What?

THE ACTRESS. I am going to tell you I shall never see you again.

THE COUNT. But why?

THE ACTRESS. Never, never. You are too dangerous! You drive a woman mad. You stand in front of me, all of a sudden, as if nothing had happened.

THE COUNT. But . . .

THE ACTRESS. Please remember, Count, I have just become your mistress.

THE COUNT. I shall never forget it!

THE ACTRESS. And what about to-night?

THE COUNT. What do you mean?

THE ACTRESS. Well, you wanted to wait for me after the theater?

THE COUNT. Very well, let's make it the day after to-morrow.

THE ACTRESS. What do you mean, the day after to-morrow? We were talking about to-night.

THE COUNT. There wouldn't be much sense in that.

THE ACTRESS. You—you *are* getting old!

THE COUNT. You don't quite understand me. What I am talking about has to do rather—how shall I express myself—rather concerns the soul.

THE ACTRESS. What do I care about your soul?

THE COUNT. Believe me, the soul enters into this. I am sure it is a mistake to believe that the spiritual and the physical are separable.

THE ACTRESS. Don't bother me with your philosophy. If I want any of that, I will read books.

THE COUNT. One never learns from books.

THE ACTRESS. Quite true! And that's why you ought to wait for me to-night. We will come to some agreement regarding the soul, you villain!

THE COUNT. Well, then, if I may, I shall wait in my carriage . . .

THE ACTRESS. You shall wait for me here in my home—

THE COUNT. After the play . . .

THE ACTRESS. Naturally.

(THE COUNT *buckles on his sword.*)

What are you doing?

THE COUNT. I believe it is time for me to go. For a formal call I have stayed a little too long as it is.

THE ACTRESS. Well, this evening it shan't be any formal call.

THE COUNT. You think not?

THE ACTRESS. I'll take care of that. And now give me one more kiss, my darling little philosopher. Here, you seducer, you . . . sweet child, you seller of souls, you . . . skunk . . . you . . . (*After she has ardently kissed him several times, she thrusts him violently away.*) Count, you have done me a great honor.

THE COUNT. I kiss your hand, Fraülein. (*At the door.*) Au revoir.

THE ACTRESS. Good-bye, Hungarian hole!

X

THE COUNT AND THE PROSTITUTE

(*About six in the morning. A poorly furnished room with one window. Dirty yellow shutters closed. Tattered green curtains. On the dresser several photographs, and beside them a woman's hat, cheap and terrible. Behind the mirror cheap Japanese fans. On the table which has a red cover, is an oil lamp with a shade of yellow paper. The lamp is burning low and makes a disagreeable odor. Beside it a pitcher with a bit of left-over beer, and a half-empty glass. On the floor beside the bed woman's clothes in disorderly heap, as if they had just been hastily flung off.* THE PROSTITUTE *lies in the bed asleep, breathing quietly.* THE COUNT *is lying on the sofa fully dressed with his light overcoat on. His hat is on the floor at the head of the sofa.*)

THE COUNT (*stirs, rubs his eyes, sits up suddenly, and looks around*). Where am I? Oh, yes. So I actually went home with that woman. (*He rises quickly, notices her bed.*) Oh, there she is. So it can all happen, even at my age. I haven't the least idea—did they carry me up here? No. I saw myself—coming into this room. I was still awake then or they waked me up or . . . or maybe it's only the room that reminds me of something? Yes . . . just yesterday I saw it. (*Looks at his watch.*) What! yesterday, a couple of hours ago!—But, I knew something had to happen. I felt it in my bones. When I began to drink yesterday, I felt it . . . and what has happened? Nothing. Or did it? 'Pon my soul . . . for . . . ten years I haven't done anything like this. Well, the long and short of it is that I got good and god damn drunk. If I only knew when I began. I remember perfectly when Louis and I went into the night-club, and . . . no, no. We left together, so it must have been on the way. Yes, that's it, Louis and I were riding in my carriage. But why do I rack my brain about it? It really doesn't matter. Let's see how we get out of here. (*Rises. The lamp shakes.*) Oh! (*Looks at the sleeping girl.*) She's a good healthy sleeper. I don't remember anything, but I'll put the money on the table and then . . . good-bye. If I didn't know what she is! (*Studies her.*) I've known a good many who didn't look as virtuous even in their sleep. My word! Louis would say I'm philosophizing again, but it's true, sleep is the great leveler—like its brother death. Hm, I should like to know, whether—No, I'd certainly remember that. No, no, I just passed out on the sofa . . . and nothing happened. It is incredible how much alike all women look. Well, let's go. (*He is about to go.*) Oh, of course. (*He takes his wallet, and is about to take out a banknote.*)

THE PROSTITUTE (*awakening*). Well . . . who's there so early in the morning? (*Recognizing him.*) Hello, honey!

THE COUNT. Good morning. Have a good sleep?

THE PROSTITUTE (*stretching*). Oh, come here. Give's a little loving.

THE COUNT (*bends down to her, considers, and draws back*). I was just going . . .

THE PROSTITUTE. Going?

THE COUNT. It's really quite time.

THE PROSTITUTE. You want to go away?

THE COUNT (*slightly embarrassed*). Well . . .

THE PROSTITUTE. Well, good-bye, you'll come some other time.

THE COUNT. Yes, good-bye. But, won't you give me your hand?

(THE PROSTITUTE *reaches out her hand from under the cover.* THE COUNT *takes her hand, and kisses it mechanically, and becoming aware of what he is doing, he smiles.*)

Just as if she were a princess. Besides, if one only . . .

THE PROSTITUTE. Why do you look at me that way?

THE COUNT. If one sees nothing but the head, as I do now . . . anyway, they all look innocent when they first wake up . . . My word, one might imagine almost anything if there weren't such a stench of kerosene.

THE PROSTITUTE. Yes, the lamp's rotten.

THE COUNT. How old are you, really?

THE PROSTITUTE. Well, what would you guess?

THE COUNT. Twenty-four.

THE PROSTITUTE. Like hell I am!

THE COUNT. Older?

THE PROSTITUTE. I'm just going on twenty.

THE COUNT. And how long have you been . . .

THE PROSTITUTE. In this business? A year.

THE COUNT. You began early.

THE PROSTITUTE. Better early than late.

THE COUNT (*sits down upon her bed*). Tell me, are you really happy?

THE PROSTITUTE. Huh?

THE COUNT. I mean, are you getting along all right?

THE PROSTITUTE. I always get along O. K.

THE COUNT. I see . . . Well, did it never occur to you that you might do something else?

THE PROSTITUTE. What else?

THE COUNT. Well . . . You are a very pretty girl. You might take a lover, for instance.

THE PROSTITUTE. Do you think I haven't got any?

THE COUNT. Yes, I know. But I mean just one, understand? Just one, who would take care of you, so that you wouldn't have to go with everybody.

THE PROSTITUTE. I don't go with everybody. I don't have to, thank God. I can pick and choose.

(THE COUNT *looks around the room.*)

THE PROSTITUTE (*noticing*). We're moving uptown next month.

THE COUNT. We? Who?

THE PROSTITUTE. Well, the Madam, and a couple of other girls that live here.

THE COUNT. There are others?

THE PROSTITUTE. Next door . . . don't you hear? . . . that's Milly. She was in the cafe too.

THE COUNT. I hear some one snoring.

THE PROSTITUTE. That's Milly. She'll snore all day long, until ten o'clock to-night. Then she'll get up, and go to the cafe.

THE COUNT. This is a terrible life.

THE PROSTITUTE. Sure is. And believe me the Madam gives her hell. I'm always on my beat by noon.

THE COUNT. What do you do on your beat?

THE PROSTITUTE. What do you suppose? I go lookin' for business.

THE COUNT. Oh, yes . . . of course . . . (*Rises, takes out his wallet, and puts a banknote on the table.*) Good-bye!

THE PROSTITUTE. Going already? . . . Good-bye . . . Call again soon. (*Turns on her side.*)

THE COUNT (*stands still*). Tell me, are you fed up with everything?

THE PROSTITUTE. Huh?

THE COUNT. I mean you don't get any fun out of it anymore?

THE PROSTITUTE (*yawning*). I wanna sleep.

THE COUNT. It's all the same to you whether a man is young or old or whether he . . .

THE PROSTITUTE. What's it to you?

THE COUNT. Well . . . (*Suddenly hitting upon a thought.*) My word, now I know who you remind me of . . .

THE PROSTITUTE. Do I look like some baby you know?

THE COUNT. Incredible, incredible. Now please, don't talk, at least not for a minute . . . (*Looking at her.*) The very same features. (*Suddenly he kisses her eyes.*) The very image.

THE PROSTITUTE. What the . . .

THE COUNT. My word, it's too bad that you . . . aren't something else. You could make your fortune!

THE PROSTITUTE. You gab just like Franz.

THE COUNT. Who is Franz?

THE PROSTITUTE. The waiter in the cafe where us girls hang out.

THE COUNT. In what way am I just like Franz?

THE PROSTITUTE. He is always telling me "You could make your fortune," and wanting me to marry him.

THE COUNT. Why don't you?

THE PROSTITUTE. No thank you . . . I don't want to marry, no, not for all the money in the world. Maybe I'll get hooked up when I get older.

THE COUNT. The eyes . . . the very same eyes . . . Louis would certainly say I was a fool.—But I must kiss your eyes once more . . . so . . . and now "Good-bye."

THE PROSTITUTE. Good-bye . . .

THE COUNT (*at the door*). Tell me . . . aren't you a bit surprised?

THE PROSTITUTE. What by?

THE COUNT. That I don't want anything else.

THE PROSTITUTE. Lots of men don't want it in the morning.

THE COUNT. I see . . . (*To himself.*) Absurd, that I expect her to be surprised . . . Well, good-bye . . . (*He is at the door.*) But really, I'm vexed. I ought to know that women like her care only about money. What am I saying . . . "like her"? It is fine, anyway, at least she doesn't pretend; I ought to be glad . . . (*Aloud.*) May I come to see you again very soon?

THE PROSTITUTE (*with closed eyes*). Sure.

THE COUNT. When are you at home?

THE PROSTITUTE. I'm always at home. Just ask for Leocadia.

THE COUNT. Leocadia . . . All right. Well, good-bye. (*At the door.*) I can still feel the wine. But after all, this is glorious. I go with a woman like her and do nothing but kiss her eyes, because she has reminded me of some one . . . (*Turns toward her.*) Tell me, Leocadia, does it often happen that a man leaves you in this way?

THE PROSTITUTE. What way?

THE COUNT. As I am doing.

THE PROSTITUTE. In the morning?

THE COUNT. No . . . have you ever had any one with you—who didn't want anything from you?

THE PROSTITUTE. No, that has never happened to me.

THE COUNT. Well, what do you think then? Do you think I didn't like you?

THE PROSTITUTE. Why shouldn't you like me? You sure liked me enough last night.

THE COUNT. I like you now, too.

THE PROSTITUTE. But last night you sure liked me.

The Count. What makes you say so?

The Prostitute. Why ask foolish questions?

The Count. Last night . . . well, tell me, didn't I drop right down on the sofa?

The Prostitute. Certainly . . . you and me together.

The Count. Together!

The Prostitute. Sure, don't you remember?

The Count. Together . . . I . . .

The Prostitute. But you passed right out.

The Count. Right away . . . I see . . . that's what happened? . . .

The Prostitute. Sure thing, honey. But you must have been awfully stewed if you can't remember.

The Count. So . . . And yet . . . there is a faint resemblance . . . Good-bye . . . (*Listens.*) What is the matter?

The Prostitute. The house-girl is up. Give her a tip as you go out. The outside door is open, so you won't have to give anything to the janitor.

The Count (*in the anteroom*). Well . . . it would have been beautiful, if I had only kissed her eyes. It would have been almost an adventure . . . But . . . it wasn't to be . . . (*The servant opens the door.*) Ah—here . . . Good-night.

The Servant. Good morning!

The Count. Of course . . . good morning . . . Good morning.

The Snob

BY CARL STERNHEIM

Translated by ERIC BENTLEY

The Snob

CHARACTERS

Christian Maske
Sybil, *Christian's mistress*
Theobald Maske, *Christian's father*
Luise Maske, *Christian's mother*
Count Palen
Marianne, *Count Palen's daughter*
Maid
Valet

The Time: Before 1914
The Place: Somewhere in Germany

ACT I

(CHRISTIAN MASKE'S *furnished room.*)

CHRISTIAN (*opening a letter*). This is grotesque! (*At the door.*) Sybil, come here!

SYBIL (*enters*). Something of importance?

CHRISTIAN. At the age of sixty my father has brought off a bastard. He's in a fix and needs money. Listen: "So I must request you to lend me enough to meet the obligations which obstretrical services have laid upon me." What do you say?

SYBIL. Nothing. I only wish you'd follow your progenitor's example and do as well by me.

CHRISTIAN. Don't be a fool! It's absolutely awful. And I intend to do something about it. Something unexpected. Moreover, I've got to have a talk with *you.*

SYBIL. I must go home.

CHRISTIAN. Yesterday a chapter in my life came to an end. You've been living with me four years and every day you've seen me getting nearer and nearer the goal.

SYBIL. You've slaved for it.

CHRISTIAN. The African mines I helped to float are showing excellent returns. The Board of Directors met yesterday, and proposed me as President of the company. There is not the slightest doubt that the stockholders will accept the proposal.

SYBIL. What a triumph!

CHRISTIAN. I own a fifth of the stock. Bought it when nobody else would touch it—nobody knows, either. Now I'm on the way, there's no limit to the progress I'll be able to make in society. Or to the amount of money I might make.

SYBIL. Who was it that first discovered your gift for business and made you leave those dismal philological studies?

CHRISTIAN. You raised me from misery, Sybil, showed me how to wear my clothes properly, and taught me manners, as far as you knew how.

SYBIL. What a sight you were with frayed cuffs and your trousers far too short!

CHRISTIAN. In addition, you contributed yourself. Money, too, sometimes.

SYBIL. Myself. Last but not least.

CHRISTIAN. I wish to have it understood by both of us that I am profoundly in your debt. I look back from this day of decision . . .

SYBIL. Never mind.

CHRISTIAN. And am most grateful to you. I am about to make you an adequate return; and forget the whole thing.

SYBIL. That would be pleasant for you.

CHRISTIAN. I do not enter upon a new epoch in my life without paying off the debts of the last one. To the best of my knowledge and belief, the expenses you incurred on my behalf have been entered in my book here. I am paying them plus interest at five per cent.

SYBIL. Christian!

CHRISTIAN. Your association with me may possibly have caused you to miss other opportunities; I have computed these together with the rest. The total debt comes to twenty-four thousand marks. You shall receive that amount today.

SYBIL (*after a pause*). Delicacy would be—

CHRISTIAN. Delicacy! You cured me of delicacy in the affairs of this world, swept it out of me with a steel broom. So today I make up our accounts. You will find them correct. In the past, monetary ties bound me to you. Such—on the whole—was our relationship. I can no longer countenance such an arrangement. If I am to have the necessary faith in the reality of my new position, everything about me must be changed accordingly. And you must either accept my perfectly reasonable decision—

SYBIL. Which is—?

CHRISTIAN. How shall I put it? Shall we say merely a greater distance between us for the future? It will be made possible by means of the sum mentioned and a certain monthly allowance.

SYBIL. You tear my feelings to shreds.

CHRISTIAN. I follow your own teachings. You will perceive that when applied to you they hurt. I am about to embark upon public life. I can't afford false steps.

SYBIL. It's true the world allows you a paid . . .

CHRISTIAN (*holding her mouth shut*). Etcetera, etcetera.

SYBIL. Am I the only thing in your life that might embarrass you in the future? Is there no greater obstacle to your social ambition than my relations with you?

CHRISTIAN. None. As you know.

SYBIL. If you'll be sensible . . .

CHRISTIAN. I make no bones about it. I can face the world as what I am. My appearance and my brains are all I need. But my parents, as you know, are lower class.

SYBIL. So if you're going to face the world, they must . . .

CHRISTIAN. Let me think for myself as you know I can. They're lower class. My good mother especially.

SYBIL. They weren't able to teach you rudimentary manners.

CHRISTIAN. The policy I'm pursuing is most unusual for a man of my class. It would obviously be a mistake to call attention to the abyss between my origin and my present status by dragging in my honored progenitors. It would be the utmost bad form.

SYBIL. And as *good* form is what you now worship before all . . .

CHRISTIAN. Your irony cuts no ice. You have a bad conscience about your own past. Nobody knows who *your* parents were. You got rid of them, just murdered them. Perhaps your father was a jailbird. Was his name really Hull? (*Laughing.*) Well, your charm is your fortune, and you have that in any case. Still he must have had something about him to have fathered a splendid creature like you. But you interrupted me. I have explained the discrepancy between a man's origin and his attainments. In addition the thought of being indebted to others—even for my existence—is merely enfeebling. My world began with me, and with me it ends. Since I hope and fear for myself alone, consideration for others is out of the question. And so: I fear father and mother.

SYBIL. What do you propose? Bribing them to stay out of sight?

CHRISTIAN. My father is not shy. He himself is asking for money.

SYBIL. You have learned the value of money anyway.

CHRISTIAN. I have learned all sorts of things.

SYBIL. And when you're so logical, someone who loves you can hardly help agreeing with you.

CHRISTIAN. I hope my parents will be equally understanding. So we agree?

SYBIL. I am adjusting myself to the new regime already. A certain distance has come between us, and I already feel an appropriate trace of servility.

CHRISTIAN. Things don't become what they are by being talked about but by being done.

SYBIL. They do become clearer though.

CHRISTIAN. How clever!

SYBIL. Christian, I love you. You are the one mistake in my ledger. I would give the whole twenty-four thousand to have you back again.

CHRISTIAN. Then you deserve to die in misery and want. Here, here's a kiss for nothing. Now you've made a mess of my tie.

SYBIL. It looked horrible anyway.

CHRISTIAN. I have learned many things from you, but one thing I never have—to tie a tie faultlessly. Show me—for the hundredth time.

SYBIL (*tying the necktie around the neck of a large vase*). First, a plain knot—second, one end through—so—third, the other one through.

CHRISTIAN. There's a bit sticking out on the right.

SYBIL. One cuts it off with the scissors.

CHRISTIAN. Then I'll need a new one every time.

SYBIL. With the result that those who know will know that *you* know.

CHRISTIAN. Which is the purpose of everything.

SYBIL (*with a low curtsy*). Mr. President, your humble servant.

CHRISTIAN. It's no joke.

SYBIL. I quite understand.

(SYBIL *goes out.*)

CHRISTIAN. On the whole, a very pleasant creature! (*At the desk.*) But now I must concentrate. (*He writes.*) "Dear Count Palen, I accept your kind invitation for the 26th of this month with humble thanks." With humble thanks? We'll see. "Greetings to the Countess." Too familiar. Too humble on the one hand and too familiar on the other. Above all he mustn't guess how glad I am to go. This paper's wrong. Letterhead would be better: Secretary of the Monambo Mines. "Dear Count *von* Palen." The "von" indicates respect. As my first written communication to that level of society, this letter must be absolutely correct and still meaningful. How does he write himself? "Dear Herr Maske, Will you come to dinner with us on the 26th? *En tout petit comité.* Yours." On ordinary cheap paper. The tone: friendly, casually intimate. "Dinner" is superb! We shall be a shade more formal, but all the same I'd like to insert one Latin word. For the sake of the masculine touch. How can a man be important for a minute or two to such persons—in five syllables? It's a prize question, and the answer's got to be found. Five syllables now, with lots of vowels and a good rolling start. (*He walks up and down the room.*) Dum-da-dum-da-da. "Indisputable." To my ear the second syllable is longer than the first. The rhythm's wrong. Praenumerando—that's the right *sound,* but of course it doesn't make sense. Dum-da-dum-da-da. I *must* find it.

THEOBALD MASKE (*enters*). Here I am. Mother's waiting downstairs.

CHRISTIAN. Father!

THEOBALD. It was just bad luck. I didn't ask for it. Can't stand fireworks, anyway. But women never know where to stop. We must look the facts in the face!

CHRISTIAN. Since you retired, you've had a little surprise for us every year.

THEOBALD. You should have let me go on with my job. You had me idle too soon. I've as much energy now as I ever had, so I have to use it up in—er—multifarious pursuits. Now I must come to an understanding with her.

CHRISTIAN. I'm going to call mother up to begin with.

THEOBALD. There's our own business first.

CHRISTIAN. We'll settle it along with the rest. No one will understand.

THEOBALD. What?

CHRISTIAN. A sum of money will be mentioned in our conversation.

THEOBALD. How? What is this?

CHRISTIAN. A sum of money, I say, one of many thousands. If we see eye to eye on the other matters, you can quietly add a thousand marks to take care of your little—mishap.

THEOBALD. You'll make conditions?

CHRISTIAN. I'll make conditions.

THEOBALD. I'm curious to hear them.

CHRISTIAN (*at the window*). There she is. (*He waves his hand.*) She saw me. She's coming up. How unspeakably she's dressed! You used a word just now that gave me an idea.

THEOBALD. In what connection?

CHRISTIAN. It went to a different rhythm from the one I wanted, but it had a ring. Remind me of it later. Now . . .

THEOBALD. A thousand?

CHRISTIAN. If we agree on the rest.

(*He goes out.*)

THEOBALD. So I'm left up in the air!

(CHRISTIAN *and* LUISE MASKE *enter.*)

Put your hat on straight, Luise. It's down over your nose like a student's cap. We're thinking of moving into the big city here. I'll find something or other to keep me from dying of dry-rot . . .

LUISE. It's one of father's ideas!

CHRISTIAN. I must tell you both that as my attention is concentrated on the goal I've set myself, I wouldn't have a free moment to spend with you.

LUISE. Surely. Surely. I knew it.

THEOBALD. We're used to that lately. It's little enough you've bothered about us. And what may this goal of yours be?

CHRISTIAN. I expect to be made President of the Company.

LUISE. President!

THEOBALD. Of the Company!

CHRISTIAN. If I am to do big things, I shall require consideration from you, which means—above all—

THEOBALD. Now listen to me. We went without for twenty years, and gave you a good education, as everyone can see. Many's the time you cost us our Sunday roast. We loved you as the monkey loves its young . . .

LUISE (*softly to herself*). President of the Company.

CHRISTIAN (*trying to recall the word*). Dum-da-dum . . .

THEOBALD. We stayed in the background so you could make your way in the world. But we've not been growing younger, and now it's this way: if we're going to get anything out of you, we'll have to hurry.

CHRISTIAN. First of all I'd like to correct one gross mis-statement: I cannot remember that you have denied yourself anything on my account since I was sixteen years old.

THEOBALD. Good God!

LUISE. Father!

CHRISTIAN. I remember you of old, Father—how you grabbed four-fifths of all the space, how the whole household revolved around you. I earned enough at tutoring while I was still in high school to pay my way, living expenses and all. Who was it that forced a boy of seventeen to eat his dinner in his father's presence, standing . . .

THEOBALD. I loved you like a monkey. You were a dear chap. Wasn't he, Mother?

LUISE. So small . . . (*She indicates the size.*)

CHRISTIAN. You were always busy with your own affairs. You never bestowed a thought upon my life until today. But now you've changed obviously. The widening scope of my life has made a big impression on you.

THEOBALD. This is boring. Well, how do things stand?

CHRISTIAN. You happened to turn up on the very day when I am closing the books of my whole life to date. No false entries will be found in them.

LUISE. What does he mean?

THEOBALD. You'll soon know.

CHRISTIAN (*taking a book from a safe*). I have entered in this book the actual expenses which, to the best of my recollection, you have incurred on my account. Interest at the rate of five per cent has been added.

THEOBALD. You want a reckoning?

CHRISTIAN. Yes.

THEOBALD (*sitting down*). Let's see. (*He puts on his glasses.*)

LUISE. What do you mean?

CHRISTIAN. Patience, Mother.

THEOBALD (*reading*). Maintenance from his first year to his sixteenth years—six hundred marks per annum. If that includes the doctor and the druggist, it's skimpy.

CHRISTIAN. I was never ill.

THEOBALD. I remember measles. And colds. Your nose was forever running. I can see it now. We gave you camomile tea. Gobs of it.

LUISE. You had a temperature of a hundred and six once. I thought my heart had stopped beating.

CHRISTIAN. Everything is covered by the sum I have entered.

LUISE. Red spots as big as saucers all over his little body.

THEOBALD. Sixteen times six hundred makes nine thousand six hundred marks. Look here. "Miscellaneous Items"—How can you pretend to remember all the items over sixteen years? There's no counting them. This entry is suspect from the very beginning.

CHRISTIAN. Certain amounts I've given you from time to time—lately in particular—have not been entered.

THEOBALD. All right, all right.

CHRISTIAN (*to himself*). If only I could remember that word. (*He stares at the letter lying on the table.*)

LUISE (*shyly to* CHRISTIAN). And the ulcer on your neck, that time.

CHRISTIAN. That's right, Mother.

THEOBALD. "Half a dozen shirts and collars, two pairs of shoes, to go to the university with—fifty marks. A gold ring—" Well, for heaven's sake, so Luise slipped the kid that ring! And I turned everything upside down hunting for it.

CHRISTIAN. It was Mother's. She gave it to me for my start in life.

THEOBALD. It cost a hundred marks.

LUISE. You still wear it?

CHRISTIAN (*shows it on his finger*). Though it gets tighter every day.

THEOBALD. Very silly. But just like Luise. "Grand total, eleven thousand." Hm! "Plus interest, eleven thousand eight hundred marks."

CHRISTIAN (*with emphasis*). Eleven thousand eight hundred. (*Clears his throat.*)

THEOBALD. So—that's what you're paying me?

CHRISTIAN. That's what I owe you.

THEOBALD. And you wish to discharge the debt?

CHRISTIAN. I'll pay it.

LUISE (*his hand in her hands, she looks at the ring*). It could be made larger.

THEOBALD. Well—I call that simply grand, my boy. You've handled the whole thing famously. (*Embracing him.*) I like to see things done with style. I can see we're reaching complete agreement.

CHRISTIAN. You expressed the intention of coming to live here in this city. I don't wish it.

THEOBALD. Is that an order?

CHRISTIAN. I have given you back your money. One good turn deserves another.

THEOBALD. But I was all set to go.

LUISE. The boy must have his reasons.

THEOBALD. The woman drives me mad! It's impossible to speak a sane word while she's about.

CHRISTIAN (*accompanies* LUISE *to the door*). Mother, wouldn't you like to have a look around? And see how I live?

LUISE (*gently*). Don't fret yourself. Everything shall be as you say. (*She goes out.*)

CHRISTIAN. As I said, if I had you here, I should have to divide my energies. And I mustn't.

THEOBALD. Is that the condition that goes with your eleven thousand eight hundred marks and so on?

CHRISTIAN. A presupposition, rather.

THEOBALD. Then it has to be considered. Where does our advantage lie? It's all very well to love you like monkeys, we also have to live in a good neighborhood. How much will the eleven thousand bring in?

CHRISTIAN. Six hundred in industrial stocks.

THEOBALD. Are you out of your mind? *My* money goes into the savings bank.

CHRISTIAN. Five hundred.

THEOBALD. That's not much. Eleven thousand sounded like something. Five hundred wouldn't feed the cat. And you want me to give up for five hundred the common man's most precious freedom—the freedom to live where he chooses? I must think it over, weigh the pro and con. No—if I give you my word as an honest man that your mother and I'll stay where we are . . .

CHRISTIAN. That's not what I have in mind.

THEOBALD. You don't want this and you don't want that. For God's sake what *do* you want?

CHRISTIAN. This invasion of yours today shows that I should never be safe from your visits.

THEOBALD. Invasion? Invasion?

CHRISTIAN. I told you. My life is about to take an entirely new turn. For the present especially I must be free from all family considerations.

THEOBALD. Nothing like this has ever happened before in all history! We've eaten dry bread so you could have everything. One sacrifice after another, whatever you say. How can a man be a parent without making sacrifices? Don't parents have to give up some pleasure or other at every breath their little brat draws? Isn't their sleep disturbed, their dinner, their every pleasure? Always something wrong: when it isn't money it's aggravation. One day the brat throws up, and the next he won't throw down. And all the silly birthdays and christenings, nothing but a nuisance . . . (*Loudly, to* CHRISTIAN, *who is sitting silently in an armchair.*) And this is filial affection! (*Hits the table with clenched fist.*) *This* is filial affection!

LUISE (*sticks her head through the partly opened door and unseen by* THEOBALD, *motions to* CHRISTIAN *to keep calm*). I'm not disturbing anything!

THEOBALD. What? (*As* CHRISTIAN *remains quiet, he throws himself into a chair at a distance from him and says calmly.*) If I'd known, you'd have been drowned in your first bath. (*Pause.*) We're living more than a hundred miles away from you as it is. And they prate about filial affection! (*He gives a laugh.*) Ha! Have you thought about the practical side? We could only just make ends meet as it is, with my pension *and* your five hundred. No one can expect us to go through all the fuss of moving away and settling in a new place without compensation.

CHRISTIAN. No one does expect it.

THEOBALD. *Generous* compensation. But who's going to pay it?

CHRISTIAN. Under certain circumstances, I will.

THEOBALD. Well I'll be darned.

CHRISTIAN. Even in Europe there are a great many cities noted for charming scenery and economic advantages. I mean, if you don't prefer America.

THEOBALD. What?!

CHRISTIAN. Keep calm, keep calm. (*He has taken out a large atlas and a Baedeker.*) Brussels, for instance. (*Reading from the book.*) "Brussels, the capital of the kingdom of Belgium: population eight hundred thousand. The city is situated in a fertile region on the banks of the Senne, a tributary of the Scheldt. The upper city where the government buildings are is the home of the aristocracy and polite society."

THEOBALD (*who has been sitting comfortably and listening devoutly*). Not bad, let's see. (*He reads aloud.*) "And polite society. Language and customs French." Can you see a 100% German turning himself into a damned foreigner? No!

CHRISTIAN. The place I had most in mind was Zurich. A perfectly ideal spot, a little paradise in every respect. And the language is German.

THEOBALD. Let's hear about it.

CHRISTIAN (*reading from another volume*). "Zurich, with approximately two hundred thousand inhabitants, is the most important city in Switzerland. It is situated on Lake Zurich and the evergreen Limmat."

THEOBALD. Evergreen, they call pine trees evergreen.

CHRISTIAN. "On the west side flows the Sihl, in spring a rushing torrent."

THEOBALD. I could do without that. There's water enough already. I'm afraid I can't swim.

CHRISTIAN. "The city is magnificently situated on a crystal lake whose gently rising banks are dotted with tall houses, orchards and vineyards."

THEOBALD. Very pretty.

CHRISTIAN (*reading*). "In the background the snow-covered Alps; to the left we behold the mighty ridge of the Glärnisch." (*Pointing in the atlas.*) This white spot here!

THEOBALD. Good God!

CHRISTIAN (*reading*). "The cooking is good, the people simple and unspoiled."

THEOBALD. As you might say.

CHRISTIAN. "The enchanting surroundings invite the excursionist."

THEOBALD. The Promised Land!

CHRISTIAN. "Lucerne and Interlaken, in short the entire Alpine region will always be at hand—your own property, so to speak." Have you any notion what is meant by "Alpine glow"?

THEOBALD. Well, what?

CHRISTIAN. It is a scenic drama of incredible and unparalleled magnificence. If you accept Zurich, also the condition that you leave me alone entirely for the next few years, I could round out your income to very considerable proportions.

THEOBALD (*after a pause*). I have moral scruples.

CHRISTIAN. Comment is superfluous.

THEOBALD. I prefer to discuss it.

CHRISTIAN. The life of a man like me is built on facts. Your conversation only holds me up. One other important matter is still undecided.

THEOBALD. I'm sixty years old today, your mother is nearly the same. We haven't had many of the good things of life, and we'll not be with you much longer.

CHRISTIAN. My mind is on more important matters: the tone you're using makes no impression. The day will soon come when we shall discuss these things comfortably and in detail. But now I'm wasting chances every second. You shall have two thousand four hundred francs from me each year. You move in three weeks. Make haste, Father, decide. I'm impatient. I'm running in a race. For a position in the world. And there are many other runners. I stop for an instant, and they rush by in a flood.

THEOBALD. You've got me dizzy. Never saw anything like you. How am I to swallow all these new ideas? And man shall not live by bread alone: where in all this can I find the -er- higher motive? The -er- spiritual purpose?

CHRISTIAN. Here and now. I give you five minutes.

THEOBALD. But I'm not convinced. I'm all mixed up.

CHRISTIAN. Trust me!

THEOBALD. When can I find the -er- spiritual purpose?

CHRISTIAN. Later. Is it settled, Father?

THEOBALD. God's whiskers! You've turned me inside out.

CHRISTIAN. Two thousand four hundred, that makes nineteen hundred marks.

THEOBALD. Plus five hundred. With what I've got already that will make close on five thousand six hundred.

CHRISTIAN. Seven thousand francs. (*At the door.*) Mother!

THEOBALD. On the Limmat? I'm stunned.

CHRISTIAN (*handing him the atlas and guide books*). Inform yourself.

LUISE (*enters, softly to* CHRISTIAN). Everything will be as you want it, I'll see to that . . . That cover on your night table, those underclothes lace and batiste—Oh, Christel, do be careful with women! I know pleasure's a temptation that comes to each of us at one time or another. But one has children, one is President of the Company and can swear before God: my mother was a spotless woman!

THEOBALD (*still stunned*). In the Tyrol!

LUISE. That's something. A good sum of money.

CHRISTIAN. Certainly, Mother. (*Embraces her.*)

LUISE (*as she leaves*). My Christel!

(LUISE, THEOBALD, CHRISTIAN *go out.* CHRISTIAN *quickly returns.*)

CHRISTIAN. I had it on the tip of my tongue that time—(*Looking at the letter.*) He was talking about his premature retirement; dissipate his strength in . . . in . . . what *could* it have been? . . . in *multifarious,* multifarious pursuits! I've got it! (*Writing.*) "Dear Count Palen, I regret that the *multifarious* demands of business prevent my accepting your kind invitation." So it's turned into a refusal, but it may be better so, who knows? (*He has rung the bell. Goes out. Enters again immediately with* COUNT PALEN.)

COUNT. I have come to discuss again the matter of your appointment. A personal discussion. Before the board of directors can make a definite announcement to the stockholders they naturally require to know what the Company can expect from you. Disliking business conversations as I do, I asked Baron Rohrschach to make the investigation. But it was thought more suitable that I should settle the matter as I am on more intimate terms with you.

CHRISTIAN. Thank you, Count.

COUNT. The Monambo Mines are, as you know, an enterprise run by a small group of people whose views are essentially the same. Business is one thing, a man's political philosophy is another. The man at the head of a syndicate like this should be—er—one of ourselves. In outlook, I mean. (CHRISTIAN *bows.*) We consider that in you we have found a man in whom competence is united with the far rarer gift of a sense of values, a feeling for the hard-won niceties of life. That of course is indispensable in cases where the brutal candor of figures has to be met with—er—an adequate counterforce. (CHRISTIAN *bows.*) You have frequently expressed opinions that coincide perfectly with our own. Indeed you have shown an almost greater perspicacity. In the vocabulary of the liberal party, I should call you an—er—aristocratic reactionary. (*He laughs.*) In fact, what has most deeply impressed me is your fervor. It is a mark of sincerity. Yes?

CHRISTIAN. Very true.

COUNT. Remarkable. And something to reflect upon. In short, I am quite taken with you. You come of an excellent family. Your education is perfect even to your recognition of the fact that—in view of the obviously special qualities we have acquired—inconspicuous uniformity is the thing. One sees it in gesture, in the tying of a tie. Well and good, all we need now is some sort of statement from you that we can present to our shareholders as, so to speak, your confession of faith.

CHRISTIAN. I understand.

COUNT. The case of a Rohrschach is a little different; the title of "Baron" suffices, assuming a man's not *déclassé.* Otherwise, certain guarantees are desirable. Many a man of the middle class has behind him the achievements of notable ancestors.

CHRISTIAN. Nothing of the sort in my case.

COUNT. No reproach, my dear sir. Middle-class people of high repute also stand upon the achievements of their families, of their traditions. Your ancestors too have built up a stock of superiority. You need only draw on it, and there's your statement. I have not yet had the privilege of meeting your father, your parents, in short . . .

CHRISTIAN. Dead. All of them—dead.

COUNT. May I say, then, with emphasis, that you are their very adequate representative? I see you are moved?

CHRISTIAN. I am, Count. At last the time has come when I may give voice to a longing which has possessed me since boyhood, when I may confess that I have always longed to resemble those whose titles are the outward token of their forebears, of their achievements. I have longed for the opportunity to second their labors and impose upon the world the principles whose historic guardians they are. It is not for me to tell what sacrifices I have already made in the good cause, but here in your presence I am ready to swear that my whole life is dedicated to it.

COUNT. You are a splendid fellow, Maske, the real thing. And now you have entirely convinced me. I thank you. And I think you may take your appointment for granted. May I smoke? Can you accept my invitation for Friday?

CHRISTIAN. Well, I—

COUNT. What is it?

CHRISTIAN. Then I will. Despite the—er—*multifarious* demands of business.

COUNT. I know how busy you are. And you'll find my daughter Marianne is the sort to appreciate a man of your type.

CHRISTIAN. I have often heard that the Countess is uncommonly gifted.

COUNT. *Enchanté,* my dear Maske.

CHRISTIAN. I am greatly obliged to you, Herr Count.

COUNT. *Herr* Count—sensitive to nuance too, I see!

CHRISTIAN. Otherwise inconspicuous uniformity is the thing!

COUNT. Witty and very charming, my dear friend!

(*Exit.*)

CHRISTIAN (*who has escorted him to the door, returns, looks hastily in the mirror and then begins to tie a necktie on a vase*). First a plain knot

. . . Second, one end through . . . so . . . Then the other end . . . And now the scissors. (*He cuts.*) If thine eye offend thee, pluck it out! At last I've got it right! Victory!

ACT II

(*Drawing room at* CHRISTIAN MASKE'S.)

COUNT. The servant says he'll be back at any moment.

MARIANNE. We came ten minutes early. That's the Corot over there.

COUNT. The pretext for our visit!

MARIANNE. It's a lovely picture. What luck, to be able to live among such things.

COUNT. It can be yours.

MARIANNE. If I'm his wife? Are you serious, Father?

COUNT. Yes, Marianne. We haven't mentioned it, but what else has occupied our minds these past weeks? And lately there has been no mistaking the man.

MARIANNE. Is he in love with me?

COUNT. Put it another way. Suppose he had none of this wealth which could rescue us from so many difficulties—would you still take him?

MARIANNE. That is a question I cannot answer. The first time you brought him to the house, I knew little about him and nothing about his circumstances. My feelings made their own choice. It seems to me that everything is borne down by his will as by a force of nature. And willingly, too.

COUNT. *Tiens!*

MARIANNE. Yes, Father: Marianne has decided.

COUNT. I had taken it for granted that you would have a certain resistance to overcome.

MARIANNE. I have. We're by no means intimate. Our conversation has never been anything but small-talk. The moment he came near me I felt under attack. But I felt that he—and he alone—could conquer me.

COUNT. He gives me the creeps.

MARIANNE. Why? Have you found him incorrect? In the smallest detail?

COUNT. No.

MARIANNE. Isn't he one of us?

COUNT. Absolutely. That's the thing I resent. I have been watching him for two years, and the very thing I found sympathetic in the beginning almost horrifies me now. If this bourgeois is really following his natural bent in living our life, where does class distinction come in? I have always considered nobility a product of breeding; I thought noble qualities took centuries to produce. At least they could never be acquired in a single generation. As the Duke of Devonshire said to a parvenu who envied him the beauty of his lawns and asked advice: All you have to do is have them well swept every morning for several hundred years. *Voilà!* I have never in all my life attempted to accomplish anything in particular. I've only been a nobleman—conscious of special innate qualities. If this man proves that such priceless values can be acquired without ancestors, I am mocked. I lose my self-respect.

MARIANNE. Might not an exceptional mind understand our special qualities? And with effort accomplish the work of many generations in one?

COUNT. Nothing can be a true possession except by long tenure. Whatever is not so possessed is merely borrowed, and sooner or later the fraud is revealed. The lighting is wrong, a mishap occurs. I'm waiting for one to occur to Herr Maske.

MARIANNE. You are rather deeply involved in his career.

COUNT. Not to the extent of becoming his victim. Rather to discover the wound that will eventually kill him. Perhaps even to give it him myself.

MARIANNE. Then fate might set me against you.

COUNT. God prevent it!

MARIANNE. *You* prevent it! That man stirred me for the first time in my life. And the excitement he aroused has not subsided! I still feel a mixture of pleasure and repulsion—a sacred and secret emotion which will declare itself when the time comes but which cannot be forced.

COUNT. Will he unmask himself before our eyes?

MARIANNE. On the contrary, he will become more and more inscrutable and surprising. Even the little I've seen of him makes me quite certain he is no ordinary man. He stands far beyond the scope of our predictions.

COUNT. Marianne!

MARIANNE. I believe this. I feel it, Father. But whatever happens you gave me a glorious youth—twenty-five happy years—I'm grateful to you for that.

COUNT. I've spoiled you.

MARIANE. And will continue to do so.

COUNT. Only to the limit of the possible.

MARIANNE (*tensely*). The limits of love are not easily reached.

CHRISTIAN (*enters in riding clothes*). Ah! Most gracious Countess! Count! Forgive me, I can at least plead that the Colonial Minister kept me all this time. He wanted advice.

COUNT. He is forever singing your praises and is anxious to present you to our Gracious Emperor.

CHRISTIAN. His question would require more talent to answer than I possess. In matters of state, the responsibilities are enormous. Only opinions directly inspired by God are of use.

COUNT. *Magnifique!* What were you riding today?

CHRISTIAN. A colt by Charmant out of Miss Gorse.—You like the picture, Countess?

MARIANNE. I am not expert in such things. But I find it moving.

CHRISTIAN. It's not Corot's masterpiece. But the tonality and values are unique.

COUNT. How is it you are so positive?

CHRISTIAN. I have seen a good two or three hundred Corot's in my time.

COUNT. Where do you find the time?

CHRISTIAN. I don't. The first picture I ever saw was a flash of lightning to me. I struck fire. And was wise to all the others. (*To* MARIANNE.) That's how I am.

COUNT. We must go. (*To* MARIANNE.) You are due at the Friesen's at half past eleven.

CHRISTIAN (*to the* COUNT). Are you accompanying the Countess, or may I ask you to stay a moment?

COUNT (*to* MARIANNE). Do you need me?

MARIANNE. No, stay.

CHRISTIAN (*to* MARIANNE). Let me take you to your carriage.

(MARIANNE *and* CHRISTIAN *exeunt.*)

COUNT (*takes a book from table*). Almanach de Gotha. Handbook of the Nobility. Investigation, eh? (*He turns the pages and reads.*) Palen. Old Westphalian nobility, appears in records for the first time with Rütger Palen, 1220. Augustus Aloysius to Elizabeth Countess of Fürstenbach, died at Ernegg, July sixteen, 1901. My good Elizabeth. Children: Friedrich Mathias, the last of our male line, and Marianne Josefa, who is about to marry a Herr Maske.

CHRISTIAN (*enters*). The Countess hopes to pick you up here when she comes by about twelve o'clock. Count Augustus von Palen, I ask for the hand of your daughter Marianne.

COUNT. You are brief. You must have thought this request over very carefully.

CHRISTIAN. As carefully as you and your daughter have thought over the answer, Count.

COUNT. You are mistaken. I don't definitely know the Countess' decision.

CHRISTIAN. Indefinitely, then? But forgive me, I should like to have your views first.

COUNT. Personally I disapprove. But that is merely a point of view, and has no real weight. Had you counted on my consent?

CHRISTIAN. I felt you were strongly opposed to the idea.

COUNT. Despite my admiration for you, I find that the gulf between us does not diminish. To be quite truthful, however, you seem to have made an enormous impression upon my daughter.

CHRISTIAN. Would you like to have more detailed information as to my circumstances?

COUNT. I have watched your progress with my own eyes and am only too well aware of the financial and social successes your gifts have brought you. I am certain of your future.

CHRISTIAN. Is there something to complain of in my character?

COUNT. Nothing.

CHRISTIAN. Then might I ask—?

COUNT. I will be frank. It is a case of class prejudice.

CHRISTIAN. Thank you. That was inevitable. The quality I have always honored most in your class is your utter inaccessibility. If your objection had been directed towards me personally I should have minded much more.

COUNT. How can you both honor a principle and try to infringe it?

CHRISTIAN. I love your daughter.

COUNT. And if she were not the Countess Palen would you *still* wish to marry her?

CHRISTIAN. That I cannot say. Her charm is indivisible.

COUNT. Assuming the Countess' consent—

(CHRISTIAN *makes an involuntary movement which betrays his agitation.*)

I thought I knew you. But now that I have to face the possibility of a closer association, I realize that you are still a stranger.

CHRISTIAN. In my class we have no books to tell us where our pedigree began. We are left groping in obscurity.

COUNT. True. A middle-class name is a mere label on anonymity. You have no records, you are not observed. We whose record is in this book live and die under the eyes of our peers. We renounce the joys of a free life among nameless masses. And in return we have the right to see our services noted and rewarded.

CHRISTIAN. Undoubtedly. But a social circle such as yours should have a place for any man who is strong enough to hold the same views and stand by them.

COUNT. That is a strength which only time and many generations can prove.

CHRISTIAN. A son of the middle-class may also be known by his forefathers.

COUNT. Who are your parents? Who are your parents' parents?

CHRISTIAN. Civil servants. They were devoted to the service of the State —if only as petty officials. My father . . .

COUNT. The individual's accomplishments shine all the brighter against a humble background, as our Royal Master lately taught us. The case of the Minister of Posts and Telegraphs, whose background is the same as yours, is most instructive.

CHRISTIAN (*laughing loudly*). A procession of shabbily but cleanly clad parents approaches from all sides.

COUNT. It does, indeed. Well, now we know each other's opinions. The decision isn't ours to make, anyhow . . . we can only wait. There is just one thing more that I must mention: My daughter has no dowry. You got rich, we lost nearly everything. We have had to practice the most rigid economy to pay my son's allowance. His regiment needs him.

CHRISTIAN (*bows*). A matter we need not discuss.

THE SERVANT (*enters*). The Countess' carriage.

COUNT. I shall let you know the decision. (*Exit.*)

CHRISTIAN. I could have told him they're living in Zurich. He has no money. He'd have had to swallow it, and sponsor their social debut. Well, I let the opportunity slip. But the situation is still under control. Why wait? They must come here. At once! The moment has come to introduce them. To take the plunge. What a sight! How the old folks will enjoy it! (*He writes, then reads aloud.*) Come by the next train. Wonderful surprise awaits you. (*He rings.*) Everything will astonish them. From the carriage I meet them in at the station to the rooms they'll stay in. Rooms with bath! Mother shall take her bolster to bed with her too. I think of her lying in bed looking back on the days when we used to dream about my future together—she will feel she has not lived in vain, when she sees how immensely the reality has surpassed the dream. We'll cure her of her worst vulgarities, and dressmakers and milliners will do the rest.

(SYBIL *enters.*)

I'm glad to see you, my child. Who do you think is coming here?

SYBIL. Your parents!

CHRISTIAN. Who told you?

SYBIL. Necessity. For two years after they left you simply longed to have them back. I could tell what was in your mind as you dropped off to sleep. And why your eyes lit up when you talked of big profits. In your own peculiar way you've been quite keen on your old people since you've had them at a safe distance. In the end you talked of nothing without referring to them. If only by roundabout inference.

CHRISTIAN. I have missed them very much.

SYBIL. By now you're convinced of that.

CHRISTIAN. Mother and I were twin souls. She did not exist except in me. I was a little god to her and she foresaw my great career and approved. We had ceased even to talk about it, a look and a smile said it all. Father was the bass accompaniment.

SYBIL. Was my confidence any less than hers?

CHRISTIAN. You insisted on being thanked. But *there* was a person forever unthanked and forever happy in my happiness!

SYBIL. But your father behaved shamelessly. He always knew he could scare you to death by threatening to turn up. And he got plenty of money out of you by doing so.

CHRISTIAN. He didn't do so to any great extent. What's a couple of thousand?

SYBIL. If he had the least idea of the style you're living in now, he'd play the game to better purpose. He'd take good care of himself.

CHRISTIAN. Let him. I ask nothing better. That is the fiendish thing about families with no roots in the past. They have no feeling of unity, of—er—togetherness. They don't understand what it means to derive life and energy from a single center. One of them gorges while the other starves. But if we could only acquire the idea that we spring from a common root, that we are tied to the tree by every vein and fibre, that we are dependent upon its well-being for our own, the happiness of any of our branches would bring pleasure to us all.

SYBIL. A frightfully venerable idea. *Our* generation never inspired that.

CHRISTIAN. How dare you take that position, my girl? Do you know more of the upheavals of our time than I? You are drunk on the catchwords of Social Democracy. The rights of the poor and such drivel.

SYBIL. I see what exists: Millions who—if they are to eat—must trample on those who block the pantry door!

CHRISTIAN. The struggle for existence! I've been through it. But I dug myself out *another* way. An urge came from within. I took the path of comfort: I knew that real life was at the end of it. And you saw me reach my goal, tearing the rags off my back, exchanging the flapping ribbon at my neck for a well-knotted tie, and gaining, little by little, that knowledge of form which is the mark of the higher man.

SYBIL. There is no end to that climb. On the top step you will still find someone stronger waiting for you—the mortal enemy whom you will have to overcome or be destroyed in the attempt.

CHRISTIAN. Communist propaganda! You are generations short of the truth.

SYBIL. To think it was I who taught him—

CHRISTIAN. Not to eat fish with his knife and not to pick his teeth? You never went beyond the superficial things. Outwardly you are a woman of the world, Sybil, but inwardly? I wonder.

SYBIL. I never wanted to be a woman of the world—inwardly.

CHRISTIAN. The grapes are sour.

SYBIL. And because you've at last made up your mind to bring back your parents . . .

CHRISTIAN. Whom I love . . .

SYBIL. Yes, ever since the talk of Humble Progenitors began.

CHRISTIAN. . . . and adore!

SYBIL. Because it's the fashion. If you really cared for them, you couldn't let . . .

CHRISTIAN. Not another word!

SYBIL. You couldn't let your mother's Sunday straw bonnet and your father's shoes provide entertainment for those new friends of yours. Your first plan saved them from ridicule and you from humiliation. It was the greatest kindness you could have done them. It was clever, too, and served its purpose.

CHRISTIAN. I made money. And need no longer be concerned with the mere necessities of life. I have earned the right to relax and contemplate life's amenities. The first luxury a man of fortune can afford is his family.

SYBIL. Your father and mother are not luxuries you can afford or not afford. If you honestly love them, and feel like worshiping at the shrine of the Family—do it in private. Don't sacrifice *them* to your vanity, your passion for form. Marry your countess if you want to, but don't give her your parents to judge you by. Remain strange and mysterious, you have so much that others have not. You don't have to have parents, too.

CHRISTIAN. But I've set my heart on the idea. I have done the utmost to get an appointment for Father—took every bit of influence I could bring to bear. Don't cross me! I have made up my mind! There are things you are not qualified to judge. *Your* life is but a succession of accidents!

SYBIL. You are trying to put an impassable gulf between us.

CHRISTIAN. It was there long before today. In thought *and* deed we are strangers. Go!

SYBIL. Such utter strangers as all that? Wasn't it you who borrowed 20 marks from me not long ago?

CHRISTIAN. You're dreaming. I paid for your services. And now I'm paying you for the last time. No more words.

SYBIL. There *is* no word that expresses what I think of you. Or if there is I'd give my life to know it.

CHRISTIAN. Go home and consult the dictionary. If you believe I am what you have just suggested, you are creating a false likeness of me, and so ruining your memories of the great love of your life. However, that is your own affair. But if you tell tales, I shall see that the law deals with you. Ruthlessly.

(SYBIL *stands looking at him as though unable to believe her ears, then dashes out.*)

So much for that. The bridge is now closed. But one no longer saw where it led in any case. The attempts of a miserable embryo to make one disloyal to one's nature, to necessary decisions. With mere talk. (*He has a rapier in his hand and is doing fencing exercises.*) But since you well know the colors of your temperament, don't grow pale before your own image, form a picture of yourself, make it good, and never mind what spectators write underneath.

(*The bell rings insistently.*)

Who's there?

(*He goes to the door.*)

(*A moment later, his voice is heard outside in a cry.*)

Mother!

(*He returns with* THEOBALD *in deep mourning.*)

THEOBALD (*after a pause, during which* CHRISTIAN *leans against the door sobbing*). There's no arguing with fate, Christian. We must look the facts in the face! If it hadn't come on me like a thunderbolt, I could have let you down easier. But your mother always was one for surprises. So her death was a surprise, too.

CHRISTIAN. We must bring her here and see that she is buried with all due pomp . . .

THEOBALD. She was—yesterday.

CHRISTIAN. And I was never sent for.

THEOBALD. I thought, why put you to all the trouble? Besides, how was I to know you could arrange to leave? A funeral is a public event after all. The thing came over her all of a sudden, she knew her end had come, and she just managed to say: "don't you let my Christel know." Her wishes. Are you cold?

(CHRISTIAN *goes out.*)

It's bowled him over. Well, I'll be darned.

CHRISTIAN (*returns with a black suit over his arm. He changes his clothes during the following, partially concealed by a screen*). Now you can tell me all about it.

THEOBALD. It's soon told. She was sitting on her bench drinking coffee. You know how she always did, with a lump of sugar on her tongue. She said she was hot, and fell in a heap.

CHRISTIAN (*sobbing spasmodically*). No illness before, no pain?

THEOBALD. Nothing.

CHRISTIAN. What were her last days like? Was she happy?

THEOBALD. She always made you think she was. That was Luise.

CHRISTIAN. How did things stand between you after that—regrettable event?

THEOBALD. I didn't overdo it. Only every now and then at stated intervals. She never found out.

CHRISTIAN. You didn't break with that person then and there?

THEOBALD. No—she was a queer one, so I thought I'd better put off the split. But I kept it well in hand. And so your mother's last days were calm.

CHRISTIAN. I shall call in an architect, a sculptor at once. She shall have the monument *my mother* deserved. I could never express how much she was to me. Perhaps an artist will be able to express it.

THEOBALD. Perhaps. (*Pause.* CHRISTIAN *is apparently grief-stricken. He puts the finishing touches to his mourning garments.*)

CHRISTIAN. What a tragic chain of events! A telegram is at your house now, asking you both to come and hear some glorious news.

THEOBALD. You *wired* for us?

CHRISTIAN. I was counting the hours.

THEOBALD. What on earth can have happened?

CHRISTIAN. If you had arrived a few hours later, you would have found your son engaged to be married!

THEOBALD. Well! Is she pretty?

CHRISTIAN. She is a countess.

THEOBALD. Christian! Where do you find the courage?

CHRISTIAN. Is it a matter of courage?

THEOBALD. That depends on the man. I thought you might take after me. What a mad leap this is!

CHRISTIAN. A step up, Father.

THEOBALD. It's weird! What about the other girl?

CHRISTIAN. So that is all you have to say?

THEOBALD. If it'd been me, they'd all talk about fireworks!

CHRISTIAN. It is the logical outcome of a perfectly natural sequel of events.

THEOBALD. With a lower civil servant for a father and a tailor's daughter for a mother, I'd call it highway robbery. And her father a count and all her relations—you're crazy, my boy!

CHRISTIAN. What nonsense!

THEOBALD. It's crazier than all the comedies in the whole world. You're making us ridiculous, that's all. You don't seem to have a scrap of consideration for us left. Why, I've never even set eyes on a count! Whenever I come near you, you turn everything upside down. Remember: your father is a civil servant on the retired list!

CHRISTIAN. Rubbish.

THEOBALD. It's a misfortune! How dare you do this to me? You're making me a laughing stock!

CHRISTIAN (*disconcerted*). But . . .

THEOBALD. It's the Seyfferts in you. Your mother was queer, too. I'll go daft. It's worse than when you sent us away. It's worse than your mother's death.

CHRISTIAN. But, Father . . .

THEOBALD (*with increasing excitement*). Trying to mate a mouse with a giraffe, are you? Tight rope tricks! Going in for the abnormal now! Sixty years old and your mother goes and dies on my hands. It was a blow. I'd got used to her. Still it was a natural thing to happen. But the Maskes—Theobald Maske that everyone knows what he is—with a family of counts! You'll drive me insane!

(CHRISTIAN *has picked up the rapier with an air of resignation.* THEOBALD *is beside himself.*)

Going to murder me now, are you? I'd do a lot better to die quietly now as a decent civil servant in his right mind than later as a victim of public ridicule. Don't you remember what you began as any more? Have you forgotten the little room and the canary and the walks we used to take together round the cemetery? You had to be extra respectful to the chief clerk in those days. But what is a clerk to a count?

CHRISTIAN (*anxiously*). Please listen though . . .

THEOBALD. How far have we got up the ladder? Oh, I'm going daft!

CHRISTIAN. I fail to understand this outburst.

THEOBALD. And the consequences? Have you overlooked the absolutely fatal consequences? Any child could see 'em. When you got rid of me and your mother and sent us to live amongst strangers in our old age, I was fairly boiling with rage. But Luise helped me over it and I ended up seeing a reason in it, though a cruel one, a—a—higher purpose for you, if not for me. You saw that we wanted for nothing—you know—live and let live, so gradually I calmed down. (*He jumps up.*) And now you've got the impudence to . . .

CHRISTIAN. I must interrupt you. Before I thought of this marriage, I felt myself gripped by a desire that had been growing in me ever since I parted from you; I wanted to live in close touch with you and Mother again. And now that I can't have both of you, I want you by yourself—to live here with me—in this house.

THEOBALD (*drops into a chair*). Well, I'm damned!

CHRISTIAN. You . . .

THEOBALD. You're not serious.

CHRISTIAN. Perfectly. I couldn't know you'd oppose the idea with such violence.

THEOBALD. You're serious?

CHRISTIAN. I don't understand.

THEOBALD (*going towards him*). What?

CHRISTIAN (*involuntarily steps back*). I don't understand.

THEOBALD. Not now either, eh?

CHRISTIAN. I mean, I see what you mean, but your scruples seem to me exaggerated—partly.

THEOBALD. Exaggerated?

CHRISTIAN. On the other hand . . .

THEOBALD. Exaggerated?

CHRISTIAN (*timorously*). Of course on the other hand—if you really—then, of course. But good Lord, doesn't it cost a man something to give up the dearest wish of his heart? However, I'll insist on your coming to the wedding.

THEOBALD. The answer to that is: either you make this suggestion in sheer thoughtlessness, in which case I say that it's improper to make a clown of your old father . . . a fine joke for you, I must say, me, in my get-up, walking the plank down the aisle with a countess on my arm . . . and at the meal afterwards, sitting there among the nobility . . . as the Common Man!

CHRISTIAN. Father!

THEOBALD. Either that's your idea, or else you're trying to take it out of me for the way I made you feel I was your father when you were a boy. So now you want to demean me before all those people! Or maybe you think this invitation will be a poultice for the pain of mother's death. No, Christian, in heaven's name. Go on doing what you've been doing for me, I've been well satisfied with that, and if you want to do more, don't do it like this with no thought of what it'll lead to. Anyway just remember what I'm like, a worthy fellow who has nothing to do with all this, who won't interfere with you the least bit, either, under any circumstances. That's why I came up the back stairs just now. I don't want anything but a few new clothes—that's all.

CHRISTIAN. Certainly—my tailor, my haberdashers . . .

THEOBALD. Not for me! I know where to get mine from. I'm taking the train back home tonight.

(*He takes his hat and stick.*)

CHRISTIAN (*anxiously*). Oh, but you can stay a day or two surely?

THEOBALD. I can *not!* And stop that flim-flam. Why don't you talk to me sensibly as you used to? Nobody saw me come and nobody'll see me go again. No need for you to come with me. I'll get a bite at the first good tavern I come to. If you'd like to drop by some day to visit her grave, I'll be glad to see you. Aside from all this nonsense, you're a good sort, Christel. But live and let live.

SERVANT (*enters*). Count Palen!

COUNT (*follows immediately*). Marianne's first impulse—which showed her fine feeling—was to come herself with your answer, my dear Maske. She is very happy, very deeply so, I assure you.

(THEOBALD *has been trying to disappear.*)

Won't you introduce me?

CHRISTIAN (*in the utmost confusion*). My father . . .

COUNT. *Tiens!* Now this is—ah—an agreeable surprise. Most happy, my dear sir! (*He extends both hands to* THEOBALD.) And I'd always had the impression—how was that I wonder?—that our friend here was an orphan . . ! (*Laughs.*) I honestly did. All the more agreeable. Ah, splendid!

CHRISTIAN. Zurich has been my father's home for some time. He comes to day to tell me my mother—suddenly died. I have won Marianne when I need her most.

(*He sinks on the* COUNT'S *breast.*)

COUNT. My sincere sympathy! (*To* THEOBALD.) With you, too, my dear sir.

THEOBALD (*bowing*). Thank you, Herr Count.

COUNT. The best advice I can offer is: run to your fiancée at once. The old gentleman will stay here. (*To* THEOBALD.) Have you had lunch? No? Let's go then. I can't replace your wife with a fiancée for you, but what a decent meal will do, I . . .

CHRISTIAN. My father planned to return at once.

COUNT. I won't hear of it.

THEOBALD. In any case one must have lunch.

COUNT. My prerogative. We'll get our condolences and congratulations over as soon as possible. Your son has kept you under lock and key too long. We'll have a bottle of claret and sniff each other over!

THEOBALD. Sniff—that's good.

COUNT. Is it the wrong word?

THEOBALD (*laughing*). No. 'Sniff'—just what I'd say, Herr Count.

CHRISTIAN (*in* THEOBALD'S *ear fiercely*). Count! (*To the* COUNT.) My father insists upon taking the mid-day train.

COUNT (*energetically*). Oh, let us alone! Old gentlemen must eat a good lunch. All that can wait. Come!

(COUNT *and* THEOBALD *exeunt.*)

CHRISTIAN. What was that sudden tone he took with me? Have I made a mistake? (*At the window.*) He's making him get into the car first! Is my face red? Am I pale? (*He runs to the mirror.*) I'm shaking like an aspen leaf! (*He jumps on a chair at the window.*) He's offering him a cigar. And they're laughing—roaring. What at? At me? O my God, what a mistake! What a mistake! Didn't I *want* to play a trump-card after all? Wasn't I swearing only five minutes ago that I'd brag and boast about him? I had the right idea! And now he'll tell Marianne and the whole family I wanted to deny my father. He can tell them I had even proclaimed him dead! But I'll simply deny it. Countermeasures, quick! (*He rings. A servant enters.*) Get the guestroom ready. My father has arrived. See that he's well looked after. (*Follows servant to the door.*) Stop! Hadn't one better wait and see what will happen? Maybe I could still get rid of the old man without attracting attention? No, no, no, no! What I felt this morning proves to be the case: I must make a big gesture. Present him as a Remarkable Phenomenon. Bring him onto the scene at once. Preparations must be made. The whole family must be dragged into it. If the worst hasn't already occurred. (*He runs up and down.*) What will they do at the winetable? What will he get out of the old man? When he's drunk, for instance. Why am I not with them? (*Beside himself.*) In heaven's name, in heaven's name! (*He howls.*) Why didn't I follow my simple childlike impulse? I could slap myself!

ACT III

(*Drawing room of a hotel suite. Flowers everywhere. At rear, a wide curtain screening entrance to bedroom. Enter* CHRISTIAN *in evening clothes and cape, wearing many decorations, and* MARIANNE *in bridal dress and cloak.*)

CHRISTIAN. A breath of air and peace. At last.

MARIANNE. What flowers! (*Looking at bouquet.*) From Father! (*She picks up a card and reads.*) For my lost angel, Marianne! And what divine orchids! (*Reading.*) From an unknown.

CHRISTIAN. Well, sentiment! What could those two have been chattering about? Did you hear them?

MARIANNE. Who?

CHRISTIAN. Didn't you notice? They absolutely ignored their partners. The fat countess . . .

MARIANNE. Aunt Ursula's almost stone-deaf. And she had to spill half her meal on her table napkin.

CHRISTIAN. Who was the Knight of St. John two away from you to the right?

MARIANNE. Mother's cousin, Albert Thüngen.

CHRISTIAN. The fellow stared at me all the time as if I'd been a ghost. He forgot to eat.

MARIANNE. We call him Frog-face—he looks it, doesn't he?

CHRISTIAN. All the orders and decorations: rare ones, too! Are you as intimate with the princess as she tried to suggest?

MARIANNE. We were together for seven years—when we were little.

CHRISTIAN. For seven years. So you're close friends.

MARIANNE. We had the same great-grandmother.

CHRISTIAN. The archduchess?

MAID (*enters*). Are you ready for me, your ladyship?

MARIANNE. I'm only madam now, Anna.

MAID. Very well, your ladyship.

MARIANNE. Stop your "ladyship" and all nonsense. I demand respect!

MAID (*sobbing*). Yes, madam.

MARIANNE. What's the matter?

MAID (*bending over* MARIANNE'S *hand*). It's so sad, madam—you don't belong to us any more.

MARIANNE. I don't belong to myself any more. That's the fate of girls. Yours too.

(*Both exit through the curtain.*)

(CHRISTIAN *rushes over to listen to what goes on behind the curtain.*)

CHRISTIAN. This Anna. What a face she has. To think of the tales a girl like that picks up behind locked doors and carries away with her . . .

MAID'S VOICE. . . . Looked heavenly. The pastor was crying . . .

MARIANNE'S VOICE. . . . Old Jansen . . . rubbish!

MAID'S VOICE. . . . Genuine Brussels . . . flounces of Brussels—so wide . . . rosebuds . . .

MARIANNE'S VOICE. . . . Ilse Zeitlow in light blue satin to set off her blond hair . . .

MAID'S VOICE. . . . You could see (*In a lower voice.*) her bosom . . . on purpose.

MARIANNE'S VOICE. For heaven's sake! (*Giggling, then whispering.*)

(CHRISTIAN *leans closer.*)

CHRISTIAN. Ah, whispering! Whispering again! Wherever I go they lower their voices, look down at the floor, and whisper!

(*Laughter from time to time comes through curtain.*)

MAID'S VOICE. . . . pointed moustache.

CHRISTIAN. That's me. But this day is my Waterloo.

MAID'S VOICE. . . . Rather silly-looking.

MARIANNE'S VOICE. Quiet!

CHRISTIAN. Canaille! I heard that, Marianne. But this evening I enter the temple of your heart and find out what you know.

(*Renewed laughter.*)

Laughter! *Schadenfreude*—well, out with it! Open all the sluices, viper! Afterwards I'll rinse that wife of mine clean of your poison to the last molecule.

THE MAID'S VOICE. It was *too* funny!

CHRISTIAN. Not so, monkey. And the day isn't done yet. My countermines are laid. Once released, they'll out-thunder anything ever heard. (*It is now quiet within.*) Quiet? What are they up to now? (*He kneels on the floor and tries to look under the curtain.*) Underwear, flesh, and gestures. But a word must be spoken—the confession, telling how much gossip the world has poured into your ears, from your father down to this insect of a maid. I've laid so deep a plot to get it out of you, you'll hardly be able to hold back a single item. You don't enter the Maske family, woman, till it inspires respect and emotion in you.

THE MAID (*entering*). May I go to madam's trunk?

(*She takes something out of it and disappears through the curtain.*)

CHRISTIAN. Up to now they've shielded me from you. They shield themselves from everyone. But today you're given over to me. Who in your family is my worst enemy? I shall explore the question with much finesse. With all his tricks he must be exposed, if I have to strain your conscience to the breaking point. (*He stares into the trunk.*) What did they fill your pocket with? What sort of books are in the trunk? Lampoons? (*He pulls a book out of the trunk.*) The New Testament. What charges have they been piling up against me in their hearts? When opportunity offers, we'll strip them to the blast.

(THEOBALD *in evening clothes pokes his head through the door.*)

This is an outrage!

THEOBALD. Only for a minute.

CHRISTIAN. What is the matter?

THEOBALD. A father's tenderness.

CHRISTIAN. You're drunk.

THEOBALD. Partly. But also full of tenderness. Tried to blow a kiss to you all evening; couldn't catch you though. Don't argue, boy. You're a wizard, and I'm proud of you. So proud of you. You've torn my old notions off of me like so many paper shirts. Principles—opinions—trampled on 'em. *You* win! All my life I lived off proverbs: Cobbler, stick to your last, and all the rest. But *you* lived off yourself. The way you treated those people today, as if they weren't even your equals. And the way they looked at you. With the greatest respect. And here you are taking a juicy little piece of the nobility to bed with you! My unaristocratic blood boils at the thought! You wear me out! I fall upon thy breast! (*Embraces him.*)

CHRISTIAN. Be quiet. She's in there! Are you drunk or not?

THEOBALD. Partly. But what I say goes. At the table, with everyone wearing their decorations, it was your proud little head . . .

CHRISTIAN. Father!

THEOBALD. Proud little head, my darling boy. Mother ought to have seen you. It was as if I was looking at a sunrise—sunrise. Can you believe it?

CHRISTIAN. Do you mean it?

THEOBALD. You've let the Maske family's belt out several holes, my boy. All of me that matters is in you. No—don't say anything. I've got to the confession at last—a question of dignity, not a thing fathers say to their sons: I'm in the way here, I'm going to do the disappearing stunt. That higher motive of mine, that higher purpose in life—I've found it: in you. You've been wanting to get rid of me: you've thought of it before, and it looked a bit brutal to me, quite a battle. But it's all plain sailing now. We'll both be everlastingly grateful to each other. (*Singing.*) "Adieu—adieu—I'll think of you!" Zurich, Mainstreet, Number 16. There resides Maske, retired civil servant, watching his son with rapture from afar!

CHRISTIAN. Someone's coming.

THEOBALD. Let 'em! Go on as you've begun and don't put your foot in it. They distrust you and despise you and hate you and so on, but they've enormous respect for you. Because they find you incomprehensible.

CHRISTIAN. How did you know?

THEOBALD. They were all dead drunk, so I crept into their confidence. When they don't know the Eagle of Hohenzollern from the Iron Cross, they'll let anybody see their insides.

CHRISTIAN. And the old man? What about my famous *faux pas?*

THEOBALD. Oh, he'd suspected the truth before, and maybe he still remembers. But at the reception today when I was basking in your glory, I could see he was basking in it, too! Besides his heart had been softened in advance by your little lovebird in there. His resistance was completely overcome.

CHRISTIAN. So they're beaten?

THEOBALD. Done for. Now hold tight. Don't let go. As a matter of fact, I've always believed our stock stood for something but I could only pass on the idea to my nearest and dearest.

CHRISTIAN. Me!

THEOBALD. Yes, and you along.

CHRISTIAN. I bent the bow! The string is now vibrating under my hand.

THEOBALD. The first arrow's for her. Let it strike home!

CHRISTIAN. We shall stick.

THEOBALD. In the old fabric!

CHRISTIAN. I hold the trump. I'll play it!

(THEOBALD *goes to curtain and looks through.* CHRISTIAN *whispers "Hey!"* THEOBALD *echoes "Hey! Hey!" They giggle and fall into each other's arms.*)

CHRISTIAN. *Vive les Maske!*

THEOBALD. I'm on to you, boy, and all the rest of it. Blood's thicker than water. (*He trots to the door, turns to throw a kiss to* CHRISTIAN *and goes out.*)

CHRISTIAN. Here life achieved the majesty of a drama. A goal was reached. The enemy crushed, obeisance made before the victor. Exit stage center.

But now comes something yet more important. How far was the territory really subdued? The woman, on whom the whole thing hangs, must give token of boundless respect. It must be a knock-down triumph for me.

MARIANNE (*enters in negligée*). How do you like me?

CHRISTIAN (*to himself*). Right now that's hardly the point.

MARIANNE. This lace has associations. On the same night in *her* life my mother wore it.

CHRISTIAN. There's no such thing as "the same."

MARIANNE. No? Am I not the same as some other woman in your past—at this moment? You must tell me everything. You must have no secrets from me. What number am I on the list, and which of the others meant a great deal to you? Do memories of any of them linger in your mind?

CHRISTIAN. What talk! How shall I bring you to reason?

MARIANNE (*her arms around his neck*). I was in love with an ensign once. I was only sixteen. A pink and white boy with a little blond moustache. That was all I ever knew about him.

CHRISTIAN. What do you know about me?

MARIANNE. When I shut my eyes, I see you are tall and dark, thick set, and you roll when you walk.

CHRISTIAN. Do I? (*He goes to the mirror and takes a few steps.*) A slight swaying gait, perhaps. There's rhythm in the movement.

MARIANNE (*gives a clear laugh*). And how do *I* walk? (*Raises her skirt and trips along.*)

CHRISTIAN. What else? What do I do?

MARIANNE. You're in business.

CHRISTIAN. Of what sort?

MARIANNE. What does it matter?

CHRISTIAN. At the age of thirty-six I am president of the greatest commercial enterprise in the Reich. I control one-fifth of the national wealth.

MARIANNE. *Tiens!*

CHRISTIAN. Your father's word! Has he discussed my affairs with you?

MARIANNE. Sort of.

CHRISTIAN. Sort of, that means he's discussed everything.

MARIANNE. I'm tired.

CHRISTIAN (*to himself*). The invitation to the dance. (*To her.*) Not yet. Am I not after all still a stranger to you, since your father never spoke seriously to you about me. Never? Are you sure? Think! Didn't he come home one day in a state of wild excitement? Try and remember.

MARIANNE. I've never seen him wildly excited in my life.

CHRISTIAN. I give in then. But at any rate it's an achievement to be in such a position at my age. It's like becoming a general at thirty-six.

MARIANNE. Only a prince can do that. (*She sits on his lap.*)

CHRISTIAN. Or?

MARIANNE. Or who?

CHRISTIAN. Think!

MARIANNE. I don't know.

CHRISTIAN. Or a genius. In the course of this past year they tried to make forty-one companies issue new stock to a total of about three quarters of a billion marks. I said I was opposed to the idea for the following reason: in return for those seven hundred and fifty millions the public would not be given cheap goods but the product of the labor of some half a million more workers which the land will be encouraged to produce. The stock capital of manufacturing concerns as to principal and interest consists entirely in manpower and output. You follow me?

MARIANNE (*still on his knee*). I'm trying.

CHRISTIAN. Pay attention! If there's no work, the productive apparatus is clogged by the mass of unwanted workers. But when new chimneystacks go up, the valves are soon open. So we stand—I told them—as captains of industry at the switchboard that controls population. It is therefore our task to see that capital is proportionate to—and not in excess of—natural increase. You understand?

MARIANNE. I think so.

CHRISTIAN. We should do better to slow up production and thereby improve quality. There you have a slight idea of Political Economy as I practice it. (*Lost in his theme he dumps her off his knee and marches around the room.*) Huh? That's high-class, as Helmholtz would have said. (*He seizes* MARIANNE *by a button on her gown and shakes her gently backwards and forwards, looking straight into her eyes as he speaks.*) I could tell you another of my superb utterances on the question of the reduction of rates for steerage passengers on our steamship lines. The vast majority of people are short-sighted, that's why the economic destiny of millions lies in the hands of a few of us.

MARIANNE. Are you so rich?

CHRISTIAN. That is a shopkeeper's word: I have power to achieve everything that my blood gives me strength to achieve. You've seen my father a few times. A personality, isn't he? The dominant traits of our family are strongly marked in him. Nothing superfluous, nothing without a purpose. Did you notice at the reception, how impressively he reached for his glass? A pity you never knew my grandfather. A gay dog—but —so you see what my ancestors planted in me. I am the end product of their combined efforts!

MAID (*enters*). Madam—your diamonds. You would rather have them with you here—these hotels—you never know. Or, you, sir?

(CHRISTIAN *takes the coronet.*)

Good-night. (*Exit.*)

CHRISTIAN. What an odd shape.

MARIANNE. The coronet of a marquise. A great-aunt of my mother's, the Marquise d'Urfés, left it to all the women of our family to wear on their wedding day.

CHRISTIAN. *Bon.*—What was I saying?—Never mind, I've a surprise for you.

MARIANNE (*clapping her hands*). Oh, do let me see.

CHRISTIAN. Turn around a minute while I unwrap it and set it up for you.

MARIANNE (*her back turned*). One, two, three—

CHRISTIAN (*uncovers a picture which has been leaning against the wall, and stands it up in front of him, his legs supporting it. It is the portrait of a woman*). You may look now.

(MARIANNE *looks at it.*)

My mother, Marianne. She too wants to see you face to face today. My mother who loved her boy so dearly.

MARIANNE. What a striking face!

CHRISTIAN. Isn't it? It's a Renoir.

MARIANNE (*flies to* CHRISTIAN'S *arms. To the portrait*). I shall love him better than myself. Your son! *My* Christian!

CHRISTIAN. Careful. It's a great work of art; you mustn't hurt it.

(*He has stood the picture against a table.*)

MARIANNE. Such lovely thick brown hair. *Your* complexion. Exquisite skin.

CHRISTIAN. She came of a peasant family many centuries old. Rumors of Viking ancestry. See those substantial jewels?—heirlooms, of course, that red coral ear-ring. A remote forebear had some official post at Halarö in the Swedish straits. There's a story of how he met Charles XII.

MARIANNE. Such marvelous hair!

CHRISTIAN. It came down to her knees. Renoir saw her in the Bois de Boulogne one day. Instantaneously he decided he must paint her.

MARIANNE. I don't wonder.

CHRISTIAN. But hear the way it happened. That's the best part. Open your ears for the prettiest calamity you ever heard of. She and Father were walking in the Bois after a ceremonious luncheon at the Cascades. Complete with Burgundy. All of a sudden she is rooted to the ground. Refuses to budge. Father, with his grey top hat at a festive angle—he's told the story a thousand times—called her and coaxed her and begged her. But there she stood.

MARIANNE. What was the matter?

(CHRISTIAN *whispers in her ear.*)

(*With a peal of gay laughter.*) Her drawers! How charming! Perfect![1]

CHRISTIAN (*laughing unrestrainedly*). And Renoir! You can well imagine, he often told me the story. (*Roaring with laughter.*) It must have been a sight for the gods.

MARIANNE. That delicious woman. Standing there in the sun!

CHRISTIAN. In short, he contrived admittance to the Maske household, taking with him a French vicomte, who was also present at the scene.

MARIANNE. How long ago was that?

CHRISTIAN. About a year before I was born, I believe.

MARIANNE. Such stories bring people so much closer to each other. I feel I know her so much better now. But it must have been a most unpleasant predicament for your father.

CHRISTIAN. He was the same *bon garçon* he is today—with the same taste for comedy. He adored his bride and was utterly taken by her charming appearance.

MARIANNE. She knew how to dress.

CHRISTIAN. She certainly did.

MARIANNE. How lovely the fashions were! How becoming, those ruffled capes! And all the exquisite women who wore them are dead!

CHRISTIAN. I'm having a monument put up in Buchow to her memory.

(*He hangs the picture on the wall.*)

MARIANNE. Have you bought the land?

CHRISTIAN. I'm going to. It's a fine estate. Especially for the monument. She was in every way so much above life size, a monument is no more than she deserved.

MARIANNE. I have misjudged your family dreadfully. But now I begin to correct my idea of them. When you talk of people, you make them come so vividly alive!

CHRISTIAN. Put it better and say I am capable of ideas. Most people are capable only of words and words and more words.

MARIANNE. I need Anne again.

CHRISTIAN. That girl again?

MARIANNE. I can't open my dress behind.

CHRISTIAN. Come here. (*He begins to look for hooks and eyes.*) Words by which no two minds understand the same thing and which are there-

---

[1]The true version of this anecdote is to be found in Sternheim's play *Die Hose*, translated by Eugene Jolas as *A Pair of Drawers* (in *transition* 6, 7, 8, 9.).

fore inadequate in bringing people to complete understanding of each other.

(MARIANNE *yawns.*)

Pure reason assembles groups of similar phenomenal or volitional forms in a single expression which determines the complex—or whole—in its essence and is called the Concept.

(MARIANNE *yawning loudly.*)

Such is the conquest of multifariousness. The slip too?

MARIANNE. Please.

CHRISTIAN. Now let me have your attention, Marianne. Every accomplishment of the human mind is directed to a single end, namely, orientation in the infinity of the world about it—thus achieving its victory over multifariousness. Hence, the words beech and oak, and so forth, names which have been forced to contain their own multifariousness, become simply "woods." (*He has come to the last hook.*)

MARIANNE. Thank you. (*She puts her foot on a chair and unbuttons her shoes.*)

CHRISTIAN. Only a fool would say even in jest "He can't see the wood for the trees."

(MARIANNE *goes behind the curtain into the bedroom.*)

Where are you going? What they mean is of course: "He can't see the trees for the wood." (*He follows her and stands at the curtain.*) To master this principle is to have the entire theory of knowledge in your pocket. (*He comes toward the front and says loudly over his shoulder.*) At any rate, there's an inkling for you of the way a brain like mine works, huh? (*Rubbing his hands, to himself.*) *Ca marche ce soir.* (*Remains standing in front of the picture, deeply moved.*) My Mother! (*Loud.*) As a young girl she went with friends on a visit to the United States, returning via the South Sea Islands and Asia. In Honolulu King Kalakawa fell madly in love with her.

(*Sound of going to bed behind the curtain.*)

That was in eighteen-eighty or eighty-one.

(*He has taken off his shoes; and only now removes his coat, so that he stands revealed in the full magnificence of his decorations. He raises his arms and looks around expectantly. Pause.*)

MARIANNE'S VOICE. What became of the vicomte?

CHRISTIAN. What vicomte?

MARIANNE'S VOICE. The one who was with Renoir in the Bois de Boulogne and went to your parents' house afterwards.

CHRISTIAN. Ah, the vicomte! Yes, of course—why, he—

(*He looks at the picture. Stands still. Pause.*)

MARIANNE'S VOICE. Well, what became of him?

CHRISTIAN. Good heavens! (*He strides across the room past the mirror.*) Ahem.

MARIANNE'S VOICE. Is it a secret?

CHRISTIAN (*to himself*). I wish I knew—but of course—Oh my God! Ah, my little countess—you're for it this time. (*He goes to the curtains and whispers through.*) Marianne!

MARIANNE (*agitated*). I'm coming. (*She enters in nightgown hastily donned.*)

CHRISTIAN. That question of yours. There was destiny in it.

MARIANNE. What did I say?

CHRISTIAN. The vicomte, what happened to him?

MARIANNE. Well?

CHRISTIAN. The truth would never have passed my lips.

MARIANNE. Christian! What *is* it?

CHRISTIAN. No! I cannot tell you.

MARIANNE. Christian! I am your wife—it is my right . . . !

CHRISTIAN. I am also a son.

MARIANNE. You have duties to me.

CHRISTIAN. There is also a son's respect for his mother.

MARIANNE. That . . . ?

CHRISTIAN. Not a word from me, Marianne.

MARIANNE. That . . . vicomte . . . ?

CHRISTIAN (*sternly*). Marianne, I forbid you ever—so long as we live—to broach this subject again. Nobody, not even I, must ever so much as guess what you imagine or suspect. My name is Maske, there's an end.

MARIANNE (*overwhelmed*). Saviour in Heaven! Of course, I'll not say a word. But what you mean to me, now I know this—that is my own affair! (*Softly.*) Ah, my Christian, the last barrier between us has fallen now. From this day forward I am all yours. (*With outstretched arms before the picture.*) Mother! Blessed Adulteress! (*Sinking into* CHRISTIAN'S *arms.*) My dearest lord and master!

(CHRISTIAN *smiles and makes a big gesture of relief.*)

Sweeney Agonistes

TWO FRAGMENTS OF AN ARISTOPHANIC MELODRAMA

BY T. S. ELIOT

ORESTES: You don't see them, you don't—but I see them: they are hunting me down, I must move on.—*Choephoroi.*

Hence the soul cannot be possessed of the divine union, until it has divested itself of the love of created beings.—*St. John of the Cross.*

CHARACTERS

Dusty
Doris
Wauchope
Horsfall
Klipstein
Krumpacker
Sweeney
Swarts
Snow

I. FRAGMENT OF A PROLOGUE

(DUSTY. DORIS.)
DUSTY. How about Pereira?
DORIS. What about Pereira?
I don't care.
DUSTY. You don't care?
Who pays the rent?
DORIS. Yes he pays the rent
DUSTY. Well some men don't and some men do
Some men don't and you know who
DORIS. You can have Pereira
DUSTY. What about Pereira?
DORIS. He's no gentleman, Pereira:
You can't trust him!
DUSTY. Well that's true.
He's no gentleman if you can't trust him
And *if* you can't trust him—
Then you never know what he's going to do.
DORIS. No it wouldn't do to be too nice to Pereira.
DUSTY. Now Sam's a gentleman through and through.
DORIS. I like Sam
DUSTY. *I* like Sam
Yes and Sam's a nice boy too.
He's a funny fellow
DORIS. He *is* a funny fellow
He's like a fellow once I knew.
He could make you laugh.
DUSTY. Sam can make you laugh:
Sam's all right
DORIS. But Pereira won't do.
We can't have Pereira
DUSTY. Well what you going to do?
TELEPHONE. Ting a ling ling
Ting a ling ling
DUSTY. That's Pereira
DORIS. Yes that's Pereira
DUSTY. Well what you going to do?

TELEPHONE. Ting a ling ling
Ting a ling ling
DUSTY. That's Pereira.
DORIS. Well can't you stop that horrible noise?
Pick up the receiver
DUSTY. What'll I say!
DORIS. Say what you like: say I'm ill,
Say I broke my leg on the stairs
Say we've had a fire
DUSTY. Hello Hello are you there?
Yes this is Miss Dorrance's *flat*—
Oh Mr. Pereira is that you? how do you do!
Oh I'm *so* sorry. I *am* so sorry
But Doris came home with a terrible chill
No, just a chill
Oh I *think* it's only a chill
Yes indeed I hope so too—
Well I *hope* we shan't have to call a doctor
Doris just hates having a doctor
She says will you ring up on Monday
She hopes to be all right on Monday
I say do you mind if I ring off now
She's got her feet in mustard and water
I said I'm giving her mustard and water
All right, Monday you'll phone through.
Yes I'll tell her. Good bye. Goooood bye.
I'm sure, that's very kind of *you.*
Ah-h-h
DORIS. Now I'm going to cut the cards for to-night.
Oh guess what the first is
DUSTY. First is. What is?
DORIS. The King of Clubs
DUSTY. That's Pereira
DORIS. It might be Sweeney
DUSTY. It's Pereira
DORIS. It might *just* as well be Sweeney
DUSTY. Well anyway it's very queer.
DORIS. Here's the four of diamonds, what's that mean?
DUSTY (*reading*). 'A small sum of money, or a present
Of wearing apparel, or a party.'
That's queer too.
DORIS. Here's the three. What's that mean?
DUSTY. 'News of an absent friend.'—Pereira!

DORIS. The Queen of Hearts!—Mrs. Porter!
DUSTY. Or it might be you
DORIS. Or it might be you
We're all hearts. You can't be sure.
It just depends on what comes next.
You've got to *think* when you read the cards,
It's not a thing that anyone can do.
DUSTY. Yes I know you've a touch with the cards
What comes next?
DORIS. What comes next. It's the six.
DUSTY. 'A quarrel. An estrangement. Separation of friends.'
DORIS. Here's the two of spades.
DUSTY. The *two* of *spades!*
THAT'S THE COFFIN!!
DORIS. THAT'S THE COFFIN?
Oh good heavens what'll I do?
Just before a party too!
DUSTY. Well it needn't be yours, it may mean a friend.
DORIS. No it's mine. I'm sure it's mine.
I dreamt of weddings all last night.
Yes it's mine. I know it's mine.
Oh good heavens what'll I do.
Well I'm not going to draw any more,
You cut for luck. You cut for luck.
It might break the spell. You cut for luck.
DUSTY. The Knave of Spades.
DORIS. That'll be Snow
DUSTY. Or it might be Swarts
DORIS. Or it might be Snow
DUSTY. It's a funny thing how I draw court cards—
DORIS. There's a lot in the way you pick them up
DUSTY. There's an awful lot in the way you feel
DORIS. Sometimes they'll tell you nothing at all
DUSTY. You've got to know what you want to ask them
DORIS. You've got to know what you want to know
DUSTY. It's no use asking them too much
DORIS. It's no use asking more than once
DUSTY. Sometimes they're no use at all.
DORIS. I'd like to know about that coffin.
DUSTY. Well I never! What did I tell you?
Wasn't I saying I always draw court cards?
The Knave of Hearts!

(*Whistle outside of window.*)

Well I *never!*
What a co*in*cidence! Cards *are* queer!

(*Whistle again.*)

DORIS. Is that Sam?
DUSTY. Of course it's Sam!
DORIS. Of course, the Knave of Hearts *is* Sam!
DUSTY (*leaning out of the window*). Hello Sam!
WAUCHOPE. Hello dear!
How many's up there?
DUSTY. Nobody's up here
How many's down there?
WAUCHOPE. Four of us here.
Wait till I put the car around the corner
We'll be right up
DUSTY. All right, come up.
WAUCHOPE. We'll be right up.
DUSTY (*to* DORIS). Cards are queer.
DORIS. I'd like to know about that coffin.
KNOCK KNOCK KNOCK
KNOCK KNOCK KNOCK
KNOCK
KNOCK
KNOCK
(DORIS. DUSTY. WAUCHOPE. HORSFALL. KLIPSTEIN. KRUMPACKER.)
WAUCHOPE. Hello Doris! Hello Dusty! How do you do!
How come? how come? will you permit me—
I think you girls both know Captain Horsfall—
We want you to meet two friends of ours,
American gentlemen here on business.
Meet Mr. Klipstein. Meet Mr. Krumpacker.
KLIPSTEIN. How do you do
KRUMPACKER. How do you do
KLIPSTEIN. I'm very pleased to make your acquaintance
KRUMPACKER. Extremely pleased to become acquainted
KLIPSTEIN. Sam—I should say Loot Sam Wauchope
KRUMPACKER. Of the Canadian Expeditionary Force—
KLIPSTEIN. The Loot has told us a lot about you.
KRUMPACKER. We were all in the war together
Klip and me and the Cap and Sam.
KLIPSTEIN. Yes we did our bit, as you folks say,
I'll tell the world we got the Hun on the run
KRUMPACKER. What about that poker game? eh what Sam?
What about that poker game in Bordeaux?

Yes Miss Dorrance you get Sam
To tell about that poker game in Bordeaux.
DUSTY. Do you know London well, Mr. Krumpacker?
KLIPSTEIN. No we never been here before
KRUMPACKER. We hit this town last night for the first time
KLIPSTEIN. And I certainly hope it won't be the last time.
DORIS. You like London, Mr. Klipstein?
KRUMPACKER. Do we like London? do we like London!
Do we like London!! Eh what Klip?
KLIPSTEIN. Say, Miss—er—uh London's swell.
We like London fine.
KRUMPACKER. Perfectly slick.
DUSTY. Why don't you come and live here then?
KLIPSTEIN. Well, no, Miss—er—you haven't quite got it
(I'm afraid I didn't quite catch your name—
But I'm very pleased to meet you all the same)—
London's a little too gay for us
Yes I'll say a little too gay.
KRUMPACKER. Yes London's a little too gay for us
Don't think I mean anything *coarse*—
But I'm afraid we couldn't stand the pace.
What about it Klip?
KLIPSTEIN. You said it, Krum.
London's a slick place, London's a swell place,
London's a fine place to come on a visit—
KRUMPACKER. Specially when you got a real live Britisher
A guy like Sam to show you around.
Sam of course is at *home* in London,
And he's promised to show us around.

II. FRAGMENT OF AN AGON

(SWEENEY. WAUCHOPE. HORSFALL. KLIPSTEIN.
KRUMPACKER. SWARTS. SNOW. DORIS. DUSTY.)
SWEENEY. I'll carry you off
To a cannibal isle.
DORIS. You'll be the cannibal!

SWEENEY. You'll be the missionary!
You'll be my little seven stone missionary!
I'll gobble you up. I'll be the cannibal.
DORIS. You'll carry me off? To a cannibal isle?
SWEENEY. I'll be the cannibal.
DORIS. I'll be the missionary.
I'll convert you!
SWEENEY. I'll convert *you*!
Into a stew.
A nice little, white little, missionary stew.
DORIS. You wouldn't eat me!
SWEENEY. Yes I'd eat you!
In a nice little, white little, soft little, tender little,
Juicy little, right little, missionary stew.
You see this egg
You see this egg
Well that's life on a crocodile isle.
There's no telephones
There's no gramophones
There's no motor cars
No two-seaters, no six-seaters,
No Citroën, no Rolls-Royce.
Nothing to eat but the fruit as it grows.
Nothing to see but the palmtrees one way
And the sea the other way,
Nothing to hear but the sound of the surf.
Nothing at all but three things
DORIS. What things?
SWEENEY. Birth, and copulation, and death.
That's all, that's all, that's all, that's all,
Birth, and copulation, and death.
DORIS. I'd be bored.
SWEENEY. You'd be bored.
Birth, and copulation, and death.
DORIS. I'd be bored.
SWEENEY. You'd be bored.
Birth, and copulation, and death.
That's all the facts when you come to brass tacks:
Birth, and copulation, and death.
I've been born, and once is enough.
You don't remember, but I remember,
Once is enough.
(Song by WAUCHOPE *and* HORSFALL. SWARTS *as* TAMBO. SNOW *as* BONES.)

Under the bamboo
Bamboo bamboo
Under the bamboo tree
Two live as one
One live as two
Two live as three
Under the bam
Under the boo
Under the bamboo tree.

Where the breadfruit fall
And the penguin call
And the sound is the sound of the sea
Under the bam
Under the boo
Under the bamboo tree.

Where the Gauguin maids
In the banyan shades
Wear palmleaf drapery
Under the bam
Under the boo
Under the bamboo tree.

Tell me in what part of the wood
Do you want to flirt with me?
Under the breadfruit, banyan, palmleaf
Or under the bamboo tree?
Any old tree will do for me
Any old wood is just as good
Any old isle is just my style
Any fresh egg
Any fresh egg
And the sound of the coral sea.

DORIS. I don't like eggs; I never liked eggs;
And I don't like life on your crocodile isle.

(*Song by* KLIPSTEIN *and* KRUMPACKER
SNOW *and* SWARTS *as before.*)

My little island girl
My little island girl
I'm going to stay with you

And we wont worry what to do
We wont have to catch any trains
And we wont go home when it rains
We'll gather hibiscus flowers
For it wont be minutes but hours
For it wont be hours but years

diminuendo {
And the morning
And the evening
And noontime
And night
Morning
Evening
Noontime
Night

DORIS. That's not life, that's no life
Why I'd just as soon be dead.
SWEENEY. That's what life is. Just is
DORIS. What is?
What's that life is?
SWEENEY. Life is death.
I knew a man once did a girl in—
DORIS. Oh Mr. Sweeney, please don't talk,
I cut the cards before you came
And I drew the coffin
SWARTS. *You* drew the coffin?
DORIS. I drew the COFFIN very last card.
I don't care for such conversation
A woman runs a terrible risk.
SNOW. Let Mr. Sweeney continue his story.
I assure you, Sir, we are very inter*es*ted.
SWEENEY. I knew a man once did a girl in
Any man might do a girl in
Any man has to, needs to, wants to
Once in a lifetime, do a girl in.
Well he kept her there in a bath
With a gallon of lysol in a bath
SWARTS. These fellows always get pinched in the end.
SNOW. Excuse me, they don't all get pinched in the end.
What about them bones on Epsom Heath?
I seen that in the papers

You seen it in the papers
They *don't* all get pinched in the end.
DORIS. A woman runs a terrible risk.
SNOW. Let Mr. Sweeney continue his story.
SWEENEY. This one didn't get pinched in the end
But that's another story too.
This went on for a couple of months
Nobody came
And nobody went
But he took in the milk and he paid the rent.
SWARTS. What did he do?
All that time, what did he do?
SWEENEY. What did he do? what did he do?
That don't apply.
Talk to live men about what they do.
He used to come and see me sometimes
I'd give him a drink and cheer him up.
DORIS. Cheer him up?
DUSTY. Cheer him up?
SWEENEY. Well here again that don't apply
But I've gotta use the words when I talk to you.
But here's what I was going to say.
He didn't know if he was alive and the girl was dead
He didn't know if the girl was alive and he was dead
He didn't know if they both were alive or both were dead
If he was alive then the milkman wasn't and the rent-collector wasn't
And if they were alive then he was dead.
There wasn't any joint
There wasn't any joint
For when you're alone
When you're alone like he was alone
You're either or neither
I tell you again it don't apply
Death or life or life or death
Death is life and life is death
I gotta use words when I talk to you
But if you understand or if you don't
That's nothing to me and nothing to you
We all gotta do what we gotta do
We're gona sit here and drink this booze
We're gona sit here and have a tune
We're gona stay and we're gona go
And somebody's gotta pay the rent.

DORIS. I know who
SWEENEY. But that's nothing to me and nothing to you.

(*Full Chorus:* WAUCHOPE, HORSFALL, KLIPSTEIN, KRUMPACKER.)
When you're alone in the middle of the night and you wake in a sweat and a hell of a fright
When you're alone in the middle of the bed and you wake like someone hit you on the head
You've had a cream of a nightmare dream and you've got the hoo-ha's coming to you.
Hoo hoo hoo
You dreamt you waked up at seven o'clock and it's foggy and it's damp and it's dawn and it's dark
And you wait for a knock and the turning of a lock for you know the hangman's waiting for you.
And perhaps you're alive
And perhaps you're dead
Hoo ha ha
Hoo ha ha
Hoo
Hoo
Hoo
KNOCK KNOCK KNOCK
KNOCK KNOCK KNOCK
KNOCK
KNOCK
KNOCK

The Threepenny Opera

BY BERTOLT BRECHT

Translated by DESMOND VESEY *and* ERIC BENTLEY

Und die Einen sind im Dunkeln
Und die Andern sind im Licht
Und man siehet die im Lichte
Die im Dunkeln sieht man nicht

CHARACTERS

A Ballad Singer
Mr. J. J. Peachum
Mrs. Peachum
Polly Peachum
MacHeath, *called Mackie the Knife*

The Gang:
Ginny Jenny
Filch
Money Matthew
Hookfinger Jacob
Robert, *called Robert the Saw*
Ede
Jimmy the Second
Walter, *called Wally the Weeper*

Reverend Kimball
John Brown, *called Tiger Brown*

Whores:
Vixen
Dolly
Betty
Molly

Smith
Lucy Brown
Beggars, Whores, Policemen, etc.

(Note: The numbers inserted in the text refer to the numbered Hints for the Actors in Brecht's notes to the play.)

PROLOGUE

BALLAD OF MACKIE THE KNIFE

(Market Day in Soho. Beggars are begging, thieves thieving, whores whoring. A ballad singer sings a ballad.)

And the shark, he has his teeth and
In his face they glisten white.
And MacHeath, he has his jack-knife
But he keeps it out of sight.

When the shark bites through his victim
There is scarlet on shagreen.
But MacHeath has fancy gloves on
So the blood is never seen.

By the river's cold green waters
People suddenly drop down.
But it's neither plague nor chol'ra
And 'tis said MacHeath's in town.

On the pavement, one fine Sunday,
Lies a body robbed of life.
And a man slips round the corner
Whom they call MacHeath the Knife.

Solly Meyer now has vanished—
Just another rich young man.
And MacHeath has all his money.
Try to prove it, if you can!

(PEACHUM *with his wife and daughter walk slowly across the stage from left to right.*)

Jenny Towler was discovered
With a jack-knife in her breast,
And MacHeath strolls down the quayside,
Knows no more than all the rest.

Where is Alphonse Glite, the coachman,
Missing seven days ago?
Maybe someone has the answer,
But MacHeath would never know.

Seven children and their granddad
Burnt to death in old Soho
In the crowd MacHeath stands watching—
Isn't asked and doesn't know.

And the seventeen-year-old widow,
She whose name has spread abroad,
Woke one night and was assaulted.
Mackie, what was your reward?

(There is a burst of laughter from the whores, and a man steps out from among them and walks quickly across the stage and exits.)

GINNY JENNY. Look! That was Mackie the Knife!

ACT I

SCENE I

IN ORDER TO COMBAT THE INCREASING HARD-HEARTEDNESS OF MANKIND, MR. J. J. PEACHUM, MERCHANT, HAS OPENED A SHOP IN WHICH THE POOREST OF THE POOR MAY ACQUIRE AN APPEARANCE CALCULATED TO MOVE EVEN THE STONIEST OF HEARTS.

(The wardrobe room of Jonathan Jeremiah Peachum's establishment for beggars. MR. PEACHUM *sings his* MORNING ANTHEM.*)*

Wake up, you old Image of Gawd!
Get on with your sinful existence
Just prove you're a rascal and fraud
And the Lord will reward your persistence.

Double-cross your own brother, you sot!
And sell your wife's honor, you knave!
Is *your* life dependent on God?
You'll know when you rise from the grave!

PEACHUM (*to the audience*). I see I shall have to try something new. This business is far too difficult: trying to arouse human pity! You know there *are* a few things that will move people to pity, a very few; but after they've been used once or twice, they no longer work. Man has the horrid capacity of being able to make himself heartless at will. So it happens, for example, that a man who sees a man standing at the street corner with only a stump of an arm will probably be so horrified the first time that he will give him sixpence. But the second time he will only give threepence; and if he sees him a third time, he'll brutally hand him over to the police. It's just the same with these old spiritual aids.

(*A large board is let down from above, and on it is written: "To give is more blessed than to receive."*)

What is the use of the finest and most appealing slogans painted on the most enticing posters, when they so quickly lose their effect? In the Bible there are some four or five sayings that really touch the heart; but as soon as they're used up, one's starving again. Take an example—this one hanging here—"Give and it shall be given unto you"—that lasted exactly three weeks. One must always be offering some new attraction. So one has to turn to the Bible again. But how often can *that* be done?

(*There is a knock,* PEACHUM *opens the door, and a young man named* FILCH *enters.*)

FILCH. Peachum & Co.?

PEACHUM. Peachum.

FILCH. Then you're the owners of the firm called "The Beggars' Friend"? I was told to come to you. Oh! Those are fine slogans. They're a goldmine. I suppose you've got a whole library full of such things? That's something quite new. Fellows like us—we'd never get an idea like that, never; and then, not being properly educated, how could we make a good business out of it?

PEACHUM. Your name?

FILCH. Well, you see, Mr. Peachum, I've had bad luck ever since I was a boy. My mother was a drunkard and my father gambled, and so from an early age I had to fend for myself; and without the loving hand of a mother to guide me I sank deeper and deeper into the morass of the great city. I never knew a father's care or the blessings of a happy home. And so now you see me . . .

PEACHUM. And so now I see you . . .

FILCH (*confused*). . . . see me . . . completely destitute, a prey to my own miserable desires.

PEACHUM. Like a wreck on the high seas, and so on. Now tell me, you worm-eaten wreck, in which district do you recite this nursery rhyme?

FILCH. What do you mean, Mr. Peachum?

PEACHUM. I presume you deliver this speech in public?

FILCH. Well, you see, Mr. Peachum, there was an unfortunate little incident yesterday in Highland Street. I was standing quietly and miserably yesterday at the corner, hat in hand, not intending any harm . . .

PEACHUM (*turning over the pages of a notebook*). Highland Street. Yes. That's the one. You're the crawling blackleg whom Honey and Sam found yesterday. You had the impertinence to solicit passers-by in District 10. We let it go at a good beating, since we took it you didn't know where God lives. But if you let yourself be seen there again, we shall have to use the saw. Understand?

FILCH. But please, Mr. Peachum, please. What can I *do* then, Mr. Peachum? The gentlemen really beat me black and blue, and then they gave me your business card. If I were to take off my coat, you'd think you were looking at a haddock.

PEACHUM. My young friend, if you don't look like a flounder my people were a sight too easy with you. Pah! This young sprout comes along and imagines that if he sticks out his paws, he'll be all set for a fine living. What would you say if somebody came and took the best fish out of *your* pond?

FILCH. But you see, Mr. Peachum—I haven't got a pond.

PEACHUM. Well, licenses are only supplied to professionals. (*Points in business-like way to a large map of London.*) London is divided into fourteen districts. Every man-jack who wishes to practice the trade of begging in any of them has to have a license from Jonathan Jeremiah Peachum and Company. Ha! Anyone could come along—a prey to his own miserable desires!

FILCH. Mr. Peachum. Only a few shillings stand between me and complete ruin. Something must turn up, with only two shillings . . .

PEACHUM. One pound.

FILCH. Mr. Peachum!

(*He points beseechingly at a poster which reads: "Shut not your ears to misery."* PEACHUM *points to a curtain in front of a show-case, on which is written: "Give and it shall be given unto you."*)

Ten shillings.

PEACHUM. And fifty per cent of the weekly takings. Including outfit, seventy per cent.

FILCH. And what does the outfit consist of?

PEACHUM. The Firm decides that.

FILCH. Well, what district can I start on?

PEACHUM. 2-104 Baker Street. That will be a little cheaper. It is only fifty per cent there, including outfit.

FILCH. Thank you.

PEACHUM. Your name?

FILCH. Charles Filch.

PEACHUM. Correct. (*Writes.*) — Mrs. Peachum!

(MRS. PEACHUM *enters.*)

This is Filch. Number three hundred and fourteen. Baker Street District. I'll enter it myself.—Of course, you would want to start now, just before the Coronation; the one opportunity in a lifetime when it's possible to earn a little money.—Outfit C. for you. (*He draws back the linen curtain in front of a show-case in which are standing five wax models.*)

FILCH. What's that?

PEACHUM. These are the five best types of misery for touching the human heart. The sight of them rouses a man to that unnatural condition in which he is actually willing to give money away. Outfit A: Victim of Modern Traffic Development. The cheerful cripple, always good-tempered, always carefree. (*He demonstrates it.*) Effect heightened by a mutilated arm.

Outfit B: Victim of the Art of War. The troublesome twitcher, annoys the pedestrians, works by arousing disgust. (*He demonstrates it.*) Modified by medals.

Outfit C: Victim of the Industrial Boom. The Pitiable Blind, or the High School of the Art of Begging.

(PEACHUM *displays him, advancing unsteadily towards* FILCH. *At the moment when he bumps into* FILCH, *the latter screams with horror.* PEACHUM *immediately stops, gazes at him in astonishment, and suddenly shouts.*)

He feels *pity! Pity! You'll* never make a beggar—not in a hundred years. A creature like you is only fit to be begged *from*! Then it's outfit D!—Celia, you've been drinking again, and now you're cockeyed! Number 136 has been complaining about his neck-rag. How often must I tell you that a gentleman will *not* have filthy clothing next to his skin. Number 136 has paid for a new costume. Stains—the only thing about it that could arouse pity—stains have to be produced—by ironing in candle wax. You never trouble to think! I always have to do everything myself! *(To* FILCH.) Undress and put this on. But mind you keep it in good condition.

FILCH. And what happens to *my* things?

PEACHUM. Property of the Firm.—Outfit E: Young man who's seen better days, preferably one who "never thought he would come down to this."

FILCH. Oh, so you use that as well? Why can't *I* have the better days outfit?

PEACHUM. Because nobody believes in another's real misery, my lad. If you've got the stomach-ache and say so, it only sounds disgusting.—And besides, it's not for you to ask questions, just put these things on.

FILCH. Aren't they rather dirty?

(PEACHUM *gives him a piercing glance.*)

I'm sorry, Mr. Peachum, I didn't mean that.

MRS. PEACHUM. Come on, hurry up, young man. I'm not going to hold your trousers till Christmas.

FILCH (*suddenly, with great determination*). But I'm not going to take off my shoes! Not for anyone. I'd rather chuck the whole thing. They were the only present I had from my poor mother, and never never, however low I may have fallen . . .

MRS. PEACHUM. Don't talk rubbish. I know you've got dirty feet.

FILCH. And where do you expect me to wash my feet? In the middle of winter!

(MRS. PEACHUM *leads him behind a folding screen, then sits down left and begins ironing candle-grease into a suit.*)

PEACHUM. Where is your daughter?

MRS. PEACHUM. Polly? Upstairs.

PEACHUM. Was that man here again yesterday? The one who always comes when I'm out.

MRS. PEACHUM. Don't be so suspicious, Jonathan! There isn't a finer gentleman alive, and the Captain seems to take quite an interest in our Polly.

PEACHUM. Um.

MRS. PEACHUM. And if I can see an inch before my nose, Polly is fond of him too.

PEACHUM. There you go, Celia! Throwing my daughter about as if I were a millionaire! So she's going to marry! And do you think our miserable business would last another week if these filthy customers had only *our* legs to look at?—A husband! *He'd* soon have us in his clutches. I know he would! D' you think your daughter would be any better than you at keeping her mouth shut in bed?

MRS. PEACHUM. You've got a nice opinion of your daughter!

PEACHUM. The worst! The very worst! She's nothing but a lump of sensuality!

MRS. PEACHUM. Well, she certainly doesn't get that from you!

PEACHUM. Marry!—My daughter should be to me what bread is to the starving.

(*He thumbs through a book.*)

That's even in the Bible somewhere. Marriage is a nasty business, anyhow. I'll soon beat the marriage out of her.

MRS. PEACHUM. Jonathan, you're just ignorant.

PEACHUM. Ignorant! Then what's his name, this gentleman?

MRS. PEACHUM. People just call him "the Captain."

PEACHUM. So you haven't even asked him his name! Ve-ery nice!

MRS. PEACHUM. Well, we wouldn't be so ill-bred as to ask him for his birth certificate; especially him being such a gentleman, inviting us to the Octopus for a dance.

PEACHUM. *Where!?*

MRS. PEACHUM. To the Octopus. For a little dance.

PEACHUM. Captain? Octopus Hotel? I see—

MRS. PEACHUM. The gentleman never touched me and my daughter except with kid gloves on his hands.

PEACHUM. Kid gloves!

MRS. PEACHUM. Now I come to think, he always had kid gloves on—white kid gloves.

PEACHUM. Ah. He had white kid gloves and a stick with an ivory handle and spats on his shoes and patent leather shoes and a nice polite manner and a scar . . .

MRS. PEACHUM. On his neck. How do you know all this about him?

(FILCH *comes out from behind the screen.*)

FILCH. Mr. Peachum, could you give me a few tips on what to do? I always prefer to have a system and not go at things haphazard.

MRS. PEACHUM. So he wants a system now!

PEACHUM. He can go and be an idiot; it'll come natural.—Come back this evening at six and you'll be given the necessaries.—Now, get out!

FILCH. Thank you so much, Mr. Peachum, thank you very much.

(*Exit* FILCH.)

PEACHUM. Fifty per cent!—And now I'll tell you who this gentleman with the kid gloves is—Mackie the Knife!

(*He runs up the stairs into* POLLY'S *bedroom.*)

MRS. PEACHUM. Lord save us! Mackie the Knife! Heaven help us!—Polly! Where's Polly?

(PEACHUM *comes slowly downstairs.*)

PEACHUM. Polly? Polly hasn't been home. Her bed's not touched.

MRS. PEACHUM. Then she's been having supper with that wool-merchant. I'm certain of it, Jonathan.

PEACHUM. For our sake, I hope it was the wool-merchant.

(MR. *and* MRS. PEACHUM *step in front of the curtain and sing. Song illumination: a golden light. The organ is lit up. Three lights come down on a bar from above, and on a board is written:* THE DESPITE-THE-FACT SONG.)

PEACHUM. Despite the fact
That they should be at home now, sleeping in their beds,
They want to act
Just as though some special treat had sent them almost off their heads.

MRS. PEACHUM. But that is the moon over Soho
That is the seductive "Can-you-feel-my-heart-beating" sigh
That is the "Wherever you go, I shall go with you, Johnny"
When their love grows warmer and the moon is high.

PEACHUM. Despite the fact
That they should do the useful things which we intend,
They go and act
As they think best and then come to a dirty end.

BOTH. And where is then their moon over Soho?
What's left of their seductive "Can-you-feel-my-heart-beating" sigh?
Where is then their "Wherever you go, I shall go with you, Johnny"?
When love has faded and in filth they die?

ACT I

SCENE II

DEEP IN THE HEART OF SOHO, MACKIE THE KNIFE CELEBRATES HIS WEDDING WITH POLLY PEACHUM, DAUGHTER OF THE KING OF THE BEGGARS.

(An empty stable.)

MATTHEW (*carrying a lantern and pointing a revolver round the stable*). Hands up! Anyone there?

(MACHEATH *enters and walks across the front of the stage.*)

MACHEATH. Well, is anyone here?

MATTHEW. Not a soul. We can have the marriage here safe enough.

POLLY (*enters in a wedding dress*). But this is a stable!

MACHEATH. Sit down on the crib for a little while, Polly. (*To the audience.*) Today, in this stable, will be celebrated my marriage to Miss Polly Peachum, who for love has followed me and promised to spend the rest of her life with me.

MATTHEW. A lot of people will be saying this is the riskiest thing you've ever done, enticing Mr. Peachum's daughter out of his own house.

MACHEATH. Who *is* Mr. Peachum?

MATTHEW. If you were to ask him, he'd say he was the poorest man in London.

POLLY. But surely you're not thinking of having our marriage here? This is a nasty, common stable. You can't invite the clergyman here—and besides, it isn't even ours. We really ought not to begin our new life with a burglary, Mac. And this is the happiest day in our lives.

MACHEATH. My dearest, everything shall be just as you wish. Not so much as a stone shall be left to touch your little feet. The furnishings are being brought along at this very moment.

MATTHEW. Here comes the furniture.

(*There is a sound outside of heavy wagons arriving. Half a dozen men come in, carrying carpets, furniture, crockery, etc., and soon the stable is transformed into an over-ornate living-room.*[1]*)*

MACHEATH. Junk!

(*The* GENTLEMEN *place their presents down on the left, congratulate the bride, and report to the bridegroom.*[2]*)*

JACOB. Here's luck! At 14 Ginger Street there were some people on the second floor and we had to smoke 'em out first.

ROBERT THE SAW. Good luck! A copper in the Strand got in our way. We had to beat him up, I'm afraid.

MACHEATH. Amateurs!

EDE. We did what we could, but three people down West are goners. Good luck!

MACHEATH. Amateurs and bunglers.

JIMMY. An old gentleman got something he wasn't expecting, but I don't think it's serious. Luck!

MACHEATH. My orders were: bloodshed to be avoided. It makes me feel quite sick when I think of it. *You'll* never make business-men. Cannibals—but never business-men!

WALTER. Good luck! Half an hour ago, madam, that piano still belonged to the Duchess of Devizes.

POLLY. Whatever furniture is this?

MACHEATH. How do you like it, Polly?

POLLY (*crying*). All those poor people robbed, just for a few bits of furniture.

MACHEATH. And what furniture! Junk! You're quite right to be angry. A rosewood piano—and a Renaissance sofa. That's unforgivable. And where is a table?

WALTER. A table?

(*They lay planks across the feeding troughs.*)

POLLY. Oh, Mac, I'm so unhappy. I do hope the clergyman won't come here.

MATTHEW. Of course he will. *We* told him the way all right.

WALTER (*pushes forward the improvised table*). A table!

MACHEATH (*seeing* POLLY *crying*). My wife is upset. And where are the other chairs? A piano and no chairs! Never trouble to think! How often does that happen when I have a wedding? Shut your trap, Weeper! How often does it happen, I'm asking, that I leave anything to you? It makes my wife unhappy from the start.

EDE. Dear Polly . . .

MACHEATH *(knocking his hat from his head[3])*. "Dear Polly"! I'll knock your head into your chest with your "Dear Polly," you sewer rat! Whoever heard such a thing—"Dear Polly." Perhaps you've slept with her, too?

POLLY. But Mac!

EDE. I swear that . . .

WALTER. If there's anything more you'd like, we'll go out again . . .

MACHEATH. A rosewood piano and no chairs! *(Laughs.)* What do *you* say to that, as the bride?

POLLY. Oh, well, it might be worse.

MACHEATH. Two chairs and a sofa, and the bridal pair sit on the ground!

POLLY. Yes, that would be a fine thing.

MACHEATH *(sharply)*. Saw the legs off the piano! Come on! Get on with it!

(Four men saw the legs off the piano and sing.)

FOUR MEN. Bill Lawton took Mary Sawyer
To be his true and lawful wedded wife.
But when they stood before the Registrar,
He didn't know she lived at Temple Bar
And *she* learnt his name for the first time in her life.
Ho!

WALTER. And so, miss, all's well and we have another bench.

MACHEATH. Might I now request you gentlemen to take off your rags and dress yourselves respectably. After all, this isn't the wedding of a mere Nobody. And Polly, may I ask *you* to get busy with the food hampers?

POLLY. Is that the wedding-breakfast? Is it all stolen, Mac?

MACHEATH. Of course, of course.

POLLY. I'd like to know what you'd do if the Police Commissioner were to knock on the door and come in now.

MACHEATH. I'd show you what your husband *can* do.

MATTHEW. Not a chance of it today. All the police are guarding the streets. The queen's arriving for the coronation on Friday.

POLLY. Two knives and fourteen forks! A knife for each chair!

MACHEATH. What a fine job of work! You're more like a lot of apprentices than trained men! Haven't you any idea what style means? You should be able to tell the difference by now between Chippendale and Louis Quatorze.

(The rest of the gang now return, wearing smart evening dress, but their behavior during the rest of the scene is not in keeping with their attire.)

WALTER. We wanted to bring the most valuable things. Look at that wood! The material is all of the very best.

MATTHEW. Ssst! Ssst! Permit me, Captain . . .

MACHEATH. Come here, Polly.

(*The two of them pose for congratulation.*)

MATTHEW. Permit me, Captain, on behalf of all, on the finest day of your life, the springtide of your career—its turning-point, one might say—to offer you our heartiest and most—er—importunate congratulations and so on and so forth. I hate this long-winded stuff. Well, what I mean is: (*Shakes* MACHEATH'S *hand.*) heads up, old pal!

MACHEATH. Thank you. That was kind of you, Matthew.

MATTHEW (*shaking* POLLY'S *hand, after having patted* MACHEATH *affectionately on the back*). I mean it. Well, never let your head get down, you old rascal. That is, never let down what you can keep up.

(*Roars of laughter from the guests.* MACHEATH *suddenly catches hold of* MATTHEW *and jerks him to the floor.*)

MACHEATH. Hold your gab. And keep your dirty jokes for your beautiful Kitty: she's the right slut to hear them.

POLLY. Mac, don't be so common.

MATTHEW. I object to your calling Kitty a slut . . .

MACHEATH. So you object, do you?

MATTHEW. And what's more, I never tell a dirty joke when I'm with her. I respect Kitty far too much for that. Which you perhaps can't understand, being like you are. And *you* ought to know about sluts! Do you think Kitty hasn't told me what *you've* said to her? And what's more, I'm a kid-glove gent compared to that.

(MACHEATH *gives him a fierce glance.*)

JACOB. Stop it. After all, this is a wedding.

(*They pull him back.*)

MACHEATH. A fine wedding, eh, Polly? Having to see these gutter-rats all round you on the day of your marriage. You didn't think your husband would be let down by his friends like this! But you live and learn.

POLLY. I think it's quite nice.

ROBERT. There's no one letting you down. A little difference of opinion can happen any time. (*To* MATTHEW.) Your Kitty is as good as any other. But now come on with your wedding present, cocky.

ALL. Come on, get on with it!

MATTHEW (*offended*). There.

POLLY. Oh! A wedding present! But that's sweet of you, Mr. Cocky-Matthew. Look, Mac, what a lovely nightdress.

MATTHEW. Perhaps a dirty joke too, eh, Captain?

MACHEATH. All right. No offence meant on this great day.

WALTER. Well, and this? Chippendale! (*He uncovers an immense grandfather clock.*)

MACHEATH. Quatorze.

POLLY. That's wonderful. I'm so happy. I can't think of words to thank you. Your attentions are so marvelous. It's a pity we haven't got a house for it, isn't it, Mac?

MACHEATH. Well, think of it as a beginning. It's always difficult to begin. Thanks too, Walter. Now clear the stuff away. The food!

JACOB (*while the others are laying the table*). Of course *I've* forgotten to bring anything. (*Emphatically to* POLLY.) Believe me, young woman, I feel very embarrassed.

POLLY. Don't mention it, Mr. Hook-Finger Jacob.

JACOB. All the boys throw their presents around and I stand here with nothing. Put yourself in my place.—But that always happens to me. I could tell you of some fixes I've been in! You wouldn't believe me! The other day I met Ginny Jenny, and I said to her: "Well, my little bitch . . ."

(*Suddenly sees* MACHEATH *standing behind him and walks away without a word.*)

MACHEATH. Come on. (*Leads* POLLY *to her seat.*) This is the finest food you'll get anywhere today, Polly. Shall we start?

(They all sit down to the wedding breakfast.[4]*)*

EDE (*pointing to the service*). Lovely plates. Savoy Hotel.

JACOB. The mayonnaise eggs are from Selfridge's. We had a jar of goose-liver, too. But on the way here Jimmy ate it out of spite, because he said he had an empty belly.

WALTER. One doesn't say "belly" among respectable people.

JIMMY. Don't gobble your eggs so, Ede, specially today!

MACHEATH. Can't someone sing something? Something edifying?

MATTHEW (*choking with laughter*). Something edifying! That's a proper word!

(*Under* MACHEATH'S *annihilating glance, he sits down, embarrassed.*)

MACHEATH (*knocking a dish out of someone's hand*). As a matter of fact, I didn't wish to start eating yet. Instead of this "on-with-the-food-and-into-the-trough" exhibition from you men, I'd rather hoped you would have given us something festive to start with. Other people always have some such thing on an occasion like this.

JACOB. What sort of thing?

MACHEATH. Must I think of everything myself? I'm not asking for an opera here. But you might have arranged something more than just eating and telling dirty jokes. Well, a day like this just shows how much one can count on one's friends.

POLLY. The salmon's wonderful, Mac.

EDE. Yes, I'll bet you've never ate one like that. But Mac has them every day. You're in the honeypot all right. I always have said: Mac will make a fine match for a girl who has higher feelings. I said that to Lucy yesterday.

POLLY. Lucy? Who is Lucy, Mac?

JACOB *(embarrassed)*. Lucy? Well, you know, you mustn't take it too seriously.

(MATTHEW *has stood up and is making furious gestures behind* POLLY *to silence* JACOB.)

POLLY *(sees him)*. Are you wanting something? The salt perhaps? What were you going to say, Mr. Jacob?

JACOB. Oh, nothing. Nothing at all. I really wanted to say nothing. I'll be getting into trouble here.

MACHEATH. What have you got in your hand, Jacob?

JACOB. A knife, Captain.

MACHEATH. And what have you got on your plate?

JACOB. A trout, Captain.

MACHEATH. I see, and with the knife, I believe, you are eating the trout. Jacob, that is disgusting. Have you ever seen such a thing, Polly? Eating fish with a knife! A person who does that is a pig, do you understand me, Jacob? You'll live and learn. You'll have a lot to do, Polly, before you can teach these oafs to behave like proper men. Do you even know what that means: a proper man?

WALTER. I know the difference from a woman!

POLLY. But Mr. Walter!

MACHEATH. So you don't want to sing a song. Nothing to brighten up the day a bit. This is to be just another sad, ordinary damned day like always.—And is anyone standing outside the door? I've got to see to that myself, I suppose. Perhaps you'd like me to stand at the door today of all days, so you can stuff yourselves here at my expense?

WALTER *(sullenly)*. What d'you mean: at your expense?

JIMMY. Shut up, Wally. I'll go out. Who'd come here anyway?

(*Exit* JIMMY.)

JACOB. It would be funny if all the wedding guests were copped today!

JIMMY *(bursts in)*. 'St! Captain, cops!

WALTER. Tiger Brown!

MATTHEW. Gerr, it's the Reverend Kimball.

(KIMBALL *enters.*)

ALL *(shout)*. Good evening, Mr. Kimball!

KIMBALL. Ah, well, I've found you at last. A small place, indeed, but your own.

MACHEATH. The Duke of Hampstead's.

POLLY. Good day, sir. Oh, I'm so happy that you've come on the most wonderful day of my life . . .

MACHEATH. And now I request an anthem for the Reverend Kimball.
MATTHEW. How would "Bill Lawton and Mary Sawyer" do?
JACOB. That's right, Bill Lawton.
KIMBALL. It would be most pleasant to hear your voices raised in song, my men.
MATTHEW. Then let's begin.

(Three men stand up and sing, hesitating, flat and uncertain, THE WEDDING SONG FOR POORER PEOPLE.)

Bill Lawton took Mary Sawyer
To be his true and lawful wedded wife.
Long may they live, ho, ho, ho!
But when they stood before the Registrar
He didn't know she lived at Temple Bar
And *she* learnt his name for the first time in her life.

HO!

D'you know what your wife is doing? No!
D'you let her do what she used to do? No!
Long may they live, ho, ho, ho!
Billy Lawton said to me: It's fine
So long as just one part of her is mine.
The swine!

HO!

MACHEATH. Is that all? Contemptible!
MATTHEW *(choking again)*. Contemptible! That's a good word, boys—contemptible!
MACHEATH. Hold your trap!
MATTHEW. No, that's what I meant—no life, no swing, nothing.
POLLY. If nobody will do anything, then I myself will sing a little song as best I can, and in it I am going to imitate a girl I once saw in a tiny bar in Soho. She was the barmaid, and you must understand that everyone always laughed at her, and then one day she spoke to the customers and told them the things that I am going to sing to you now. So this is the little bar—you must imagine it being very dirty—which she stood behind every morning and every evening. There is the washing-up bowl and that's the cloth which she used for drying the glasses. Where you are sitting, sat the men who laughed at her. You can laugh, too, so that everything is just as it was; but if you can't, then you needn't. *(She begins, pretending to wash glasses and muttering to her-*

self.) Now one of you must say — you for instance: (*Pointing at* WALTER.) And when is your ship coming home, Jenny?

WALTER. And when is your ship coming home, Jenny?

POLLY. And another says—you, perhaps: Do you still wash up glasses, oh! Jenny the Pirate's Bride?

MATTHEW. Do you still wash up glasses, oh! Jenny the Pirate's Bride?

POLLY. Good, and now I begin.

(Song illumination: golden light. The organ is lit up. Three lights on a bar come down from above, and on a board is written: JENNY THE PIRATE'S BRIDE.)

Gentlemen, today you see me washing up the glasses
And making beds for each who stays here.
And you throw me a penny and I thank you for it as well,
And you see my shabby costume and this dirty old hotel
And you think that I shall end my days here.
But one fine evening there'll be a shout down by the harbor,
And you'll ask: what's the reason for that shout?
And you'll see me smiling as I wash my glasses,
And you'll ask: what has she to smile about?
For a ship with eight sails
And with fifty great cannon
Sailed in with the tide.

But you'll say: go wash your glasses, my girl.
And you'll throw your pennies to me,
And I'll take all your pennies
And tuck the beds up tight
But no one is going to sleep in them tonight,
For you still have no idea who I may be.
But one evening there'll be a roar down by the harbor
And you'll ask: what's the reason for that roar?
And you'll see me standing staring through the window
And you'll ask: now what's she grinning for?
And the ship with eight sails
And with fifty great cannon
Will start shooting the town.

Then, gentlemen, you'll soon take that laugh off your faces,
For your houses will fly in the air
And when the whole town is razed to the ground
Just a dirty old hotel will be standing safe and sound
And you'll ask: what famous person lives in there?
And all through night there'll be a shouting round the hotel

And you'll ask: why has that hotel survived?
And you'll see me step out of the front door in the morning
And you'll ask: is that where *she* once lived?
    And the ship with eight sails
    And with fifty great cannon
    Will run flags up the mast.

And at midday you will see a hundred men come ashore
Who will search the shadows so still now.
And they'll capture every single living person they can see
And put them in chains and bring them to me
And ask: which of these shall we kill now?
And when the sun stands at noon there'll be a hush down by the harbor
As they ask me which of these are doomed to die
And then you'll hear me saying to them: All o' them!
And when their heads fall, I shall shout: Hoppla!
    And the ship with eight sails
    And with fifty great cannon
    Will sail homewards with me.

MATTHEW. Very nice, that's good, eh? And how she does it all, the young lady!

MACHEATH. What do you mean, nice? That's not nice, you fool! That's art. You did it wonderfully, Polly. But in front of such scum—pardon me, your reverence—it's wasted. (*In an undertone to* POLLY.) And what's more I don't like you doing this play-acting, so oblige me by stopping it in future.

(*Loud laughter at the table. The gang are making fun of the parson.*)

And what have you got in your hand, your reverence?

JACOB. Two knives, Capt'n.

MACHEATH. What have you got on your plate, your reverence?

KIMBALL. Smoked salmon, I think.

MACHEATH. I see. And with the knife you're eating salmon, is that it?

JACOB. Have you ever seen the like, eating his fish with a knife; a person who does that is nothing more than a . . .

MACHEATH. Pig. Understand me, Jacob? You'll learn in time.

JIMMY (*bursting in*). Hi, Captain! Police! The Commissioner himself.

WALTER. Brown! Tiger Brown!

MACHEATH. Tiger Brown. The same Tiger Brown who is Commissioner of Police, the pillar of the Old Bailey; and who will shortly enter Captain MacHeath's miserable dwelling. Now you'll live and learn!

(*The gang creep away.*)

JACOB. Then it's the gallows for us.

(BROWN *enters.*)

BROWN. Hallo, Mac! I haven't much time and I've got to leave almost at once. Why *must* you pick on somebody else's stable? That's another burglary!

MACHEATH. But Jacky, it's so convenient. I'm glad you've come to partake of old Mac's wedding feast. May I introduce my wife, Polly, née Peachum. Polly, this is Tiger Brown. What do you think of her, old man? (*Slaps him on the back.*) And these are my friends, Jacky; you've probably seen them all before.

BROWN (*in embarrassment*). But I'm here privately, Mac.

MACHEATH. So are they.

(*He calls them. They come, one by one, hands up.*)

Hi, Jacob!

BROWN. That's Hook-Finger Jacob, the biggest scoundrel living.

MACHEATH. Here! Jimmy! Robert! Walter!

BROWN. Well, we'll forget everything for today.

MACHEATH. Hi, Ede! Matthew!

BROWN. Sit down, gentlemen, sit down.

ALL. Thank you, sir.

BROWN. Happy to meet the charming wife of my old friend Mac.

POLLY. Don't mention it, sir.

MACHEATH. Sit yourself down, you old rascal, and start in on the whiskey! —Polly! Gentlemen! Today you see in your midst a man whom the king's inscrutable wisdom has chosen to set high over his fellow men, and who yet has remained through fair weather and foul—*my friend.* You all know who I mean, and you do too, Jacky. Ah, Jacky, do you remember when you were a soldier and I was a soldier and we served together in India? Well, Jacky, old man, shall we sing the Army Song? (*They sit side by side on the table. Song illumination: a golden light. The organ is lit up. Three lights come down from above on a bar, and on a board is written:* THE ARMY SONG.)

Johnny and Jimmy were both on the scene
And George had his promotion order
For the Army doesn't ask what a man has been:
They were all marching north to the border.

The Army's story
Is guns and glory
From the Cape to Cutch Behar
When they are at a loss
And chance to come across
New and unruly races
With brown or yellow faces
They chop them into little bits of beefsteak tartare!

Warm whiskey went to Johnny's head
And Jimmy was cold every night,
But George took them both by the arm and said:
The Army lasts forever, and might is right.
The Army's story
Is guns and glory
From the Cape to Cutch Behar.
When they are at a loss
And chance to come across
New and unruly races
With brown or yellow faces
They chop them into little bits of beefsteak tartare!

Now Jim is missing and George is dead
And whiskey has sent Johnny barmy
But blood is blood and still runs red—
They're recruiting again for the army! !

(*As they all sit there, they march in time with their feet.*)
The Army's story
Is guns and glory
From the Cape to Cutch Behar
When they are at a loss
And chance to come across
New and unruly races
With brown or yellow faces
They chop them into little bits of beefsteak tartare!

MACHEATH. We were boyhood friends together, and yet, though life in its great flood has torn us far apart, although our professional interests are so different—some people might even say, diametrically opposed—our friendship has survived it all. Take a lesson from that! Castor and Pollux. Hector and Andromache. Seldom have I, the simple workman —well, you know what I mean—seldom have I undertaken even the smallest job of work without giving my friend Brown a share of the proceeds (a considerable share, my good Brown) as a present and a proof of my unswerving loyalty to him; and seldom has the all-powerful Commissioner—take that knife out of your mouth, Jacob—organized a raid without previously giving a little tip to me, the friend of his youth. Well, and so it goes on; everything depends on reciprocity. Learn from that. *(He takes* BROWN *by the arm.)* And now, Jacky, I'm glad you've come. That's real friendship.

(*A pause while* BROWN *sorrowfully regards a carpet.*)
Genuine Persian Shirah.

BROWN. From the Oriental Carpet Company.

MACHEATH. Yes, we get all our carpets there. Do you know, I had to have you here today, Jacky. I hope you don't feel too uncomfortable, being in the position you are.

BROWN. You know, Mac, I can't refuse you anything. But I must go, I have so much to do; if anything should happen at the coronation . . .

MACHEATH. Jacky, my father-in-law is an unpleasant old swine. If he were to raise some kind of a stink, are there any records in Scotland Yard that could be used against me?

BROWN. In Scotland Yard there is absolutely nothing against you, Mac.

MACHEATH. Of course.

BROWN. I saw to all that. And now, good-night.

MACHEATH. Aren't you going to stand up?

BROWN (*to* POLLY). The best of luck.

(*Exit* BROWN, *accompanied by* MACHEATH.)

JACOB (*who meanwhile with* MATTHEW *and* WALTER *has been talking to* POLLY). I must admit I could not help getting the needle, when I heard Tiger Brown was coming.

MATTHEW. You know, ma'am, we have our connections with the highest official circles.

WALTER. Yes. Mac always has an extra iron in the fire which we never suspect. But we have our little irons in the fire too. Gentlemen, it is half past nine.

MATTHEW. And now comes the high spot.

(*All retire to the back left, behind a hanging carpet which conceals something.* MACHEATH *enters.*)

MACHEATH. Well, what's up?

MATTHEW. A little surprise, Captain.

(*Behind the carpet they sing* THE WEDDING SONG FOR POORER PEOPLE, *but this time quite softly and full of feeling. However, when they get to the end of the first verse,* MATTHEW *tears down the carpet and they sing on, bawling at the tops of their voices and beating time on a bed which stands behind.*)

Bill Lawton took Mary Sawyer
To be his true and lawful wedded wife.
Long may they live, ho, ho, ho!
But when they stood before the Registrar
He didn't know she lived at Temple Bar
And she learnt his name for the first time in her life.

HO!

D'you know what your wife is doing? No!
D'you let her do what she used to do? No!
Long may they live, ho, ho, ho!
Billy Lawton said to me: It's fine
So long as just one part of her is mine.
The swine!

HO!

MACHEATH. I thank you, friends, I thank you.

WALTER. And now the unobtrusive departure.

(The gang exeunt.)

MACHEATH. And now sentiment must come into its own, lest a man become a mere slave to his work. Sit down, Polly. Do you see the moon over Soho?

(Music.)

POLLY. I see it, dearest. Can you feel my heart beating, beloved?

MACHEATH. I can feel it, beloved.

POLLY. Wherever you go, I shall go with you.

MACHEATH. And where you stay, there too shall I stay.

TOGETHER *(singing)*. And though there's no license to show your name
Also no flowers for the happy pair
And though you don't know whence your wedding dress came
And no myrtles are twined in your hair—
The platter from which you are eating your bread,
Don't you keep it long, throw it down;
For love endures or does not endure
In many and many a town.

ACT I

SCENE III

FOR PEACHUM, WHO KNOWS THE HARDNESS OF THE WORLD, THE LOSS OF HIS DAUGHTER MEANS NOTHING SHORT OF COMPLETE RUIN.

PEACHUM'S *establishment for beggars. Right,* PEACHUM *and* MRS. PEACHUM. *In the doorway stands* POLLY, *in hat and coat, a small suitcase in her hand.)*

MRS. PEACHUM. Married? First we hang her back and front with dresses and hats and gloves and finery, and then when she's cost as much as a

sailing ship to rig out, she throws herself away in the gutter like a rotten tomato. So you've gone and got married?
(*Song illumination; golden light. The organ is lit up. Three lights come down on a bar, and on a board is written:* IN THE BARBARA SONG POLLY TELLS HER PARENTS OF HER MARRIAGE WITH MACHEATH.)

1.

Once I believed when I was pure and young—
And that I was once, just as much as you—
Perhaps one day a man will come to me
And then I'll have to know what to do.
And if he's a rich man
And if he's a nice man
And keeps his collar clean as collars go
And if he knows how to behave when with a lady
Then I shall say to him: "No"
And so one holds one's head up higher
And is still on public show.
I know the moon shines bright the whole night long
I know the boat will gently drift along
But further things can't go.
Oh! one cannot just lie down peacefully
Oh no, one must be cold as winter snow
Oh! there's so much can happen suddenly
The only thing to say is: NO

2.

The first who came was a man from Kent
He was all that a man should be.
The second had three ships of his own
And the third was mad about me.
And since they were rich men
And since they were nice men
And they kept their collars clean as collars go
And since they knew how to behave when with a lady
I said to each one: "No"
And so I held my head up higher
And remained on public show.
I knew the moon shone bright the whole night long
I knew the boat would gently drift along
But further things couldn't go.
Oh! one cannot just lie down peacefully
I had to be as cold as winter snow
For so much might have happened suddenly
The only thing to say is: NO

3.

But one summer's day, and the day was blue,
Came a man who didn't ask when
And he hung his hat up on the nail inside my bedroom
And I didn't know what I did then.
And since he wasn't rich
And since he wasn't nice
And his collar was not clean as collars go
And he didn't know how to behave when with a lady
To him I never said: "No"
So I didn't hold my head up high
Being no longer for public show.
Ah, the moon shone bright the whole night long
And the boat this time was tied up fast and strong
And it all had to be just so
Oh! one must simply lie down peacefully,
Oh! one couldn't be cold as winter snow
For so much had to happen suddenly
And there wasn't such a word as NO

PEACHUM. So that's the sort of a crook's hussy she's become. Very nice. That's lovely.

MRS. PEACHUM. If you're already so immoral as to have to marry at all, why must it be a horse-thief and a murderer? That'll cost you dear some day! I should have seen it coming. Even as a child she had a head as swollen as if she'd been queen of England.

PEACHUM. So she has really got married.

MRS. PEACHUM. Yes. Yesterday afternoon at five o'clock.

PEACHUM. To a notorious criminal! Come to think it over, it shows great courage on the part of this man. But if I have to give away my daughter, the last support of my old age, my house will fall in on me and my last dog will desert me. Why, I couldn't even give away the dirt under my fingernails without risking death from starvation. If all three of us can live through the winter on one log of wood, we may perhaps see the next year. Perhaps.

MRS. PEACHUM. What are you thinking of? This is the reward for all we've done, Jonathan. I shall go mad. Everything is going round in my head. I can't control myself any longer. Oh! (*She faints.*) A glass of brandy!

PEACHUM. There! Now you see what you have done to your mother. Quick! Just a crook's hussy, that's fine. Strange how the poor old woman has taken it to heart.

(POLLY *returns with a bottle of brandy.*)

That's the last consolation left to your poor mother.

POLLY. Go on, give her two glasses. Mother can carry twice as much when she's not quite herself. That'll put her on her legs again. (*During the whole of this scene she has had a radiantly happy expression on her face.*)

MRS. PEACHUM (*revived*). Oh, now she's showing her wicked false sympathy and kindness again.

(*Five men enter.*[5])

A BEGGAR. I won't have it. This thing isn't a proper stump, and I'm not going to waste my money on it.

PEACHUM. What do you want? That's as good a stump as all the others, only you don't keep it clean.

BEGGAR. Is that so? Then why don't I earn as much as all the others? No, you can't put that over me. (*Hurls the stump away.*) I might as well cut off my own leg, if I wanted junk like that.

PEACHUM. Well, what *do* you want? What can I do about it if people have hearts as hard as granite. I can't give you five stumps! In five minutes I can make such a miserable wreck out of a man that a dog would weep if he saw him. What can I do, if *people* won't weep? There's another stump, if one's not enough for you. But take care of your things!

BEGGAR. That'll do.

PEACHUM (*tries a mutilated arm on another beggar*). Leather is bad, Celia. Rubber is more horrible. (*To the third.*) The boil is going down, and it's your last. Now we can start from the beginning again. (*Examining the fourth.*) Of course natural scars are never the same as artificial ones. (*To the fifth.*) What's the matter with you? You have been eating again. I shall have to make an example of you.

BEGGAR. Mr. Peachum, I really haven't eaten much, my fat's just unnatural, I can't help it.

PEACHUM. Neither can I. You're dismissed. (*Turning to the second beggar.*) Between "arousing pity" and "getting on people's nerves" there naturally exists a considerable difference, my friend. Yes, I need artists. Only an artist can arouse pity in people's hearts. If you'd work properly, your public would be forced to appreciate and applaud you. But you never think of anything. So, of course, I cannot extend your engagement.

(THE BEGGARS *exeunt.*)

POLLY. Please consider him. Is he handsome? No. But he makes a living. He offers me an existence. He is a first class burglar—and also a far-sighted and experienced thief. I know exactly the amount of his savings. I could even tell you the figure. A few more successful enterprises and we shall be able to retire to a little house in the country, just like Mr. Shakespeare whom Father admires so much.

PEACHUM. Well, it's all quite simple.—You're married. What does one do when one's married? Don't bother to think. One gets a divorce, eh? It's not so difficult, is it?

POLLY. I don't know what you mean.

MRS. PEACHUM. Divorce.

POLLY. But I love him, so how can I think of divorce?

MRS. PEACHUM. Polly, aren't you ashamed of yourself?

POLLY. Mother, if you've ever been in love . . .

MRS. PEACHUM. In love! Those damned books you've been reading have turned your head. Polly, everyone does it.

POLLY. Then I shall be an exception.

MRS. PEACHUM. Then I'll tan your bottom, you exception!

POLLY. Yes, all mothers do that, but it doesn't do any good. Love is greater than a tanned bottom.

MRS. PEACHUM. Polly, don't try my patience too far.

POLLY. I won't be robbed of my love.

MRS. PEACHUM. Another word and you'll get a box on the ears.

POLLY. But love is the greatest thing in the world.

MRS. PEACHUM. That creature has several women. When he's hanged, there'll be a half dozen females presenting themselves as widows, and each one will have a brat in her arms. Oh, Jonathan!

PEACHUM. Hanged! How did you come to think of hanging? It's an idea! Go outside, Polly.

(*Exit* POLLY *who remains listening outside the door.*)

You're right. That'll be worth forty pounds.

MRS. PEACHUM. I think I know what you mean. Tell the police.

PEACHUM. Naturally. And besides, like that we can get him hanged free . . . It'll be two birds with one stone. Only we've got to find out where he's hiding.

MRS. PEACHUM. I can tell you that, my dear. He's hiding with his whores.

PEACHUM. But they won't give him up.

MRS. PEACHUM. Just leave it to me. Money rules the world. I'll go straight to Wapping and talk to the girls there. If this fine gentleman meets one of them two hours from now, he's done for.

POLLY (*enters*). My dear Mama, you can save yourself the trouble of going all that way. Before Mac would meet such women, he'd give himself up to the police. And if he did go to the police, the Commissioner would offer him a drink and a cigar, and then they'd discuss a certain business in this street where things aren't quite as they should be either. For, dear Papa, this Commissioner was very jolly at my wedding.

PEACHUM. What is the name of the Commissioner?

POLLY. He's called Brown. But you'd only know him as Tiger Brown. All who are afraid of him call him Tiger Brown. But my husband, you might like to know, calls him Jacky. To him he's just his dear Jacky. They were boyhood friends.

PEACHUM. I see, they're friends. The Commissioner and the notorious criminal. Then they're probably the only friends in this fine city.

POLLY (*poetically*). Whenever they had a drink together, they would stroke one another's cheeks and say: "If you'll have another, I'll have another." And whenever one went out, the other one's eyes grew moist and he would say: "Wherever you go, I shall go with you." There's nothing against Mac in Scotland Yard.

PEACHUM. Well, well. From Tuesday evening till Thursday morning Mr. MacHeath—a gentleman who has certainly been married several times—enticed my daughter Polly Peachum from her parental home under the pretence of marriage. Before the week is over this will prove a sufficient excuse for bringing him to the gallows, which he so richly deserves. "Mr. MacHeath, you once had white kid gloves and a stick with an ivory handle and a scar on your neck, and you frequented the Octopus Hotel. All that now remains is your scar, which is probably the least valuable of your distinguishing marks, and now you only frequent gaols, and very soon you won't frequent anywhere . . ."

MRS. PEACHUM. Oh, Jonathan, you'll never succeed; you know you're dealing with Mackie the Knife, the most dangerous criminal in London. He takes what he wants.

PEACHUM. Who is Mackie the Knife? Get ready, we're going to the Sheriff of London. And you're going to Wapping.

MRS. PEACHUM. To his whores.

PEACHUM. For the wickedness of the world is so great that one has to run one's legs off, to avoid having them stolen.

POLLY. And I, Papa, will be very glad to shake Mr. Brown by the hand again.

(*All three walk to the front of the stage, and, to song illumination, sing the first finale. On a board is written:* FIRST FINALE—THE UNCERTAINTY OF HUMAN CIRCUMSTANCES.)

POLLY. What I ask for, is it much?
Just a man who's strong and tender
One to whom I can surrender.
Is that then so very much?

PEACHUM (*holding a Bible in his hand*)
There is one right to which man is entitled—
That he may call some happiness his own
Enjoying all the pleasures life can offer
Being given bread to eat and not a stone.
That is one right to which he is entitled.
But sad to say there's been no case recorded

Of any man who got his share—oh no!
Who wouldn't claim this right, if chance afforded,
But force or circumstance won't have it so!

MRS. PEACHUM. Gladly would I give to you
All the things you ever wanted,
Let your dearest wish be granted.
Such things give us pleasure too.

PEACHUM. Be good and kind! Could anything be dearer?
Each giving to the poor in brotherly love.
If all were good, *His* Kingdom would be nearer
And we could bask in radiance from above.
Be good and kind! Could anything be dearer?
But sad to say this happy state comes never
For means are scarce and man is far too low.
Who wouldn't choose to live in peace forever?
But force of circumstance won't have it so!

POLLY & MRS. PEACHUM. And sad to say, he states the case.
The world is poor and man is base.

PEACHUM. Of course I state the very case
The world is poor and man is base.
Who wouldn't like a Paradise below?
But would our circumstances have it so?
No, that could never be the case.
Your brother may be fond of you
But when the food's too short for two
He'll go and slap you in the face.
Oh Loyalty!—we need that grace.
But when your wife, who's fond of you,
Decides your love for her won't do
She'll go and slap you in the face.
Oh Gratitude!—we need that grace.
And then your child who's fond of you,
If your pension's not enough for two
He'll go and slap you in the face.
Oh Kindness!—we all need that grace.

POLLY & MRS. PEACHUM. Yes, that's the truth about it,
The silly truth about it.
The world is poor and man is base,
And sad to say he states the case.

PEACHUM. Of course I state the very case
The world is poor and man is base.
We should be good—instead of low,
But force of circumstance won't have it so.

ALL THREE. So there is nothing we can do
The world is rotten through and through!
PEACHUM. The world is poor and man is base,
And sad to say I state the case.
ALL THREE. Yes, that's the truth about it,
The silly truth about it.
And so there's nothing we can do
For the world is rotten through and through!

ACT II

SCENE I

THURSDAY AFTERNOON. MACHEATH TAKES LEAVE OF HIS WIFE, BEFORE FLEEING TO HIGHGATE TO ESCAPE HIS FATHER-IN-LAW.

(The stable.)

POLLY (*enters*). Mac! Mac! Don't be afraid, it's me.

MACHEATH (*lying on a bed*). What's the matter? What are you looking like that for, Polly?

POLLY. I've just been to see Brown, and my father was there, too, and they've arranged that they're going to catch you; my father threatened something terrible and Brown stuck up for you, but then he gave in and he thinks you ought to go as quickly as possible and disappear for a time. Mac, you must pack!

MACHEATH. What! Pack? Nonsense! Come here, Polly. We're going to do something quite different from packing.

POLLY. No, we can't do it now. I'm so frightened. They talked about hanging all the time.

MACHEATH. I don't like it, Polly, when you're moody. There's nothing against *me* in Scotland Yard.

POLLY. Maybe not yesterday, but today there's something awful against you all of a sudden. Listen, I can tell you—I've brought the list of charges with me, I don't know whether I shall get through it, it's so long it never seems to end—listen, you've killed two shop-keepers, and committed more than thirty burglaries, twenty-three street-robberies, arson, attempted murder, forgeries, perjury—and all in six months. You're a terrible person, Mac. And in Winchester you seduced two young sisters under the age of consent.

MACHEATH. They told me they were over twenty-one. And what did Brown say?

(*He stands up slowly and walks to the right, along the footlights, whistling.*)

POLLY. He caught me up in the corridor and said he couldn't do anything more for you. Oh, Mac! (*She throws her arms around his neck.*)

MACHEATH. Well then, if I *must* go you'll have to take over the running of the business.

POLLY. Don't talk of business now. I can't bear to hear of it! Mac, kiss your poor Polly again and swear you'll never, never . . .

(MACHEATH *interrupts her and leads her to the table where he pushes her down into a chair.*)

MACHEATH. These are the account books. Listen carefully. This is a list of the staff. (*Reads.*) Hook-Finger Jacob, a year and a half in the business; let's see what he's brought in. One, two, three, four, five gold watches. It's not much, but it's skilled work. Don't sit on my lap, I'm not feeling like it any more. And here's Wally the Weeper, an unreliable swine. Fences stuff of his own accord. Three weeks' grace for him, then up. You will simply report him to Brown.

POLLY (*sobbing*). I will simply report him to Brown.

MACHEATH. Jimmy the Second, an impudent customer; profitable but impudent. Pinches the sheets from under the finest ladies in the land. Give him a rise.

POLLY. I'll give him a rise.

MACHEATH. Robert the Saw, a petty thief, without a trace of genius. He won't end on the gallows, but he'll never come to anything.

POLLY. Never come to anything.

MACHEATH. Otherwise you'll carry on the same as before: get up at seven, wash, take one bath a day, and so on.

POLLY. You're quite right, Mac, I shall just have to set my teeth and keep an eye on the business. What's yours is now mine, too, isn't it, Mackie? And Mac, what about your rooms? Shall I give them up? It would be such waste to pay the rent!

MACHEATH. No, I need them still.

POLLY. But why? They only cost us money.

MACHEATH. You seem to think I'm never going to come back.

POLLY. What do you mean? You can take them again![6] Mac . . . Mac, I can't stand it any longer. I keep looking at your mouth and yet I don't hear what you're saying. Will you be faithful to me, Mac?

MACHEATH. Of course I shall be faithful to you. I shall repay like for like. Do you think I don't love you? It's just that I look further ahead than you.

POLLY. I'm so glad, Mac. Think only of me when the others are after you like bloodhounds . . .

(*At the word "bloodhounds" he stiffens, stands up, crosses to the right, takes off his coat and starts washing his hands.*)

MACHEATH (*hurriedly*). Send all the profits to Jack Poole's banking house in Manchester. Between ourselves, it's only a question of weeks before I change over to banking exclusively. It's safer as well as more profitable. In six weeks at the most the money must all be out of this business, and then you'll go to Brown and hand the list over to the police. In eight weeks at the most all this scum of humanity will be sitting in the Old Bailey.

POLLY. But, Mac! How can you look them in the eyes when you're going to doublecross them like this and they're as good as hanged? Can you still shake them by the hand?

MACHEATH. Who? Robert the Saw, Money Matthew, Hook-Finger Jacob? Those gaol-birds?

(*Enter the gang.*)

Gentlemen, I'm glad to see you.

POLLY. Good-day, gentlemen.

MATTHEW. Capt'n, I've got the plans for the Coronation here. It looks as though there's days of good hard work ahead of us. The Archbishop of Canterbury arrives in half an hour.

MACHEATH. When?

MATTHEW. Five-thirty. We must start at once, Captain.

MACHEATH. Yes, you must go at once.

ROBERT. What do you mean: *you*?

MACHEATH. As far as I'm concerned I'm afraid I've got to take a short trip to the country.

ROBERT. What! Are they going to nab you?

MATTHEW. And just before the Coronation, too! The Coronation without you will be like tea without sugar.

MACHEATH. Shut up! Because of this, I'm handing over the management of the business to my wife for a short time. Polly!

(*He pushes her to the front and then retires to the back, where he watches her.*)

POLLY. Men, I think our Captain can go away without having to worry. We shall manage all right and get along fine, eh?

MATTHEW. I've got nothing to say. But I don't know if a woman at a time like this . . . I'm not saying anything against *you*, ma'am.

MACHEATH (*from the back*). What do you say to that, Polly?

POLLY. You lousy swine, that's a good beginning. (*Screaming.*) Of course you're not saying anything against me: or these men here would have had your trousers off and tanned your bottom long ago. Isn't that so, gentlemen?

(*A short pause, then they all clap like mad.*)

JACOB. She's all right, and she means what she says.

WALTER. Bravo, our new captain knows all the answers. Hurrah for Polly!

ALL. Hurrah for Polly!

MACHEATH. A pity, I can't be in London for the Coronation. It'll be a hundred per cent business. During the day every house empty, and at night all the best people drunk. That reminds me, Matthew—you drink too much. Last week you made it obvious that it was *you* who set fire to the children's hospital at Greenwich. If that sort of thing happens again, you're sacked. Who set fire to the children's hospital?

MATTHEW. I did.

MACHEATH (*to the others*). Who set it on fire?

THE OTHERS. You did, Captain.

MACHEATH. Well, who did?

MATTHEW (*sullenly*). You. Going on this way, ones like us will never come up in the world.

MACHEATH (*with a gesture of hanging*). You'll come up all right if you think you can compete with me. Have you ever heard of an Oxford professor letting his scientific mistakes be made by some assistant or other? Of course not, he makes them himself.

ROBERT. Ma'am, you're in command of us while your husband is away. Accounts settled every Thursday, ma'am.

POLLY. Every Thursday, men.

(*Exit gang.*)

MACHEATH. And now, good-bye, my love. Keep fresh and don't forget to make up every day, just as if I were there. That's very important, Polly.

POLLY. And you, Mac, promise me you'll never look at another woman and that you'll go away immediately. Believe me, your little Polly doesn't say this out of jealousy, but because it's very important, Mac.

MACHEATH. But, Polly, why should *I* bother with any second-hand goods? I only love you. When it's dark enough I shall start out, and before you can see the moon from your window, I shall be far beyond Highgate.

POLLY. Oh, Mac, don't tear my heart from my body. Stay with me and let us be happy together.

MACHEATH. But I have to tear my own heart from my body: I have to go and no one knows when I shall return.

POLLY. It lasted such a little while, Mac.

MACHEATH. Is it over already?

POLLY. Mac, last night I had a dream. I was looking out of the window and I heard laughter in the street, and when I looked up, I saw our moon, and the moon was quite thin, like a penny that is all worn away. Don't forget me, Mac, in strange places.

MACHEATH. Of course I shall never forget you, Polly. Kiss me, Polly.
POLLY. Good-bye, Mac.
MACHEATH. Good-bye, Polly.

(*Music.*)

POLLY. And he will never come back again.

(*The bells begin to ring.*)

The Queen is now in London on her way.
Where shall we be on Coronation Day?

(*Sings.*)

Sweet while it lasted, and now it is over,
Tear out your heart, say "Good-bye, my lover."
What use is my weeping (O Virgin restore me!)
When 'tis plain my mother knew all this before me?

MACHEATH (*sings*). For love endures or does not endure
In many and many a town.

INTERLUDE

(MRS. PEACHUM *and* GINNY JENNY *step out in front of the curtain.*)

MRS. PEACHUM. So if you see Mackie the Knife, run to the nearest policeman and report him; and you'll get ten shillings for it.

GINNY JENNY. But do you think we'll see him if the police are after him? When the hunt starts, he won't be wasting any time with us.

MRS. PEACHUM. I can tell you this much, Jenny: even if the whole of London were after him, MacHeath is not the man to give up his old habits. *(She sings* THE BALLAD OF SEXUAL SLAVERY.*)*

Now here's a man who fights the devil's battle.
The butcher, he! And all the others, cattle!
A dirty crook! No man has taken him in!
Who gets him down, that gets 'em all down? Women!
Whether he will or not,—he must comply.
Such is the law of sexual slavery.
He pays no heed to the Bible. He laughts at the S. P. G.
He will persist that he's an egoist
Knows that with a woman no one can resist.
So keeps them all from his vicinity.
But in the day he need not feel elated
For when the night falls, he's again prostrated.

And many a man saw many a man's confusion:
The noble soul descends to prostitution!
And they who saw it swore no one took them in—
Yet when they were corpses, who interred 'em? Women!
Whether they will or not,—they must comply.
Such is the law of sexual slavery.

He fastens on to the Bible. He enlists in the S. P. G.
He's Methodist! Becomes an Anarchist!
Has celery deleted from his midday dinner list
The afternoon is spent in thinking patiently.
By evening he says: I feel elevated
And when the night falls, he's again prostrated.

ACT II

SCENE II

THE CORONATION BELLS HAVE NOT YET RUNG OUT AND MACKIE THE KNIFE IS ALREADY SITTING AMONG HIS WHORES AT WAPPING. THE GIRLS BETRAY HIM. IT IS THURSDAY EVENING.

(A brothel in Wapping. An ordinary early evening. The girls, mostly in their underclothes, are ironing, playing draughts, washing themselves; a peaceful bourgeois idyll'. HOOK-FINGER JACOB *is reading the newspaper, paying not the slightest attention to anyone around him. In fact, he is rather in the way.)*

JACOB. He won't come today.

WHORE. Do you think so?

JACOB. I don't think he'll *ever* come again.

WHORE. That would be a pity.

JACOB. Would it? If I know him, he's already well away by now. This time it's—clear out!

(*Enter* MACHEATH, *hangs his hat on a nail, sits on the sofa behind the table.*)

MACHEATH. My coffee!

VIXEN (*astounded*). "My coffee"! (*Repeats this in amazement several times.*)

JACOB (*horrified*). Why aren't you in Highgate?

MACHEATH. Today is my Thursday. I cannot let such trifles disturb my habits. (*Throws his charge-sheet on the floor.*) Besides, it's raining.

GINNY JENNY (*reads the charge-sheet*). In the name of the Queen, Captain MacHeath is herewith charged with triple . . .

JACOB (*snatching it from her*). Am I there too?

MACHEATH. Of course, the whole staff.

GINNY JENNY (*to the other whore*). Look, those are the charges. (*Pause.*) Mac, give me your hand. (*He holds out his hand.*)

DOLLY. Yes, Jenny, read his hand; you know how to do it better than anyone. (*Holds forward a paraffin lamp.*)

MACHEATH. A rich legacy!

GINNY JENNY. No, not a rich legacy.

BETTY. Why are you looking like that, Jenny? It's enough to give anyone the shivers.

MACHEATH. A long journey in the near future?

GINNY JENNY. No, not a long journey.

VIXEN. What do you see then?

MACHEATH. Only good news, please—no bad!

GINNY JENNY. Oh well! I see a narrow darkness there and a little light. And then I see a large T, which means the treachery of a woman. Then I see . . .

MACHEATH. Stop. I'd like to know a few details about the narrow darkness and the treachery; for example, the name of the treacherous woman.

GINNY JENNY. I can only see that it begins with J.

MACHEATH. Then it's wrong. It begins with P.

GINNY JENNY. Mac, when the Coronation bells ring out in Westminster, you will have a difficult time.

MACHEATH. Go on.

(JACOB *laughs raucously.*)

What's the matter? (*He goes across to* JACOB, *and reads too.*) Quite wrong, there were only three.

JACOB (*laughs*). I know.

MACHEATH. Nice underclothes you have here.

WHORE. From the cradle to the coffin, underclothes always come first.

OLD WHORE. I never use silk. The gentlemen always think you're ill if you do.

(GINNY JENNY *edges quietly out of the door.*)

2ND WHORE *(to* GINNY JENNY). Where are you going, Jenny?

GINNY JENNY. You'll see.

(*Exit.*)

MOLLY. But homespun linen puts them off.

OLD WHORE. I have had great success with linen.

VIXEN. That's because the gentlemen feel quite at home.

MACHEATH (*to* BETTY). Have you still got the black braid?

BETTY. Yes, still got the black braid.

MACHEATH. And what sort of underclothes do *you* wear?

2ND WHORE. Oh dear, I'm quite ashamed. I can never bring anyone into my room, my aunt is so mad about men; and in doorways, you know, I can't wear any underclothes at all.

(JACOB *laughs.*)

MACHEATH. Have you finished?

JACOB. No, I'm just at the rapes.

MACHEATH (*again sitting on the sofa*). But where's Jenny now? Ladies, long before my star rose over this town . . .

VIXEN. Long before my star rose over this town . . .

MACHEATH. . . . I lived in the direst poverty with one of you ladies. And even though I am Mackie the Knife now, in present happiness I shall never forget the companions of darker days: above all Jenny, whom I loved best of all the girls. Listen to me!

(As MACHEATH *sings* THE BALLAD OF THE FANCY-MAN, GINNY JENNY *stands outside the window right and beckons to a* POLICEMAN. *Then* MRS. PEACHUM *joins her. The three stand under the street lamp and look towards the left.)*

MACHEATH. There was a time, in days now long ago,
When we two lived together, I and she
And my brains told her body what to do,
I guarded her and she took care of me.
One can do different, but that way does too.
And when a stranger came, I left our little bed
And had a drink or two and showed myself well-bred
And when he paid, I said: Auf Wiederseh'n
If any time you'd care to—come again.
So six months long we lived a happy life
In that bordel where we were man and wife.

(*Enter* GINNY JENNY *through the door: behind her the* POLICEMAN.)

GINNY JENNY. But in that time of days so long ago
Between us there was many an angry rift
And when the cash was short he'd curse and shout
And he would say: now I must pawn your shift.
A shift will do, but one can do without
But sometimes I grew angry—all come to it—
And I would ask him outright, how he dared to do it
And then he'd start to knock my face about
And then I'd sometimes really feel put out!

BOTH. Those six long months we lived a happy life
In that bordel where we were man and wife.

BOTH *(together and alternating)*. That was a time of days now long ago.[8]

HE. Before our simple happiness was broken

SHE. When every day we shared a bed for two

HE. For nightly, as I said, she was bespoken
(The night is usual, but the day will do)

SHE. And one fine day I felt a young MacHeath

HE. And so we worked it out: that I lay underneath

SHE. Because he knew an unborn child so often crushes

HE. Though the child was always destined for the rushes.
Too soon we ended our six months of life
In that bordel where we were man and wife.

(*Dance.* MACHEATH *picks up his swordstick; she hands him his hat; and he is still dancing when* CONSTABLE SMITH *lays a hand on his shoulder.*)

SMITH. Well, now we can get going.

MACHEATH. Has this rat-hole *still* only got one exit?

(SMITH *attempts to handcuff* MACHEATH. MACHEATH *thrusts against his chest, so that he stumbles over backwards. Then* MACHEATH *jumps out of the window. But outside are standing* MRS. PEACHUM *and the* POLICE.)

MACHEATH (*calmly and very politely*). Good evening, madam.

MRS. PEACHUM. My dear Mr. MacHeath. My husband always says: the greatest heroes of history always tripped up over such small obstacles.

MACHEATH. May I enquire how your husband is?

MRS. PEACHUM. Better again. Unfortunately you must now take leave of these charming ladies here. Constable! Take this gentleman to his new lodgings.

(*He is led off.* MRS. PEACHUM *speaks through the window.*)

Ladies, if any of you should wish to visit him, you will always find him at home. The gentleman lives from now on in the Old Bailey.—I knew he'd be here with his whores. I myself will pay what is owing. Farewell, ladies.

(*Exit* MRS. PEACHUM.)

GINNY JENNY. Hey, Jacob! Something's happened.

JACOB (*who, on account of his intensive reading, has noticed nothing*). Where is Mac?

GINNY JENNY. The police were here!

JACOB. God save us! And here I was, reading and reading and reading . . . Boys, boys, boys!

(*Exit.*)

ACT II

SCENE III

BETRAYED BY HIS WHORES, MACHEATH IS FREED FROM PRISON BY THE LOVE OF ANOTHER WOMAN.

(*Prison in the Old Bailey. A barred cage. The death cell. Enter* BROWN.)

BROWN. If only my men don't catch him! Oh God, I hope he's far beyond Highgate by now and thinking of his old friend Jacky. But he's so light-hearted, like all great men. If they should bring him in now, and he were to look at me with his faithful friendly eyes, I couldn't stand it. Thank God, there's at least a moon shining, and when he gets into the country he won't get lost. *(Noise outside.)* What's that? Oh God, they've got him.

MACHEATH (*tied with heavy ropes and guarded by six policemen, he enters proudly*). Well, my faithful minions, here we are again, thank God, once more in our old home. (*He sees* BROWN *who has retreated to the farthest corner of the cell.*)

BROWN (*after a long pause, under the fearful gaze of his former friend*). Mac, I didn't do it . . . I did everything I could . . . don't look at me like that, Mac . . . I can't bear it . . . Your silence is too terrible. (*Shouts at a policeman.*) Don't pull him with that rope, you swine! Say something, Mac. Say something to your old friend . . . Give him a word in his dark . . . (*Rests his head against the wall and weeps.*) He doesn't think me worth even a word.

(*Exit.*)

MACHEATH. That miserable Brown. That evil conscience incarnate. And such a creature is made commissioner of police. Lucky I didn't bawl him out. At first I thought of doing something of the sort. But then I thought a good, piercing, punishing stare would send the shivers down his back. The idea found its mark. I looked at him and he wept bitterly. That's a trick I got from the Bible.

(*Enter* SMITH *with handcuffs.*)

Well, Mr. Overseer, I suppose those are the heaviest you could find. With your permission, I should like to ask for a more comfortable pair. (*He draws out his check book.*)

SMITH. Certainly, Captain, we have them here at all prices. It depends what you want to pay. From one to ten guineas.

MACHEATH. How much do none at all cost?

SMITH. Fifty.

MACHEATH (*writes out a check*). The devil of it is, that all that business with Lucy will now come out. And when Brown hears what I've done to his daughter behind his friendly back, he'll turn into a real tiger for the first time in his life.

SMITH. Yes, you've made your bed: now lie on it.

MACHEATH. I'll bet that slut is waiting outside. I shall have a fine time from now till the execution.

So, gentlemen, is this what you'd call living?
I find no pleasure in such ribaldry

When still a child I heard with great misgiving:
Only the well-to-do live pleasantly.

(*Song illumination: golden light. The organ is illuminated. Three lights come down on a bar from above—and on a board is written:* THE BALLAD OF THE PLEASANT LIFE.[9])

Some say that we should live like famous sages
On empty stomachs and ascetic reading
Within a hovel where the rats are breeding.
Preserve me from such lunatics in cages!
Let those who like it live the simple way
I've had (between ourselves) too much by far.
No animal from here to Zanzibar
Would live that simple life a single day.
What help is freedom? What good to me?
Only the well-to-do live pleasantly!

Those brave adventurers of light and leading
Who risk their skins in search of new sensations
In order that their truthful publications
May give the bourgeoisie exciting reading—
Just look at them in their domestic station
See how they go with frigid wives to bed,
Their gloomy thoughts five thousand years ahead
And one ear cocked for further acclamation.
Can we call that living? Don't you agree:
Only the well-to-do live pleasantly?

And I myself have felt the inclination
To lead a great and solitary existence
But when I saw such men at shorter distance
I told myself—that's not your occupation.
Poverty makes you sad as well as wise
And bravery brings with fame a bitter grave:
So you are poor and lonely, wise and brave,
And now not even greatness satisfies.
Then let this adage your motto be:
Only the well-to-do live pleasantly!

(*Enter* LUCY.)

LUCY. You miserable wretch, you—how can you look me in the face after all that has happened between us?

MACHEATH. Lucy, haven't you a heart? When you see your own husband before you in this condition!

LUCY. My husband! You brute! So you think I know nothing of what's been happening with Miss Peachum. I could scratch your eyes out!

MACHEATH. Lucy, seriously, you're not so stupid as to be jealous of Polly?

LUCY. So you're not married to her, you beast?

MACHEATH. Married! That's a good one! I go to a certain house. I talk to her. Now and then I give her a sort of kiss, and now the silly bitch runs around boasting all over the place that she's married to me. My darling Lucy, I'm ready to do anything to reassure you, if you really believe that she and I are married. What more can a gentleman say? He cannot say more.

LUCY. Oh, Mac, I only want to become an honest woman.

MACHEATH. If you think you'll become an honest woman by marrying me—good. What more can a gentleman say? He cannot say more.

(*Enter* POLLY.)

POLLY. Where's my husband? Oh, Mac, there you are. Don't look away, you needn't be ashamed in front of me. After all, I am your wife.

LUCY. Oh, you miserable wretch.

POLLY. Mackie in prison! Why didn't you escape? You told me you wouldn't go to those women any more. I knew what they'd do to you; but I didn't say anything because I believed you. Mac, I shall stay with you to the death.—Not a word, Mac, not a look! Oh, Mac, think what your Polly's suffering when she sees you like this before her!

LUCY. The slut!

POLLY. What's that? Mac, who is that woman? Tell her at least who I am. Tell her, please, that I'm your wife. Am I not your wife? Look at me—am I not your wife?

LUCY. You treacherous brute, have you got two wives, you monster?

POLLY. Say something, Mac. Am I not your wife? Haven't I done everything for you? When I married, I was pure and innocent, you know that. And you handed everything over to me as we arranged, and I was to tell Jacob to . . .

MACHEATH. If you two would shut your mouths for five minutes I could explain everything. This is more than any man can stand.

POLLY. Yes, my love, it's clear that the wife . . .

LUCY. The wife!!

POLLY. . . . The wife has a sort of natural priority. At least outwardly, my love. It's too bad. It's enough to drive anyone mad, this aggravation.

LUCY. Aggravation, that's a good one. And what have you picked up for yourself? This dirty slut! That's your great conquest! That's your beauty of Soho!

(*Song illumination: golden light. The organ is illuminated. Three lights come down on a bar from above and on a board is written:* THE JEALOUSY DUET.)

LUCY. Come right out, you beauty of Soho!
Show your lovely legs for my inspection!

I too would like to see a thing of beauty
For there's no one can rival your perfection!
You seem to have thought it was you my husband was after!
POLLY. Did I then, did I then?
LUCY. Yes, that really makes me roar with laughter!
POLLY. Does it then, does it then?
LUCY. Ha, how everyone would laugh!
POLLY. You think everyone would laugh?
LUCY. If Mac should fall for such a calf!
POLLY. If Mac should fall for such a calf?
LUCY. Ha, ha, ha, ha, ha! A man for her!
No one cares a damn for her!
POLLY. Well, we'll soon find out the truth
LUCY. Yes, we'll soon find out the truth!
TOGETHER. Mackie and me, we're two birds of a feather
He loves me, we'll always stick together.
And so I must contend it
Our love cannot be ended
When such a creature crops up!
Ridiculous!
POLLY. Yes, I'm called the beauty of Soho
My lovely legs are worthy of inspection.
LUCY. D'you think so?
POLLY. For people like to see a thing of beauty
And they say no one can rival my perfection.
LUCY. You hussy!
POLLY. Hussy yourself!
I knew it was always me that my husband was after.
LUCY. Was it so? Was it so?
POLLY. So I can afford to roar with laughter.
LUCY. Can you then? Can you then?
POLLY. And how everyone would laugh!
LUCY. You think everyone would laugh?
POLLY. If no one loved my pretty calf!
LUCY. If no one loved your pretty calf?
POLLY (*to the audience*). D'*you* think there's no man for me?
No one cares a damn for me?
LUCY. Well, we'll soon find out the truth.
POLLY. Yes, we'll soon find out the truth.
TOGETHER. Mackie and me, we're two birds of a feather
He loves just me, we'll always stick together.
And so I must contend it
Our love cannot be ended

When such a creature crops up!
Ridiculous!

MACHEATH. And now, dear Lucy, be calm. This is simply a trick of Polly's. She wants to make trouble between you and me. They are going to hang me, and she wants to be able to call herself my widow. Really, Polly, this is not the right time for such things.

POLLY. You have the heart to deny me?

MACHEATH. And you have the heart to go on chattering about my being married to you? Why must you add to my misery, Polly? *(Shakes his head reproachfully.)* Polly, Polly!

LUCY. Really, Miss Peachum, you're only making a show of yourself. Quite apart from the fact that it is monstrous of you to excite a poor gentleman in this condition!

POLLY. The simplest rules of behavior, my dear madam, would teach you, I believe, that a person should behave with somewhat more modesty towards a man in the presence of his wife.

MACHEATH. Seriously, Polly, that's carrying a joke too far.

LUCY. And if you, madam, want to start a row in the prison here, I shall find myself compelled to summon a warder and tell him to show you the door. I should be sorry to have to do it, Miss Peachum.

POLLY. Mrs! Mrs! Mrs! Permit me to tell you this—Miss!—these airs that you're giving yourself don't suit you in the least. My duty compels me to remain by my husband.

LUCY. What do you say to that! What do you say to that! So she won't go! She stands there and waits to be thrown out and won't go! Shall I speak more plainly?

POLLY. Hold your filthy mouth, you slattern, or else I'll give you a smack on the jaw, dear madam!

LUCY. You're going to be thrown out, you impertinent creature! It's no use mincing words with you. You don't understand delicacy.

POLLY. Your delicacy! Oh, I'm only compromising my own dignity! And I'm too good for that . . . I am. (*She cries.*)

LUCY. Well, look at me, you slut! *(She has a fat stomach.)* Does *that* come out of thin air? *(Pause.)* Now are your eyes beginning to open?

POLLY. Oh! So that's how you are! I suppose you're hoping to make something out of it? You shouldn't have let him in, you fine lady!

MACHEATH. Polly!

POLLY *(sobbing)*. That's really too much. Mac, this shouldn't have happened. I don't know what I shall do now.

(*Enter* MRS. PEACHUM.)

MRS. PEACHUM. I knew it. She's with that man. You hussy, come here immediately. When your husband is hanged, you can hang yourself with him. A fine way to behave to your poor mother: she has to come and fetch you out of prison. And he has two at the same time—that Nero!

POLLY. Leave me alone, mama; you don't know . . .

MRS. PEACHUM. Come home—*immediately*!

LUCY. Listen to that, your mother has to tell you how to behave.

MRS. PEACHUM. Quick.

POLLY. All right. Only I must . . . I must tell him something else . . . Really . . . It's very important.

MRS. PEACHUM (*giving her a box on the ear*). And that's important too. Get on!

POLLY. Oh, Mac! (*She is dragged off.*)

MACHEATH. Lucy, you behaved wonderfully. Of course I was sorry for her. That's why I couldn't treat the girl as she deserved. You thought at first there was some truth in what she said? Am I right?

LUCY. Yes, I did think so, dearest.

MACHEATH. If it had been true, her mother would never have got me into this mess. Have you heard what she did to me? A mother only behaves like that to a seducer, never to a son-in-law.

LUCY. It makes me so happy, when you speak from the bottom of your heart like that. I love you so much, I'd almost rather see you hanged than in the arms of another girl.

MACHEATH. Lucy, I would like to owe my life to you.

LUCY. It's wonderful the way you say that; say it again.

MACHEATH. Lucy, I would like to owe my life to you.

LUCY. Shall I escape with you, dearest?

MACHEATH. But you know it will be hard to hide if we escape together; as soon as the search is over, I'll have you fetched and by express post!

LUCY. How can I help you?

MACHEATH. Bring me my hat and stick.

(LUCY *exits and returns with his hat and stick and throws them into his cell.*)

Lucy, the fruit of our love which you carry beneath your heart will forever bind us together.

(*Exit* LUCY. SMITH *enters, goes into the cage and says to* MACHEATH.)

SMITH. Give me that stick.

(*After a short chase in which* SMITH, *armed with a chair and crow-bar, drives* MACHEATH *before him,* MACHEATH *climbs over the bars. The Police start to pursue him.*)

BROWN (*off*). Hello, Mac. Mac, please answer! It's Jacky here. Mac, please be kind and answer, I can't bear it any longer. (*Enters.*) Mackie! What's up? He's gone, thank God! (*He sits down on the bench.*)

(*Enter* PEACHUM.)

PEACHUM (*to* SMITH). My name is Peachum. I have come to claim the forty pounds which is offered for the capture of the robber, MacHeath. (*Appears in front of the cage.*) Hey! Is Mr. MacHeath there? (BROWN *remains silent.*) Ah! So the other gentleman has gone out for a little walk? I come here to visit a criminal and whom do I find but Mr. Brown! Tiger Brown in prison and his friend MacHeath out.

BROWN (*groaning*). Mr. Peachum, it's not my fault.

PEACHUM. Of course not. You would never be . . . to get yourself into this situation . . . impossible, Brown.

BROWN. Mr. Peachum, I am beside myself.

PEACHUM. I believe you. You must feel horrible.

BROWN. Yes, it's this feeling of helplessness that paralyses one. The men do just what they like. It's terrible, terrible.

PEACHUM. Wouldn't you like to lie down a little? Just shut your eyes and behave as though nothing had happened. Imagine you're lying on a beautiful green field with little white clouds overhead. The main thing is to get this nasty affair off your mind. Everything that's happened, and above all what's still to come.

BROWN (*uneasily*). What do you mean by that?

PEACHUM. It's wonderful the way you're taking it. If I were in your position, I'd simply collapse and go to bed and drink hot tea. And what's more I'd arrange to have a nice cool hand stroking my forehead.

BROWN. Damn you! I can't help it if the man escapes. The police can't do anything about it.

PEACHUM. So the police can't do anything about it? You don't think we shall see Mr. MacHeath here again?

(BROWN *shrugs his shoulders.*)

Then it will be a nasty injustice, what happens to you. Of course people will say the police shouldn't have let him escape. And so I can't see that brilliant coronation procession quite yet.

BROWN. What do you mean?

PEACHUM. I might remind you of an historic example which, although it aroused considerable excitement in its time, fourteen hundred years before Christ, is unknown to the larger public today. After the Egyptian king, Rameses the Second, died, the chief of police of Nineveh, and also of Cairo, was guilty of some petty injustice towards the lower classes of the people. The results at that time were terrible. The coronation procession of the new queen, Semiramis, was, as the history books state, "a succession of catastrophes caused by the all too lively participation of the lower classes." The historians are far too squeamish to describe what Semiramis had done to her chief of police. I only remember vaguely; but there was some talk of snakes which she nourished at his bosom.

BROWN. Really?

PEACHUM. The Lord be with you, Brown.

(*Exit.*)

BROWN. Now only an iron hand can do any good. Sergeant, a conference. Send out a general alarm.

(*Curtain.* MACHEATH *and* GINNY JENNY *step in front of the curtain and sing. On a board is written:* SECOND FINALE—THE SURVIVAL OF MANKIND.)

MACHEATH. All you who try in righteous paths to lead us,
Who tell us to avoid all carnal sin
Your elementary duty is to feed us
Then start your preaching: that's how to begin.
You who love your stomachs and praise our honesty
Read, mark, and learn before it is too late:
However you may use your ingenuity,
Till we've had dinner, morality can wait.
First even poorer people must be able
To satisfy their appetites at table.

VOICE OFF. For how can man survive?

MACHEATH. For how can man survive? By simply getting
Others under, cheating and exploiting all he can.
He only can survive by sheer forgetting—
Forgetting that he ever was a man.

CHORUS OFF. So gentlemen, to this fact be alive:
That only by misdeeds can man survive.

GINNY JENNY. You think that moral laws should be decreed us
On when to lift our skirts and when to grin
But first of all your duty is to feed us
Then start your preaching: that's how to begin.
You need our shame to feed your promiscuity
But here is something you should take to heart:
However you may use your ingenuity
First comes the cart horse—afterwards the cart.
First even poorer people must be able
To satisfy their appetites at table.

VOICE OFF. For how can man survive?

GINNY JENNY. For how can man survive? By simply getting
Others under, cheating and exploiting all he can.
He only can survive by sheer forgetting—
Forgetting that he ever was a man.

CHORUS OFF. So gentlemen, to this fact be alive:
That only by misdeeds can man survive!

ACT III

SCENE I

THE SAME NIGHT PEACHUM PREPARES FOR ACTION. BY MEANS OF A DEMONSTRATION OF MISERY HE HOPES TO DISORGANIZE THE CORONATION PROCESSION.

(The wardrobe-room of Peachum's establishment. The Beggars are painting boards with such inscriptions as "I gave my eye for my King," etc.)

PEACHUM. Gentlemen, at this very hour, in our eleven branches between here and Wapping, there are one thousand four hundred and thirty-two men working on such boards as these in order to attend the Coronation of our Queen.

MRS. PEACHUM. Come on, come on! If you won't work, you can't beg. You hope to be a blind man, and you can't even write a proper K. That's supposed to be a child's handwriting, not an old man's.

(Roll of drums.)

BEGGAR. There's the guard of honor lining up, and they'd never dream that today, the grandest day of their military life, they've got to deal with us.

(FILCH *enters and announces.)*

FILCH. A dozen benighted birds are coming along this way, Mrs. Peachum. They say they're to be given money here.

(Enter the Whores.)

GINNY JENNY. Madam . . .

MRS. PEACHUM. Well, well, well, you look as though you've all fallen off your perches. I suppose you've come for the money for your Mr. MacHeath. Well, you'll get nothing, do you understand me, absolutely nothing.

GINNY JENNY. And how may we understand that, madam?

MRS. PEACHUM. Bursting into my room in the middle of the night! Coming to a respectable house at three in the morning! You'd do better to sleep off the effects of business. You all look like skimmed milk.

GINNY JENNY. So we're not going to get our reward for having Mr. MacHeath arrested, madam?

MRS. PEACHUM. Quite correct. In fact, you'll get something you don't like, instead of your blood-money.

GINNY JENNY. And why, madam?

MRS. PEACHUM. Because this wonderful Mr. MacHeath has again vanished into thin air. That's why. And now get out of my house, ladies.

GINNY JENNY. Don't you try that on with us. I give you fair warning. Not with us.

MRS. PEACHUM. Filch, the ladies wish to be shown the door.

(FILCH *approaches the girls.* GINNY JENNY *pushes him away.*)

GINNY JENNY. I'd advise you to keep your dirty mouth shut, or it might happen that . . .

(*Enter* PEACHUM.)

PEACHUM. What's happening here? I hope you haven't given them any money. Well, what's the matter, ladies? Is Mr. MacHeath in prison or is he not?

GINNY JENNY. Let me in peace with your Mr. MacHeath. You're not a patch on him. I had to send a gentleman away tonight because I wanted to cry in the pillow every time I thought how I had sold Mackie to you. Yes, and what do you think happened this morning? Not an hour ago I had just cried myself to sleep when I heard a whistle, and there in the street below stood the gentleman for whom I'd been weeping for, and he asked me to throw the key down to him. He wished to forget the wrong I had done him in my arms. He's the last gentleman left in London, ladies. And if our colleague, Sukey Tawdry, isn't with us now, it's because he went from me to her, to comfort her as well.

PEACHUM (*to himself*). Sukey Tawdry . . .

GINNY JENNY. So now you know you're dirt compared to him. You low-down, dirty, sneaking spies.

PEACHUM. Filch, run quickly to the nearest police station and say that Mr. MacHeath is staying with Sukey Tawdry.

(*Exit* FILCH.)

But, ladies, why are we quarreling? The money will be paid you, of course. My dear Celia, it would be better if you went and made coffee for the ladies instead of insulting them.

MRS. PEACHUM. Sukey Tawdry! (*Sings.*)

Now here's a man is facing execution
The burning lime awaits his dissolution.
It won't be long before the noose does him in
But what absorbs his whole attention? Women!
Though near the gallows—still he must comply.
Such is the law of sexual slavery.
    And now he has been sold. There's nothing left to save.
    A female Judas has the money in her hand.
    And now he just begins to understand:
    The charms of women lead but to the grave.
    And, though his fury rages unabated,
    Before the night falls he's again prostrated.

(*Exit* MRS. PEACHUM.)

PEACHUM. Come on, come on! You'd all be rotting in the sewers of Wapping if I hadn't spent sleepless nights discovering how to earn a few pence from your poverty. And I did discover something:—that the rich of the earth indeed *create* misery, but cannot bear to *see* misery. For they are weaklings and fools, just like you. So long as they have enough to eat to the end of their days and can grease their floors with butter, so that even the crumbs that fall from their tables grow fat, they cannot look with indifference on a man collapsing from hunger—although, of course, it must be in front of *their* house that he collapses.

(*Enter* MRS. PEACHUM *with a tray full of coffee cups.*)

MRS. PEACHUM. You can come to the shop tomorrow and fetch your money; but *after* the Coronation.

GINNY JENNY. Mrs. Peachum, you leave me speechless.

PEACHUM. Fall in! We assemble in an hour outside Buckingham Palace. Quick!

(*The Beggars fall in.*)

FILCH (*bursts in*). The police! I never got as far as the station. The police are already here! !

PEACHUM. Hide yourselves! (*To* MRS. PEACHUM.) Get the orchestra ready, quickly. And when you hear me say "harmless," understand me, "harmless" . . .

MRS. PEACHUM. Harmless? I understand nothing.

PEACHUM. Of course you understand nothing. But when I say "harmless" . . .

(*There is a knocking on the door.*)

That's the cue, *harmless*, then play some sort of music or other. Now get out!

(*Exit* MRS. PEACHUM. *The Beggars, excepting a girl with the board "A victim of Military Despotism," hide with their things behind the clothes racks right. Enter* BROWN *and several policemen.*)

BROWN. And now, Mr. Beggars' Friend, we take action. Handcuff him, Smith. Ah, so those are a few of your charming notices. (*To the girl.*) "A Victim of Military Despotism"—is that you?

PEACHUM. Good morning, Mr. Brown, good morning. Slept well?

BROWN. Eh?

PEACHUM. Morning, Brown.

BROWN. Is he speaking to me? Does he know any of you? I don't think I have the pleasure of your acquaintance.

PEACHUM. Haven't you? Morning, Brown.

BROWN. Knock his hat off his head.

(SMITH *does so.*)

PEACHUM. Listen, Brown, since your way leads you *by* my house—I said *by*, Brown—I can now ask you to put a certain MacHeath finally under lock and key.

BROWN. The man is mad. Don't laugh, Smith. Tell me, Smith, how is it possible that this notorious criminal is allowed to be at large in London?

PEACHUM. Because he's your friend, Brown.

BROWN. Who?

PEACHUM. Mackie the Knife. Not me. I'm not a criminal. I'm only a poor man, Brown. You can't treat me badly. And listen to me, Brown. You're on the verge of the worst hour of your life. Would you like a cup of coffee? (*To the whores.*) Children, give the Commissioner of Police a drink, that's not the way to behave. After all, we're all friends here. We all obey the law! And the law is simply and solely made for the exploitation of those who do not understand it. Or of those who, for naked need, cannot obey it. And whoever would pick up the crumbs of this exploitation must keep strictly to the law.

BROWN. So you think our judges are bribable!

PEACHUM. On the contrary, sir, on the contrary. Our judges are totally unbribable; there's no amount of money can bribe them to dispense justice!

(*A second roll of drums.*)

Departure of the troops to line the route. The departure of the poorest of the poor takes place half an hour later.

BROWN. Quite right, Mr. Peachum. The departure of the poorest of the poor takes place in half an hour. They're departing for their winter-quarters in prison. *(To the policemen.)* Well, boys, gather in everything that you can find. All the patriots that are here. *(To the beggars.)* Have you ever heard of Tiger Brown? Tonight, Mr. Peachum, I have found the solution, and, I may also add, I have saved a friend from death. I shall smoke out your whole nest. And then I shall lock you all up for—yes, what for? For street-begging. You seem to have warned me that you were going to bother me and the Queen with your beggars. These beggars I shall now arrest. That will teach you.

PEACHUM. Very nice, only—what beggars?

BROWN. Well, these cripples here. Smith, we'll take the gentlemen with us right away.

PEACHUM. Brown, I can save you from overstepping your duty. Thank God, you came to me. Of course you can arrest these few people, they are harmless, *harmless* . . .

(Music starts and plays a few introductory bars of the SONG OF THE INADEQUACY OF HUMAN ENDEAVOR.)

BROWN. What's that?

PEACHUM. Music. They're playing as well as they can. "The Song of Inadequacy." Don't you know it? It will teach you something.

(*Song illumination: golden light. The organ is lit up. Three lights come down from above on a bar, and on a board is written:* THE SONG OF THE INADEQUACY OF HUMAN ENDEAVOR.)

A man lives by his head
But it does not suffice.
Just try it, and you'll find your head
Won't raise a pair of lice.
In this world forever
Man cannot be sharp enough
Ever to discover
All the tricks and bluff.

Well, make yourself a plan
Just be a leading light!
And then work out a second plan
And neither will come right.
In this world forever
Man is never bad enough.
Yet his high endeavor
Shows that he's good stuff.

Well, run in search of luck
But take care not to fall
For all men run in search of luck
And luck runs last of all.
In this world forever
Man is never meek and mild enough
So all his endeavor
Is a great self-bluff.

Your plan was ingenious, Brown, but impracticable. All that you can arrest here are a few young people who have arranged a small fancy-dress dance in celebration of the Coronation of their Queen. But when the really poor ones come—there's not a single one here now—they'll come in thousands. That's it: you have forgotten the monstrous number of the poor. If they were to stand there in front of the Abbey, it would not be a very cheerful sight. They don't look very nice. Do you know what erysipelas is, Brown? Well, think of a hundred people with erysipelas on their faces. And then these mutilated creatures. At the door of the Abbey. We would rather avoid that, Brown. You say the police will make short work of us poor people. But you do not believe that yourself. And what will it look like if six hundred poor cripples have to be struck down with your truncheons because of the Coronation? It will look very bad. It will be disgusting. Enough to make one sick. I feel ill, Brown, when I think of it. A small chair, please.

BROWN *(to* SMITH*)*. It's a threat. It's blackmail. One can't do anything to this man; in the interests of public safety it's impossible to do anything to him. Such a thing has never happened before.

PEACHUM. But it has happened now. I'll tell you something: you can do what you like to the Queen of England, but you can't even tread on the toes of the poorest man in London—or you're done for, Mr. Brown.

BROWN. So I'm to arrest Mackie the Knife? Arrest him? But it's all very well for you to talk. You've got to catch your man before you can arrest him.

PEACHUM. When you say that, I cannot contradict you. So I shall produce the man for you; we'll soon see if there's any morality left. Jenny, where is Mr. MacHeath at the present moment?

GINNY JENNY. With Sukey Tawdry, at 21 Oxford Street.

BROWN. Smith, go immediately to 21 Oxford Street, Sukey Tawdry's flat, arrest MacHeath, and bring him to the Old Bailey. In the meantime I must change into my full-dress uniform. At times like these I have to wear full-dress.

PEACHUM. Brown, if he's not hanged by six . . .

BROWN. Oh, Mac, it was no good.

(Exit BROWN *with the Policemen.)*

PEACHUM *(calling after him)*. Now you've learnt something, Brown!

(A third roll of drums.)

Drums for the third time. A fresh plan of campaign. New destination: the Old Bailey. Quick march!

(Exeunt the Beggars singing.)

Since man is far from good
Just hit him on the head
And if you do it properly
He's either good or dead.
In this world forever
Man is never good enough
So to make him clever
You must treat him rough!

INTERLUDE

(In front of the curtain appears GINNY JENNY *with a hurdy-gurdy. She sings* THE SONG OF SOLOMON.*)*

You've heard of wise old Solomon
You know his history.
He understood all things on earth

And saw that all was vanity
And cursed the moment of his birth.
How great and wise was Solomon!
And then, behold, ere it was night
The world saw all that followed on:
His wisdom brought him to that dreadful plight—
Oh, who would envy such a one!

You've heard of lovely Cleopatra
You know her history!
All men were victim to her lust
And yet she died in agony
And passed away and fell to dust.
How fine and great was Babylon!
And then, behold, ere it was night
The world saw all that followed on:
Her beauty brought her to that dreadful plight—
Oh, who would envy such a one!

You've heard of Caesar bold and brave
You know his history!
He sat like god enthroned in light
And yet he was murdered openly
When his career had reached its height.
And loud he cried "You too, my son!"
And then, behold, ere it was night
The world saw all that followed on:
His boldness brought him to that dreadful plight—
Oh, who would envy such a one!

You know the studious-minded Brecht
You've sung him now and then.
Too often he inquired the source
Of all the wealth of wealthy men
They hunted him out of his home, of course.
How studious was my poor old mother's son!
And then, behold, ere it was night
The world saw all that followed on:
His studiousness had brought him to this plight—
Oh, who would envy such a one!

And now you see our friend MacHeath
His head hangs by a hair!
So long as he had commonsense
And robbed his victims everywhere
His fame and fortune were immense.
But then his heart got on the run!
And now, behold, ere it is night
The world sees all that follows on:
His passions brought him to this dreadful plight—
Oh, who would envy such a one!

ACT III

SCENE II

THE BATTLE FOR POSSESSION

(A room in the Old Bailey.[10]*)*

SMITH. Miss. Mrs. Polly MacHeath would like to speak to you.

LUCY. Mrs. MacHeath? Show her in.

POLLY. Good morning, madam. Madam, good morning!

LUCY. What can I do for you?

POLLY. You recognize me?

LUCY. Of course I recognize you.

POLLY. I've come here to-day to beg your pardon for my behavior yesterday.

LUCY. Well?

POLLY. I have really no excuse for my behavior yesterday except—my unhappiness.

LUCY. Yes, yes.

POLLY. Miss Brown, you must forgive me. I was very upset yesterday by Mr. MacHeath's behavior. He really shouldn't have placed us in this position, don't you agree? And you can tell him so, too, when you see him.

LUCY. I—I—don't see him.

POLLY. You've already seen him.

LUCY. I have not seen him.

POLLY. I'm sorry.

LUCY. After all, he's very fond of you.

POLLY. Oh no, he only loves you, I know that well enough.

LUCY. Very kind of you.

POLLY. But, Miss Brown, a man is always afraid of a woman who loves him too much. Naturally, the result is that he neglects that woman and avoids her. I saw at first glance that he was bound to you in a way which I naturally couldn't all at once guess.

LUCY. Do you mean that honestly?

POLLY. Certainly, of course, very honestly. Believe me.

LUCY. Dear Miss Peachum, we have both loved him too much.

POLLY. Perhaps that was it. (*Pause.*) And now, Miss Brown, I'll explain to you how it all came about. Ten days ago I saw Mr. MacHeath for the first time in the Octopus Hotel. My mother was there too. About a week later, that is, the day before yesterday, we were married. Yesterday I discovered that the police wanted him for a great many crimes. And today I don't know what will happen. Twelve days ago I wouldn't have dreamt I could ever have fallen for a man.

(*Pause.*)

LUCY. I quite understand now, Miss Peachum.

POLLY. Mrs. MacHeath.

LUCY. Mrs. MacHeath.

POLLY. And indeed, during the last few hours I have been thinking a lot about this man. It's not so simple. For you see, Miss Brown, I have every reason to envy you for his behavior towards you the other day. When I had to leave you, compelled, I must admit, by my mother, he showed not the slightest sign of regret. But perhaps he hasn't got a heart at all, just a stone in his breast instead. What do you think, Lucy?

LUCY. Yes, dear Miss Peachum. But I am not quite sure if the fault lies entirely with Mr. MacHeath. You should have kept to your own sort, Miss Peachum.

POLLY. Mrs. MacHeath.

LUCY. Mrs. MacHeath.

POLLY. You're quite right—or at least I ought to have conducted everything, as my father says, "on a business basis."

LUCY. Of course.

POLLY (*weeps*). He was my only possession.

LUCY. My dear, that's a misfortune that can happen even to the cleverest woman. But you are legally his wife, you can comfort yourself with that. But, child, I can't bear to go on seeing you so depressed. Can I offer you a little something?

POLLY. What?

LUCY. Something to eat!

POLLY. Oh, yes, please, a little something to eat.

(*Exit* LUCY.)

(*To herself.*) The great fool!

(LUCY *returns with coffee and cakes.*)

LUCY. Now, that should be enough.

POLLY. You're really giving yourself too much trouble. (*Pause. She eats.*) That's a lovely picture you have of him. When did he bring it?

LUCY. What do you mean—bring?

POLLY (*innocently*). I meant, when did he bring it up to you?

LUCY. He didn't bring it.

POLLY. Did he give it to you right in this room?

LUCY. He never was in this room.

POLLY. I see. But it wouldn't have mattered, would it? The paths of fate are terribly complicated.

LUCY. Don't go on talking such nonsense. You came here to spy around.

POLLY. It's true, isn't it, that you know where he is?

LUCY. I? Don't *you* know?

POLLY. Tell me where he is immediately.

LUCY. I haven't the slightest idea.

POLLY. Then you don't know where he is? Word of honor?

LUCY. No, I do not know. And don't you know either?

POLLY. No, this is terrible.

(POLLY *laughs and* LUCY *weeps.*)

He's got two responsibilities, and he's gone.

LUCY. I can't bear it any longer. Oh, Polly, it's so awful.

POLLY (*happily*). But I'm so glad that at the end of this tragedy I've found a friend like you. In spite of everything. Will you have something more to eat? Another cake?

LUCY. Something more. Oh, Polly, don't be so kind to me. Really, I don't deserve it. Oh, Polly, men aren't worth it.

POLLY. Of course men aren't worth it, but what can one do?

LUCY. Nothing! I'll tell you the truth. Polly, will you be very angry with me?

POLLY. What is it?

LUCY. It's not real.

POLLY. What isn't real?

LUCY. *That! (She points to her fat stomach.)* And all on that cheap crook's account.

POLLY (*laughs*). Oh, that's wonderful. So it was all a trick? Oh, you're a card. Listen—do you want Mackie? I'll give him to you. Take him as you find him!

(*There is a sound of voices and steps outside.*)

What's that?

LUCY (*at the window*). Mackie! They've caught him again.

POLLY (*collapses*). Then everything is over.

(*Enter* MRS. PEACHUM.)

MRS. PEACHUM. Ah, Polly, so here you are. Change your dress quickly;

your husband is about to be hanged. I've brought the mourning clothes with me.

(POLLY *undresses and puts on her widow's weeds.*)

You'll look lovely as a widow. But try and look a little cheerful, too.

ACT III

SCENE III

FRIDAY MORNING, FIVE O'CLOCK, MACKIE THE KNIFE, WHO ONCE MORE WENT BACK TO HIS WHORES, HAS AGAIN BEEN BETRAYED BY THEM. HE IS NOW ABOUT TO BE HANGED.

(Barred cage. The Death Cell. The bells of the City are ringing. Police bring MACHEATH, *handcuffed, into the cell.)*

SMITH. In here with him. The bells have already rung for the first time. Try and behave like a man. I don't know how you manage to make yourself look such a broken-down wreck. I believe you're ashamed. (*To the policemen.*) When the bells ring for the third time, and that will be at six o'clock, he's to be hanged. Get everything ready.

A CONSTABLE. Every street outside has been jammed with people for the last quarter of an hour. It's impossible to get through now.

SMITH. Extraordinary! How do they know already?

CONSTABLE. If it goes on like this, the whole of London will know in half an hour. Then the people who were going to the Coronation will all come here instead. And the Queen will have to drive through empty streets.

SMITH. So we shall have to be quick about it. If we're finished by six, the people will be able to be back at their places on the Coronation route by seven. Now get on with it.

MACHEATH. Hi, Smith, what's the time?

SMITH. Haven't you got eyes? Four minutes past five.

MACHEATH. Four minutes past five.

(*As* SMITH *shuts the door of the cell from the outside,* BROWN *enters.*)

BROWN (*questioning* SMITH, *with his back to the cell*). Is he in there?

SMITH. Do you want to see him?

BROWN. No, no, no, for God's sake, manage it all yourself.

(*Exit* BROWN.)

MACHEATH (*suddenly bursting into a soft and rapid torrent of speech*). But, Smith, I won't say anything, nothing about bribery, don't be afraid of that. I know everything. If you let yourself be bribed, you must at least flee from the country. Yes, you must. Also you must have enough money to live on. A thousand pounds, will that do? Don't say anything. In twenty minutes I'll let you know whether you can have that thousand pounds by mid-day. I'm not talking about anyone's feelings. Go outside and think it over carefully. Life is short and so is money. And I'm not even sure whether I can raise any. But let anyone in here who wants to see me.

SMITH (*slowly*). You're talking nonsense, Mr. MacHeath.

(*Exit* SMITH.)

MACHEATH *(sings softly and very quickly* THE EPISTLE TO HIS FRIENDS).

Now hear the voice which calls on you to save.
MacHeath lies not on leaves of gentle brown,
Nor under hawthorn trees—but in a grave
Where Fate in bitter wrath has struck him down!
God grant that you may hear his final plea!
For now thick walls surround and hold him fast!
My friends, do you not ask where he may be?
If he is dead, then drink to all the past.
But while he lives, stand by and set him free!
Or shall his torment last eternity?[11]

(MATTHEW *and* JACOB *appear in the passage. Both approach* MACHEATH.)

Five twenty-five. You've taken your time.

JACOB. Well, after all, we had to . . .

MACHEATH. After all, after all, I'm going to be hanged, man![12] But I've got no time left to quarrel with you. Five twenty-eight. Well, how much can you draw out of your private deposits immediately?

MATTHEW. From our banks, at five o'clock in the morning?

JACOB. Is it really as bad as all that?

MACHEATH. Four hundred pounds, can you manage that?

JACOB. Yes, and what about us? That's all we've got.

MACHEATH. Are you going to be hanged, or am I?

MATTHEW *(excitedly)*. Did *we* go and sleep with Sukey Tawdry instead of making ourselves scarce? Do *we* have Sukey Tawdry or do you?

MACHEATH. Shut up! I'll soon be sleeping somewhere else, and not with that slut. Five-thirty.

JACOB. Then I suppose we shall have to do it, Matthew.

SMITH (*enters*). Mr. Brown told me to ask you what you would like to have—for breakfast.

MACHEATH. Leave me alone. (*To* MATTHEW.) Now will you or will you not? (*To* SMITH.) Asparagus.

MATTHEW. I'm certainly not going to be shouted at.

MACHEATH. I'm not shouting at you. That's only because . . . Now, Matthew, are you going to let me be hanged?

MATTHEW. Of course I won't let you be hanged. Whoever suggested I would? But that's all. Four hundred pounds is all that's there. One's still allowed to say that, I suppose.

MACHEATH. Five thirty-eight.

JACOB. Then hurry, Matthew, or it will be no use at all.

MATTHEW. If only we can get through; the streets are blocked. This rabble!

MACHEATH. If you're not here by five minutes to six, you'll never see me again. (*Shouts.*) You'll never see me again . . .

SMITH. They're off. Well, how goes it? (*Makes a gesture of paying out money.*)

MACHEATH. Four hundred.

(SMITH *goes away, shrugging his shoulders.* MACHEATH, *calling after him.*)

I must speak to Brown.

SMITH (*returns with policeman*). You've got the soap?

POLICEMAN. But not the right sort.

SMITH. You will be able to set up the thing in ten minutes.

POLICEMAN. But the trap is not working yet.

SMITH. It *must* work, the bells have already rung for the second time.

POLICEMAN. A fine piece of apparatus!

(*Exit policeman.*)

MACHEATH (*sings* THE EPISTLE TO HIS FRIENDS).

O come and see his wretched destiny
Now he is really done for, as you say.
And you who think the last authority
Is vested in the dirty cash you pay
Beware lest you go down as well as he!
Now hurry all of you to see the queen
And speak to her of him and plead his cause
Run headlong like the swine of Gadarene
For still his teeth are long as eagles' claws.
Or shall his torment last eternity?

SMITH. I can't let you in. Your number is sixteen and it's not your turn yet.

POLLY. What do you mean: my number is sixteen? You're not a bureaucrat. I am his wife, I must speak to him.

SMITH. Then five minutes at the most.

POLLY. What do you mean, five minutes! It's ridiculous. Five minutes! You can't say it. It's not as simple as all that. This is farewell forever.

There's a terrible lot to be said between man and wife . . . Where is he then?

SMITH. Can't you see him?

POLLY. Of course. Thank you

MACHEATH. Polly!

POLLY. Yes, Mackie, here I am.

MACHEATH. Of course.

POLLY. How are you? Are you very done up? It's terribly difficult!

MACHEATH. And what will *you* do? What will become of you?

POLLY. Oh, our business is doing very well. That's the least of our troubles. Mackie, are you very nervous? . . . Who actually was your father? There's so much you haven't told me. I don't understand it at all. You were really quite healthy always.

MACHEATH. Polly, can't you help me out?

POLLY. Yes, of course.

MACHEATH. With money, I mean. I talked to the warder here . . .

POLLY (*slowly*). The money has gone to Manchester.

MACHEATH. And you have none?

POLLY. No, I've got nothing. But do you know, Mac, I could perhaps speak to someone . . . I might even be able to ask the Queen personally. (*She breaks down.*) Oh, Mackie!

SMITH (*pulling* POLLY *away*). Now have you got your thousand pounds?

POLLY. Good luck, Mac, take care of yourself and never forget me.

(*Exit* POLLY. A CONSTABLE *brings on a table with a plate of asparagus on it.*)

SMITH. Is the asparagus tender?

CONSTABLE. It is.

(*Exit* CONSTABLE. BROWN *enters and walks over to* SMITH.)

BROWN. Smith, what does he want with me? I'm glad you waited for me with the table. We'll take it with us when we go in to him, so he'll see how thoughtful we are.

(*They both carry the table into the cell. Exit* SMITH. *Pause.*)

Hallo, Mac. Here's your asparagus. Won't you have a little?

MACHEATH. Don't trouble yourself, Mr. Brown, there are other people who will do me the last honors.[13]

BROWN. But Mackie!

MACHEATH. I should like the account! Forgive me if I eat in the meanwhile. After all, this is my last meal. (*Eats.*)

BROWN. Good appetite! Oh, Mac, you wound me with red-hot irons.

MACHEATH. The account, sir, please, the account. No sentimentality.

BROWN (*sighing, draws a little notebook out of a pocket*). I've brought it with me, Mac. Here is the account for the last six months.

MACHEATH (*cuttingly*). I see. So you have only come to get your money out of me.

BROWN. But you know that's not true . . .

MACHEATH. All right, I don't want you to be the loser. What do I owe you? I'm sorry, but I shall need a detailed statement. Life has made me mistrustful . . . And you're the one who will understand that best.

BROWN. Mac, when you speak like that, I can't even think.

(*There is a sound of loud banging behind.*)

SMITH (*voice*). All right, that will hold.

MACHEATH. The account, Brown.

BROWN. Very well, if you really want it—first of all there are the rewards for the arrests of the murderers which you or your people made possible. You received from the Government in all . . .

MACHEATH. Three cases at forty pounds each makes a hundred and twenty pounds. So a quarter of that for you is thirty pounds, which we therefore owe you.

BROWN. Yes—yes—but I really don't know, Mac, at the last minute like this if we can . . .

MACHEATH. Please leave that stuff out. Thirty pounds, and for the one in Dover eight pounds.

BROWN. Why only eight pounds, that was . . .

MACHEATH. Do you or do you not believe me? As a result of the last half year you receive thirty-eight pounds.

BROWN (*sobbing loudly*). A whole lifetime . . . I've known your every thought . . .

BOTH. By just looking in your eyes.

MACHEATH. Well, well, three years in India—Johnny and Jimmy were both on the scene—five years in London, and that's all the thanks I get. (*In the meanwhile he shows what he will look like when hanged.*)
Here hangs MacHeath who never did you wrong,
Sold by a faithless friend of former days.
And dangling from a rope a fathom long
He knows at last how much his bottom weighs.

BROWN. Mac, if you're going to behave to me like that . . . who attacks my honor attacks me. (*Runs angrily out of the cage.*)

MACHEATH. Your honor . . .

BROWN. Yes, my honor. Smith, begin! Let the people in! (*To* MACHEATH.) Excuse me, please.

SMITH (*quickly to* MACHEATH). I can still get you away, but in a minute it will be too late. Have you got the money?

MACHEATH. Yes, as soon as the boys get back.

SMITH. They're not in sight. Well—that's off.

(*People are let in:* PEACHUM, MRS. PEACHUM, POLLY, LUCY, THE WHORES, THE CLERGYMAN, MATTEW *and* JACOB.)

GINNY JENNY. They didn't want to let us in, but I said to them: if you don't take your something heads out of my way, you'll know Ginny Jenny better than you like.

PEACHUM. I am his father-in-law. Pardon me, but which of these present is Mr. MacHeath?

MACHEATH (*presents himself*). I am MacHeath.

PEACHUM (*walks past the cage and stands right, as do all the others subsequently*). Fate, Mr. MacHeath, decreed that you should become my son-in-law without my knowing you. The circumstances in which I meet you for the first time are very tragic. Mr. MacHeath, you once had white kid gloves, a stick with an ivory handle and a scar on your neck, and you frequented the Octopus Hotel. There remains the scar on your neck, which is probably the least valuable of your distinguishing marks, and now you only frequent gaols, and very soon you won't frequent anywhere . . .

(POLLY *walks sobbing past the cage and stands right.*)

MACHEATH. What a pretty dress you're wearing.

(MATTHEW *and* JACOB *come past the cage and stand right.*)

MATTHEW. We couldn't get through on account of the crowd. But we ran so fast I thought Jacob was going to have a stroke. If you don't believe us . . .

MACHEATH. What do the men say? Have they got good places?

MATTHEW. There, Captain, we knew you'd understand us. But look, we don't get a Coronation every day. The men have to earn when they can. They asked to be remembered to you.

JACOB. Kindly.

MRS. PEACHUM (*walks past the cage and stands right*). Mr. MacHeath, who would have thought of this when a week ago we had a little dance together in the Octopus Hotel.

MACHEATH. Yes, a little dance.

MRS. PEACHUM. But Fate is cruel.

BROWN (*to the clergyman at the back*). And with this man I stood at Aserbaijan, shoulder to shoulder, under withering fire.

GINNY JENNY (*comes past the cage*). Us girls are all in an awful fix. Not a soul has gone to the Coronation. They all want to see you. (*Stands right.*)

MACHEATH. To see me.

SMITH. Now, come on. Six o'clock.

MACHEATH. We will not keep the people waiting. Ladies and gentlemen, you see here the vanishing representative of a vanishing class. We artisans of the lower middle class, who work with honest jemmies on the cash-boxes of small shop-keepers, are being ruined by large concerns backed by the banks. What is a picklock to a bank-share? What is the burglary of a bank to the founding of a bank? What is the murder of a man to the employment of a man? Fellow citizens, I herewith take my leave of you. I thank you all for coming. Some of you have been very close to me. That Jenny should have given me up astonishes me greatly. It is a clear proof that the world will always be the same. The concurrence of several unfortunate circumstances has brought about my fall. Good—I fall.

(*Song illumination: golden light. The organ is lit up. Three lights come down from above on a bar and on a board is written:* BALLADE IN WHICH MACHEATH BEGS THE FORGIVENESS OF ALL.)

You people who survive us when we die
Let not your hearts be hard against our action
And laugh not when we hang against the sky
A stupid laugh of bitter satisfaction.
Nor curse against us, though we be defeated,
Be not, as was the Law to us, unkind.
Not all of us possess a lawful mind.
My friends, be not light-hearted nor conceited.
My friends, let this our fate a warning be
And pray to God that He will pardon me.

The rains now wash us down and wash us clean
And wash the flesh we overfed before.
And those which saw too much and asked for more—
Our eyes—are pecked by ravens perched between.
We tried indeed to climb above our station
And now we hang on high as though in pride
Attacked by hungry birds on every side
Like refuse waiting for disintegration.
Oh brothers, let our fate a warning be
And pray to God that He will pardon me.

And girls who flaunt their buxom beauty
To catch the eyes of men with yearnings
And thieves who watch them when on duty
To confiscate their sinful earnings
And murderers and brothel-keepers
And pickpockets and such as we
Abortionists and crossing-sweepers
I pray that they will pardon me.

Not so the police, scum of the nation,
Who every evening, every morning
Caused me endless tribulation
And usually without a warning.
Oh, I could curse them to damnation
But for today I'll let that be
To save all further explanation
I pray they too will pardon me.

With iron hammers smash their faces
And smash them till they cease to be
But now I would forget their faces
And pray that they will pardon me.

SMITH. If you please, Mr. MacHeath.

MRS. PEACHUM. Polly and Lucy, stand by your husband in his last hour.

MACHEATH. Ladies, whatever there may have been between us . . .

SMITH (*leads him off*). Come on!

(Passage to the Gallows. All exeunt then re-enter from the other side of the stage, carrying hurricane-lamps. When MACHEATH *is standing on the gallows,* PEACHUM *speaks.)*

PEACHUM. Most honored public, thus far we have come
MacHeath should now be hanged and justice done
For in the whole of Christendom
There's nothing granted free to anyone.

But just in case you should have been misled
And think that *we* approve this execution
MacHeath will *not* be hanged till he be dead,
For we've thought out a different solution.

In order that, in opera anyway,
Mercy may prevail over justice once a year
And also since we wish you well today
The royal messenger will now appear.

(On a board is written: THIRD FINALE—THE ARRIVAL OF THE MOUNTED MESSENGER.)

CHORUS. Hark, who comes! Hark, who comes!
The royal messenger riding comes!

BROWN (*enters on horseback and sings recitative*).
On account of her Coronation, our gracious Queen commands that a certain MacHeath shall at once be released. (*All cheer.*)

At the same time he is raised to the permanent ranks of the nobility. (*Cheers.*) The castle Marmorell and an income of ten thousand pounds are his as long as he shall live. And to the happy couples here the Queen presents her royal and cordial felicitations.

MACHEATH. A rescue! A rescue! I was sure of it! Where the need is greatest, there God's help will be nearest.

POLLY. A rescue! A rescue! My dearest MacHeath has been rescued. I am so happy.

MRS. PEACHUM. So the whole thing has a happy ending. How calm and peaceful would our life be always, if a messenger came from the king whenever we wanted.

PEACHUM. Therefore all remain standing where you are now and sing the chorale of the poorest of the poor, of whose difficult life you have shown us something today. But in real life their end is always bad. Mounted messengers from the queen come far too seldom, and if you kick a man he kicks you back again. Therefore never be too ready to condemn injustice.

ALL (*singing to the accompaniment of the organ, they advance to the front of the stage. The words they sing appear on a board or screen.*)

Condemn injustice not with overboldness
Since it is cold, its death is sure but slow.
Consider all the darkness and the coldness
Which fill this vale of misery and woe.

The Love of Don Perlimplin and Belisa in the Garden

AN EROTIC ALLELUJAH IN FOUR SCENES

BY FEDERICO GARCÍA LORCA

Translated by RICHARD L. O'CONNELL AND JAMES GRAHAM LUHAN

CHARACTERS

Perlimplin
Marcolfa
Belisa
The Mother
First Sprite
Second Sprite

PROLOGUE

(*House of* DON PERLIMPLIN. *Green walls; chairs and furniture painted black. At the rear, a deep window through which Belisa's balcony may be seen.* PERLIMPLIN *wears a green cassock and a white wig full of curls.* MARCOLFA, *the servant, wears the classic striped dress.*)

PERLIMPLIN. Yes?
MARCOLFA. Yes.
PERLIMPLIN. But why, "yes"?
MARCOLFA. Just because yes.
PERLIMPLIN. And if I should say no?
MARCOLFA (*acidly*). No?
PERLIMPLIN. No.
MARCOLFA. Tell me, Master, the reason for that "no."
PERLIMPLIN. You tell me, you persevering domestic, the reasons for that "yes."

(*Pause.*)

MARCOLFA. Twenty and twenty are forty . . .
PERLIMPLIN (*listening*). Proceed.
MARCOLFA. And ten, fifty.
PERLIMPLIN. Go ahead.
MARCOLFA. At fifty years one is no longer a child.
PERLIMPLIN. Of course!
MARCOLFA. I may die any minute.
PERLIMPLIN. Of course!
MARCOLFA (*weeping*). And what will happen to you all alone in the world?
PERLIMPLIN. What will happen?
MARCOLFA. That's why you have to marry.
PERLIMPLIN (*distracted*). Yes?
MARCOLFA (*sternly*). Yes.
PERLIMPLIN (*miserably*). But Marcolfa . . . why "yes"? When I was a child a woman strangled her husband. He was a shoemaker. I can't forget it. I've always said I wouldn't marry. My books are enough for me. What good will marriage do me?
MARCOLFA. Marriage holds great charms, Master. It isn't what it appears on the outside. It's full of hidden things . . . things which it would not be becoming for a servant to mention. You see that . . .
PERLIMPLIN. That what?
MARCOLFA. That I have blushed.

(*Pause. A piano is heard.*)

VOICE OF BELISA (*within, singing*).

Love, love.
Enclosed within my thighs,
the sun swims like a fish.
Warm water in the rushes,
love.
Morning cock, the night is going!
Don't let it vanish, no!

MARCOLFA. My master will see the reason I have.

PERLIMPLIN (*scratching his head*). She sings prettily.

MARCOLFA. She is the woman for my master. The fair Belisa.

PERLIMPLIN. Belisa . . . but wouldn't it be better . . . ?

MARCOLFA. No. Now come. (*She takes him by the hand and goes toward the window.*) Say, "Belisa."

PERLIMPLIN. Belisa . . .

MARCOLFA. Louder.

PERLIMPLIN. Belisa!

(*The balcony of the house opposite opens and* BELISA *appears, resplendent in her loveliness. She is half naked.*)

BELISA. Who calls?

(MARCOLFA *hides behind the window curtains.*)

MARCOLFA. Answer!

PERLIMPLIN (*trembling*). I was calling.

BELISA. Yes?

PERLIMPLIN. Yes.

BELISA. But why, "yes"?

PERLIMPLIN. Just because yes.

BELISA. And if I should say no?

PERLIMPLIN. I would be sorry, because . . . we have decided that I want to marry.

BELISA (*laughs*). Marry whom?

PERLIMPLIN. You.

BELISA (*serious*). But . . . (*Calling.*) Mama! Mama-a-a!

MARCOLFA. This is going well.

(*Enter the* MOTHER *wearing a great eighteenth-century wig full of birds, ribbons, and glass beads.*)

BELISA. Don Perlimplin wants to marry me. What must I do?

MOTHER. The very best of afternoons to you, my charming little neighbor. I always said to my poor little girl that you have the grace and elegance of that great lady who was your mother whom I did not have the pleasure of knowing.

PERLIMPLIN. Thank you.

MARCOLFA (*furiously, from behind the curtain*). I have decided that we are going . . .

PERLIMPLIN. We have decided that we are going . . .

MOTHER. To contract matrimony. Is that not so?

PERLIMPLIN. That is so.

BELISA. But, Mama, what about me?

MOTHER. You are agreeable, naturally. Don Perlimplin is a fascinating husband.

PERLIMPLIN. I hope to be one, madam.

MARCOLFA (*calling to* DON PERLIMPLIN). This is almost settled.

PERLIMPLIN. Do you think so?

(*They whisper together.*)

MOTHER (*to* BELISA). Don Perlimplin has many lands. On these are many geese and sheep. The sheep are taken to market. At the market they get money for them. Money produces beauty . . . and beauty is sought after by all men.

PERLIMPLIN. Then . . .

MOTHER. She is ever so thrilled. Belisa, go inside. It isn't well for a maiden to hear certain conversations.

BELISA. Until later. (*She leaves.*)

MOTHER. She is a lily. You've seen her face? (*Lowering her voice.*) But if you should see further! Just like sugar. But, pardon. I need not call these things to the attention of a person as modern and competent as you . . .

PERLIMPLIN. Yes?

MOTHER. Why, yes. I said it without irony.

PERLIMPLIN. I don't know how to express our gratitude.

MOTHER. Oh, "our gratitude." What extraordinary delicacy! The gratitude of your heart and yourself . . . I have sensed it. I have sensed it . . . in spite of the fact that it is twenty years since I have had relations with a man.

MARCOLFA (*aside*). The wedding.

PERLIMPLIN. The wedding . . .

MOTHER. Whenever you wish. Though . . . (*She brings out a handkerchief and weeps.*) . . . to every mother . . . until later! (*Leaves.*)

MARCOLFA. At last!

PERLIMPLIN. Oh, Marcolfa, Marcolfa! Into what world are you going to thrust me?

MARCOLFA. Into the world of matrimony.

PERLIMPLIN. And if I should be frank, I would say that I feel thirsty. Why don't you bring me some water?

MARCOLFA (*approaching and whispering in his ear*). Who could believe it?

(*The piano is heard. The stage is in darkness.* BELISA *opens the curtains of her balcony, almost naked, singing languidly.*)

BELISA. Love, love.
Enclosed within my thighs,
The sun swims like a fish.

MARCOLFA. Beautiful maiden.

PERLIMPLIN. Like sugar . . . white inside. Will she be capable of strangling me?

MARCOLFA. Woman is weak if frightened in time.

BELISA. Love.
Morning cock, the night is going!
Don't let it vanish, no!

PERLIMPLIN. What does she mean, Marcolfa? What does she mean?

MARCOLFA. What is this I feel? What is it?

(*The piano goes on playing. Past the balcony flies a band of black paper birds.*)

THE ONLY ACT

SCENE I

(*Don Perlimplin's room. At the center there is a great bed piled high with pillows, spread with down comforters, and topped by a canopy with plume ornaments. It is arranged slanting, as if in an old picture with bad perspective. In the round back wall there are six doors. The first one on the right serves as entrance and exit for* DON PERLIMPLIN. *It is the wedding night.* MARCOLFA, *with a candelabrum in her hand, speaks at the first door on the left side.*)

MARCOLFA. Good-night.

BELISA (*offstage*). Good-night, Marcolfa.

(DON PERLIMPLIN *enters, magnificently dressed in the style of the eighteenth-century, wearing a green coat trimmed with fur and a cravat of real lace.*)

MARCOLFA. May my master have a good wedding night.

PERLIMPLIN. Good-night, Marcolfa.

(MARCOLFA *leaves.* PERLIMPLIN *tiptoes toward the room in front and looks from the door.*)

Belisa, in all that froth of lace you look like a wave, and you give me the same fear of the sea that I had as a child. Since you came from the church my house is full of secret whispers, and the water grows warm of its own accord in the glasses. Oh! Perlimplin . . . Where are you, Perlimplin?

(*Tiptoes back.* BELISA *appears, dressed in a great sleeping garment full of laces. Her hair is loose and her arms bare.*)

BELISA. The maid perfumed this room with lavender and not with musk as I ordered . . . (*Goes toward the bed.*) Nor did she put on the fine linen and the bedcover she has. Marcolfa . . . (*At this moment there is a soft music of guitars.* BELISA *crosses her hands over her breast.*) Ah! Whoever seeks me ardently will find me. My thirst is never quenched, just as the thirst of the gargoyles who spurt water in the fountains is never quenched. (*The music continues.*) Oh, what music! *What music!* Like the soft warm downy feathers of a swan! Oh! Is it I? Or is it the music?

(*She throws a great cape of red velvet over her shoulders and walks about the room. The music is silent and five whistles are heard.*)

BELISA. Five of them!

(PERLIMPLIN *appears.*)

PERLIMPLIN. Do I disturb you?

BELISA. How could that be possible?

PERLIMPLIN. Are you sleepy?

BELISA (*ironically*). Sleepy?

PERLIMPLIN. The night has become a little chilly. (*Rubs his hands. Pause.*)

BELISA (*with decision*). Perlimplin.

PERLIMPLIN (*trembling*). What do you want?

BELISA (*vaguely*). It's a pretty name, "Perlimplin."

PERLIMPLIN. Yours is prettier, Belisa.

BELISA (*laughing*). Oh! Thank you! (*Short pause.*)

PERLIMPLIN. I wanted to tell you something.

BELISA. And that is?

PERLIMPLIN. I have been late in deciding . . . but . . .

BELISA. Say it.

PERLIMPLIN. Belisa, I love you.

BELISA. Oh, you little gentleman! That's your duty.

PERLIMPLIN. Yes?

BELISA. Yes.

PERLIMPLIN. But why "yes"?

BELISA (*coyly*). Because.

PERLIMPLIN. No.

BELISA. Perlimplin!

PERLIMPLIN. No, Belisa, before I married you, I didn't love you.

BELISA (*jokingly*). What are you saying?

PERLIMPLIN. I married . . . for whatever reason, but I didn't love you. I couldn't have imagined your body until I saw it through the keyhole when you were putting on your wedding dress. And then it was that I felt love come to me. Then! Like the deep thrust of a lancet in my throat.

BELISA (*intrigued*). But, the other women?

PERLIMPLIN. What women?

BELISA. Those you knew before.

PERLIMPLIN. But, the other women?

BELISA. You astonish me!

PERLIMPLIN. The first to be astonished was I. (*Pause. Five whistles are heard.*) What's that?

BELISA. The clock.

PERLIMPLIN. Is it five?

BELISA. Bedtime.

PERLIMPLIN. Do I have your permission to remove my coat?

BELISA. Of course, little husband. (*Yawning.*) And put out the light, if that is your wish.

(PERLIMPLIN *puts out the light.*)

PERLIMPLIN (*in a low voice*). Belisa.

BELISA (*loudly*). What, child?

PERLIMPLIN (*whispering*). I've put the light out.

BELISA (*jokingly*). I see that.

PERLIMPLIN (*in a much lower voice*). Belisa . . .

BELISA (*in a loud voice*). What, my enchanter?

PERLIMPLIN. I adore you!

(*Two* SPRITES, *entering from opposite sides of the stage, run a curtain of misty gray. The theatre is left in darkness. Flutes sound with a sweet, sleepy tone. The* SPRITES *should be two children. They sit on the prompt box facing the audience.*)

FIRST SPRITE. And how goes it with you in this tiny darkness?

SECOND SPRITE. Neither well nor badly, little friend.

FIRST SPRITE. Here we are.

SECOND SPRITE. And how do you like it? It's always nice to cover other people's failings . . .

FIRST SPRITE. And then to let the audience take care of uncovering them.

SECOND SPRITE. And without this covering and uncovering . . .

FIRST SPRITE. What would the poor people do?

SECOND SPRITE (*looking at the curtain*). Don't leave even a crack.

FIRST SPRITE. For the cracks today are darkness tomorrow.

(*They laugh.*)

SECOND SPRITE. When things are quite evident . . .

FIRST SPRITE. Man figures that he has no need to investigate them . . .

SECOND SPRITE. And he goes to dark things to discover in them secrets he already knew.

FIRST SPRITE. But that's what we're here for. We Sprites!

SECOND SPRITE. Did you know Perlimplin?

FIRST SPRITE. Since he was a child.

SECOND SPRITE. And Belisa?

FIRST SPRITE. Well. Her room exhaled such intense perfume that I once fell asleep and awoke between her cat's paws.

(*They laugh.*)

SECOND SPRITE. This affair was . . .

FIRST SPRITE. Ever so clear!

SECOND SPRITE. All the world imagined it.

FIRST SPRITE. And the gossip must have turned then to more mysterious things.

SECOND SPRITE. That's why our efficient and most sociable screen should not be opened yet.

FIRST SPRITE. No, don't let them find out.

SECOND SPRITE. The soul of Perlimplin, tiny and frightened like a newborn duckling, becomes enriched and sublime at these moments.

(*They laugh.*)

FIRST SPRITE. The audience is impatient.

SECOND SPRITE. And with reason. Shall we go?

FIRST SPRITE. Let's go. I feel a fresh breeze on my back already.

SECOND SPRITE. Five cool camellias of the dawn have opened in the walls of the bedroom.

FIRST SPRITE. Five balconies upon the city.

(*They rise and throw on some great blue hoods.*)

SECOND SPRITE. Don Perlimplin, do we help or hinder you?

FIRST SPRITE. Help: because it is not fair to place before the eyes of the audience the misfortune of a good man.

SECOND SPRITE. That's true, little friend, for it's not the same to say: "I have seen," as "It is said."

FIRST SPRITE. Tomorrow the whole world will know about it.

SECOND SPRITE. And that's what we wish.

FIRST SPRITE. One word of gossip and the whole world knows.

SECOND SPRITE. Sh . . .

(*Flutes begin to sound.*)

FIRST SPRITE. Shall we go through this tiny darkness?

SECOND SPRITE. Let us go now, little friend.

FIRST SPRITE. Now?

SECOND SPRITE. Now.

(*They open the curtain.* DON PERLIMPLIN *appears on the bed, completely dressed; on his forehead are two enormous horns, gilded and beflowered.* BELISA *is at his side. The five balconies of the stage are wide open, and through them the white light of dawn enters.*)

PERLIMPLIN (*awakening*). Belisa! Belisa! Answer me!

BELISA (*pretending to awaken*). Perlimplinpinito . . . what do you want?

PERLIMPLIN. Tell me quickly.

BELISA. What do you want me to tell you? I didn't fall asleep much before you did.

PERLIMPLIN (*leaps from the bed. He has on his cassock*). Why are the balconies open?

BELISA. Because this night the wind has blown as never before.

PERLIMPLIN. Why do the balconies have five ladders that reach to the ground?

BELISA. Because that is the custom in my mother's country.

PERLIMPLIN. And whose are those five hats which I see under the balconies?

BELISA (*leaping from the bed*). The little drunkards who come and go. Perlimplinillo! Love!

(PERLIMPLIN *looks at her, staring stupefied.*)

PERLIMPLIN. Belisa! Belisa! And why not? You explain everything so well. I am satisfied. Why couldn't it have been like that?

BELISA (*coyly*). I'm not a little fibber.

PERLIMPLIN. And I love you more every minute!

BELISA. That's the way I like it.

PERLIMPLIN. For the first time in my life I am happy! (*He approaches and embraces her, but, in that instant, turns brusquely from her.*) Belisa, who has kissed you? Don't lie, for I know!

BELISA (*gathering her hair*). Of course you know! What a playful little husband I have! (*In a low voice.*) You! You have kissed me!

PERLIMPLIN. Yes. I have kissed you . . . but . . . if some one else had kissed you . . . if some one else had kissed you . . . do you love me?

BELISA (*lifting a naked arm to embrace him*). Yes, little Perlimplin.

PERLIMPLIN. Then, what do I care? (*Embraces her.*) Are you Belisa?

BELISA (*coyly, and in a low voice*). Yes! Yes! Yes!

PERLIMPLIN. It almost seems like a dream!

BELISA (*recovering*). Look, Perlimplin, close the balconies because, before you know it, people will be getting up.

PERLIMPLIN. What for? Since we have both slept enough, we shall see the dawn. Don't you like that?

BELISA. Yes, but . . . (*She sits on the bed.*)

PERLIMPLIN. I had never seen the sunrise.

(BELISA, *exhausted, falls on the pillows of the bed.*)

It is a spectacle which . . . this may seem an untruth . . . thrills me! Don't you like it? (*Goes toward the bed.*) Belisa, are you asleep?

BELISA (*in her dreams*). Yes.

(PERLIMPLIN *tiptoes over and covers her with the red cape. An intense golden light enters through the balconies. Bands of paper birds cross them amidst the ringing of the morning bells.* PERLIMPLIN *has seated himself on the edge of the bed.*)

PERLIMPLIN. Love, love
that here lies wounded.
So wounded by love's going;
so wounded,
dying of love.
Tell every one that it was just
the nightingale.
A surgeon's knife with four sharp edges;
the bleeding throat—forgetfulness.
Take me by the hands, my love,
for I come quite badly wounded,
so wounded by love's going.
So wounded!
Dying of love!

SCENE II

(*Perlimplin's dining room. The perspectives are deliciously wrong. All the objects on the table are painted as in a primitive Last Supper.*)

PERLIMPLIN. Then you will do as I say?

MARCOLFA (*crying*). Don't worry, master.

PERLIMPLIN. Marcolfa, why do you keep on crying?

MARCOLFA. Your grace knows. On your wedding night five men entered your bedroom—one through each balcony—and left forgotten behind them their hats and you quite tranquil! Five. My lord, five! Representatives of the five races of the earth. The European, with his beard—the Indian—the Negro—the Yellow Man—and the American. And you unaware of it all.

PERLIMPLIN. That is of no importance.

MARCOLFA. Just imagine: yesterday I saw her with another one.

PERLIMPLIN (*intrigued*). Really?

MARCOLFA. And she didn't even hide from me.

PERLIMPLIN. But I am happy, Marcolfa.

MARCOLFA. The master astonishes me.

PERLIMPLIN. You have no idea how happy I am. I have learned many things and above all I can imagine many others.

MARCOLFA. My master loves her too much.

PERLIMPLIN. Not as much as she deserves.

MARCOLFA. Here she comes.

PERLIMPLIN. Please leave.

(MARCOLFA *leaves and* PERLIMPLIN *hides in a corner. Enter* BELISA *dressed in a red dress of eighteenth-century style. The skirt, at the back, is slit allowing silk stockings to be seen. She wears huge earrings and a red hat trimmed with big ostrich plumes.*)

BELISA. Again I have failed to see him. In my walk through the park they were all behind me except him. His skin must be dark, and his kisses must perfume and burn at the same time—like saffron and cloves. Sometimes he passes underneath my balconies and moves his hand slowly in a greeting that makes my breasts tremble.

PERLIMPLIN. Ahem!

BELISA (*turning*). Oh! What a fright you gave me.

PERLIMPLIN (*approaching her affectionately*). I observe you were speaking to yourself.

BELISA (*distastefully*). Go away!

PERLIMPLIN. Shall we take a walk?

BELISA. No.

PERLIMPLIN. Shall we go to the confectioner's?

BELISA. I said no!

PERLIMPLIN. Pardon.

(*A letter rolled about a stone falls through the balcony.* PERLIMPLIN *picks it up.*)

BELISA. Give that to me.

PERLIMPLIN. Why?

BELISA. Because it's for me.

PERLIMPLIN (*jokingly*). And who told you that?

BELISA. Perlimplin! Don't read it!

PERLIMPLIN (*jokingly severe*). What are you trying to say?

BELISA (*weeping*). Give me that letter!

PERLIMPLIN (*approaching her*). Poor Belisa! Because I understand your feelings I give you this paper which means so much to you.

(BELISA *takes the note and hides it in her bosom.*)

I can see things. And even though it wounds me deeply, I understand you live in a drama.

BELISA (*tenderly*). Perlimplin!

PERLIMPLIN. I know that you are unfaithful to me, and that you will continue to be so.

BELISA (*fondly*). I've never known any man other than my Perlimplinillo.

PERLIMPLIN. That's why I want to help you as any good husband should when his wife is a model of virtue . . . look. (*He closes the door and adopts a mysterious air.*) I know everything! I realized immediately.

You are young and I am old . . . what are we going to do! But I understand perfectly. (*Pause. In a low voice.*) Has he come by here?

BELISA. Twice.

PERLIMPLIN. And has he signalled to you?

BELISA. Yes . . . but in a manner that's a little disdainful . . . and that hurts me!

PERLIMPLIN. Don't be afraid. Two weeks ago I saw that young man for the first time. I can tell you with all sincerity that his beauty dazzled me. I have never seen another man in whom manliness and delicacy meet in a more harmonious fashion. Without knowing why, I thought of you.

BELISA. I haven't seen his face . . . but . . .

PERLIMPLIN. Don't be afraid to speak to me. I know you love him . . . and I love you now as if I were your father. I am far from that foolishness; therefore . . .

BELISA. He writes me letters.

PERLIMPLIN. I know that.

BELISA. But he doesn't let me see him.

PERLIMPLIN. That's strange.

BELISA. And it even seems . . . as though he scorns me.

PERLIMPLIN. How innocent you are!

BELISA. But there's no doubt he loves as I wish . . .

PERLIMPLIN (*intrigued*). How is that?

BELISA. The letters I have received from other men . . . and which I didn't answer because I had my little husband, spoke to me of ideal lands—of dreams and wounded hearts. But these letters from him . . . they . . .

PERLIMPLIN. Speak without fear.

BELISA. They speak about me . . . about my body . . .

PERLIMPLIN (*caressing her arms*). About your body!

BELISA. "What do I want your soul for?" he tells me. "The soul is the patrimony of the weak. Of frozen heroes and sickly people. Beautiful souls are at death's door, leaning upon whitest hairs and lean hands. Belisa, it is not your soul that I desire, but your white and soft trembling body."

PERLIMPLIN. Who could that beautiful youth be?

BELISA. No one knows.

PERLIMPLIN (*inquisitive*). No one?

BELISA. I have asked all my friends.

PERLIMPLIN (*inscrutably and decisively*). And if I should tell you I know him?

BELISA. Is that possible?

PERLIMPLIN. Wait. (*Goes to the balcony.*) Here he is.

BELISA (*running*). Yes?

PERLIMPLIN. He has just turned the corner.

BELISA (*choked*). Oh!

PERLIMPLIN. Since I am an old man, I want to sacrifice myself for you. This that I do no one ever did before. But I am already beyond the world and the ridiculous morals of its people. Good-bye.

BELISA. Where are you going?

PERLIMPLIN (*at the door, grandiosely*). Later you will know everything. Later.

SCENE III

(*A grove of cypresses and orange trees. When the curtain rises,* MARCOLFA *and* PERLIMPLIN *appear in the garden.*)

MARCOLFA. Is it time yet?

PERLIMPLIN. No, it isn't time yet.

MARCOLFA. But what has my master thought?

PERLIMPLIN. Everything he hadn't thought before.

MARCOLFA (*weeping*). It's my fault!

PERLIMPLIN. Oh, if you only knew what gratitude there is in my heart for you!

MARCOLFA. Before this, everything went smoothly. In the morning I would take him his milk and coffee and grapes . . .

PERLIMPLIN. Yes . . . the grapes! The grapes! But . . . I? It seems to me that a hundred years have passed. Before, I could not think of the extraordinary things the world holds. I was merely on the threshold. On the other hand . . . today! Belisa's love has given me a precious wealth that I ignored before . . . don't you see? Now I can close my eyes and . . . I can see what I want. For example, my mother, when she was visited by the elves. Oh, you know how elves are . . . tiny. It's marvelous! They can dance upon my little finger.

MARCOLFA. Yes, yes, the elves, the elves, but . . . how about this other?

PERLIMPLIN. The other? Ah! (*With satisfaction.*) What did you tell my wife?

MARCOLFA. Even though I'm not very good at these things, I told her what the master had instructed me to say . . . that that young man . . . would come tonight at ten o'clock sharp to the garden, wrapped, as usual, in his red cape.

PERLIMPLIN. And she?

MARCOLFA. She became as red as a geranium, put her hands to her heart, and kissed her lovely braids passionately.

PERLIMPLIN (*enthusiastic*). So she got red as a geranium, eh? And, what did she say?

MARCOLFA. She just sighed; that's all. But, oh! such a sigh!

PERLIMPLIN. Oh, yes! As no woman ever sighed before! Isn't that so?

MARCOLFA. Her love must border on madness.

PERLIMPLIN (*vibrantly*). That's it! What I need is for her to love that youth more than her own body. And there is no doubt that she loves him.

MARCOLFA (*weeping*). It frightens me to hear you . . . but how is it possible? Don Perlimplin, how is it possible that you yourself should encourage your wife in the worst of sins?

PERLIMPLIN. Because Perlimplin has no honor and wants to amuse himself! Now do you see? Tonight the new and unknown lover of my lady Belisa will come. What should I do but sing? (*Singing.*) Don Perlimplin has no honor! Has no honor!

MARCOLFA. Let my master know that from this moment on I consider myself dismissed from his service. We servants also have a sense of shame.

PERLIMPLIN. Oh, innocent Marcolfa! Tomorrow you will be as free as a bird. Wait until tomorrow. Now go and perform your duty. You will do what I have told you?

MARCOLFA (*leaving, drying her tears*). What else is there for me to do? What else?

(*A sweet serenade begins to sound.* DON PERLIMPLIN *hides behind some rosebushes.*)

BELISA (*within, singing*). Upon the river shores
the passing night is moistened.

VOICES. The passing night is moistened.

BELISA. And in Belisa's breasts
the flowers die of love.

VOICES. The flowers die of love.

PERLIMPLIN. The flowers die of love!

BELISA. The night is naked singing
upon the bridge of March.

VOICES. Upon the bridge of March.

BELISA. Belisa bathes her body
with briny water and oils.

PERLIMPLIN. The flowers die of love!

BELISA. The night of anis and silver
is shining on the rooftops.

VOICES. Is shining on the rooftops.

BELISA. Silver of streams and mirrors
and anis of white thighs.

VOICES. The flowers die of love!

(BELISA *appears in the garden splendidly dressed. The moon lights the stage.*)

BELISA. What voices fill the air with the sweet harmony of one nocturne alone? I have felt your warmth and your weight, delicious youth of my soul. Oh! The branches are moving . . .

(*A young man dressed in a red cape appears and crosses the garden cautiously.*)

BELISA. Sh! Here! Here!

(*The young man signals with his hand that he will return immediately.*)

Oh! Yes . . . come back my love! Like a jasmine floating and without roots, the sky will fall over my moistening shoulders. Night! My night of mint and lapislazuli . . .

(PERLIMPLIN *appears.*)

PERLIMPLIN (*surprised*). What are you doing here?

BELISA. I was walking.

PERLIMPLIN. Only that?

BELISA. In the clear night.

PERLIMPLIN (*severely*). What were you doing here?

BELISA (*surprised*). Don't you know?

PERLIMPLIN. I don't know anything.

BELISA. You sent me the message.

PERLIMPLIN. Belisa . . . are you still waiting for him?

BELISA. With more ardor than ever.

PERLIMPLIN (*loudly*). Why?

BELISA. Because I love him.

PERLIMPLIN. Well, he will come.

BELISA. The perfume of his flesh passes beyond his clothes. I love him, Perlimplin, I love him! It seems to me that I am another woman!

PERLIMPLIN. That is my triumph.

BELISA. What triumph?

PERLIMPLIN. The triumph of my imagination.

BELISA. It's true that you helped me love him.

PERLIMPLIN. As now I will help you mourn him.

BELISA (*puzzled*). Perlimplin! What are you saying?

(*The clock sounds ten. A nightingale sings.*)

PERLIMPLIN. It is the hour.

BELISA. He should be here this instant.

PERLIMPLIN. He's leaping the walls of my garden.

BELISA. Wrapped in his red cape.

PERLIMPLIN (*drawing a dagger*). Red as his blood.

BELISA (*holding him*). What are you going to do?

PERLIMPLIN (*embracing her*). Belisa, do you love him?

BELISA. Yes!

PERLIMPLIN. Well, since you love him so much, I don't want him ever to leave you. And in order that he should be completely yours, it has come to me that the best thing would be to stick this dagger in his gallant heart. Would you like that?

BELISA. For God's sake, Perlimplin!

PERLIMPLIN. Then, dead, you will be able to caress him in your bed—so handsome and well groomed—without the fear that he should cease to love you. He will love you with the infinite love of the dead, and I will be free of this dark little nightmare of your magnificent body. (*Embracing her.*) Your body . . . that I will never possess! (*Looking into the garden.*) Look where he comes. Let go, Belisa. Let go! (*He exits running.*)

BELISA (*desperately*). Marcolfa! Bring me the sword from the dining room; I am going to run my husband's throat through. (*Calling . . .*)
Don Perlimplin
Evil husband!
If you kill him,
I'll kill you!

(*A man wrapped in a large red cape appears among the branches. He is wounded and stumbling.*)

BELISA (*embracing him*). Who opened your veins so that you fill my garden with blood? Love, let me look at your face for an instant. Oh! Who has killed you . . . who?

PERLIMPLIN (*uncovering himself*). Your husband has just killed me with this emerald dagger. (*He shows the dagger stuck in his chest.*)

BELISA (*frightened*). Perlimplin!

PERLIMPLIN. He ran away through the fields and you will never see him again. He killed me because he knew I loved you as no one else . . . While he wounded me he shouted: "Belisa has a soul now!" Come near. (*He has stretched out on the bench.*)

BELISA. Why is this? And you are truly wounded.

PERLIMPLIN. Perlimplin killed me . . . Ah, Don Perlimplin! Youngish old man, manikin without strength, you couldn't enjoy the body of Belisa . . . the body of Belisa was for younger muscles and warm lips . . . I, on the other hand, loved your body only . . . your body! But he has killed me . . . with this glowing branch of precious stones.

BELISA. What have you done?

PERLIMPLIN (*near death*). Don't you understand? I am my soul and you are your body. Allow me this last moment, since you have loved me so much, to die embracing it.

(BELISA *draws near and embraces him.*)

BELISA. Yes . . . but the young man? Why have you deceived me?

PERLIMPLIN. The young man!

(*Closes his eyes. The stage is left in its natural light.* MARCOLFA *enters.*)

MARCOLFA. Madame . . .

BELISA (*weeping*). Don Perlimplin is dead!

MARCOLFA. I knew it! Now we shall bind him in the youthful red suit in which he used to walk under his own balconies.

BELISA (*weeping*). I never thought he was so devious.

MARCOLFA. You have found out too late. I shall make him a crown of flowers like the noon-day sun.

BELISA (*confused, as if in another world*). Perlimplin, what have you done, Perlimplin?

MARCOLFA. Belisa, now you are another woman. You are dressed in the most glorious blood of my master.

BELISA. But who was this man? Who was he?

MARCOLFA. The beautiful adolescent whose face you never will see.

BELISA. Yes, yes, Marcolfa—I love him—I love him with all the strength of my flesh and my soul—but where is the young man in the red cape? Where is he?

MARCOLFA. Don Perlimplin, sleep peacefully . . . Do you hear? Don Perlimplin . . . Do you hear her?

(*The bells sound.*)

The Infernal Machine

BY JEAN COCTEAU

Translated by CARL WILDMAN

The Infernal Machine

CHARACTERS

The Voice
The Young Soldier
The Soldier
The Chief, *their captain*
Jocasta, *the queen, widow of Laïus*
Tiresias, *a soothsayer, nearly blind*
The Phantom of Laïus, *the dead king*
The Sphinx
Anubis, *Egyptian God of the Dead*
The Theban Matron
A Little Boy
A Little Girl
Oedipus, *son of Laïus*
Creon, *brother of Jocasta*
The Messenger from Corinth
The Shepherd of Laïus
Antigone, *daughter of Oedipus*

The four scenes should be planted on a little platform in the center of the stage, surrounded by nocturnal curtains. The slope of the platform varies according to the requirements of the scenes. Besides the lighting of details, the four acts should be flooded in the livid mythical light of quicksilver.

ACT I

THE PHANTOM OF LAIUS

THE VOICE

'He will kill his father. He will marry his mother.'

To thwart this oracle of Apollo, Jocasta, Queen of Thebes, leaves her son on the mountain-side with his feet pierced and bound. A shepherd of Corinth finds the nursling and carries it to Polybius. Polybius and Merope, king and queen of Corinth, were bemoaning a sterile marriage. The child, Oedipus or *Pierced-feet,* respected by bears and wolves, is to them a heaven-sent gift. They adopt him.

When a young man, Oedipus questions the oracle of Delphi.

The god speaks: *You will murder your father and marry your mother.* He must therefore fly from Polybius and Merope. The fear of parricide and incest drives him on towards his fate.

One evening, arriving at the cross-roads of Delphi and Daulis, he meets an escort. A horse jostles him; a quarrel starts; a servant threatens him; he replies with a blow from his stick. The blow misses the servant and kills the master. This dead man is Laïus, the old king of Thebes. Parricide!

The escort, fearing an ambush, took to its heels. Oedipus, unsuspecting, passed on. Besides, he is young, enthusiastic; this accident is soon forgotten.

During one of his halts, he learns of the scourge of the Sphinx. The Sphinx, 'the Winged Virgin,' 'the Singing Bitch,' is killing off the young men of Thebes. This monster asks a riddle and kills those who do not guess it. Queen Jocasta, widow of Laïus, offers her hand and her crown to the conqueror of the Sphinx.

Like the young Siegfried to come, Oedipus rushes on. He is consumed with curiosity and ambition. The meeting takes place. What was the nature of this meeting? Mystery. Be that as it may, Oedipus enters Thebes a conqueror, he marries the queen. Incest!

For the gods really to enjoy themselves, their victim must fall from a great height. Years come and go in prosperity. Two daughters and two sons complicate the monstrous union. The people love their king. But the plague suddenly descends upon them. The gods accuse an anonymous criminal of infecting the country and demand that he shall be driven out.

From one discovery to another, and as if intoxicated by misfortune, Oedipus, in the end, finds himself up against the wall. The trap shuts. All becomes clear. With her red scarf, Jocasta hangs herself. With the golden brooch of the hanging woman, Oedipus puts out his eyes.

Spectator, this machine, you see here wound up to the full in such a way that the spring will slowly unwind the whole length of a human life, is one of the most perfect constructed by the infernal gods for the mathematical destruction of a mortal.

(*A patrol path round the ramparts of Thebes. High walls. A stormy night. Summer lightning. The din and bands of the popular district can be heard.*)

THE YOUNG SOLDIER. They're having a good time!

THE SOLDIER. Trying to.

YOUNG SOLDIER. Well, anyway, they dance all night.

SOLDIER. They can't sleep, so they dance.

YOUNG SOLDIER. All the same, they're getting tight and going with women, and spending their nights in night clubs, while I am tramping up and down with you. Well I, for one, can't stand it any longer! I can't stand it! I can't! D'you see? That's flat. I can't stand it any longer.

SOLDIER. Desert.

YOUNG SOLDIER. Oh! no. I've made up my mind. I'm going to put my name down for the Sphinx.

SOLDIER. What for?

YOUNG SOLDIER. What do you mean? Why, to do something, of course. To put an end to this nerve-racking business and this ghastly inaction.

SOLDIER. Out of a stew into a funk.

YOUNG SOLDIER. Funk?

SOLDIER. Yes, just that . . . funk! I've seen brighter and sturdier lads than you who got the wind up. Unless the gentleman wishes to down the Sphinx and draw the first prize.

YOUNG SOLDIER. And why not, after all? The only man to come back alive from the Sphinx became an idiot, I know. But, supposing what he jibbers is true. What if it is a riddle. What if I guess it. What . . .

SOLDIER. But, my poor son of a bitch, don't you realize that hundreds upon hundreds of chaps who've been to the stadium and college and everything have left their carcasses behind there, and you, a poor little second-class soldier like you wants to . . .

YOUNG SOLDIER. I shall go! I shall, because I can't bear any longer counting the stones of this wall, hearing that band, and seeing your rotten mug, and . . . (*He stamps.*)

SOLDIER. That's the stuff, my hero! I was expecting this attack of nerves. I like that better. Now . . . Now . . . enough crying. . . . Let's calm ourselves . . . there, there, there . . .

YOUNG SOLDIER. I hate you!

(*The* SOLDIER *bangs his spear against the wall behind the* YOUNG SOLDIER *who becomes rigid.*)

SOLDIER. What's up?

YOUNG SOLDIER. Didn't you hear anything?

SOLDIER. No . . . where?

YOUNG SOLDIER. Ah! . . . I seemed . . . I thought for a moment . . .

SOLDIER. You're like a sheet. . . . What's the matter? Are you going to pass out?

YOUNG SOLDIER. It's silly . . . I seemed to hear a knock. I thought it was him!

SOLDIER. The Sphinx?

YOUNG SOLDIER. No, him, the ghost, the phantom, you know!

SOLDIER. The phantom? Our dear old phantom of Laïus? And is that what turns your stomach over? Really!

YOUNG SOLDIER. Sorry.

SOLDIER. You're sorry, old son of a gun? Don't be so silly! To start with, there's a good chance that our phantom will not appear again after last night's business. That's that. And besides, what are you sorry about? Look at things squarely. We can hardly say this phantom has scared us. Oh! well, . . . the first time perhaps. . . . But, after that, eh? . . . He was a decent old phantom chap, almost a pal, a relief. Well, if the idea of this phantom makes you jumpy, it's because you're in a real state of nerves, like everybody in Thebes, rich or poor alike, except a few big pots who make something out of everything. There's not much fun in war, but do you imagine it's amusing to fight an unknown enemy? We're beginning to get fed up with oracles, happy deaths and heroic mothers. Do you think I should pull your leg as I do if my nerves weren't on edge, and do you think you'd burst into tears, and that lot over there'd get tight and dance? No, they would stay tucked securely in bed, and we'd be playing dice while waiting for friend phantom.

YOUNG SOLDIER. I say . . .

SOLDIER. Well? . . .

YOUNG SOLDIER. What d'you think it's like . . . the Sphinx?

SOLDIER. Oh! give the Sphinx a rest. If I knew what it was like I shouldn't be here doing guard-duty with you tonight.

YOUNG SOLDIER. Some make out it's no bigger than a hare, and is timid, and has a sweet little woman's head. But I think it has a woman's head and breast, and sleeps with the young men.

SOLDIER. Oh, look here! Shut up and forget it!

YOUNG SOLDIER. Perhaps it doesn't ask anything and doesn't even touch you. You meet it, look at it, and die of love.

SOLDIER. All we needed was for you to go and fall in love with the public scourge. After all, public scourge . . . between ourselves, do you know what I think about this public scourge? . . . It's a vampire! Yes, a common or garden vampire! Some old man who is in hiding from the police, and somehow they don't manage to lay hands on him.

YOUNG SOLDIER. A vampire with a woman's head?

SOLDIER. Oh! not him! Oh! no! A real old vampire with a beard and moustache, and a belly. He sucks your blood and that's how it is they bring corpses back to their families, all with the same wound in the same place: the back of the neck! And now, go and see for yourself if you're still keen.

YOUNG SOLDIER. You say that . . .

SOLDIER. I say that . . . I say that . . . Hi! . . . The chief.

(*They stand up to attention. The* CHIEF *enters and folds his arms.*)

CHIEF. Easy! . . . Well, my lads . . . Is this where we see phantoms?

SOLDIER. Chief . . .

CHIEF. Silence! You will speak when I ask you. Which of you two has dared . . .

YOUNG SOLDIER. It's me, chief.

CHIEF. Good lord! whose turn to speak is it? Are you going to keep quiet? I was asking: which of you two has dared to make a report touching the service, in a high place, without it passing through the accepted channels? Right over my head. Answer.

SOLDIER. It wasn't his fault, chief, he knew . . .

CHIEF. Was it you or he?

YOUNG SOLDIER. Both of us, but *I* . . .

CHIEF. Silence! I want to know how the High Priest came to hear of what happens at night at this post, while I myself heard nothing.

YOUNG SOLDIER. It's my fault, chief, my fault. My comrade here didn't want to say anything about it. But I thought I ought to speak and, as this incident didn't concern the service . . . and, well . . . I told his uncle everything; because his uncle's wife is sister to one of the queen's linen-maids, and his brother-in-law is in Tiresias' temple.

SOLDIER. That's why I said it was my fault, chief.

CHIEF. All right! Don't burst my ear-drums. So . . . this incident doesn't concern the service. Very good, oh! very good! . . . And it seems . . . this famous incident which doesn't concern the service is a ghost story?

YOUNG SOLDIER. Yes, chief.

CHIEF. A ghost appeared to you one night when you were on sentry-duty, and this ghost said to you . . . Just what did this ghost say to you?

YOUNG SOLDIER. He told us, chief, he was the spectre of King Laïus, and he had tried to appear several times since his murder, and he begged us to find some way of warning Queen Jocasta and Tiresias with all speed.

CHIEF. With all speed! Fancy that! What a nice old phantom! And . . . didn't you ask him, say, why you had the honor of this visit and why he doesn't appear directly before the queen or Tiresias?

SOLDIER. Yes, chief, I asked him, I did. His answer was that he wasn't free to put in an appearance anywhere, and that the ramparts were the most favorable spot for people who had died violent deaths, because of the drains.

CHIEF. Drains?

SOLDIER. Yes, chief. He said drains, meaning the fumes you only find there.

CHIEF. 'Struth! A very learned spectre, and he doesn't hide his light under a bushel. Did he scare you much? And what did he look like? What was his face like? What clothes did he wear? Where did he stand, and what language did he speak? Are his visits long or short? Have you seen him on different occasions? Although this business doesn't concern the service, I must admit I am curious to learn from your lips a few details about the manners and customs of ghosts.

YOUNG SOLDIER. We were scared the first night, chief, I admit. I ought to have said he appeared very suddenly, like a lamp lighting up, there in the thickness of the wall.

SOLDIER. We saw it together.

YOUNG SOLDIER. It was hard to make out the face and the body; the mouth when it was open, was clearer, and a white tuft of his beard, and a large red stain, bright red, near the right ear. He spoke with difficulty and couldn't somehow manage to get out more than one sentence at a time. But you'd better ask my comrade here about that, chief. He explained to me how it was the poor man couldn't manage to get it over.

SOLDIER. Oh! you know, chief, it's nothing very difficult! He spent all his energy in the effort to appear, that is, in leaving his new shape and taking on the old, so that we could see him. That's the reason why each time he spoke a little better, he began to disappear, became transparent like, and you could see the wall through him.

YOUNG SOLDIER. And as soon as he spoke badly you could see him very well. But you saw him badly as soon as he spoke well, and began saying the same thing over again. 'Queen Jocasta. You must . . . you must . . . Queen . . .Queen . . . Queen Jocasta . . . You must . . . You must warn the queen. . . . You must warn Queen Jocasta . . . I ask you, gentlemen, I ask you, I . . . I . . . Gentlemen . . . I ask . . . you must . . . you must . . . I ask you, gentlemen, to warn . . . I ask you . . . The queen . . . Queen Jocasta . . . to warn, gentlemen, to warn . . . Gentlemen . . . Gentlemen . . .' That's how he went on.

SOLDIER. And you could see he was afraid of disappearing before he'd said all his words right to the end.

YOUNG SOLDIER. And see here, listen a mo', d'you remember? Every time the same business. The red stain went last. Just like a ship's light on the wall, chief.

SOLDIER. The whole business was over in a second!

YOUNG SOLDIER. He has appeared in the same place five times, every night, a little before dawn.

SOLDIER. But, last night which was unlike the others, we . . . well, we had a bit of a dust-up, and my comrade here decided to tell the royal house everything.

CHIEF. Well! Well! And how was this night 'unlike the others,' which, if I'm not mistaken, caused a dispute between you . . . ?

SOLDIER. It was like this chief. . . . You know, guard-duty isn't exactly all beer and skittles.

YOUNG SOLDIER. So really we were waiting for the phantom.

SOLDIER. We betted, saying:

YOUNG SOLDIER. Will come . . .

SOLDIER. Won't . . .

YOUNG SOLDIER. Will come . . .

SOLDIER. Won't . . . and it may seem a funny thing to say, but it was a comfort to see him.

YOUNG SOLDIER. A habit, as you might say.

SOLDIER. We ended by imagining we saw him when he wasn't there. We'd say to each other: 'It's moving! The wall is lighting up. Don't you see anything? No. But you must do. Over there, I tell you. . . The wall isn't the same. Don't you see, look, look!'

YOUNG SOLDIER. And we looked and stared our eyes out. We dared not move.

SOLDIER. We watched for the least change.

YOUNG SOLDIER. And when, at last, it came, we could breathe again, and weren't the least bit afraid.

SOLDIER. The other night, we watched and watched, and stared ourselves nearly blind; we thought he'd not show up, when he began to come stealthily . . . not at all quickly like on the first nights. And once he was visible, he changed his sentences and told us as well as he could that something fearful had happened, a thing of death which he couldn't explain to the living. He spoke of places where he could go and places where he couldn't go, and that he had been where he shouldn't and knew a secret which he shouldn't know, and that he would be discovered and punished, and afterwards he wouldn't be allowed to appear, he wouldn't be able to appear any more. (*Solemn voice.*) 'I shall die my last death,' he said, 'and it will be finished, finished. You see, gentlemen, there is not a moment to lose. Run! Warn the queen! Find Tiresias! Gentlemen! Gentlemen! have pity! . . .' He was begging away and day was breaking. And there he stuck!

YOUNG SOLDIER. Suddenly we thought he'd go mad.

SOLDIER. We understood from sentences without beginning or end that he had left his post, you know, . . . didn't know how to disappear, and was lost. We saw him going through the same performance to disappear as to appear, and he couldn't manage it. So then he asked us to insult him, because, he said, insulting ghosts is the way to make them go. The silliest thing about it was that we hadn't the guts to do it. The more he repeated: 'Come on! young men, insult me! Let yourselves go, do your best . . . Oh, come on!'—the more idiotic we looked.

YOUNG SOLDIER. And the less we found to say! . . .

SOLDIER. Yes, that is the limit! And yet, it's not for lack of blasting the chiefs.

CHIEF. Very nice of you, gentlemen, I'm sure! Thank you for the chiefs.

SOLDIER. Oh! I didn't mean that, chief. . . . I meant . . . I meant the princes, crowned heads, ministers, the government, what . . . the powers that be. We had even chatted about injustices. . . . But the king was such a good old phantom, poor King Laïus, that the swearwords wouldn't come. He was urging us on and we were dithering: 'Go on then! Hop it, you son of a bitch!' In short, we gave him bouquets!

YOUNG SOLDIER. Because, you see, chief: son of a bitch is a friendly way of speaking among soldiers.

CHIEF. It's as well to know.

SOLDIER. Go on! Go on then! . . . son of a . . . you old . . . Poor phantom! He hung there between life and death and he was outside himself with fear because of the cocks and the sun. When, all of a sudden, we saw the wall become the wall again, and the red stain go out. We were dog tired.

YOUNG SOLDIER. It was after that night that I decided to speak to his uncle as he refused to speak himself.

CHIEF. Your phantom doesn't seem to be very punctual.

SOLDIER. Oh! chief, you know, he may not show himself again.

CHIEF. I am in his way, no doubt.

SOLDIER. No, chief. But after last night . . .

CHIEF. But I understand from what you say that your phantom is very polite. He will appear, I'm quite sure. In the first place, the politeness of kings is punctuality, and the politeness of phantoms consists in taking on human form, according to your ingenious theory.

SOLDIER. Possibly, chief, but it's also possible that with phantoms there are no more kings, and they may mistake a century for a minute. So if the phantom appears in a thousand years instead of this evening . . .

CHIEF. You're a clever sort of chap, but patience has its limits. I tell you this phantom will appear. I tell you my presence is upsetting him, and I tell you that no one outside the service must pass along this sentry path.

SOLDIER. Yes, chief.

CHIEF (*in an outburst*). So, phantom or no phantom, I order you to stop the first person who turns up unless he gives the password, got it?

SOLDIER. Yes, chief.

CHIEF. And don't forget to patrol. That's all!

(*The two* SOLDIERS *stand stiffly at shoulder-arms.*)

CHIEF (*false exit*). Don't try any clever tricks! I've got my eye on you.

(*He disappears. Long silence.*)

SOLDIER. That's that.

YOUNG SOLDIER. He thought we were trying to pull his leg.

SOLDIER. Oh, no, my friend! He thought some one was trying to pull our legs.

YOUNG SOLDIER. Ours?

SOLDIER. Yes, my friend. I get to know lots of things through my uncle. The queen is nice, but at bottom she isn't liked; they find her . . . (*He strikes his head.*) They say she is eccentric and has a foreign accent, and is under the influence of Tiresias. This Tiresias advises the queen to do everything that will harm her. Do this . . . and do that. . . . She tells him her dreams, and asks him if she ought to get up right foot or left foot first; he leads her by the nose and licks her brother's boots, and plots with him against the sister. They are a low lot there. I wouldn't mind betting the chief thought the phantom was from the same source as the Sphinx. A priest's trick to attract Jocasta and make her believe anything they want.

YOUNG SOLDIER. No?

SOLDIER. Pretty flabbergasting, eh? But that's how it is. . . . (*In a very low voice.*) As for me, I believe in the phantom, take it from me. But, for that very reason and because they don't believe in it, I advise you to keep your mouth shut. You've already succeeded in making a fine hash of things. Take down this report: 'Has given proof of an intelligence well above his rank. . . .'

YOUNG SOLDIER. Still, if our king . . .

SOLDIER. Our king! . . . Our king! . . . Half a mo'! . . . A dead king isn't a living king. It's like this, if King Laïus were living, well, between ourselves, he would manage on his own and wouldn't come looking for you to do his errands in town.

(*They move off towards the right by the patrol path.*)

THE VOICE OF JOCASTA (*at the bottom of the steps. She has a very strong accent: the international accent of royalty*). Still another flight! I hate steps! Why all these steps? We can see nothing! Where are we?

THE VOICE OF TIRESIAS. But, Madam, you know what I think of this escapade, and *I* didn't . . .

VOICE OF JOCASTA. Stop it, Zizi. You only open your mouth to say silly things. This is not the time for moral lessons.

VOICE OF TIRESIAS. You should have taken another guide. I am nearly blind.

VOICE OF JOCASTA. What is the use of being a soothsayer, I wonder! Why, you don't even know where the steps are. I shall break my leg! It will be your fault, Zizi, your fault, as usual.

TIRESIAS. My fleshly eyes have gone out to the advantage of an inner eye which has other uses than counting steps.

JOCASTA. And now he's cross all over his eye! There! There! We love you, Zizi; but these flights of steps upset me so. We had to come, Zizi, we simply had to!

TIRESIAS. Madam . . .

JOCASTA. Don't be obstinate. I had no idea there were all these wretched steps. I am going to go up backwards. You will steady me. Don't be afraid. *I* am leading you. But if I looked at the steps, I should fall. Take my hands. Forward!

(*They appear on the set.*)

There . . . there . . . there . . . four, five, six, seven . . .

(JOCASTA *arrives on the platform and moves to the right.* TIRESIAS *treads on the end of her scarf. She utters a cry.*)

TIRESIAS. What is it?

JOCASTA. It's your foot, Zizi! You're walking on my scarf.

TIRESIAS. Forgive me . . .

JOCASTA. Ah! he's cross! But it isn't you I am annoyed with, it's the scarf! I am surrounded by objects which hate me! All day long this scarf is strangling me. At one time, it catches in the branches, at another, it gets wound on the hub of a carriage, another time, you tread on it. It's a positive fact. I am afraid of it, but I dare not be separated from it! Awful! It will be the death of me.

TIRESIAS. Look what a state your nerves are in.

JOCASTA. And what is the use of your third eye, I should like to know? Have you found the Sphinx? Have you found the murderers of Laïus? Have you calmed the people? Guards are stationed at my door and I am left with things that hate me, that want my death!

TIRESIAS. From mere hearsay . . .

JOCASTA. I feel things. I feel things better than all of you! (*She puts her hand on her belly.*) I feel them there! Has every stone been turned to discover the murderers of Laïus?

TIRESIAS. Madam knows very well the Sphinx made further searches impossible.

JOCASTA. Well, I for one don't care a jot about your fowls' entrails. . . . I feel, there . . . that Laïus is suffering and wants to complain. I am determined to get to the bottom of this story, and to hear this young guard for myself; and I *shall* hear him. I am your queen, Tiresias, don't you forget it.

TIRESIAS. My dear child, you must try and understand a poor blind man who adores you, watches over you, and wishes you were sleeping in your room instead of running after a shadow on the ramparts.

JOCASTA (*with mystery*). I do not sleep.

TIRESIAS. You don't sleep?

JOCASTA. No, Zizi, I don't sleep. The Sphinx and the murder of Laïus have put my nerves all on edge. You were right there; even better than that, if I fall asleep for so much as a minute I have a dream, one dream only, and I am ill for the whole day.

TIRESIAS. Isn't it my business to interpret dreams? . . .

JOCASTA. The place of the dream is rather like this platform, so I'll tell you. I am standing in the night, cradling a kind of nursling. Suddenly, this nursling becomes a sticky paste which runs through my fingers. I shriek and try to throw this paste away, but . . . Oh! Zizi . . . if only you knew, it's foul . . . This thing, this paste stays hanging on to me, and when I think I'm free of it, the paste flies back and strikes me across the face. And this paste is living. It has a kind of mouth which fixes itself on mine. And it creeps everywhere, it feels after my belly, and my thighs. How beastly!

TIRESIAS. Calm yourself.

JOCASTA. I don't want to sleep any more, Zizi . . . I don't want to sleep any more. Listen to that music. Where is it? They don't sleep either. It's lucky for them they have that music. They are afraid, Zizi . . . and rightly. They must dream horrible things and they don't want to sleep. And while I think of it, why this music? Why is it allowed? Do I have music to keep me from sleeping? I didn't know these places stayed open all night. How is it there is this scandal, Zizi? Creon must send out orders! This music must be stopped! This scandal must stop at once.

TIRESIAS. Madam, I implore you to calm yourself and to give up this idea. You're beside yourself for lack of sleep. We have authorized these bands so that the people don't become demoralized, to keep up their courage. There would be crimes . . . and worse than that if there were no dancing in the working-class district.

JOCASTA. Do I dance?

TIRESIAS. That's different. You are in mourning for Laïus.

JOCASTA. So are they all, Zizi. All of them! Every one! And yet they can dance and I can't. It's too unfair . . . I shall . . .

TIRESIAS. Some one coming, Madam.

JOCASTA. I say, Zizi, I'm shaking. I have come out with all my jewels.

TIRESIAS. There's nothing to fear. You won't meet prowlers on the patrol path. It must be the guards.

JOCASTA. Perhaps the soldier I am looking for?

TIRESIAS. Don't move. We'll find out.

(*The* SOLDIERS *enter. They see* JOCASTA *and* TIRESIAS.)

YOUNG SOLDIER. Steady, looks like somebody.

SOLDIER. Where have they sprung from? (*Aloud.*) Who goes there?

TIRESIAS (*to the* QUEEN). We are going to get into hot water. (*Aloud.*) Listen, my good men . . .

YOUNG SOLDIER. Password.

TIRESIAS. You see, Madam, we ought to have the password. You're getting us into an awful mess.

JOCASTA. Password? Why? What password? How silly, Zizi. I shall go and speak to him myself.

TIRESIAS. Madam, I implore you. They have instructions. These guards might not recognize you, nor believe me. It's very dangerous.

JOCASTA. How romantic you are! You see dramas everywhere.

SOLDIER. They're whispering together. Perhaps they will jump out on us.

TIRESIAS (*to the* SOLDIERS). You have nothing to fear. I am old and nearly blind. Let me explain my presence on these ramparts, and the presence of the person who accompanies me.

SOLDIER. No speeches. The password!

TIRESIAS. One moment. Just a moment. Listen, my good men, have you seen any gold coins?

SOLDIER. Attempted bribery.

(*He goes towards the right to guard the patrol path and leaves the* YOUNG SOLDIER *opposite* TIRESIAS.)

TIRESIAS. You're wrong. I meant: have you seen the queen's portrait on a gold coin?

YOUNG SOLDIER. Yes!

TIRESIAS (*gets out of the way and shows the* QUEEN, *who is counting the stars, in profile*). And . . . don't you recognize . . . ?

YOUNG SOLDIER. I don't see the connection you mean between the queen, who is quite young, and this matron.

JOCASTA. What does he say?

TIRESIAS. He says he finds Madam very young to be the queen. . . .

JOCASTA. He's entertaining!

TIRESIAS (*to the* SOLDIER). Fetch your chief.

SOLDIER. Not necessary. I have orders. Clear off! Look sharp!

TIRESIAS. You'll learn of this!

JOCASTA. Zizi, what is it now? What does he say?

(*The* CHIEF *enters.*)

CHIEF. What's this?

YOUNG SOLDIER. Chief! Two people here are wandering about without the password.

CHIEF (*going towards* TIRESIAS). Who are you? (*He suddenly recognizes* TIRESIAS.) My lord! (*He bows.*) How can I ever apologize enough?

TIRESIAS. Phew! Thanks, Captain. I thought this young warrior was going to run us through.

CHIEF. How can you forgive me? (*To the* YOUNG SOLDIER.) Idiot! Leave us.

(*The* YOUNG SOLDIER *goes to his comrade on the extreme right.*)

SOLDIER (*to the* YOUNG SOLDIER). What a brick!

TIRESIAS. Don't scold him! He was obeying orders . . .

CHIEF. Such a visit . . . in such a place! What can I do for you, my lord?

TIRESIAS (*standing back to show the* QUEEN). Her Majesty!

(*The* CHIEF *starts back.*)

CHIEF (*bows at a respectful distance*). Madam! . . .

JOCASTA. No ceremony, please! I should like to know which guard saw the phantom?

CHIEF. The clumsy young oaf who allowed himself to ill-use my lord Tiresias, and if Madam . . .

JOCASTA. See, Zizi. What luck! I was right in coming. . . . (*To the* CHIEF.) Tell him to approach.

CHIEF (*to* TIRESIAS). My lord, I don't know if the queen fully realizes that this young soldier would explain himself better through the medium of his chief; and that, if he speaks alone, Her Majesty risks . . .

JOCASTA. What now, Zizi? . . .

TIRESIAS. The chief was pointing out to me that he is used to the men and he might serve as a kind of interpreter.

JOCASTA. Send the chief away! Has the boy a tongue, or not? Let him come near.

TIRESIAS (*aside to the* CHIEF). Don't insist, the queen is overwrought. . . .

CHIEF. Very well. . . . (*He goes to his* SOLDIERS. *To the* YOUNG SOLDIER.) The queen wants to speak to you. And control your tongue. I'll pay you out for this, young fellow-me-lad.

JOCASTA. Come here!

(*The* CHIEF *pushes the* YOUNG SOLDIER *forward.*)

CHIEF. Go along then! Go on, booby, forward. You won't be eaten. Excuse him, Your Majesty. Our boys are scarcely familiar with court ways.

JOCASTA. Ask that man to leave us alone with the soldier.

TIRESIAS. But, Madam . . .

JOCASTA. And no but-Madams. . . . If this Captain stays a moment longer, I shall kick him.

TIRESIAS. Listen, chief. (*He leads him aside.*) The queen wants to be alone with the guard who has seen something. She has whims. She might become displeased with you and I couldn't do anything about it.

CHIEF. Right. I'll leave you. . . . If I stayed it was because . . . well . . . I don't mean to give you advice, my lord . . . But, between you and me, be on your guard about this phantom story. (*He bows.*) My lord. . . . (*A long salute to the* QUEEN. *He passes near the* SOLDIER.) Hi! The queen wishes to stay alone with your comrade.

JOCASTA. Who is the other soldier? Has he seen the phantom?

YOUNG SOLDIER. Yes, Your Majesty, we were on guard-duty together.

JOCASTA. Then let him stop. Let him stay there! I'll call him if I want him. Good evening, Captain, you are free.

CHIEF (*to the* SOLDIER). We'll have this out later!

(*He goes out.*)

TIRESIAS (*to the* QUEEN). You have mortally offended that Captain.

JOCASTA. About time too! Generally it's the men who are mortally offended and never the chiefs. (*To the* YOUNG SOLDIER.) How old are you?

YOUNG SOLDIER. Nineteen.

JOCASTA. Exactly his age! He would be his age. . . . He looks splendid! Come nearer. Look, Zizi, what muscles! I adore knees. You can tell the breed by the knees. He would look like that too. . . . Isn't he fine, Zizi. Feel these biceps, like iron. . . .

TIRESIAS. I am sorry, Madam, but you know . . . I'm no authority. I can scarcely see what they're like.

JOCASTA. Then feel. . . . Test them. Thighs like a horse! He steps away! Don't be afraid . . . The old grandpa is blind. Heaven knows what he's imagining, poor lad. He's quite red! He's adorable! And nineteen!

YOUNG SOLDIER. Yes, Your Majesty!

JOCASTA (*mocking him*). Yes, Your Majesty! Isn't he just too delicious? Ah! what a shame! Perhaps he doesn't even know he's handsome. (*As one speaks to a child.*) Well, . . . did you see the phantom?

YOUNG SOLDIER. Yes, Your Majesty!

JOCASTA. The phantom of King Laïus?

YOUNG SOLDIER. Yes, Your Majesty! The king told us he was the king.

JOCASTA. Zizi . . . what do you know with all your fowls and stars? Listen to this boy. . . . And what did the king say?

TIRESIAS (*leading the* QUEEN *away*). Madam! Be careful, these young people are hotheaded, credulous . . . pushful . . . Be on your guard. Are you certain this boy has seen the phantom, and, even if he has seen it, is it really the phantom of your husband?

JOCASTA. Gods! How unbearable you are! Unbearable and a spoilsport. Every time you come and break the spell and you stop miracles with your intelligence and incredulity. Please, let me question this boy on my own. You can preach afterwards. (*To the* YOUNG SOLDIER.) Listen. . . .

YOUNG SOLDIER. Your Majesty! . . .

JOCASTA (*to* TIRESIAS). I'll find out straight away whether he has seen Laïus. (*To the* YOUNG SOLDIER.) How did he speak?

YOUNG SOLDIER. He spoke quickly and a lot, Your Majesty, ever such a lot, and he got mixed up, and he didn't manage to say what he wanted to.

JOCASTA. That's he! Poor dear! But why on these ramparts? The stench. . . .

YOUNG SOLDIER. That's it, Your Majesty. . . . The phantom said it was because of the swamps and the rising fumes that he could appear.

JOCASTA. How interesting! Tiresias, you would never learn that from your birds. And what did he say?

TIRESIAS. Madam, Madam, you must at least question him with some order. You'll muddle this youngster's head completely.

JOCASTA. Quite right, Zizi, quite right. (*To the* YOUNG SOLDIER.) What was he like? How did you see him?

YOUNG SOLDIER. In the wall, Your Majesty. A sort of transparent statue, as you might say. You can see the beard most clearly, and the black hole of the mouth as it speaks, and a red stain on the temple, bright red.

JOCASTA. That's blood!

YOUNG SOLDIER. Fancy! We didn't think of that.

JOCASTA. It's a wound! How dreadful! (LAÏUS *appears.*) And what did he say? Did you understand anything?

YOUNG SOLDIER. It wasn't easy, Your Majesty. My comrade noticed that he had to make a big effort to appear, and each time he made an effort to express himself clearly, he disappeared; then he was puzzled as to how to set about it.

JOCASTA. Poor dear!

THE PHANTOM. Jocasta! Jocasta! My wife! Jocasta!

(*They neither hear nor see him during the whole of the scene.*)

TIRESIAS (*addressing the* SOLDIER). And were you not able to grasp anything intelligible?

PHANTOM. Jocasta!

SOLDIER. Well, yes, my lord. We understood he wanted to warn you of a danger, put you on your guard, both the queen and you, but that's all. The last time he explained he knew some secrets he ought not to have known, and if he was discovered, he would not be able to appear again.

PHANTOM. Jocasta! Tiresias! Can't you see me? Can't you hear me?

JOCASTA. And didn't he say anything else? Didn't he say anything particular?

SOLDIER. Ah, well, Your Majesty! Perhaps he didn't want to say anything particular in our presence. He was asking for you. That is why my comrade tried to inform you.

JOCASTA. Dear boys! And I have come. I knew very well. I felt it there! You see, Zizi, with all your doubts. And tell us, young soldier, where the spectre appeared. I want to touch the spot.

PHANTOM. Look at me! Listen to me, Jocasta! Guards, you always saw me before. Why not see me now? It's a torment. Jocasta! Jocasta! (*While these words are being uttered, the* SOLDIER *goes to the place where the* PHANTOM *is. He touches it with his hand.*)

SOLDIER. There. (*He strikes the wall.*) There, in the wall.

YOUNG SOLDIER. Or in front of the wall. It was difficult to make out.

JOCASTA. But why doesn't he appear tonight? Do you think he will still be able to appear?

PHANTOM. Jocasta! Jocasta! Jocasta!

SOLDIER. I am sorry, Madam, I don't think so, after what happened last night. I'm afraid there may have been a bit of a dust-up, Your Majesty may be too late.

JOCASTA. What a shame! Always too late. Zizi, I am always the last person in the whole kingdom to be informed. Think of the time that has been wasted with your fowls and oracles! We ought to have run, to have guessed. We shall learn absolutely nothing! And there will be disasters. And it will be your fault, Zizi, your fault, as usual.

TIRESIAS. Madam, the queen is speaking in front of these men.

JOCASTA. Yes, I am speaking in front of these men! I suppose I ought to restrain myself? When King Laïus, the dead King Laïus, has spoken in front of these men. But he has not spoken to you, Zizi, nor to Creon. He hasn't been to the temple to show himself. He showed himself on the patrol path to these men, to this boy of nineteen who is so handsome and looks like . . .

TIRESIAS. I implore you . . .

JOCASTA. Yes, I am overwrought, you must try to understand. These dangers, this spectre, this music, this pestilential smell. . . . And there's a storm about. I can feel it in my shoulder. I am stifling, Zizi, stifling.

PHANTOM. Jocasta! Jocasta!

JOCASTA. I think I hear my name. Didn't you hear anything?

TIRESIAS. My poor lamb. You're worn out. Day is breaking. You are dreaming where you stand. Are you even sure this phantom business hasn't come from the fatigue of these young men on the watch who force themselves not to sleep and live in this depressing, swampy atmosphere?

PHANTOM. Jocasta! For pity's sake, listen to me! Look at me! Gentlemen, you are kind. Keep the queen. Tiresias! Tiresias!

TIRESIAS (*to the* YOUNG SOLDIER). Step aside a moment, I want to speak to the queen.

(*The* YOUNG SOLDIER *goes to his comrade.*)

THE SOLDIER. Well, old son! You've clicked! She's fallen for it! Petted by the queen, eh!

YOUNG SOLDIER. Look here! . . .

SOLDIER. You're made for life. Don't forget your pals.

TIRESIAS. . . . Listen! Cockcrow. The phantom will not return. Let us go home.

JOCASTA. Did you see how handsome he is?

TIRESIAS. Don't revive those sad things, my lamb. If you had a son . . .

JOCASTA. If I had a son, he would be handsome, brave, he would guess the riddle and kill the Sphinx. He would return victor.

TIRESIAS. And you would go without a husband.

JOCASTA. Little boys always say: 'I want to become a man so that I can marry mother.' It's not such a bad idea, you know, Tiresias. Is there a sweeter union, a union that is sweeter and more cruel, and prouder, than that couple: a son and a young mother? Listen, Zizi, just now, when I touched that young guard, Heaven alone knows what he must have thought, the poor lad, and I myself nearly fainted. He would be nineteen, Tiresias, nineteen! The same age as this soldier. Can we be sure Laïus did not appear to him because of this likeness?

(*Cockcrows.*)

PHANTOM. Jocasta! Jocasta! Jocasta! Tiresias! Jocasta!

TIRESIAS (*to the* SOLDIERS). My friends, do you think it is any use waiting?

PHANTOM. For pity's sake!

SOLDIER. Frankly, no, my lord. The cocks are crowing. He will not appear now.

PHANTOM. Gentlemen! Mercy! Am I invisible? Can't you hear me?

JOCASTA. Come along! I will be obedient. But I am very glad I questioned the boy. You must find out his name and where he lives. (*She goes towards the steps.*) I had forgotten these steps, Zizi! . . . That band is making me ill. Listen, we can go back through the higher town by the little streets and we can visit the night clubs.

TIRESIAS. Madam, you don't mean it.

JOCASTA. Oh! now he's beginning again! He'll send me simply raving! Mad and off my head. I've got my veils on, Zizi, how do you expect I should be recognized?

TIRESIAS. My child, you said yourself you have come out wearing all your jewels. Your brooch alone has pearls as large as an egg.

JOCASTA. I am a martyr! Others can laugh and dance and amuse themselves. Do you imagine I am going to leave this brooch at the palace where it simply strikes everybody's eye? Call the guard. Tell him to help me down these steps. And you can follow us.

TIRESIAS. But, Madam, since the presence of this young man affects you . . .

JOCASTA. He is young and strong. He will help me, and I shan't break my neck. Obey your queen once, at least.

TIRESIAS. Hi! . . . No, he . . . Yes, you. . . . Help the queen down the steps. . . .

SOLDIER. You see, old man!

YOUNG SOLDIER (*approaching*). Yes, my lord.

PHANTOM. Jocasta! Jocasta! Jocasta!

JOCASTA. He's nervous! And flights of steps hate me. Steps, hooks, and scarves. Oh! yes, they do, they hate me! They're after my death. (*A cry.*) Ho!

YOUNG SOLDIER. Has the queen hurt herself?

TIRESIAS. No, silly! Your foot! Your foot!

YOUNG SOLDIER. What foot?

TIRESIAS. Your foot on the end of the scarf. You nearly strangled the queen.

YOUNG SOLDIER. Ye gods!

JOCASTA. Zizi, you are utterly ridiculous. Poor darling. There you go calling him a murderer because he walks, as you did, on this scarf. Don't upset yourself, my boy. My lord is absurd. He never misses an opportunity of hurting people's feelings.

TIRESIAS. But, Madam, . . .

JOCASTA. You are the one who is clumsy. Come along. Thank you, my boy. Send your name and address to the temple. One, two, three, four. . . . Marvelous! Zizi! Do you see how well I'm getting down. Eleven, twelve. . . . Zizi, are you following? Two more steps. (*To the* SOLDIER.) Thank you. I can manage now. Help grandpa!

(JOCASTA *disappears left, with* TIRESIAS. *Cocks are heard.*)

VOICE OF JOCASTA. Through your fault, I shall never know what my poor Laïus wanted.

PHANTOM. Jocasta!

VOICE OF TIRESIAS. That story is all very vague.

VOICE OF JOCASTA. What? Very vague? What do you mean, vague? It's you who are vague with your third eye. That boy knows what he has seen, and he has seen the king. Have you seen the king?

VOICE OF TIRESIAS. But . . .

VOICE OF JOCASTA. Have you seen him? . . . No. . . . Well . . . It's amazing . . . it's like . . .

(*The voices die away.*)

PHANTOM. Jocasta! Tiresias! Have pity!

(*The two* SOLDIERS *turn to each other and see the* PHANTOM.)

THE TWO SOLDIERS. Oh! the spectre!

PHANTOM. Gentlemen, at last! I am saved! I kept calling, begging. . . .

SOLDIER. You were there?

PHANTOM. During the whole of your talk with the queen and Tiresias. Then why was I invisible?

YOUNG SOLDIER. I'll run and fetch them!

SOLDIER. Halt!

PHANTOM. What? You stop him?

YOUNG SOLDIER. Let me go . . .

SOLDIER. When the joiner comes, the chair stops wobbling; when you get to the shoemender, your sandal stops hurting you; when you get to the doctor, you no longer feel the pain. Fetch them! They would only have to arrive to make the phantom disappear.

PHANTOM. Alas! Do these simple souls then know what the priests cannot divine?

YOUNG SOLDIER. I shall go.

PHANTOM. Too late. . . . Stay. It is too late. I am discovered. They are coming; they are going to take me. Ah! they're here! Help! Help! Quick! Tell the queen a young man is approaching Thebes, and on no account . . . No! No! Mercy! Mercy! They've got me! Help! Ended! I . . . I . . . Mercy . . . I . . . I . . .

(*Long silence. The two* SOLDIERS, *back to the audience, contemplate endlessly the place in the wall where the* PHANTOM *disappeared.*)

SOLDIER. Not so gay!

YOUNG SOLDIER. No!

SOLDIER. These things are beyond us, old man.

YOUNG SOLDIER. But what is clear is that, in spite of death, that fellow wanted, at all costs, to warn his wife of a danger which is threatening her. My duty is to overtake the queen and the high priest and repeat to them word for word what we have just heard.

SOLDIER. Do you want the queen?

(*The* YOUNG SOLDIER *shrugs his shoulders.*)

Then . . . he only had to appear to them and talk to them, they were here. We saw him all right ourselves and they didn't, and they even prevented us from seeing him, and that takes the biscuit. This proves that dead kings become private individuals. Poor Laïus! Now he knows how easy it is to get into touch with the great of the earth.

YOUNG SOLDIER. But us?

SOLDIER. Oh! us! It's easy to get into touch with men, you coon. . . . But, don't you see . . . chiefs, queens, and high priests . . . they always go before it happens, or come when it's all over.

YOUNG SOLDIER. What's 'it'?

SOLDIER. How should I know? . . . I understand myself, that's the chief thing.

YOUNG SOLDIER. And you wouldn't go and warn the queen?

SOLDIER. A word of advice: let princes deal with princes, phantoms with phantoms, and soldiers with soldiers.

(*Flourish.*)

ACT II

THE MEETING OF OEDIPUS AND THE SPHINX

THE VOICE

Spectators, let us imagine we can recall the minutes we have just lived through together and relive them elsewhere. For, while the Phantom of Laïus was trying to warn Jocasta on the ramparts of Thebes, the Sphinx and Oedipus met on a hill overlooking the town. The bugle-calls, moon, stars, and crowing cocks will be the same.

(*An unpeopled spot on a hill overlooking Thebes, by moonlight. The road to Thebes from right to left passes over the fore-stage. It gives the impression of rounding a high leaning stone whose base is fixed at the lower end of the platform and forms the support for the wings on the right. Behind the ruins of a little temple is a broken wall. In the middle of the wall stands a complete pedestal which used to indicate the entrance to the temple and bears the trace of a chimera: a wing, a foot, a haunch.*
Broken and overturned columns. For the Shades of Anubis and Nemesis at the end, a record by the actors can declaim the dialogue, whilst the actress mimes the part of the dead girl with the head of a jackal.
When the curtain rises a girl in a white dress is seen sitting among the ruins. The head of a jackal lies in her lap, its body remaining hidden behind her. Distant bugle-calls.)

THE SPHINX. Listen.
THE JACKAL. Well?
THE SPHINX. That's the last call. We're free.
(ANUBIS *gets up and the* JACKAL'S *head is seen to belong to him.*)
THE JACKAL, ANUBIS. It's the first. There'll be two more before the gates are closed.
THE SPHINX. It's the last. I'm quite sure it's the last.
ANUBIS. You're sure because you want the gates closed, but I'm sorry duty forces me to contradict you; we're not free. That was the first bugle call. We'll wait.
THE SPHINX. I may have been mistaken, but . . .
ANUBIS. May have been mistaken! You were. . . .

THE SPHINX. Anubis!

ANUBIS. Sphinx?

THE SPHINX. I've had enough of killing, enough of dealing out death.

ANUBIS. We must obey. There are mysteries within mystery, gods above gods. We have our gods and they have theirs. That's what is called infinity.

THE SPHINX. You see, Anubis, there is no second call. It's you who are mistaken, let us go. . . .

ANUBIS. Do you mean you would like this night to pass without any deaths?

THE SPHINX. Yes! I do, indeed! Yes! Although it's growing late, I tremble to think some one may still come by.

ANUBIS. You're getting sensitive.

THE SPHINX. That's my business.

ANUBIS. Don't get cross.

THE SPHINX. Why must we always be acting without aim, without end, without understanding? Why, for example, should you have a dog's head, Anubis? Why have the god of the dead in the shape given to him by credulous people? Why must we have an Egyptian god in Greece and why must he have a dog's head?

ANUBIS. It's marvelous, how like a woman you look when it comes to asking questions.

THE SPHINX. That is no answer!

ANUBIS. Well, my answer is: that logic forces us to appear to men in the shape in which they imagine us; otherwise, they would see only emptiness. Moreover, neither Egypt nor Greece nor death, neither the past nor the future has any meaning for us. Further, you know only too well to what use I must put this jaw. And finally, our masters prove their wisdom by giving me a material form which is not human and so preventing me from losing my head, however beastly it may be; for I am your keeper, remember. I can see that if they had given you a mere watchdog we should already be in Thebes with me on a leash and you sitting in the middle of a band of young men.

THE SPHINX. How stupid you are!

ANUBIS. Then try and remember that these victims who touch the girl-figure you have assumed are no more than noughts wiped off a slate, even if each of these noughts were an open mouth calling for help.

THE SPHINX. That may be. But here the calculations of gods are hard to follow. . . . Here we kill. Here the dead really die. Here I do kill.

(*While the* SPHINX *was speaking with her eyes on the ground,* ANUBIS *pricked up his ears, looked round, and moved silently off over the ruins where he disappears. When the* SPHINX *raises her eyes, she looks for* ANUBIS *and finds herself face to face with a small group of people who enter down stage right, and whom* ANUBIS *had scented. The group is composed of a Theban* MATRON, *her little boy and girl. The* MATRON *is dragging her daughter along. The boy is walking ahead.*)

THE MATRON. Look where you're going! Get along now! Don't look behind you! Leave your sister alone! Go on. . . . (*She sees the* SPHINX *as the little boy stumbles into her.*) Look out! I told you to look where you're going! Oh! I'm so sorry, madam. . . . He never looks where he's going. . . . He hasn't hurt you, has he?

THE SPHINX. No! not at all, madam.

THE MATRON. I didn't expect to meet any one on my path at such an hour.

THE SPHINX. I'm new to these parts, I haven't been long in Thebes; I was on my way to a relative who lives in the country and got lost.

THE MATRON. Poor dear! And where does your relative live?

THE SPHINX. . . . Near the twelfth milestone.

THE MATRON. The very part I come from! I had lunch with my family, at my brother's place, you know. He made me stay to dinner. And then you know you begin gossiping and don't notice the time, and so here I am going home after curfew with my brats half-asleep already.

THE SPHINX. Good-night, madam.

THE MATRON. Good-night. (*She makes to go.*) And . . . I say . . . don't linger on the way. I know the likes of you and me haven't much to fear . . . but I wouldn't be too bold, if I were you, till I was inside the walls.

THE SPHINX. Are you afraid of thieves?

THE MATRON. Thieves! Ye gods, what could they get out of me? Oh! no, my dear. Where *do* you come from? Any one can see you're not from the town. Thieves! I should think so! I mean the Sphinx!

THE SPHINX. Do you really, madam, honestly and truly believe in that nonsense yourself?

THE MATRON. That nonsense indeed! How young you are. Young people are so disbelieving these days. Oh! yes, they are. That's how disasters happen. Let alone the Sphinx, I'll give you a case from my family. . . . My brother that I've just left. . . . (*She sits down and lowers her voice.*) He married a beautiful tall blonde from the north. One night he wakes up and what does he find? His wife in bed without head or entrails. She was a vampire. When he'd got over the first fright, what does my brother do? Without a moment's hesitation he finds an egg and lays it on the pillow in the place of his wife's head. That's how you stop vampires getting back into their body. All at once he hears a moaning. It was the head and entrails flying wildly across the room and begging my brother to take away the egg. My brother wouldn't, and the head went from moans to anger, from anger to tears, from tears to kisses. To cut a long story short, my idiot brother takes away the egg and lets his wife get back into her body. Now he knows his wife is a vampire and my sons make fun of their uncle. They maintain that he made up this entire vampire story to disguise the fact that his wife really did go out, but with her body, and that he let her come back, and that he's a coward and ashamed of himself. But *I* know very well my sister-in-law is a vampire. . . . And my sons are in danger of marrying fiends from the Underworld, all because they are obstinate and *disbelieving*.

And the same with the Sphinx—I'm sorry if I hurt your feelings, but it's only the likes of my sons and you who don't believe in it.

THE SPHINX. Your sons . . . ?

THE MATRON. Not the little brat who just bumped into you. I mean my boy of seventeen. . . .

THE SPHINX. You have several sons, have you?

THE MATRON. I had four. Now I have three. Seven, sixteen, and seventeen. And I can tell you ever since that wicked beast appeared the house has been impossible.

THE SPHINX. Your sons quarrel . . . ?

THE MATRON. I mean, my dear, that it's impossible to live under the same roof. The one who's sixteen is only interested in politics. According to him the Sphinx is a bugbear used to scare the poor and to impose on them. There may have been something like your old Sphinx at one time —that's how my son speaks—but now the old Sphinx is dead; and he's merely a priest's demon and an excuse for police jobbery. They fleece and loot and terrorize the masses and then blame it all on the Sphinx. It's a good thing the Sphinx has broad shoulders. Whose fault is it that we starve to death, that prices go up, and that bands of looters swarm over the countryside? Why, the Sphinx's, of course. And the Sphinx is to blame because business is bad, and the government's weak and one crash follows another; because the temples are glutted with rich offerings whilst mothers and wives are losing the bare necessities of life, and because foreigners with money to spend are leaving town. . . . Ah, you should see him, miss, how he gets up on the table, shouting, waving his arms, and stamping his feet; and then he denounces those who are responsible for it all, preaches revolt, eggs on the anarchists, shouting at the top of his voice names that are enough to get us all hanged. And between ourselves, miss . . . I know . . . you can take it from me . . . the Sphinx exists all right, but they're making the most of it. You can be sure of that. What we want is a man, a dictator!

THE SPHINX. And . . . what about the brother of your young dictator?

THE MATRON. Oh! he's another kettle of fish. He despises his brother, he despises me, he despises the gods, he despises everything. He makes you wonder where he can get hold of all he comes out with. He says, if you please, that the Sphinx would interest him if it killed for killing's sake, but that this Sphinx of ours is in league with the oracles, and so it doesn't interest him.

THE SPHINX. And your fourth son? When was it . . . ?

THE MATRON. I lost him nearly a year ago. He was just nineteen.

THE SPHINX. Poor woman. . . . What did he die of?

THE MATRON. The Sphinx.

THE SPHINX (*gloomily*). Ah! . . .

THE MATRON. It's all very well for his younger brother to maintain he was a victim of police intrigues. . . . Oh! no. There's no mistake, he died through the Sphinx. Ah! my dear . . . if I live to a hundred I'll never forget that scene. One morning (he hadn't been home that night) I thought I heard him knock; I opened the front door and saw the underneath of his poor feet and then there followed a long way off, ever so far away, his poor little face, and in the back of his neck—look, just here—a large wound from which the blood had already stopped flowing. They brought him to me on a stretcher. Then I went: Ho! and fell, all of a heap. . . . A blow like that, you know, you don't get over in a hurry. You may be thankful you don't come from Thebes, thankful if you have no brothers. . . . You're lucky. . . . My other boy, the orator, wants to avenge him. What's the good? But he hates the priests, and my poor son was one of a series of human offerings.

THE SPHINX. Human offerings?

THE MATRON. To be sure. During the first months of the Sphinx the soldiers were sent to avenge the fine young men who were found dead all over the place, and they returned empty-handed. The Sphinx couldn't be found. Then, as there was a rumor that the Sphinx asked riddles, young people from the schools were sacrificed; and then the priests stated that the Sphinx demanded human offerings. At that, the youngest and weakest and fairest were chosen.

THE SPHINX. Poor woman!

THE MATRON. I tell you, my dear, what we want is a man of action. Queen Jocasta is still young. At a distance you would say she was twenty-nine or thirty. What we want is a ruler to fall from the sky, marry her, and kill the beast; some one to make an end of corruption, lock up Creon and Tiresias, improve the state of finance and liven up the people, some one who would care for the people and save us, yes, that's it, save us. . . .

THE SON. Mummy!

THE MATRON. Sh!

THE SON. Mummy . . . I say, mummy, what does the Sphinx look like?

THE MATRON. I don't know. (*To the* SPHINX.) And what d'you think is the latest? They're asking us to contribute our last farthings for a monument to those killed by the Sphinx! Will that bring them back to us, I should like to know.

THE SON. Mummy . . . what is the Sphinx like?

THE SPHINX. Poor little chap! His sister's asleep. Come along. . . . (*The son clings to the skirt of the* SPHINX.)

THE MATRON. Now don't worry the lady.

THE SPHINX. He's all right. (*She strokes his neck.*)

THE SON. I say, mummy, is this lady the Sphinx?

THE MATRON. Little silly. (*To the* SPHINX.) I hope you don't mind. At that age children don't know what they're saying. . . . (*She gets up.*) Oh my! (*She takes the little girl who is asleep in her arms.*) Come along now! Off we go, lazy-bones!

THE SON. Mummy, is that lady the Sphinx? I say, mummy, is the Sphinx that lady? Is that the Sphinx, mummy?

THE MATRON. Sh! Don't be silly. (*To the* SPHINX.) Well, good evening. Excuse my gossiping to you. I was glad to stop for a breather. . . . And . . . take care. (*Fanfare.*) Quickly. There's the second bugle. After the third we'll be shut out.

THE SPHINX. Go along, quickly. I'll hurry my way. You've put me on my guard.

THE MATRON. Believe me, we'll not feel safe until there comes a man who will rid us of this scourge.

(*She goes out left.*)

THE SON'S VOICE. I say, mummy, what's the Sphinx look like? Why wasn't it that lady? Then, what's he like?

THE SPHINX. A scourge!

ANUBIS (*coming from among the ruins*). That woman *would* have to come along here just now.

THE SPHINX. I've been unhappy for the past two days, for two days now I've been carrying on in this miserable way in the hope that this massacre would come to an end.

ANUBIS. Don't worry. You're all right.

THE SPHINX. Listen. This is my secret wish and these the circumstances which would allow me to mount my pedestal for a last time. A young man will climb the hill, I shall fall in love with him. He'll have no fear. And when I ask my question he will answer as to an equal. He will give *the answer*, d'you hear, Anubis, and I shall fall dead.

ANUBIS. Make no mistake: only your mortal form will fall dead.

THE SPHINX. And isn't that the form I should want to live in to make him happy?

ANUBIS. It's nice to see that human form doesn't make a great goddess become a little woman.

THE SPHINX. You see how right I was. That bugle we heard was the last after all!

ANUBIS. Daughter of men! One is never finished with you. I tell you no! No!

(*He leaves her side and mounts an overturned column.*)

That was the second. When I've heard another one you can go. Oh!

THE SPHINX. What is it?

ANUBIS. Bad news.

THE SPHINX. Some one coming?

ANUBIS. Yes.

(*The* SPHINX *gets up beside* ANUBIS *and looks into the wings, right.*)

THE SPHINX. I can't! I can't and I won't question this young man. You needn't ask me to.

ANUBIS. I should say, if you're like a young mortal, he's like a young god.

THE SPHINX. What grace, Anubis, and what shoulders! He's coming.

ANUBIS. I'll hide. Don't forget you are the Sphinx. I'm keeping my eye on you. I'll be with you at the first sign.

THE SPHINX. Anubis, listen . . . quickly . . .

ANUBIS. Sh! . . . He's here. (ANUBIS *hides.*)

(OEDIPUS *enters up stage right. He is walking along with his eyes on the ground. He starts.*)

OEDIPUS. Oh! I'm sorry. . . .

THE SPHINX. I startled you.

OEDIPUS. Well . . . no . . . I was dreaming, I was miles away, and suddenly, before me . . .

THE SPHINX. You took me for an animal.

OEDIPUS. Almost.

THE SPHINX. Almost? Almost an animal, that's the Sphinx.

OEDIPUS. Yes, I know.

THE SPHINX. You admit you took me for the Sphinx. Thank you.

OEDIPUS. Oh! I soon realized my mistake.

THE SPHINX. Too kind. The truth of the matter is, it can't be so amusing to find yourself suddenly face to face with the Sphinx, if you're a young man.

OEDIPUS. And . . . if you're a girl?

THE SPHINX. He doesn't attack girls.

OEDIPUS. Because girls avoid his haunts and are not supposed to go out alone when the light is failing.

THE SPHINX. You do well to mind your own business, young man, and let me go my way.

OEDIPUS. Which way?

THE SPHINX. You're simply amazing. Must I give my reasons for being out to a complete stranger?

OEDIPUS. And suppose I guessed your reason?

THE SPHINX. You amuse me.

OEDIPUS. Aren't you moved by curiosity, the curiosity which is raging amongst all modern young women, the curiosity to know what the Sphinx looks like? If he has claws, or a beak, or wings, and whether he takes after the tiger or the vulture?

THE SPHINX. Oh! come, come.

OEDIPUS. The Sphinx is the criminal of the day. Who's seen him? No one. Fabulous rewards are promised to the first person who discovers him. The faint of heart tremble. Young men die. . . . But a girl, couldn't she venture into the forbidden area, setting orders at defiance, and dare what no reasonable person would dare, to unearth the monster, surprise him in his lair, get a view of him?

THE SPHINX. You're on the wrong track, I tell you. I'm going back to a relative who lives in the country, and as I had forgotten the very existence of a Sphinx and that the outskirts of Thebes are not safe, I was resting a moment on the stones of these old ruins. You see how far you're out.

OEDIPUS. What a pity! For some time now I've only run across people as dull as ditch water; so I hoped for something more unusual. Pardon me.

THE SPHINX. Good evening!

OEDIPUS. Good evening!

(*They pass each other. But* OEDIPUS *turns back.*)

I say! Pardon me. I may appear unpleasant, but, I must say, I can't bring myself to believe you. Your presence in these ruins still intrigues me enormously.

THE SPHINX. You're simply incredible.

OEDIPUS. Because if you were like other girls you would already have made off as fast as your legs would carry you.

THE SPHINX. My dear boy, you're quite absurd.

OEDIPUS. It seemed to me so marvelous to find in a girl a worthy competitor.

THE SPHINX. A competitor? Then you are looking for the Sphinx?

OEDIPUS. Looking for him? Let me tell you, I've been on the march for a whole month. Probably that's why I appeared ill-mannered just now. I was so wild with excitement as I drew near Thebes that I could have shouted my enthusiasm to the merest block of stone, when, instead of a block of stone, what stands in my path but a girl in white. So I couldn't help talking to her about what was uppermost in my mind and attributing to her my own intentions.

THE SPHINX. But surely, a moment ago, when you saw me spring out of the shadow, you didn't seem to me very much on the alert for a man who wants to measure his strength with the enemy.

OEDIPUS. That is true. I was dreaming of fame, and the beast would have caught me unawares. Tomorrow in Thebes I shall equip myself and the hunt will begin.

THE SPHINX. You love fame?

OEDIPUS. I'm not sure about that. I like trampling crowds, trumpet-calls, flying banners, waving palm-branches, the sun, gold and purple, happiness, luck—you know, to live!

THE SPHINX. Is that what you call living?

OEDIPUS. Don't you?

THE SPHINX. No, I must say I have quite a different idea of life.

OEDIPUS. What's that?

THE SPHINX. To love. To be loved by the one you love.

OEDIPUS. I shall love my people and they me.

THE SPHINX. The public square is not a home.

OEDIPUS. The public square has nothing to do with it. The people of Thebes are looking for a man. If I kill the Sphinx I shall be that man. Queen Jocasta is a widow; I shall marry her. . . .

THE SPHINX. A woman who might be your mother!

OEDIPUS. The important thing is that she is not.

THE SPHINX. Do you imagine that a queen and her people would give themselves up to the first comer?

OEDIPUS. Would you call the vanquisher of the Sphinx a first comer? I know the promised reward is the queen. Don't laugh at me. Please listen. You must. I must prove that my dream isn't merely a dream. My father is King of Corinth. My father and mother were already old when I was born and I lived in a court of gloom. Too much fuss and comfort produced in me a feverish longing for adventure. I began to pine and waste away, when one evening a drunk shouted at me that I was a bastard and that I was usurping the place of a legitimate son. Blows and abuse followed, and the next day, despite the tears of Merope and Polybius, I decided to visit the sanctuaries and question the gods. They all replied with the same oracle: you will murder your father and marry your mother.

THE SPHINX. What?

OEDIPUS. Yes, I mean it. At first this oracle fills you with horror, but my head is firmly fixed on my shoulders! I reflected on the absurdity of the whole thing. I made allowances for the gods and the priests, and I came to this conclusion: either the oracle hid a less serious meaning which had to be discovered, or the priests who communicate from temple to temple by means of birds found it perhaps to their advantage to put this oracle into the mouth of the gods and to weaken my chances of coming into power. Briefly, I soon forgot my fears, and, I own, profiting by this threat of parricide and incest, I fled the court so that I might satisfy my thirst for the unknown.

THE SPHINX. Now it's my turn to feel dazed. I'm sorry I rather made fun of you. Will you forgive me, Prince?

OEDIPUS. Give me your hand. May I ask your name? Mine is Oedipus; I'm nineteen.

THE SPHINX. Oh! What does it matter about mine, Oedipus? You must like illustrious names. . . . That of a little girl of seventeen wouldn't interest you.

OEDIPUS. That's unkind.

THE SPHINX. You adore fame. Yet I should have thought the surest way of foiling the oracle would be to marry a woman younger than yourself.

OEDIPUS. That doesn't sound like you. That's more like a mother of Thebes where marriageable young men are few.

THE SPHINX. And that's not like you either. That was a gross, common thing to say.

OEDIPUS. So, I shall have walked the roads past mountain and stream merely to take a wife who will quickly become a Sphinx, worse than that, a Sphinx with breasts and claws!

THE SPHINX. Oedipus . . . .

OEDIPUS. No, thank you! I prefer to try my luck. Take this belt: with that you will be able to get to me when I have killed the beast.

(*Business.*)

THE SPHINX. Have you ever killed?

OEDIPUS. Yes, once. At the cross-roads of Delphi and Daulis. I was walking along like a moment ago. A carriage was approaching driven by an old man with an escort of four servants. When I was on a level with the horses, one of them reared and knocked me into a serving-man. The fool tried to strike me, I aimed a blow at him with my stick, but he dodged down and I caught the old man on the temple. He fell and the horses bolted, dragging him along. I ran after them, the servants were terrified and fled; I found myself alone with the bleeding body of the old man and the horses who screamed as they rolled about entangled, and broke their legs. It was dreadful . . . dreadful . . . .

THE SPHINX. Yes, isn't it . . . it's dreadful to kill.

OEDIPUS. Oh, well, it wasn't my fault and I think no more about it. The thing is to clear all obstacles, to wear blinkers, and not to give way to self-pity. Besides, there is my star.

THE SPHINX. Then farewell, Oedipus. I am of the sex which is disturbing to heroes. Let us go our ways, we can have little in common.

OEDIPUS. Disturbing to heroes, eh! You have a high opinion of your sex.

THE SPHINX. And . . . supposing the Sphinx killed you?

OEDIPUS. His death depends, if I'm not mistaken, on questions which I must answer. If I guess right he won't even touch me, he'll just die.

THE SPHINX. And if you do not guess right?

OEDIPUS. Thanks to my unhappy childhood, I have pursued studies which give me a great start over the riff-raff of Thebes.

THE SPHINX. I'm glad to hear it.

OEDIPUS. And I don't think this simple-minded monster is expecting to be confronted by a pupil of the best scholars of Corinth.

THE SPHINX. You have an answer to everything. A pity, for, I own, Oedipus, I have a soft spot for weak people, and I should like to have found you wanting.

OEDIPUS. Farewell.

(The SPHINX *makes one step as if to rush in pursuit of* OEDIPUS, *stops, but cannot resist the call. Until her 'I! I!' the* SPHINX *does not take her eyes off those of* OEDIPUS; *she moves as it were round this immobile, steady, vast gaze from under eyelids which do not flicker.)*

THE SPHINX. Oedipus!

OEDIPUS. Did you call me?

THE SPHINX. One last word. For the moment does nothing else occupy your mind, nothing else fire your heart, nothing stir your spirit save the Sphinx?

OEDIPUS. Nothing else, for the moment.

THE SPHINX. And he . . . or she who brought you into his presence. . . . I mean who would help you. . . . I mean who may perhaps know something to help bring about this meeting . . . would he or she in your eyes assume such prestige that you would be touched and moved?

OEDIPUS. Naturally, but what does all this mean?

THE SPHINX. And supposing I, I myself, were to divulge a secret, a tremendous secret?

OEDIPUS. You're joking!

THE SPHINX. A secret which would allow you to enter into contact with the enigma of enigmas, with the human beast, with the singing bitch, as it is called, with the Sphinx?

OEDIPUS. What! You? You? Did I guess aright, and has your curiosity led you to discover . . . ? No! How stupid of me. This is a woman's trick to make me turn back.

THE SPHINX. Good-bye.

OEDIPUS. Oh! Forgive me! . . .

THE SPHINX. Too late.

OEDIPUS. I'm kneeling, a simple fool who begs forgiveness.

THE SPHINX. You're a fatuous young man who is sorry to have lost his chance and is trying to get it back.

OEDIPUS. I am and I'm ashamed. Look, I believe you, I'll listen. But if you have played me a trick, I shall drag you by the hair and grip you till the blood flows.

THE SPHINX. Come here.

(She leads him opposite the pedestal.)

Shut your eyes. Don't cheat. Count up to fifty.

OEDIPUS (*with his eyes shut*). Take care!

THE SPHINX. It's your turn to do that.

(OEDIPUS *counts. One feels that something extraordinary is happening. The* SPHINX *bounds across the ruins, disappears behind a wall and re-appears in the real pedestal, that is, she seems to be fastened on to the pedestal, the bust resting on the elbows and looking straight ahead, whereas the actress is really standing, and only lets her bust appear and her arms in spotted gloves with her hands grasping the edge; out of the broken wing suddenly grow two immense, pale, luminous wings and the fragment of statue completes her, prolonging her, and appearing to belong to her.* OEDIPUS *is heard counting 47, 48, 49, then he makes a pause and shouts: 50. He turns round.*)

OEDIPUS. You!

THE SPHINX (*in a high distant voice, joyous and terrible*). Yes, I! I, the Sphinx!

OEDIPUS. I'm dreaming!

THE SPHINX. You are no dreamer, Oedipus. You know what you want, and did want. Silence. Here I command. Approach.

(OEDIPUS, *with his arms held stiffly by his body as if paralysed, tries frantically to free himself.*)

THE SPHINX. Come forward. (OEDIPUS *falls on his knees.*) As your legs refuse their help, jump, hop. . . . It's good for a hero to make himself ridiculous. Come along! Move yourself! Don't worry, there's nobody to see you.

(OEDIPUS, *writhing with anger, moves forward on his knees.*)

THE SPHINX. That's it. Stop! And now . . .

OEDIPUS. And now, I'm beginning to understand your methods, what moves you make to lure and slay.

THE SPHINX. . . . And now, I am going to give you a demonstration, I'm going to show you what would happen in this place, Oedipus, if you were any ordinary handsome youth from Thebes, and if you hadn't the privilege of pleasing me.

OEDIPUS. I know what your pleasantries are worth.

(*He knits up all the muscles of his body. It is obvious he is struggling against a charm.*)

THE SPHINX. Yield! Don't try to screw up your muscles and resist. Relax! If you resist you will only make my task more delicate and I might hurt you.

OEDIPUS. I shall resist!

(*He shuts his eyes and turns his head away.*)

THE SPHINX. You need not shut your eyes or turn away your head. For it is not by my look nor by my voice that I work. A blind man is not so dexterous, the net of a gladiator not so swift, nor lightning so fine, nor a coachman so stiff, nor a cow so weighty, nor a schoolboy working at his sums with his tongue out so good, nor a ship so hung with rigging, so spread with sails, secure and buoyant; a judge is not so incorruptible, insects so voracious, birds so bloodthirsty, the egg so nocturnal, Chinese executioners so ingenious, the heart so fitful, the trickster's hand so deft, the stars so fateful, the snake moistening its prey with saliva so attentive. I secrete, I spin, I pay out, I wind, I unwind, I rewind, in such a way that it is enough for me to desire these knots for them to be made, to think about them for them to be pulled tight or slackened. My thread is so fine it escapes the eye, so fluid you might think you were suffering from a poison, so hard a quiver on my part would break your limbs, so highly strung a bow stroked between us would make music in the air; curled like the sea, the column and the rose, muscled like the octopus, contrived like the settings of our dreams, above all invisible, unseen, and majestic like the blood circulating in statues, my thread coils round you in fantastic patterns with the volubility of honey falling upon honey.

OEDIPUS. Let me go!

THE SPHINX. And I speak, I work, I wind, I unwind, I calculate, I meditate, I weave, I winnow, I knit, I plait, I cross, I go over it again and again, I tie and untie and tie again, retaining the smallest knots that I shall later on have to untie for you on pain of death; I pull tight, I loosen, I make mistakes and go back, I hesitate, I correct, entangle and disentangle, unlace, lace up and begin afresh; and I adjust, I agglutinate, I pinion, I strap, I shackle, I heap up my effects, till you feel that from the tip of your toes to the top of your head you are wrapped round by all the muscles of a reptile whose slightest breath constricts yours and makes you inert like the arm on which you fall asleep.

OEDIPUS (*in a weak voice*). Let me be! Mercy! . . .

THE SPHINX. And you will cry for mercy, and you won't have to be ashamed of that, for you won't be the first. I have heard prouder than you call for their mothers, and I have seen more insolent than you burst into tears; and the more silent are even weaker than the rest: they faint before the end and I have to minister to them after the fashion of embalmers in whose hands the dead are drunk men no longer able to stand on their feet!

OEDIPUS. Merope! . . . Mother!

THE SPHINX. Then, I should command you to advance a little closer, and I should help you by loosening your limbs. So! And I should question you. I should ask you, for example: What animal is it that goes on four legs in the morning, in the afternoon on two, and in the evening on three? And you would cudgel your brains, till in the end your mind would settle on a little medal you won as a child, or you would repeat a number, or count the stars between these two broken columns; and I should make you return to the point by revealing the enigma. Man is the animal who walks on four legs when he is a child, on two when he is full-grown, and when he is old with the help of a stick as a third leg.

OEDIPUS. How idiotic!

THE SPHINX. You would shout: How idiotic! You all say that. Then, since that cry only confirms your failure, I should call my assistant, Anubis. Anubis!

(ANUBIS *appears and stands on the right of the pedestal with folded arms and his head turned to one side.*)

OEDIPUS. Oh! Sphinx. . . . Oh! Sphinx, madam! Please, no! No!

THE SPHINX. And I should make you go down on your knees. Go on. . . . Go on . . . that's right. . . . Do as you're told. And you'd bend your head . . . and Anubis would bound forward. He would open his wolf-like jaws!

(OEDIPUS *utters a cry.*)

I said: *would* bend, *would* bound forward, *would* open. . . . Haven't I always been careful to express myself in that mood? Why that cry? Why that horrified expression? It was a demonstration, Oedipus, simply a demonstration. You're free.

OEDIPUS. Free!

(*He moves an arm, a leg. . . . He gets up, he reels, he puts his hand to his head.*)

ANUBIS. Pardon me, Sphinx, this man cannot leave here without undergoing the test.

THE SPHINX. But . . . .

ANUBIS. Question him.

OEDIPUS. But . . . .

ANUBIS. Silence! Question this man.

(*A silence.* OEDIPUS *turns his back and remains motionless.*)

THE SPHINX. I'll question him. . . . All right. . . . I'll question him. . . . (*With a last look of surprise at* ANUBIS.) What animal is it that walks on four legs in the morning, on two in the afternoon, and on three in the evening?

OEDIPUS. Why, man, of course! He crawls along on four legs when he's little, and walks on two legs when he is big, and when he's old he helps himself along with a stick as a third leg.

(*The* SPHINX *sways on her pedestal.*)

OEDIPUS (*making his way to the left*). Victory!

(*He rushes out left. The* SPHINX *slips down into the column, disappears behind the wall, and reappears wingless.*)

THE SPHINX. Oedipus! Where is he? Where is he?

ANUBIS. Gone, flown. He is running breathlessly to proclaim his victory.

THE SPHINX. Without so much as a look my way, without a movement betraying feeling, without a sign of gratitude.

ANUBIS. And did you expect anything else?

THE SPHINX. Oh, the fool! Then he has not understood a single thing.

ANUBIS. Not a single thing.

THE SPHINX. Kss! Kss! Anubis. . . . Here, here, look, after him, quickly, bite him, Anubis, bite him!

ANUBIS. And now it's all going to begin afresh. You're a woman again and I'm a dog.

THE SPHINX. I'm sorry. I lost my head, I'm mad. My hands are trembling. I'm like fire. I wish I could catch him again in one bound, I'd spit in his face, claw him with my nails, disfigure him, trample on him, castrate him, and flay him alive!

ANUBIS. That's more like yourself.

THE SPHINX. Help me! Avenge me! Don't stand there idle!

ANUBIS. Do you really hate this man?

THE SPHINX. I do.

ANUBIS. The worst that could happen to him would seem too good to you?

THE SPHINX. It would.

ANUBIS (*holding up the* SPHINX's *dress*). Look at the folds in this cloth. Crush them together. Now if you pierce this bundle with a pin, remove the pin, smooth the cloth till all trace of the old creases disappears, do you think a simple country loon would believe that the innumerable holes recurring at intervals result from a single thrust of a pin?

THE SPHINX. Certainly not.

ANUBIS. Human time is a fold of eternity. For us time does not exist. From his birth to his death the life of Oedipus is spread flat before my eyes, with its series of episodes.

THE SPHINX. Speak, speak, Anubis, I'm burning to hear. What d'you see?

ANUBIS. In the past Jocasta and Laïus had a child. As the oracle gave out that this child would be a scourge . . . .

THE SPHINX. A scourge!

ANUBIS. A monster, an unclean beast . . . .

THE SPHINX. Quicker, quicker!

ANUBIS. Jocasta bound it up and sent it into the mountains to get lost. A shepherd of Polybius found it, took it away, and, as Polybius and Merope were lamenting a sterile marriage . . . .

THE SPHINX. I can't contain myself for joy.

ANUBIS. They adopted it. Oedipus, son of Laïus, killed Laïus where the three roads cross.

THE SPHINX. The old man.

ANUBIS. Son of Jocasta, he will marry Jocasta.

THE SPHINX. And to think I said to him: 'She might be your mother.' And he replied: 'The important thing is that she is not.' Anubis! Anubis! It's too good to be true. . . .

ANUBIS. He will have two sons who will kill each other, and two daughters one of whom will hang herself. Jocasta will hang herself. . . .

THE SPHINX. Stop! What more could I hope for? Think, Anubis: the wedding of Jocasta and Oedipus! The union of mother and son. . . . And will he know soon?

ANUBIS. Soon enough.

THE SPHINX. What a moment to live! I have a foretaste of its delights. Oh! to be present!

ANUBIS. You will be.

THE SPHINX. Is that true? . . .

ANUBIS. I think the moment has come to remind you who you are and what a ridiculous distance separates you from this little body which is listening to me. You who have assumed the role of Sphinx! You, the Goddess of Goddesses! You, the greatest of the great! The implacable! Vengeance! Nemesis! (ANUBIS *prostrates himself.*)

THE SPHINX. Nemesis . . . .

(*She turns her back to the audience and remains a while erect, making a cross with her arms. Suddenly she comes out of this hypnotic state and rushes up stage.*)

Once more, if he is in sight, I should like to feed my hatred, I want to see him run from one trap to another like a stunned rat.

ANUBIS. Is that the cry of the awakening goddess or of the jealous woman?

THE SPHINX. Of the goddess, Anubis, of the goddess. Our gods have cast me for the part of the Sphinx, and I shall show myself worthy of it.

ANUBIS. At last!

(*The* SPHINX *looks down on the plain, leaning over to examine it. Suddenly she turns round. The last trace of the greatness and fury which had transformed her has disappeared.*)

Dog! You lied to me.

ANUBIS. I?

THE SPHINX. Yes, you! Liar! Liar! Look along the road. Oedipus is coming back, he's running, he's flying, he loves me, he has understood!

ANUBIS. You know very well, Madam, what accompanies his success and why the Sphinx is not dead.

THE SPHINX. Look how he jumps from rock to rock, just as my heart leaps in my breast.

ANUBIS. Convinced of his triumph and your death this young fool has just realized that in his haste he's forgotten the most important thing.

THE SPHINX. Mean wretch! Do you mean to tell me he wants to find me dead?

ANUBIS. Not you, my little fury: the Sphinx. He thinks he's killed the

Sphinx; he will have to prove it. Thebes won't be satisfied with a fisherman's yarn.

THE SPHINX. You're lying. I'll tell him everything. I'll warn him. I'll save him. I'll turn him away from Jocasta, from that miserable town. . . .

ANUBIS. Take care.

THE SPHINX. I shall speak.

ANUBIS. He's coming. Let him speak first.

(OEDIPUS, *out of breath, comes in down stage left. He sees the* SPHINX *and* ANUBIS *standing side by side.*)

OEDIPUS (*saluting*). I'm happy to see, Madam, what good health the immortals enjoy after their death.

THE SPHINX. What brings you back here?

OEDIPUS. The collecting of my due.

(*Angry movement on the part of* ANUBIS *towards* OEDIPUS, *who steps back.*)

THE SPHINX. Anubis!

(*With a gesture she orders him to leave her alone. He goes behind the ruins. To* OEDIPUS.)

You shall have it. Stay where you are. The loser is a woman. She asks one last favor of her master.

OEDIPUS. Excuse me for being on my guard, but you've taught me to distrust your feminine wiles.

THE SPHINX. Ah! I was the Sphinx. No, Oedipus. . . . You will bear my mortal remains to Thebes and the future will reward you . . . according to your deserts. No . . . I ask you merely to let me disappear behind this wall so that I may take off this body in which, I must confess, I have, for some little while, felt rather . . . cramped.

OEDIPUS. Very well. But be quick. At the last bugles. . . . (*The bugles are heard.*) You see, I speak of them and they are sounded. I must waste no time.

THE SPHINX (*hidden*). Thebes will not leave a hero standing at her gates.

VOICE OF ANUBIS (*from behind the ruins*). Hurry, Madam, hurry. It looks as though you're inventing excuses and dawdling on purpose.

THE SPHINX (*hidden*). Am I the first, God of the Dead, whom you've had to drag by the clothes?

OEDIPUS. You're trying to gain time, Sphinx.

THE SPHINX (*hidden*). So much the better for you, Oedipus. My haste might have served you ill. A serious difficulty occurs to me. If you bear into Thebes the body of a girl instead of the monster which the people expect, the crowd will stone you.

OEDIPUS. That's true! Women are simply amazing; they think of everything.

THE SPHINX (*hidden*). They call me: The virgin with the claws. . . . The singing bitch. . . . They will want to identify my fangs. Don't be alarmed. Anubis! My faithful dog! Listen, since our faces are only shadows, I want you to give me your jackal's head.

OEDIPUS. Splendid idea!

ANUBIS (*hidden*). Do what you like, so long as this shameful play-acting may come to an end and you may become yourself once more.

THE SPHINX (*hidden*). I shan't be long.

OEDIPUS. I shall count up to fifty as I did before. I'll have my own back.

ANUBIS (*hidden*). Madam, Madam, what are you waiting for?

THE SPHINX. Now I'm ugly, Anubis. A monster! . . . Poor boy . . . supposing I frighten him. . . .

ANUBIS. Don't worry, he won't even see you.

THE SPHINX. Is he blind then?

ANUBIS. Many men are born blind and only realize it the day a home-truth hits them between the eyes.

OEDIPUS. Fifty!

ANUBIS (*hidden*). Go on. . . . Go on. . . .

THE SPHINX (*hidden*). Farewell, Sphinx.

(*From behind the wall comes the staggering figure of a girl with a jackal's head. She waves her arms in the air and falls.*)

OEDIPUS. About time too! (*He rushes forward, not stopping to look, lifts the body, and takes a stand down stage right. He carries the body before him on his outstretched arms.*) No! Not like that! I should look like that tragedian I saw in Corinth playing the part of a king carrying the body of his son. The pose was pompous and moved no one.

(*He tries holding the body under his left arm; behind the ruins on the mound appear two giant forms covered with rainbow veils: the gods.*)

OEDIPUS. No! I should be ridiculous. Like a hunter going home empty-handed after killing his dog.

ANUBIS (*the form on the right*). To free your goddess's body of all human contamination, perhaps it might be as well for this Oedipus to disinfect you by bestowing on himself at least a title of demi-god.

NEMESIS (*the form on the left*). He is so young. . . .

OEDIPUS. Hercules! Hercules threw the lion over his shoulder! . . . (*He puts the body over his shoulder.*) Yes, over my shoulder. Over my shoulder! Like a demi-god!

ANUBIS (*veiled*). Isn't he simply *incredible!*

OEDIPUS (*moving off towards the left, taking two steps after each of his thanksgivings*). I have killed the unclean beast.

NEMESIS (*veiled*). Anubis . . . I feel very ill at ease.

ANUBIS. We must go.

OEDIPUS. I have saved the town!

ANUBIS. Come along, mistress, let us go.

OEDIPUS. I shall marry Queen Jocasta!

NEMESIS (*veiled*). Poor, poor, poor mankind! . . . I can stand no more, Anubis. . . . I can't breathe. Let us leave the earth.

OEDIPUS. I shall be king!

(*A murmur envelopes the two huge forms. The veils fly round them. Day breaks. Cocks crow.*)

ACT III

THE WEDDING NIGHT

THE VOICE

The coronation and nuptial celebrations have been going on since dawn. The crowd has just acclaimed the queen and the conqueror of the Sphinx for the last time.

Every one goes home. In the little square of the royal palace now rises only the slight murmur of a fountain. Oedipus and Jocasta find privacy at last in the nuptial chamber. They are very tired and heavy with sleep. In spite of a few hints and civilities on the part of destiny, sleep will prevent them from seeing the trap which is closing on them for ever.

(*The platform represents Jocasta's bedroom, which is as real as a little butcher's shop amid the town buildings. A broad bed covered with white furs. At the foot of the bed, an animal's skin. On the right of the bed, a cradle.*

On the right fore-stage, a latticed bay window, looking on to the square of Thebes. On the left fore-stage, a movable mirror of human size.

OEDIPUS *and* JOCASTA *are wearing their coronation costumes. From the moment the curtain rises, they move about in the slow motion induced by extreme fatigue.*)

JOCASTA. Phew! I'm done! You are so active, dear! I am afraid, for you, this room will become a cage, a prison.

OEDIPUS. My dear love! A scented bedroom, a woman's room, yours! After this killing day, those processions, that ceremonial, that crowd which still clamoured for us under our very windows. . . .

JOCASTA. Not clamoured for us . . . for you, dear.

OEDIPUS. Same thing.

JOCASTA. You must be truthful, my young conqueror. They hate me. My dress annoys them, my accent annoys them, they are annoyed by my blackened eyelashes, my rouge, and my liveliness!

OEDIPUS. It's Creon who annoys them! The cold, hard, inhuman Creon! I shall make your star rise again. Ah! Jocasta! What a magnificent programme!

JOCASTA. It was high time you came. I can't stand it any more.

OEDIPUS. Your room a prison! Your room, dear . . . and our bed.

JOCASTA. Do you want me to remove the cradle? After the death of the child, I had to have it near me, I couldn't sleep. . . . I was too lonely. . . . But now . . .

OEDIPUS (*in an indistinct voice*). But now . . .

JOCASTA. What?

OEDIPUS. I said . . . I said . . . that it's he . . . he . . . the dog . . . I mean . . . the dog who won't . . . the dog . . . the fountain-dog. . . .

(*His head droops.*)

JOCASTA. Oedipus! Oedipus!

OEDIPUS (*awakens, startled*). What?

JOCASTA. You were falling asleep, dear!

OEDIPUS. Me? Never.

JOCASTA. Oh, yes, you were, dear. You were telling me about a dog who won't . . . a fountain-dog. And I was listening.

(*She laughs and herself seems to be becoming vague.*)

OEDIPUS. Nonsense!

JOCASTA. I was asking you if you wanted me to remove the cradle, if it worries you.

OEDIPUS. Am I such a kid as to fear this pretty muslin ghost? On the contrary, it will be the cradle of my luck. My luck will grow in it beside our love until it can be used for our first son. So you see! . . .

JOCASTA. My poor love. . . . You're dropping with fatigue and here we stand . . . (*Same business as with* OEDIPUS.) . . . stand on this wall . . .

OEDIPUS. What wall?

JOCASTA. This rampart wall. (*She starts.*) A wall. . . What? I . . . I . . . (*Haggard.*) What's happening?

OEDIPUS (*laughing*). Well, this time it's you dreaming. We're tired out, my poor sweet.

JOCASTA. I was asleep? Did I talk?

OEDIPUS. We *are* a pretty pair! Here I go telling you about fountain-dogs, and you tell me about rampart walls: and this is our wedding night! Listen, Jocasta, if I happen to fall asleep again (are you listening?), do please awaken me, shake me, and if you fall asleep, I'll do the same for you. This one night of all must not founder in sleep. That would be too sad.

JOCASTA. You crazy darling you, why? We have all our life before us.

OEDIPUS. Maybe, but I don't want sleep to spoil the miracle of passing this joyous night alone, unutterably alone with you. I suggest we remove these heavy clothes, and as we're not expecting any one . . .

JOCASTA. Listen, my darling boy, you'll be cross . . . .

OEDIPUS. Jocasta, don't tell me there's still some official duty on the programme!

JOCASTA. While my women are doing my hair, etiquette demands that you receive a visit.

OEDIPUS. A visit? At this hour?

JOCASTA. A visit . . . a visit . . . a purely formal visit.

OEDIPUS. In this room?

JOCASTA. In this room.

OEDIPUS. From whom?

JOCASTA. Now don't get cross. From Tiresias.

OEDIPUS. Tiresias? I refuse!

JOCASTA. Listen, dear. . . .

OEDIPUS. That's the limit! Tiresias playing the part of the family pouring out their farewell advice. How comic! I shall refuse his visit.

JOCASTA. You crazy dear, *I* am asking you to. It's an old custom in Thebes that the high priest must in some way bless the royal marriage bonds. And besides, Tiresias is our old uncle, our watch-dog. I am very fond of him, Oedipus, and Laïus adored him. He is nearly blind. It would be unfortunate if you hurt his feelings and set him against our love.

OEDIPUS. That's all very well . . . in the middle of the night. . . .

JOCASTA. Do! Please, for our sake and the sake of the future. It's essential. See him for five minutes, but see him and listen to him. I ask you to. (*She kisses him.*)

OEDIPUS. I warn you I shan't let him sit down.

JOCASTA. I love you, dear. (*Long kiss.*) I shall not be long. (*At the right-hand exit.*) I am going to let him know he can come. Be patient. Do it for my sake. Think of me. (*She goes out.*)

(OEDIPUS, *alone, looks at himself in the mirror and tries attitudes.* TIRESIAS *comes in left, unheard.* OEDIPUS *sees him in the middle of the room and turns about face.*)

OEDIPUS. I am listening.

TIRESIAS. Steady, My Lord. Who told you I had saved up a sermon for your especial benefit?

OEDIPUS. No one, Tiresias, no one. But I don't suppose you find it pleasant acting as kill-joy. I suggest you are waiting for me to pretend I have received your advice. I shall bow, and you will give me the accolade. That would be enough for us in our tired state and at the same time custom would be satisfied. Have I guessed right?

TIRESIAS. It is perhaps correct that there is at the bottom of this procedure a sort of custom, but for that, it would be necessary to have a royal marriage with all the dynastic, mechanical, and, I admit, even irksome business which that entails. No, My Lord. Unforeseen events bring us face to face with new problems and duties. And you will agree, I think, that your coronation, and your marriage, appear in a form which is difficult to classify, and does not fit into any code.

OEDIPUS. No one could say more graciously that I have crashed on Thebes like a tile from a roof.

TIRESIAS. My Lord!

OEDIPUS. You must know, then, that classifiable things reek of death. You must strike out in other spheres, Tiresias, quit the ranks. That's the sign of masterpieces and heroes. An original, that's the person to astonish and to rule.

TIRESIAS. Right! Then you will admit that, as I have taken on a job outside the ceremonial sphere, I am striking out on a new line for myself.

OEDIPUS. To the point, Tiresias, to the point.

TIRESIAS. Good. Then I'll go straight to the point and speak in all frankness. My Lord, your auguries look black, very black. I must put you on your guard.

OEDIPUS. Well, if I didn't expect that! Anything else would have surprised me. This is not the first time the oracles have set about me and my audacity has thwarted them.

TIRESIAS. Do you believe they can be thwarted?

OEDIPUS. I am the living proof of it. And even if my marriage upsets the gods, what about your promises, your freeing of the town, and the death of the Sphinx? And why should the gods have pushed me on as far as this room, if this marriage displeases them?

TIRESIAS. Do you think you can solve the problem of free will in a minute? Ah! power, I fear, is going to your head.

OEDIPUS. And power is slipping away from you.

TIRESIAS. Take care! You are speaking to a high priest.

OEDIPUS. Take care yourself, high priest. Must I remind you that you are speaking to your king?

TIRESIAS. To the husband of my queen, My Lord.

OEDIPUS. Jocasta notified me a little while ago that her power is to pass into my hands, in full. Say that to your master.

TIRESIAS. I serve only the gods.

OEDIPUS. Well, if you prefer that way of putting it, say that to the person who is awaiting your return.

TIRESIAS. Headstrong youth! You don't understand me.

OEDIPUS. I understand perfectly well: an adventurer is in your way. I expect you hope I found the Sphinx dead on my path. The real conqueror must have sold it to me, like those hunters who buy the hare from a poacher. And supposing I have paid for the mortal remains, whom will you find ultimately as the conqueror of the Sphinx? The same type of person who has been threatening you every minute and preventing Creon from sleeping: a poor second-class soldier whom the crowd will bear in triumph and who will claim his due . . . (*Shouting.*) *his due!*

TIRESIAS. He would not dare.

OEDIPUS. Ah! You see! I have made you say it. That's the secret of the intrigue. There go your beautiful promises. That is what you were counting on.

TIRESIAS. The queen is more to me than my own daughter. I must watch over her and defend her. She is weak, credulous, romantic. . . .

OEDIPUS. You are insulting her.

TIRESIAS. I love her.

OEDIPUS. She is in need of no one's love but mine.

TIRESIAS. About this love, Oedipus, I demand an explanation. Do you love the queen?

OEDIPUS. With all my being.

TIRESIAS. I mean: do you love to take her in your arms?

OEDIPUS. I love most of all to be taken in her arms.

TIRESIAS. I appreciate that delicate distinction. You are young, Oedipus, very young. Jocasta might be your mother. I know, oh! I know, you are going to reply . . .

OEDIPUS. I am going to reply that I have always dreamed of such a love, an almost motherly love.

TIRESIAS. Oedipus, aren't you confusing love and love of glory? Would you love Jocasta if she were not on a throne?

OEDIPUS. A stupid question which is always being asked. Would Jocasta love me if I was old, ugly, and had not appeared out of the unknown? Do you fancy you cannot be infected by love through touching purple and gold? Are not the privileges of which you speak of the very substance of Jocasta, an organic part of her? We have been each other's from all eternity. Within her body lie fold after fold of a purple mantle which is much more regal than the one she fastens on her shoulders. I love and adore her, Tiresias. At her side, I seem to occupy at last my proper place. She is my wife, she is my queen. I possess her, I shall keep her, I shall find her again, and neither by prayers nor threats can you drag from me obedience to orders from heaven knows where.

TIRESIAS. Think it over again, Oedipus. The omens and my own wisdom give me every reason to fear this wild marriage. Think it over.

OEDIPUS. Rather late, don't you think?

TIRESIAS. Have you had experience of women?

OEDIPUS. Not the slightest. And to complete your astonishment and cover myself with ridicule in your eyes, I am a virgin.

TIRESIAS. You!

OEDIPUS. The high priest of a capital is astonished that a country boy should put all his pride in keeping himself pure for a single offering. You would, no doubt, have preferred a degenerate prince, a puppet, so that Creon and the priests could work the strings.

TIRESIAS. You are going too far!

OEDIPUS. Must I order you again . . . .

TIRESIAS. Order? Has pride sent you mad?

OEDIPUS. Don't put me into a rage! My patience is at an end, my temper is ungovernable, and I am capable of any unpremeditated act.

TIRESIAS. What arrogance! . . . Weak and arrogant!

OEDIPUS. You will have brought it on yourself.

(*He throws himself upon* TIRESIAS, *seizing him by the neck.*)

TIRESIAS. Let me go. . . . Have you no shame? . . .

OEDIPUS. You are afraid that I could, from your face, there, there, close up, and in your blind man's eyes, read the real truth about your behaviour.

TIRESIAS. Murderer! Sacrilege!

OEDIPUS. Murderer! I ought to be. . . . One day, I shall probably have to repent for this foolish respect, and if I dared. . . . Oh! Oh! Why! Gods! look here . . . here . . . in his blind man's eyes, I had no idea it was possible.

TIRESIAS. Let me go! Brute!

OEDIPUS. The future! My future, as in a crystal bowl.

TIRESIAS. You will repent. . . .

OEDIPUS. I see, I see. . . . Soothsayer, you have lied! I shall marry Jocasta. . . . A happy life, rich, prosperous, two sons . . . daughters . . . and Jocasta still as beautiful, still the same, in love, a mother in a palace of happiness. . . . Now it's not so clear, not clear. I want to see! It's your fault, soothsayer. . . . I want to see! (*He shakes him.*)

TIRESIAS. Curse you!

OEDIPUS (*suddenly recoiling, letting* TIRESIAS *go, and putting his hands over his eyes*). Oh! filthy wretch! I am blind. He's thrown pepper at me. Jocasta! Help! Help! . . .

TIRESIAS. I threw nothing, I swear. You are punished for your sacrilege.

OEDIPUS (*writhing on the ground*). You lie!

TIRESIAS. You wanted to read by force the secrets my diseased eyes hold and that I myself have not yet interpreted; and you are punished.

OEDIPUS. Water, water, quickly, it's burning me. . . .

TIRESIAS (*laying his hands over* OEDIPUS' *face*). There, there. . . . Be a good boy. . . . I forgive you. Your nerves are on edge. Come, keep still. Your sight will return, I swear. I expect you got to the point which the gods wish to keep in darkness, or they may be punishing you for your impudence.

OEDIPUS. I can see a little . . . I think.

TIRESIAS. Are you in pain?

OEDIPUS. Less . . . the pain is going. Ah! . . . it was like fire, red pepper, a thousand pinpoints, a cat's paw scrabbling in my eye. Thank you. . . .

TIRESIAS. Can you see?

OEDIPUS. Not clearly, but I can see, I can see. Phew! I really thought I was blind for good and that it was one of your kind of tricks. Besides, I rather deserved it.

TIRESIAS. It's nice to believe in miracles when miracles suit us, and when they don't, it's nice to believe in them no longer but say it is a trick on the part of the soothsayer.

OEDIPUS. Forgive me. I am of a violent and vindictive disposition. I love Jocasta. I was waiting for her, impatiently, and this extraordinary phenomenon, all those images of the future in the pupil of your eyes put me under a spell, made me dizzy—as if I was drunk.

TIRESIAS. Can you see better now? It is an almost blind man asking you.

OEDIPUS. Quite, and I have no more pain. Heavens, I'm ashamed of my conduct towards an infirm old man and a priest. Will you accept my apologies?

TIRESIAS. I was only speaking for your own good and Jocasta's.

OEDIPUS. Tiresias, in a way I owe you something in return, a confession that is difficult to make, and which I had promised myself I would make to no one.

TIRESIAS. A confession?

OEDIPUS. I noticed during the coronation ceremony that you and Creon were making signs to one another. Do not deny it. Well, I wished to keep my identity secret; but I give it up. Listen carefully, Tiresias. I am not a wanderer. I come from Corinth. I am the only child of King Polybius and Queen Merope. A nobody will not soil this marriage bed. I am a king and son of a king.

TIRESIAS. My Lord. (*He bows.*) A word from you would have cleared the atmosphere of the uneasiness created by your incognito. My little girl will be so glad. . . .

OEDIPUS. But wait! I ask you as a favor to safeguard at least this last night. Jocasta still loves in me the wanderer dropped out of the clouds, the young man stepping suddenly out of the shadows. It will unfortunately be only too easy to destroy this mirage tomorrow. In the meantime, I hope the queen will become sufficiently submissive for her to learn without disgust that Oedipus is not a prince fallen from the sky, but merely a prince.

I wish you good evening, Tiresias. Jocasta will be on her way back. I am dropping with fatigue . . . and we want to remain in intimacy together. This is our desire.

TIRESIAS. My Lord, excuse me. (OEDIPUS *makes a sign to him with his hand.* TIRESIAS *stops at the left-hand exit.*) One last word.

OEDIPUS (*loftily*). What is it?

TIRESIAS. Forgive my boldness. This evening, after the closing of the temple, a beautiful young girl came into the private chapel where I work and, without a word of excuse, handed me this belt and said: 'Give it to Lord Oedipus and repeat word for word this sentence: Take this belt: with that you will be able to get to me when I have killed the beast.' I had scarcely tucked away the belt when the girl burst out laughing and disappeared, but I couldn't make out in what direction.

OEDIPUS (*snatching away the belt*). And that's your trump card. You have already built up a whole system in order to destroy my hold on the queen's head and heart. How should I know? A previous promise of marriage. . . . A girl takes her revenge. . . . The temple scandal. . . . Tell-tale find. . . .

TIRESIAS. I was fulfilling my commission. That's all.

OEDIPUS. Miscalculation and bad policy. Go . . . and carry this bad news with all speed to Prince Creon. (TIRESIAS *stays on the threshold.*) He reckoned he was going to scare me! But in point of fact, it is I who scare you, Tiresias. *I* scare you. I can see it written in large letters on your face. It wasn't so easy to terrorize the child. Confess that the child terrifies you, grandpa! Confess, grandpa! Confess I terrify you! Confess at least I make you afraid!

(OEDIPUS *is lying face down on the animal-skin.* TIRESIAS *is standing like a bronze statue. Silence. Then thunder.*)

TIRESIAS. Yes. Very afraid. (*He leaves, walking backwards. His prophetic voice can be heard.*) Oedipus! Oedipus! Listen to me. You are pursuing classic glory. There is another kind: obscure glory, the last resource of the arrogant person who persists in opposing the stars.

(OEDIPUS *remains looking at the belt. When* JOCASTA *comes in, in her night-dress, he quickly hides the belt under the animal-skin.*)

JOCASTA. Well now? What did the old bogy say? He must have tormented you.

OEDIPUS. Yes . . . no. . . .

JOCASTA. He's a monster. He must have proved to you that you are too young for me.

OEDIPUS. You are beautiful, Jocasta . . . !

JOCASTA. . . . That I am old.

OEDIPUS. He rather gave me to understand that I loved your pearls, and your diadem.

JOCASTA. Always damaging everything! Spoiling everything! Doing harm!

OEDIPUS. But you can take it from me, he didn't manage to scare me. On the contrary, I scared him. He admitted that.

JOCASTA. Well done! My love! You, dear, after my pearls and diadem!

OEDIPUS. I am happy to see you again without any pomp, without your jewels and orders, white, young, and beautiful, in our loving room.

JOCASTA. Young! Oedipus! . . . You mustn't tell lies. . . .

OEDIPUS. Again . . . .

JOCASTA. Don't scold me.

OEDIPUS. Yes, I shall scold you! I shall scold you because a woman like you ought to be above such nonsense. A young girl's face is as boring as a white page on which my eyes can read nothing moving; whereas your face! . . . I must have the scars, the tattooing of destiny, a beauty which has weathered tempests. Why should you be afraid of crow's feet, Jocasta? What would a silly little girl's look or smile be worth beside your remarkable face; struck by fate, marked by the hangman, and tender, tender and . . . *(He notices that* JOCASTA *is weeping.)* Jocasta! My dear little girl, you're crying! Whatever's the matter? . . . Oh, look here . . . What have I done? Jocasta! . . .

JOCASTA. Am I so old then . . . so very old?

OEDIPUS. My dear crazy girl! It's you who persist in . . .

JOCASTA. Women say things to be contradicted. They always hope it isn't true.

OEDIPUS. My dear Jocasta! . . . How silly I am! What a clumsy bear I am. . . . Darling. . . . Calm yourself, and kiss me. . . . I meant . . . .

JOCASTA. Never mind. . . . I am being ridiculous. (*She dries her eyes.*)

OEDIPUS. It's all my fault.

JOCASTA. It isn't. . . . There . . . the black is running into my eye now. (OEDIPUS *coaxes her.*) It's all over.

OEDIPUS. Quick, a smile. (*Slight rumbling of thunder.*) Listen.

JOCASTA. My nerves are bad because of the storm.

OEDIPUS. The sky is so bright with stars, so pure.

JOCASTA. Yes, but there is a storm brewing somewhere. When the fountain makes a still murmur like silence, and my shoulder aches, there is always a storm about and summer lightning.

(*She leans against the bay window. Summer lightning.*)

OEDIPUS. Come here, quickly. . . .

JOCASTA. Oedipus! . . . come here a moment.

OEDIPUS. What is it? . . .

JOCASTA. The sentry . . . look, lean out. On the bench on the right, he's asleep. Don't you think he's handsome, that boy? with his mouth wide open.

OEDIPUS. I'll teach him to sleep. I'll throw some water in his open mouth.

JOCASTA. Oedipus!

Oedipus. How dare he sleep when guarding the queen!

Jocasta. The Sphinx is dead and you're alive. Let him sleep in peace! May all the town sleep in peace! May they all sleep every one!

Oedipus. Lucky sentry!

Jocasta. Oedipus! Oedipus! I should like to make you jealous, but it isn't that. . . . This young guard . . .

Oedipus. What is so extraordinary about this young guard then?

Jocasta. During that famous night, the night of the Sphinx, while you were encountering the beast, I had an escapade on the ramparts with Tiresias. I had heard that a young soldier had seen the spectre of Laïus, and that Laïus was calling for me to warn me of a threatening danger. Well . . . that soldier was the very sentry who is guarding us.

Oedipus. Who is guarding us! . . . Anyway. . . . Let him sleep in peace, my kind Jocasta. I shall guard you all right on my own. Of course, not the slightest sign of the spectre of Laïus.

Jocasta. Not the slightest, I'm sorry to say. . . . Poor lad! I touched his shoulders and legs, and kept saying to Zizi, 'Touch, touch,' and I was in a state . . . because he was like you. And it's true, you know, Oedipus, he was like you.

Oedipus. You say: 'This guard was like you.' But, Jocasta, you didn't know me then; it was impossible for you to know or to guess. . . .

Jocasta. Yes, indeed, that's true. I expect I meant to say my son would be about his age. (*Silence.*) Yes . . . I am getting muddled. It's only now that this likeness strikes me. (*She shakes off this uneasy feeling.*) You're a dear, you're good-looking, I love you. (*After an attitude.*) Oedipus!

Oedipus. My goddess!

Jocasta. I approve of your not telling the story of your victory to Creon or to Tiresias, or to everybody. (*With her arms around his neck.*) But to me . . . to me!

Oedipus (*freeing himself*). I had your promise! . . . And but for that boy . . . .

Jocasta. Is the Jocasta of yesterday the Jocasta of now? Haven't I a right to share your memories without anybody else knowing anything about it?

Oedipus. Of course.

Jocasta. And do you remember, you kept saying: 'No, no, Jocasta, later, later when we are in our loving room.' Well, aren't we in our loving room? . . .

Oedipus. Persistent monkey! Charmer! She always ends by getting what she wants. Now lie still. . . . I am beginning.

Jocasta. Oh, Oedipus! Oedipus! What fun! What fun! I'm quite still.

(JOCASTA *lies down, shuts her eyes, and keeps still.* OEDIPUS *begins lying, hesitating, inventing, accompanied by the storm.*)

OEDIPUS. Now. I was nearing Thebes. I was following the goat-track which rounds the hill to the south of the town. I was thinking of the future, of you whom I imagined less beautiful than you are in reality, but still, very beautiful, painted, and sitting on a throne in the center of a group of ladies-in-waiting. Supposing you do kill it, I thought, would you, Oedipus, dare to ask for the promised reward? Should I dare to go near the queen? . . . And I kept walking and worrying myself, when all of a sudden I came to a halt. My heart was beating hard. I had just heard a sort of song. The voice that sang it was not of this world. Was it the Sphinx? My haversack contained a knife. I slipped the knife under my tunic and crept along. Do you happen to know the ruins of a little temple on that hill, with a pedestal and the hind-quarters of a chimera? (*Silence.*)

Jocasta . . . Jocasta . . . Sleeping?

JOCASTA (*awaking with a start*). What? Oedipus . . .

OEDIPUS. You were sleeping.

JOCASTA. I wasn't.

OEDIPUS. Oh, yes, you were. There's a fickle little girl for you! She demands a story and then goes and falls asleep in the middle of it instead of listening.

JOCASTA. I heard it all. You're mistaken. You were speaking of a goat-track.

OEDIPUS. A long way past the goat-track! . . .

JOCASTA. Don't be angry, darling. Are you cross with me? . . .

OEDIPUS. Me?

JOCASTA. Yes, you are cross with me, and rightly. What a stupid silly I am! That's what age does for you.

OEDIPUS. Don't be sad. I'll start the story again, I promise you, but first of all you and I must lie down side by side and sleep a little. After that, we shall get out of this glue and this struggle against sleep which is spoiling everything. The first one to wake up will wake the other. Promise.

JOCASTA. Promised. Poor queens know how to sleep sitting, for a minute between two audiences. But give me your hand. I am too old, Tiresias was right.

OEDIPUS. Perhaps so for Thebes, where girls are marriageable at thirteen. Then what about me? Am I an old man? My head is drooping; I am woken up by my chin hitting my chest.

JOCASTA. You? That's quite different, it's the dustman, as children say! But as for me . . . You began to tell me the most marvelous story in the world and I go and doze away like a grandma beside the fire. And you will punish me by never beginning it over again, and finding excuses. . . . Did I talk?

OEDIPUS. Talk? No. I thought you were being very attentive. You naughty girl, have you some secrets you are afraid you might disclose to me during your sleep?

JOCASTA. I was simply afraid of those foolish things that we sometimes say when sleeping.

OEDIPUS. You were resting as good as gold. So long, my little queen.

JOCASTA. So long, my king, my love.

(*Hand in hand, side by side, they shut their eyes and fall into the heavy sleep of people who struggle against sleep. A pause. The fountain soliloquizes. Slight thunder. Suddenly, the lighting becomes the lighting of dreams. The dream of* OEDIPUS. *The animal-skin is pushed up. It is lifted by the head of* ANUBIS. *He shows the belt at the end of his outstretched arm.* OEDIPUS *tosses about and turns over.*)

ANUBIS (*in a slow mocking voice*). Thanks to my unhappy childhood, I have pursued studies which give me a great start over the riff-raff of Thebes, and I don't think this simple-minded monster is expecting to be confronted by a pupil of the best scholars of Corinth. But if you have played a trick on me, I shall drag you by the hair. (*Up to a howl.*) I shall drag you by the hair, I shall drag you by the hair, I shall grip you till the blood flows! . . . I shall grip you till the blood flows! . . .

JOCASTA (*dreaming*). No, not that paste, not that foul paste! . . .

OEDIPUS (*in a distant, muffled voice*). I shall count up to fifty: one, two, three, four, eight, seven, nine, ten, ten, eleven, fourteen, five, two, four, seven, fifteen, fifteen, fifteen, fifteen, three, four. . . .

ANUBIS. And Anubis would bound forward. He would open his wolf-like jaws!

(*He disappears under the platform. The animal-skin resumes its normal appearance.*)

OEDIPUS. Help me! Help! Help! Come to me! Everybody! Come here!

JOCASTA. What? What is it? Oedipus! my darling! I was sleeping like a lump! Wake up! (*She shakes him.*)

OEDIPUS (*struggling and talking to the* SPHINX). Oh! Madam, Madam! Mercy! Mercy, Madam! No! No! No! No, Madam!

JOCASTA. My pet, don't scare me so. It's a dream. This is me, me, Jocasta, your wife, Jocasta.

OEDIPUS. No, no! (*He awakens.*) Where was I? How ghastly! Jocasta, is that you? . . . What a nightmare, what a horrible nightmare!

JOCASTA. There, there, it's all over, you are in our room, dear, in my arms. . . .

OEDIPUS. Didn't you see anything? Really, how silly I am, it was that animal-skin. . . . Phew! I must have talked. What did I say?

JOCASTA. It's your turn now. You were shouting: 'Madam! No, no, Madam! No, Madam. Mercy, Madam!' Who was that wicked woman?

OEDIPUS. I've forgotten now. What a night!

JOCASTA. And as for me! Your shouts saved me from an unspeakable nightmare. Look! You're soaked through, swimming in perspiration. It's my fault. I let you go to sleep in all those heavy clothes, golden chains, clasps, and those sandals which cut your heel. . . . (*She lifts him up. He falls back.*) Come along! What a big baby! I can't possibly leave you in this state. Don't make yourself heavy, help me. . . .

(*She lifts him up, takes off his tunic and rubs him down.*)

OEDIPUS (*still in a vague state*). Yes, my little darling mother. . . .

JOCASTA (*mocking him*). 'Yes, my little darling mother. . . .' What a child! Now he's taking me for his mother.

OEDIPUS (*awake*). Oh, forgive me, Jocasta, my love, I am being so silly. You see I'm half asleep, I mix up everything. I was thousands of miles away with my mother who always thinks I am too cold or too hot. You're not cross?

JOCASTA. Silly boy! Let me see to you, and sleep away. All the time he's excusing himself and asking forgiveness. My word! What a polite young man! He must have been taken care of by a very kind mother, very kind, and then you go and leave her, there. But I mustn't complain of that. I love with all the warmth of a woman in love that mother who petted you and kept you and brought you up for me, for us.

OEDIPUS. Sweet.

JOCASTA. I should say so! Your sandals. Raise your left leg. (*She takes off his sandals.*) And now the right. (*Same business; suddenly she utters a terrible cry.*)

OEDIPUS. Hurt yourself?

JOCASTA. No . . . no. . . .

(*She recoils, and stares like a mad creature at* OEDIPUS' *feet.*)

OEDIPUS. Ah! my scars. . . . I didn't know they were so ugly. My poor darling, did they alarm you?

JOCASTA. Those holes . . . how did you get them? . . . They must come from such serious injuries. . . .

OEDIPUS. From the hunt, I think. I was in the woods; my nurse was carrying me. Suddenly from a clump of trees a wild boar broke cover and charged her. She lost her head and let me go. I fell and a woodcutter killed the animal while it was belaboring me with its tusks. . . . It's true! But she is as pale as a ghost! My darling! I ought to have warned you. I'm so used to them myself, those awful holes. I didn't know you were so sensitive. . . .

JOCASTA. It's nothing. . . .

OEDIPUS. Weariness and sleepiness put us into this state of vague terror . . . you had just come out of a bad dream. . . .

JOCASTA. No, . . . Oedipus. No. As a matter of fact, those scars remind me of something I am always trying to forget.

OEDIPUS. I always strike unlucky.

JOCASTA. You couldn't possibly know. It's to do with a woman, my foster-sister and linen-maid. She was with child at the same age as myself, at eighteen. She worshipped her husband despite the difference of age and wanted a son. But the oracles predicted so fearful a future for the child that, after giving birth to a son, she had not the courage to let it live.

OEDIPUS. What?

JOCASTA. Wait. . . . Imagine what strength of mind a poor woman must have to do away with the life of her life . . . the son from her womb, her ideal on earth and love of loves.

OEDIPUS. And what did this . . . woman do?

JOCASTA. With death in her heart, she bored holes in the feet of the nursling, tied them, carried it secretly to a mountain-side and abandoned it to the wolves and bears. (*She hides her face.*)

OEDIPUS. And the husband?

JOCASTA. Every one thought the child had died a natural death, and that the mother had buried it with her own hands.

OEDIPUS. And . . . this woman . . . still lives?

JOCASTA. She is dead.

OEDIPUS. So much the better for her, for my first example of royal authority would have been to inflict on her, publicly, the worst tortures, and afterwards, to have her put to death.

JOCASTA. The oracles were clear and matter-of-fact. Before those things a woman always feels so stupid and helpless.

OEDIPUS. To kill! (*Recalling* LAÏUS.) Of course, it isn't infamous to kill when carried away by the instinct of self-defence, and when bad luck is involved. But basely to kill in cold blood the flesh of one's flesh, to break the chain . . . to cheat in the game!

JOCASTA. Oedipus, let's talk about something else . . . your furious little face upsets me too much.

OEDIPUS. Yes, let us talk about something else. I should be in danger of loving you less if you tried to defend this miserable wretch.

JOCASTA. You're a man, my love, a free man and a chief! Try and put yourself in the place of a child-mother who is credulous about the oracles, worn out, disgusted, confined, and terrified by the priests. . . .

OEDIPUS. A linen-maid! That's her only excuse. Would you have done it?

JOCASTA (*with gesture*). No, of course not.

OEDIPUS. And don't run away with the idea that to fight the oracles requires a herculean determination. I could boast and pose as a wonder;

I should be lying. You know, to thwart the oracles, I only had to turn my back on my family, my longings, and my country. But the farther I got from my native town, and the nearer I came to yours, the more I felt I was returning home.

JOCASTA. Oedipus! Oedipus, that little mouth of yours which chatters away, that little wagging tongue, those frowning eyebrows and fiery eyes! Couldn't the eyebrows relax a little, Oedipus, and the eyes close gently for once, and that mouth be used for softer caresses than words?

OEDIPUS. There I go again. A bear, a great bear, and a clumsy one at that.

JOCASTA. You are a child.

OEDIPUS. I'm not a child!

JOCASTA. Now he's off again! There, there, be a good boy.

OEDIPUS. You're right. I'm behaving very badly. Calm this talkative mouth with yours, and these feverish eyes with your fingers.

JOCASTA. One moment. I'll shut the grating. I don't like to know that grating's open at night.

OEDIPUS. I'll go.

JOCASTA. You stay lying down. . . . I'll take a look in the mirror at the same time. Do you want to embrace a fright? After all this excitement, the gods alone know what I look like. Don't make me nervous. Don't look at me. Turn the other way, Oedipus.

OEDIPUS. I'm turning over. (*He lies across the bed with his head on the edge of the cradle.*) There, I'm shutting my eyes.

(JOCASTA *goes to the window.*)

JOCASTA (*to* OEDIPUS). The little soldier is still asleep, he's half-naked . . . and it isn't warm tonight . . . poor lad!

(*She goes to the movable mirror; suddenly, she stops, listening in the direction of the square. A* DRUNK *is talking very loud with long pauses between his reflections.*)

VOICE OF THE DRUNK. Politics! . . . Pol—i—tics! What a mess! They just tickle me to death! . . . Ho! Look! a dead'un! . . . Sorry, a mistake: 's a soldier asleep. . . . Salute! Salute the sleeping army! (*Silence.* JOCASTA *stands on her toes, and tries to see outside.*)

VOICE OF THE DRUNK. Politics! . . . (*Long silence.*) It's a disgrace . . . a disgrace. . . .

JOCASTA. Oedipus, my dear!

OEDIPUS (*in his sleep*). Hi!

JOCASTA. Oedipus! Oedipus! There's a drunk and the sentry doesn't hear him. I hate drunks. I want him sent away, and the soldier woken up. Oedipus! Oedipus! Please! (*She shakes him.*)

OEDIPUS. I wind, I unwind, I calculate, I meditate, I weave, I winnow, I knit, I plait, I cross, . . .

JOCASTA. What's he saying? How beautifully he sleeps! I might die, he wouldn't notice it.

THE DRUNK. Politics!

(*He sings. As soon as the first lines are sung,* JOCASTA *leaves* OEDIPUS, *putting his head back on the edge of the cradle, and goes to the middle of the room. She listens.*)

Madam, what ever are you at?
Madam, what ever are you at?
Your husband's much too young,
Much too young for you, that's flat! . . . Flat. . . .
Et cetera. . . .

JOCASTA. Oh! The beasts . . .

THE DRUNK. Madam, what ever are you at
With this holy marriage?

(*During what follows,* JOCASTA, *bewildered, goes to the window on tiptoe. Then she returns to the bed, and leaning over* OEDIPUS, *watches his face, but still looking from time to time in the direction of the window, where the voice of the* DRUNK *alternates with the murmur of the fountain and the cock crows. She lulls the sleep of* OEDIPUS *by gently rocking the cradle.*)

THE DRUNK. Now, if I were in politics . . . I'd say to the queen: Madam! . . . a minor can't be your man. . . . Take a husband who's serious, sober, and strong . . . a husband like me. . . .

VOICE OF THE GUARD (*who has just awakened. He gradually recovers his self-assurance*). Move on!

VOICE OF THE DRUNK. Salute the waking army! . . .

THE GUARD. Move on! And look sharp!

THE DRUNK. You might at least be polite. . . .

(*As soon as the* GUARD *is heard,* JOCASTA *leaves the cradle, having first muffled* OEDIPUS' *head in the muslin.*)

THE GUARD. D'you want me to stop your mouth?

THE DRUNK. Always politics! What a mess!
Madam, what ever are you at? . . .

THE GUARD. Come on, hop it! Clear off! . . .

THE DRUNK. I'm clearing off, I'm clearing off, but you might be polite about it.

(*During these remarks,* JOCASTA *goes to the mirror. She cannot see herself owing to the moonlight conflicting with the dawn. She takes the mirror by its supports and moves it away from the wall. The mirror itself stays fastened to the scenery.* JOCASTA *drags the frame along, trying to get some light, glancing at* OEDIPUS *who sleeps on. She brings the piece of furniture carefully into the foreground, opposite the prompter's box, so that the public becomes her mirror and* JOCASTA *looks at herself in full view of all.)*

THE DRUNK (*very distant*). Your husband's much too young,
Much too young for you, that's flat! . . . Flat! . . .

(Sound of the SENTRY'S *footsteps, bugle-calls, cockcrows, a kind of snoring noise from the rhythmic, youthful breathing of* OEDIPUS. JOCASTA, *with her face up against the empty mirror, lifts her cheeks by handfuls.)*

ACT IV

OEDIPUS REX

(*17 years later*)

THE VOICE

Seventeen years soon pass. The great plague in Thebes seems to be the first set-back to that renowned good luck of Oedipus. For their infernal machine to work properly, the gods wanted all ill-luck to appear in the guise of good luck. After delusive good fortune, the king is to know true misfortune and supreme consecration, which, in the hands of the cruel gods, makes of this playing-card king, in the end, a man.

(Cleared of the bedroom, the red hangings of which are pulled away into the flies, the platform seems to be surrounded by walls which grow in size. It finally represents an inner courtyard. By a balcony high up Jocasta's room is made to communicate with this court. One gets to it through an open door below, in the center.

When the curtain rises, OEDIPUS, *aged, and wearing a little beard, stands near to the door.* TIRESIAS *and* CREON *are standing on the right and left of the court. Center right, a young boy rests one knee on the ground: he is the* MESSENGER *from Corinth.)*

OEDIPUS. What have I done to shock people now, Tiresias?

TIRESIAS. You are enlarging on things, as usual. I think, and I'll say again, it might be more decent to learn of a father's death with less joy.

OEDIPUS. Indeed. (*To the* MESSENGER.) Don't be afraid, boy. Tell me, what was the cause of Polybius' death? Is Merope so very terribly unhappy?

MESSENGER. King Polybius died of old age, my lord, and . . . the queen, his wife, is barely conscious. She is so old she can't fully realize even her misfortune.

OEDIPUS (*his hand to his mouth*). Jocasta! Jocasta!

(JOCASTA *appears on the balcony; she parts the curtain. She is wearing her red scarf.*)

JOCASTA. What is it?

OEDIPUS. How pale you are! Don't you feel well?

JOCASTA. I admit that what with the plague, the heat, and visits to the hospitals I feel quite exhausted. I was resting on my bed.

OEDIPUS. This messenger has brought me great news, worth disturbing you for.

JOCASTA (*astonished*). Good news? . . .

OEDIPUS. Tiresias blames me for finding it good: My father is dead.

JOCASTA. Oedipus!

OEDIPUS. The oracle told me I should be his murderer, and that I should be the husband of my mother. Poor Merope! She is very old, and my father, Polybius, has died a good natural death!

JOCASTA. The death of a father is never a happy event, as far as I know.

OEDIPUS. I hate play-acting and conventional tears. To be quite genuine, I was so young when I left my father and mother, that I no longer have any particular feelings for them.

MESSENGER. Lord Oedipus, if I may . . .

OEDIPUS. You may, my boy.

MESSENGER. Your indifference is not really indifference. I can explain it to you.

OEDIPUS. Something new.

MESSENGER. I ought to have begun at the end of the story. On his deathbed, the king of Corinth asked me to tell you that you are only his adopted son.

OEDIPUS. What?

MESSENGER. My father, one of Polybius' shepherds, found you on a hill, at the mercy of wild beasts. He was a poor man; he carried his find to the queen who used to weep because she had no children. This is how the honor of performing such an extraordinary mission at the Theban court has fallen to me.

TIRESIAS. This young man must be exhausted after his journey, and he has crossed our town which is full of unhealthy stenches. Perhaps it would be better if he took some refreshment and rested before being questioned.

OEDIPUS. No doubt, Tiresias, you would like the torture to last. You think my world is tottering. You don't know me well enough. Don't you rejoice too soon. Perhaps I am happy to be a child of fortune.

TIRESIAS. I was only putting you on your guard against your sinister habit of questioning, seeking to know and understand everything.

OEDIPUS. Whether I am a child of the muses or of a common tramp, I shall question without fear; I will know things.

JOCASTA. Oedipus, my love, he is right. You get excited. . . . You get excited . . . and you believe everything you're told, and then afterwards . . . .

OEDIPUS. Upon my word! That's the last straw! Unflinchingly I withstand the hardest knocks, and you all plot to make me put up with these things and not try to find out where I come from.

JOCASTA. Nobody is plotting . . . my love . . . but I know . . . .

OEDIPUS. You're wrong, Jocasta. Nobody knows me at present, neither you, nor I, nor any one else. (*To the* MESSENGER.) Don't tremble, my lad. Speak up. Tell us more.

MESSENGER. That's all I know, Lord Oedipus, except that my father untied you when you were half-dead, hanging by your wounded feet from a short branch.

OEDIPUS. Oh! So that's how we come by those fine scars!

JOCASTA. Oedipus, Oedipus, dear . . . come up here . . . Anybody would think you enjoy plunging knives into your wounds.

OEDIPUS. And so those were my swaddling clothes! . . . My story of the hunt is . . . false, like so many others. Well, if that's the way things are . . . I may come of a god of the woods and a dryad, and have been nourished by wolves. Don't you rejoice too soon, Tiresias!

TIRESIAS. You do me an injustice. . . .

OEDIPUS. At any rate, I haven't killed Polybius, but . . . now come to think of it . . . I have killed a man.

JOCASTA. You!

OEDIPUS. Yes! I! Oh! You needn't be alarmed. It was accidental, and sheer bad luck! Yes, I have killed, soothsayer, but as for parricide, you'd better officially give it up. During a brawl with the serving-men, I killed an old man at the cross-roads of Delphi and Daulis.

JOCASTA. At the cross-roads of Delphi and Daulis! . . .

(*She disappears as if drowning.*)

OEDIPUS. There's marvelous material for you to build up a really fine catastrophe. That traveller must have been my father. 'Heavens, my father!' But incest won't be so easy, gentlemen. What do *you* think, Jocasta? . . . (*He turns around and sees* JOCASTA *has disappeared.*) Splendid! Seventeen years of happiness, and a perfect reign, two sons, two daughters, and then this noble lady only has to learn that I am the stranger whom, by the way, she first loved, and she turns her back on me. Let her sulk! Let her sulk! I shall be left alone with my fate.

CREON. Your wife, Oedipus, is ill. The plague is demoralizing us all. The gods are punishing the town and desire a victim. A monster is hiding in our midst. They demand he shall be found and driven out. Day after day the police have failed and the streets are littered with corpses. Do you realize what an effort you are asking of Jocasta? Do you realize that you are a man and that she is a woman, an aging woman at that, and a mother who is disturbed about the contagion? Before blaming Jocasta for a movement of impatience, you might have tried to excuse her.

OEDIPUS. I see what you are getting at, brother. The ideal victim, the monster in hiding. . . . From one coincidence to another . . . wouldn't it be a pretty job, with the help of the priests and the police, to succeed in muddling the people of Thebes and make them believe *I* am that monster!

CREON. Don't be absurd!

OEDIPUS. I think you're capable of anything, my friend. But Jocasta, that's another matter. . . . I am astonished at her attitude. (*He calls her.*) Jocasta! Jocasta! Where are you?

TIRESIAS. She looked as though her nerves were all on edge. She is resting . . . let her be.

OEDIPUS. I am going. . . . (*He goes toward the* MESSENGER.) Now, let us come to the point. . . .

MESSENGER. My Lord!

OEDIPUS. Holes in my feet . . . bound . . . on the mountain-side. . . . How did I fail to understand at once? . . . And then I wondered why Jocasta . . . .

It's very hard to give up enigmas. . . . Gentlemen, I was not the son of a dryad. Allow me to introduce you to the son of a linen-maid, a child of the people, a native product.

CREON. What's this all about?

OEDIPUS. Poor Jocasta! One day I unwittingly told her what I thought of my mother. . . . I understand everything now. She must be terrified, and utterly desperate. In short . . . wait for me. I must question her at all costs, leaving nothing in the dark, so that this horrible farce may come to an end.

(*He leaves by the middle door.* CREON *immediately rushes to the* MESSENGER, *whom he pushes out through the door on the right.*)

CREON. He is mad. What does all this mean?

TIRESIAS. Don't move. A storm is coming to us from the most distant ages. The thunderbolt is aimed at this man, and I ask you, Creon, to let the thunderbolt follow its whims, to wait motionless and not to interfere in the slightest.

(*Suddenly,* OEDIPUS *is seen on the balcony, stranded and aghast. He leans on the wall with one hand.*)

OEDIPUS. You have killed her for me.

CREON. What do you mean, killed?

OEDIPUS. You have killed her for me. . . . That's where she is, hanging . . . hanging by her scarf. . . . She is dead . . . gentlemen, she is dead. . . . It's all over . . . all over.

CREON. Dead? I'm coming. . . .

TIRESIAS. Stay here . . . the priest orders you to. It's inhuman, I know; but the circle is closing; we must keep silent and please stay here . . . .

CREON. You wouldn't stop a brother from. . . .

TIRESIAS. I would! Let the story be. Keep out of it.

OEDIPUS (*at the door*). You have killed her for me . . . she was romantic . . . weak . . . ill . . . you forced me to say I was a murderer. . . . Whom did I murder, gentlemen, I ask you? . . . Through clumsiness, mere clumsiness . . . just an old man on the road . . . a stranger.

TIRESIAS. Oedipus: through mere clumsiness you have murdered Jocasta's husband, King Laïus.

OEDIPUS. Mean wretches! . . . I can see it now! You are carrying on your plot! . . . it was even worse than I thought. . . . You have made my poor Jocasta believe that I was the murderer of Laïus . . . that I killed the king to set her free and so that I could marry her.

TIRESIAS. Oedipus, you have murdered Jocasta's husband, King Laïus. I have known it for a long time, and you are telling lies. I haven't said a word about it either to you or to her or to Creon or to any one else. This is how you reward me for my silence.

OEDIPUS. Laïus! . . . So that's it. . . . I am the son of Laïus and of the linen-maid. The son of Jocasta's foster-sister and Laïus.

TIRESIAS (*to* CREON). If you want to, now's the time. Quickly. There are limits even to harshness.

CREON. Oedipus, through you, my sister is dead. I only kept silent to save the life of Jocasta. I think it is useless to prolong unnecessarily the false mystery and the unravelling of a sordid drama whose intrigue I have finally succeeded in discovering.

OEDIPUS. Intrigue?

CREON. The most secret of secrets are betrayed one day or another to the determined seeker. The honest man, sworn to silence, talks to his wife, who talks to an intimate friend, and so on. (*In to the wings.*) Come in, shepherd.

(*An old* SHEPHERD *comes in, trembling.*)

OEDIPUS. Who is this man?

CREON. The man who carried you bleeding and bound on to the mountain-side according to your mother's orders. Let him confess.

SHEPHERD. To speak means death to me. Princes, why haven't I died before so as not to live through this minute?

OEDIPUS. Whose son am I, old man? Strike, strike quickly!

SHEPHERD. Alas.

OEDIPUS. I am nearer to the sound of something that should not be heard.

SHEPHERD. And I . . . to the saying of something that should not be said.

CREON. You must say it. I wish you to.

SHEPHERD. You are the son of Jocasta, your wife, and of Laïus, killed by you where the three roads cross. Incest and parricide, may the gods forgive you!

OEDIPUS. I have killed whom I should not. I have married whom I should not. I have perpetuated what I should not. All is clear. . . . *(He goes out.)*

(CREON *drives out the* SHEPHERD.)

CREON. Who was the linen-maid and foster-sister he was talking about?

TIRESIAS. Women cannot hold their tongues. Jocasta must have made out that her crime had been committed by a servant to see what effect it had on Oedipus.

(*He holds his arm and listens with bent head. Forbidding murmur. The little* ANTIGONE, *with hair dishevelled, appears on the balcony.*)

ANTIGONE. Uncle! Tiresias! Come up, quickly! Hurry, it's horrible! I heard shrieks inside; mother dear doesn't move any more, she has fallen like a log, and father dear is writhing over her body and stabbing at his eyes with her big golden brooch. There's blood everywhere. I'm frightened! I'm too frightened, come up . . . come up, quickly . . .

(*She goes in.*)

CREON. This time nothing shall prevent me. . . .

TIRESIAS. Yes, I shall. I tell you, Creon, the finishing touches are being put to a masterpiece of horror. Not a word, not a gesture. It would be unkind for us to cast over it so much as a shadow of ourselves.

CREON. Sheer madness!

TIRESIAS. Sheer wisdom. . . . You must admit . . . .

CREON. Impossible. As for the rest, power falls once more into my hands.

(*He frees himself, and at the very moment when he bounds forward, the door opens.* OEDIPUS *appears, blind.* ANTIGONE *is clinging to his clothes.*)

TIRESIAS. Stop!

CREON. I shall go mad! Why, but why has he done that? Better have killed himself.

TIRESIAS. His pride does not let him down. He wanted to be the happiest of men, now he wants to be the most unhappy.

OEDIPUS. Let him drive me out, let them finish me off, stone me, strike down the foul beast!

ANTIGONE. Father!

TIRESIAS. Antigone! My soothsaying staff! Offer it to him from me. It will bring him some luck.

(ANTIGONE *kisses the hand of* TIRESIAS *and carries the staff to* OEDIPUS.)

ANTIGONE. Tiresias offers you his staff.

OEDIPUS. Is he there? . . . I accept it, Tiresias. . . . I accept it. . . . Do you remember, eighteen years ago, I saw in your eyes that I should become blind and I couldn't understand it? I see it all clearly now, Tiresias, but I am in pain. . . . I suffer. . . . The journey will be hard.

CREON. We must not let him cross the town, it would be an awful scandal.

TIRESIAS (*in a low voice*). In a town of plague? And besides, you know, they saw the king Oedipus wished to be; they won't see the king he is now.

CREON. Do you mean he will be invisible because he is blind?

TIRESIAS. Almost.

CREON. Well, I can tell you I have had enough of your riddles and symbols. *My* head is firmly fixed on my shoulders and my feet planted firmly on the ground. I shall give orders.

TIRESIAS. Your police may be well organized, Creon; but where this man goes they will not have the slightest power.

CREON. I . . . .

(TIRESIAS *seizes his arm and puts his hand over his mouth. . . . For* JOCASTA *appears in the doorway.* JOCASTA, *dead, white, beautiful, with closed eyes. Her long scarf is wound round her neck.*)

OEDIPUS. Jocasta! You, dear! You alive!

JOCASTA. No, Oedipus. I am dead. You can see me because you are blind; the others cannot see me.

OEDIPUS. Tiresias is blind. . . .

JOCASTA. Perhaps he can see me faintly . . . but he loves me, he won't say anything. . . .

OEDIPUS. Wife, do not touch me! . . .

JOCASTA. Your wife is dead, hanged, Oedipus. I am your mother. It's your mother who is coming to help you. . . . How would you even get down these steps alone, my poor child?

OEDIPUS. Mother!

JOCASTA. Yes, my child, my little boy. . . . Things which appear abominable to human beings, if only you knew, from the place where I live, if only you knew how unimportant they are!

OEDIPUS. I am still on this earth.

JOCASTA. Only just. . . .

CREON. He is talking with phantoms, he's delirious. I shall not allow that little girl . . . .

TIRESIAS. They are in good care.

CREON. Antigone! Antigone! I am calling you. . . .

ANTIGONE. I don't want to stay with my uncle! I don't want to, I don't want to stay in the house. Dear father, dear father, don't leave me! I will show you the way, I will lead you. . . .

CREON. Thankless creature.

OEDIPUS. Impossible, Antigone. You must be a good girl. . . . I cannot take you with me.

ANTIGONE. Yes, you can!

OEDIPUS. Are you going to desert your sister Ismene?

ANTIGONE. She must stay with Eteocles and Polynices. Take me away, please! Please! Don't leave me alone! Don't leave me with uncle! Don't leave me at home!

JOCASTA. The child is so pleased with herself. She imagines she is your guide. Let her think she is. Take her. Leave everything to me.

OEDIPUS. Oh! . . . (*He puts his hand to his head.*)

JOCASTA. Are you suffering, dear?

OEDIPUS. Yes, in the head, the neck, the arms. . . . It's fearful.

JOCASTA. I'll give you a dressing at the fountain.

OEDIPUS (*breaking down*). Mother . . . .

JOCASTA. Who would have believed it? That wicked old scarf and that terrible brooch! Didn't I say so time and again?

CREON. It's utterly impossible. I shall not allow a madman to go out free with Antigone. It is my duty to . . . .

TIRESIAS. Duty! They no longer belong to you; they no longer come under your authority.

CREON. And pray whom should they belong to?

TIRESIAS. To the people, poets and unspoiled souls.

JOCASTA. Forward! Grip my dress firmly . . . don't be afraid.

(*They start off.*)

ANTIGONE. Come along, father dear . . . let's go. . . .

OEDIPUS. Where do the steps begin?

JOCASTA AND ANTIGONE. There is the whole of the platform yet. . . .

(*They disappear . . .* JOCASTA *and* ANTIGONE *speak in perfect unison.*)

JOCASTA AND ANTIGONE. Careful . . . count the steps. . . . One, two, three, four, five. . . .

CREON. And even supposing they leave the town, who will look after them, who will admit them?

TIRESIAS. Glory.

CREON. You mean rather dishonor, shame. . . .

TIRESIAS. Who knows?

A Full Moon in March

BY W. B. YEATS

CHARACTERS

First Attendant
Second Attendant
The Queen
The Swineherd

(THE SWINEHERD *wears a half-savage mask covering the upper part of his face. He is bearded. When the inner curtain rises for the second time the player who has hitherto taken the part of the* QUEEN *is replaced by a dancer.*)

(*When the stage curtain rises, two* Attendants, *an elderly woman and a young man, are discovered standing before an inner curtain.*)

First Attendant.
What do we do?
What part do we take?
What did he say?
Second Attendant.
Join when we like,
Singing or speaking.
First Attendant.
Before the curtain rises on the play?
Second Attendant.
Before it rises.
First Attendant.
What do we sing?
Second Attendant.
'Sing anything, sing any old thing,' said he.
First Attendant.
Come then and sing about the dung of swine.

(*They slowly part the inner curtain.* The Second Attendant *sings—* The First Attendant *may join in the singing at the end of the first or second verse.* The First Attendant *has a soprano, the* Second *a bass voice.*)

Second Attendant.
Every loutish lad in love
Thinks his wisdom great enough,
What cares love for this and that?
Tó make all his parish stare,
As though Pythagoras wandered there.
Crown of gold or dung of swine.

Should old Pythagoras fall in love
Little may he boast thereof.
What cares love for this and that?
Days go by in foolishness.
O how great their sweetness is!
Crown of gold or dung of swine.

Open wide those gleaming eyes,
That can make the loutish wise.
What cares love for this and that?
Make a leader of the schools
Thank the Lord, all men are fools.
Crown of gold or dung of swine.

(*They sit at one side of the stage near audience. If they are musicians, they have beside them drum, flute and zither.* THE QUEEN *is discovered seated and veiled.*)

THE QUEEN (*stretching and yawning*).
What man is at the door?
SECOND ATTENDANT.
Nobody, Queen.
THE QUEEN.
Some man has come, some terrifying man,
For I have yawned and stretched myself three times.
Admit him, Captain of the Guard. . . .
SECOND ATTENDANT (*speaking as* CAPTAIN OF THE GUARD).
He comes.
(*Enter* THE SWINEHERD.)
THE SWINEHERD.
The beggars of my country say that he
That sings you best shall take you for a wife.
THE QUEEN.
He that best sings his passion.
THE SWINEHERD.
And they say
The kingdom is added to the gift.
THE QUEEN.
I swore it.
THE SWINEHERD.
But what if some blind aged cripple sing
Better than wholesome men?
THE QUEEN.
Some I reject.
Some I have punished for their impudence.
None I abhor can sing.
THE SWINEHERD.
So that's the catch.
Queen, look at me, look long at these foul rags,
At hair more foul and ragged than my rags;

Look on my scratched foul flesh. Have I not come
Through dust and mire? There in the dust and mire
Beasts scratched my flesh; my memory too is gone,
Because great solitudes have driven me mad.
But when I look into a stream, the face
That trembles upon the surface makes me think
My origin more foul than rag or flesh.

THE QUEEN.

But you have passed through perils for my sake;
Come a great distance. I permit the song.

THE SWINEHERD.

Kingdom and lady, if I sing the best?
But who decides?

THE QUEEN.

I and my heart decide.
We say that song is best that moves us most.
No song has moved us yet.

THE SWINEHERD.

You must be won
At a full moon in March, those beggars say.
That moon has come, but I am here alone.

THE QUEEN.

No other man has come.

THE SWINEHERD.

The moon is full.

THE QUEEN.

Remember through what perils you have come;
That I am crueller than solitude,
Forest or beast. Some I have killed or maimed
Because their singing put me in a rage,
And some because they came at all. Men hold
That woman's beauty is a kindly thing,
But they that call me cruel speak the truth,
Cruel as the winter of virginity.
But for a reason that I cannot guess
I would not harm you. Go before I change.
Why do you stand, your chin upon your breast?

THE SWINEHERD.

My mind is running on our marriage night,
Imagining all from the first touch and kiss.

THE QUEEN.

What gives you that strange confidence? What makes
You think that you can move my heart and me?

THE SWINEHERD.
Because I look upon you without fear.
THE QUEEN.
A lover in railing or in flattery said
God only looks upon me without fear.
THE SWINEHERD.
Desiring cruelty, he made you cruel.
I shall embrace body and cruelty,
Desiring both as though I had made both.
THE QUEEN.
One question more. You bring like all the rest
Some novel simile, some wild hyperbole
Praising my beauty?
THE SWINEHERD.
My memory has returned.
I tended swine, when I first heard your name.
I rolled among the dung of swine and laughed.
What do I know of beauty?
THE QUEEN.
Sing the best
And you are not a swineherd, but a king.
THE SWINEHERD.
What do I know of kingdoms? *(Snapping his fingers.)*
That for kingdoms!
THE QUEEN.
If trembling of my limbs or sudden tears
Proclaim your song beyond denial best,
I leave these corridors, this ancient house,
A famous throne, the reverence of servants—
What do I gain?
THE SWINEHERD.
A song—the night of love,
An ignorant forest and the dung of swine.
(QUEEN *leaves throne and comes down stage.*)
THE QUEEN.
All here have heard the man and all have judged.
I led him, that I might not seem unjust,
From point to point, established in all eyes
That he came hither not to sing but to heap
Complexities of insult upon my head.
THE SWINEHERD.
She shall bring forth her farrow in the dung.
But first my song—what nonsense shall I sing?

THE QUEEN.
  Send for the headsman, Captain of the Guard.
SECOND ATTENDANT (*speaking as* CAPTAIN OF THE GUARD).
  I have already sent. He stands without.
THE QUEEN.
  I owe my thanks to God that this foul wretch,
  Foul in his rags, his origin, his speech,
  In spite of all his daring has not dared
  Ask me to drop my veil. Insulted ears
  Have heard and shuddered, but my face is pure.
  Had it but known the insult of his eyes
  I had torn it with these nails.
THE SWINEHERD *(going up stage).*
                                    Why should I ask?
  What do those features matter? When I set out
  I picked a number on the roulette wheel.
  I trust the wheel, as every lover must.
THE QUEEN.
  Pray, if your savagery has learnt to pray,
  For in a moment they will lead you out
  Then bring your severed head.
THE SWINEHERD.
                                    My severed head. *(Laughs.)*
  There is a story in my country of a woman
  That stood all bathed in blood—a drop of blood
  Entered her womb and there begat a child.
THE QUEEN.
  A severed head! She took it in her hands;
  She stood all bathed in blood; the blood begat.
  O foul, foul, foul!
THE SWINEHERD.
                        She sank in bridal sleep.
THE QUEEN.
  Her body in that sleep conceived a child.
  Begone! I shall not see your face again.

(*She turns towards him, her back to the audience, and slowly drops her veil.* THE ATTENDANTS *close the inner curtain.*)

SECOND ATTENDANT.
  What do we sing?

FIRST ATTENDANT.
An ancient Irish Queen
That stuck a head upon a stake.
SECOND ATTENDANT.
Her lover's head;
But that's a different queen,
A different story.
FIRST ATTENDANT.
He had famished in a wilderness,
Braved lions for my sake,
And all men lie that say that I
Bade that swordsman take
His head from off his body
And set it on a stake.

He swore to sing my beauty
Though death itself forbade.
They lie that say, in mockery
Of all that lovers said,
Or in mere woman's cruelty
I bade them fetch his head.

(*They begin to part the inner curtain.*)

O what innkeeper's daughter
Shared the Byzantine crown?
Girls that have governed cities,
Or burned great cities down,
Have bedded with their fancy-man
Whether a king or clown;

Gave their bodies, emptied purses
For praise of clown or king,
Gave all the love that women know!
O they had their fling,
But never stood before a stake
And heard the dead lips sing.

(THE QUEEN *is discovered standing exactly as before, the dropped veil at her side, but she holds above her head the severed head of the* SWINEHERD. *Her hands are red. There are red blotches upon her dress, not realistically represented: red gloves, some pattern of red cloth.*)

FIRST ATTENDANT.
Her lips are moving.

SECOND ATTENDANT.
She has begun to sing.
FIRST ATTENDANT.
I cannot hear what she is singing.
Ah, now I can hear.

(*Singing as* QUEEN.)

Child and darling, hear my song,
Never cry I did you wrong;
Cry that wrong came not from me
But my virgin cruelty.
Great my love before you came,
Greater when I loved in shame,
Greatest when there broke from me
Storm of virgin cruelty.

(THE QUEEN *dances to drum-taps and in the dance lays the head upon the throne.*)

SECOND ATTENDANT.
She is waiting.
FIRST ATTENDANT.
She is waiting for his song.
The song he has come so many miles to sing.
She has forgotten that no dead man sings.
SECOND ATTENDANT *(laughs softly as Head).*
He has begun to laugh.
FIRST ATTENDANT.
No; he has begun to sing.
SECOND ATTENDANT *(singing as Head).*
I sing a song of Jack and Jill.
Jill had murdered Jack;
The moon shone brightly;
Ran up the hill, and round the hill,
Round the hill and back.
A full moon in March.

Jack had a hollow heart, for Jill
Had strung his heart on high;
The moon shone brightly;
Had hung his heart beyond the hill.
A twinkle in the sky.
A full moon in March.

(THE QUEEN *in her dance moves away from the head, alluring and refusing.*)

FIRST ATTENDANT (*laughs as* QUEEN).

SECOND ATTENDANT.
She is laughing. How can she laugh,
Loving the dead?

FIRST ATTENDANT.
She is crazy. That is why she is laughing.

(*Laughs again as* QUEEN)

(QUEEN *takes up the head and lays it upon the ground. She dances before it—a dance of adoration. She takes the head up and dances with it to drum-taps, which grow quicker and quicker. As the drum-taps approach their climax, she presses her lips to the lips of the head. Her body shivers to very rapid drum-taps. The drum-taps cease. She sinks slowly down, holding the head to her breast.* THE ATTENDANTS *close inner curtain singing and then stand one on either side while the stage curtain descends.*)

SECOND ATTENDANT.
Why must those holy, haughty feet descend.
From emblematic niches, and what hand
Ran that delicate raddle through their white?
My heart is broken, yet must understand.
What do they seek for? Why must they descend?

FIRST ATTENDANT.
For desecration and the lover's night.

SECOND ATTENDANT.
I cannot face that emblem of the moon
Nor eyelids that the unmixed heavens dart,
Nor stand upon my feet, so great a fright
Descends upon my savage, sunlit heart.
What can she lack whose emblem is the moon?

FIRST ATTENDANT.
But desecration and the lover's night.

SECOND ATTENDANT.
Delight my heart with sound; speak yet again.
But look and look with understanding eyes
Upon the pitchers that they carry; tight
Therein all time's completed treasure is:
What do they lack? O cry it out again.

FIRST ATTENDANT.
Their desecration and the lover's night.

NOTES

FANTASIO (1834)

If it is true, as many have thought, that Musset's plays are charming but formless, the charm must be either superficial or spurious: how could any profound and genuine quality find expression in art except through form? One suspects that people say "charming but formless" when they find a work impressive but cannot see why.

Francisque Sarcey, for instance—the finest dramatic critic, perhaps, of Musset's century. Musset was not in his line. He preferred the domestic dramas of the mid-century, now long dead. Of *Fantasio* he wrote: "I never had much enthusiasm for this barely finished sketch in which a few charming passages stand out—and even these little more than bravura." Nevertheless, when he comes to sum up Musset as dramatist, Sarcey grants him much more than he had ever denied. He declares that the great gift in dramatic art is that of movement and that, like Molière, Musset had it:

> Take even his most vulnerable works. They are written by a man whom the fairy of the theatre touched at his birth. I don't quite like *Fantasio* and its involved wit. But look at the first scene where he is chatting with his three friends. How it is made! How every word is *en situation!* How, from one end to the other of this conversation, one feels carried along by a big scenic movement!

And again:

> Musset flits above realities without, however, losing himself in the clouds. He is near enough to the truest truth for us to touch it with our fingers. He is ever ready to take off into the ideal where we can follow him effortlessly —hence those flights so native to his genius which transport us.
>
> This rapid transition from the vulgarities of prose to the purest poetry seems natural to us, for the writer holds us forever midway between the two, and whether he rises or falls, he does it with such ease and with so even a movement of the wings that we hardly notice. . .
>
> Yes, this Musset whom they call an imitator is distinguished in the theatre by two qualities of the first order, one of which is not common, the other extraordinarily rare.
>
> Nature gave him the gift of movement: "No one more than he has a precise feeling for interest and effect, for what should be said and what left unsaid, for the point where a scene should be begun, the point to which it has to be brought. No one ever preserved an order so precise beneath an air of abandon and negligence." It is M. Thierry who says this. . .
>
> But to this quality without which a man cannot be a writer at all, Musset adds another without which one cannot be a poet. He had the ability to introduce the miseries of ordinary life among the splendors of the ideal and to create beyond all conditions of place, space, and time types which were not the less real for floating thus in the realms of pure imagination.

Now if this summing-up is valid, almost everything said against Musset the playwright either by Sarcey himself or anyone else falls away. The man whose every word is "en situation," and whose most conversational passages have scenic movement, is no "literary" dramatist. The man who can mingle the miseries of actuality with the splendors of the ideal, who can make easy transitions from prose to poetry, whose poetry is always concrete however fanciful—such a man's work is not likely to lack dramatic tension and richness. The man who knows exactly how long a scene should be, who knows where to start and where to arrive, what to omit and what to include, who is precise yet with a fine appearance of *insouciance*—such a man does not lack a sense of dramatic form.

Look now at *Fantasio*. Has it not, in actual fact, a rather neat and obvious unity? It has two main characters, Fantasio and Elsbeth, and the action of play consists of what the one does to the other: Fantasio acts, Elsbeth is acted upon. (This pattern is very common in drama and might be called "the pedagogic pattern"—Fantasio is the teacher, Elsbeth the taught.) This inner, or essential, action is framed by an outer, or ostensible, action: the courtship of the Prince of Mantua whose arrival and departure give a clear contour to the play. But the fact that this is only the ostensible action is made utterly plain by the play's climax, at which the prince and his aide become the victims of Fantasio's practical joke. Moreover, it is through Fantasio that "the miseries of ordinary life" enter the fairy-tale world and with them the profounder elements of meaning and dramatic conflict.

The princess is "placed" between her lady-in-waiting who lives exclusively in the private realm of romance and her father who belongs to the public realm of politics and war. From both these directions Elsbeth is driven towards marriage with the Prince of Mantua. The Lady is thrilled at the prospect of a romantic affair, her illusions being most patently revealed when she imagines that it is the prince who is disguised as a jester. The King, though he declares at first that he will never sacrifice his daughter's happiness to interests of state, later prepares to do so without qualms. It is Fantasio who steps in and prevents the marriage. A pretty irony: for Fantasio, as his name indicates and his talk confirms, is supposedly a fantastic with no status in society, while the King and the Lady are supposed to know the sensible thing to do. Musset, like other Romanticists, has something to say about the wisdom of fantasy, the stupidity of official commonsense.

Fantasio's relation to Elsbeth is contrasted also with that of the Prince of Mantua, who is, in a sense, his rival. Both men insist on approaching Elsbeth in disguise. But here again there is a difference between the true and the ostensible. Ostensibly, Fantasio's is the more humiliating disguise. In fact, though, "foolishness" is again shown to be wiser than "sanity." The

Prince of Mantua who belongs more wholeheartedly to the public realm of politics and war than the King himself is the unwisest person in the play.

Fantasio is contrasted with the Prince of Mantua in not being really a suitor. The audience—represented on the stage by The Lady—expects all the time that Fantasio will take the Prince's place at the wedding. But once again Musset avoids the purely idyllic or sentimental formula. His Fantasio has put on his disguise without erotic motive. His motive was only to evade his creditors and to watch the royal comedy from the royal box. If he becomes involved in Elsbeth's fate it is as a human being not as a male animal. "Chance has bade cross on its great roadway two wheels which were not following in the same rut and which could not press the same dust." At this point one realizes, perhaps, that the *sententiae* concerning man in the very discursive second scene (the one which Sarcey calls the first) were not fancy talk. Fantasio has not changed at the end. He is still the outcast, the lonely one, the man of the nineteenth-century. At the beginning he declared that there was no such thing as love. At the end nothing has as yet happened to change his opinion. There can be no happy ending—but also no unhappy one. "Everyone has his own spectacles; no one exactly knows what is the color of his glasses. Who can tell me truly if I am happy or unhappy, good or evil, sad or gay, foolish or witty?"

DANTON'S DEATH (1835)

Goronwy Rees writes:

> *Danton's Death* might well be interpreted as a conflict between Danton's love of life and Robespierre's revolutionary dogmatism, with Danton's defeat sweetened by his preference for dying rather than spilling more blood. Presented on the stage today, the play might well be seen as a Trotskyist version of the struggle between Trotsky and Stalin. To read the play thus is to lose the impartiality which Buchner so subtly maintains . . . the conflict in his play is less a conflict between Danton and Robespierre than a conflict of both with the necessity to which both must submit.

If any writer knew how to put politics into a play, Büchner did. Yet *Danton's Death*, as Mr. Rees indicates, is not merely a political play. Its characters are not the right people and the wrong as in westerns, war movies, and proletarian literature. They are concrete and felt from within. Differing from Mr. Rees, I should say that the author's sympathies do seem to lie with Danton rather than Robespierre but that, unlike most radicals, Büchner does not let his sympathies run away with him. He prefers Danton but he is not writing down simply his preferences. Robespierre has a place in the scheme of things—unfortunately. This *unfortunately* gives us what Mr. Rees rightly diagnoses as fatalism. A famous letter of Büchner's is relevant here:

> I have been studying the history of the Revolution. I felt as if annihilated by the terrible *fatalism of history*. I see in men's nature a horrible uniformity, in human relations an unavoidable violence, exercised by all and by none. The individual only foam on the wave, greatness a mere accident, the mastery of genius a puppet play, a ridiculous struggle against an iron law, to understand which is the highest that can be achieved, to rule it impossible. . . . The "must" is one of the curses with which man is baptized. The saying: it must needs be that offences come, but woe to that man by whom the offence cometh—is horrible. What is it in us that lies, murders, steals?

This fatalism seems to me not an elaborate philosophy of pessimism secretly delighted in, like Schopenhauer's. It is an humble and tortured bewilderment before the awful problem of necessity. Büchner's attitude to the equally torturing problem of liberty and authority is similar.

Büchner was certainly a political thinker and a radical one at that. But his thinking was not bounded by politics. He wanted to know the whole meaning of life. "What is it in us that lies, murders, steals?" In *Danton's Death,* politics is put in the larger frame of history, and history in the larger frame still of human existence. Thus Büchner approaches something very like tragedy: the tragedy of history in the first place, and in the second simply the old tragedy of being a man. Mr. Rees has some good words on the first of these tragedies:

> Danton's tragedy is that he is no longer an agent of history, has no function to perform; he can no longer act, he can only protest, and his apathy and lassitude come from his awareness that his historical moment is over. Yet across the action of the play, as across the mind of Robespierre, falls the gigantic shadow of Danton's greatness during the September days. The curse of the "must" has passed to the bloodstained figures of Robespierre and Saint-Just, and in Robespierre awareness of his fate reaches an extreme intensity, most of all in the monologue in which, like Hitler, he declares himself a sleepwalker . . .

The second and more traditional tragedy is shown in Büchner's insistence on the isolation of the tragic figure, an isolation which is made to represent the loneliness of the human situation. His two carefully balanced main characters both feel it. Danton says at the outset: "We are thick-skinned, our hands reach out to each other but it's waste of time, leather rubs against leather—we are very lonely." And Robespierre, after comparing himself with Christ: "They are all leaving me—all is waste and empty—I am alone."

This second tragedy is even more apparent in the thematic treatment of death. The play is not called *Danton and Robespierre,* after all, but *Danton's Death.* Death and the imagery of death (corpses, worms, putrefaction, sleep) are prominent not merely in the execution scene but throughout the play. Robespierre and Saint-Just, the whole anti-Danton party, are the death-bringers and even the death-preachers.

So much for the theme—which cannot but be clear to the careful reader. The form of the play is less transparent. One's first impression is of brilliance in the parts. But the director of this play should beware of assuming that there is no over-all structure. He (and every good reader directs the play, if only in the theatre of his mind) should list the scenes one by one—there are from 6 to 10 in each act—and set down the names of the chief characters in each and the gist of the business transacted. After this, if he is sensitive to lyric, psychological, and thematic values, as well as to narrative values, he will not be disposed to delete very much or to change the order of the scenes.

Büchner is known in Germany as the great proto-modern of the drama, as against Schiller who looks back to Shakespeare. Yet it would not be absurd to say that Schiller preserved the letter, Büchner the spirit of Shakespeare. To be sure, Büchner is a great naturalist two generations before the official birth of dramatic naturalism. But naturalism is at its best when least natural and most poetic. The conversation of Büchner's Frenchmen is earthy but it is also, in an admirable way, artificial: ". . . for me there are no dates, no changes. I am always one thing only, an unbroken longing and desire, a flame, a stream . . ." It is one of Büchner's whores talking! The dialogue of the whole play is so rich with imagination, so dense with meaning—it is not surprising that one's first impression is of the quality of particular speeches rather than the whole.

Danton's Death will continue to seem formless to the same people who find Elizabethan drama formless—that is, to people who try to fit all drama to the Procrustean bed of the modern "well-made" play. To such readers *Danton's Death* will seem constantly to digress, to expatiate, to tail off—in a phrase, to stand in need of streamlining by Orson Welles. Those, on the other hand, who have cultivated a little sympathy for the "open," chronicling, episodic, broad-sweeping kind of play will be ready to observe the subtlety and deadly accuracy which Büchner's "loose" form permits.

Shakespearean form tends to the multiplication of persons, a multiplication which is a help, not a handicap, if the playwright has the art to exploit parallelism and contrast to the top of their bent. In a "modern" play the playwright might give force to the contrast of Danton and Robespierre by stripping everything else away from it. His play would then have that starkness and simplicity which much of the best recent drama has achieved. The Shakespearean way, however, is not to strip and subtract but to enrich and add. So Büchner. Danton is set over against Robespierre, but alongside him is Camille Desmoulins. Another "unnecessary" character is Danton's wife. But in Büchner's pattern, Danton and wife parallel Camille and wife. They also parallel Danton and harlot. Of course, the word *parallel* is too precise. With the similarity go differences. A complex pattern of similarity and difference makes up the play. The basic unit is the short scene. And the procedure is to arrange the scenes in an order that creates variety of rhythm and tempo, significant interaction of meanings, all within the steady flow of the play as a whole.

LA PARISIENNE (1885)

Obviously this play is a superb "portrait of a lady." But Aristotle was, I think, right when he said that a drama is "an imitation, not of men, but of an action and of life," that is, not portraiture, but a grouping of people and events, of a subject, and a subject that is rooted in life. More skilful than the direct strokes of portraiture is the way in which Becque defines Clotilde by her relationships with three different men.

He starts with a comic device, or joke, which expresses the initial paradox of Clotilde's situation: that she has re-shuffled conventional erotic and marital relationships. This fact is first brought sharply to the attention of the audience by the famous *coup de théâtre* in Act One: the man who seemed to be her husband, by the conventional test of domestic bickering, is her lover. This point is reiterated as a running joke throughout the play in a manner that will seem merely tiresome if we are concerned with it merely as a joke but which we can see to be dramatically functional if we are concerned with the "imitation of an Action." It is true naturalistic comedy in that the comic complication comes about not by fantastic invention but by substituting for the conventionally dramatic something a good deal closer to everyday life. Pedestrian naturalists substitute a dull reality for amusing reality. Naturalists of genius show truth to be more dramatic than fiction. They do not invent paradoxes. They find them.

In naturalistic comedy, the comic device uncovers the facts for us. Thus, in *La Parisienne,* the first sensational use of the central joke tells us that, erotically considered, Clotilde is married to Lafont. As the joke is repeated, and the little triangle better defined, we find that the cards are not so heavily stacked against the legal husband after all. The first two acts are the comedy of Lafont. At the outset he appears as the supplanter of the husband. But he is forever on the way out. We gradually realize that, if Dusmesnil is not Clotilde's favorite bedfellow, he is someone, perhaps, that she is more deeply loyal to. In the Third Act Clotilde is just signing off a third man. This relationship has been very simple. She wanted something out of Simpson—for her husband. If we are prepared to think sexual intercourse rather unimportant, this play can be regarded as highly idealistic: Clotilde's sexual attachment to other men is as nothing compared to her non-sexual attachment to her husband. Of course the action of the play changes nothing. Clotilde takes Lafont back. "We're very weak, it is true, for those who charm us, but we always come back to those who love us." She does not say "to those we love." Her attitude to eros is entirely passive. That is why her acceptance of Lafont does him no great credit. In the realm where she is active, Clotilde serves her husband like a loyal wife. That is why his cuckold's position has more dignity than her lover's. By the time we come to the last lines of the play, in which the basic joke is again repeated, a situation bristling with ironies has been very completely and very elegantly defined.

La Parisienne, in its plainness, is a highly unusual comedy. Becque is at a great distance from the classical comedy of Molière which proceeded on a ground work of *commedia dell' arte* devices (as described by Bergson). He is almost equally far from Wilde and Shaw, for there are no epigrams in his play, practically nothing that is witty when removed from its context. Yet it is, throughout, very sharply and closely comic, and Sarcey (who by temperament was as unsympathetic to Becque as to Musset) put his finger on the comic method of his dialogue. In Becque's plays, he wrote, "every retort is a trait."

In *La Parisienne,* an occasional passage is amusing out of context:

> I'm a good, staunch, reactionary. I love order, quiet, well-established principles. I want the churches to be open if I feel like going into one. I want the shops also open and full of pretty things . . .

In context these remarks have twice as much weight because, coming from Clotilde, they are only half-consciously witty: they are partly an unconscious and naive give-away.

I can think of no play so naturalistic as this which is at the same time so purely comic. In our time the comic writers penetrate very little into life, are not, in the deeper sense, naturalistic; the naturalistic writers have little sense of comedy. I say "naturalistic in the deeper sense" because Becque does not bother to be naturalistic in unnecessary ways, such as in eliminating soliloquies. Nor is his naturalism an easy propagandist device. Compare him with Brieux or Galsworthy! The propagandist naturalists would be interested in the subject of *La Parisienne* only insofar as it allowed them to make a point about, say, the double standard. The topic, indeed, arises in Becque's play and, in one passage, is explicitly mentioned. But it never jumps out of the frame of Becque's picture. Becque is a moral writer in that he brings the actions of men into high relief and, by achieving form, demonstrates his love of order. But he does not relieve you of your responsibility to make your own decisions. His business is done when he has presented an imitation of an action and of life.

ROUND DANCE (1897)

No one, I think, has ever done justice to this play *as a play*. A generation ago it bewildered the bourgeoisie throughout Central Europe and, unfortunately, was praised by its champions chiefly for that reason. Look back at the early American editions of the play, and you will see that it was presented to the public, or rather to that section of it that buys *erotica* in limited editions, as something cutely naughty, delightfully decadent. No wonder Schnitzler himself was rather embarrassed by the play and for many years tried to prevent its being performed.

For *Round Dance* is a singularly direct piece of work. Starting from the desperately gay sex life of late nineteenth-century Vienna, Schnitzler creates a sad image of modern life—and human life generally. Upon this chaos he imposed a very neat pattern: boy meets girl. The sexual game is danced in pairs and can best be shown so on the stage where dialogue, in its original sense of talk between two people, is a sort of basic dramaturgic dance-step. Thus far life and dramatic art are in harmony. But life reaches a climax in copulation, conversation being only preparation and aftermath; while on the stage—not for reasons of prudency only—climactic actions tend to be in the background, preparations and aftermaths being what is actually presented to us.

Necessarily Schnitzler adopts the pattern of *art*, but, precisely because he is an artist, what he is most concerned about is expressing *life*. Thus his play presents the preparations and the aftermaths of copulation while keeping the act itself as a sort of unseen center. Thus the pattern of art is, in a sense, played against the pattern of life. The whole play is in words—in a production we would see less love-making than in the average movie—and yet the whole subject is sex. (When the play was produced under Schnitzler's supervision he was always eager to tone down stage directions or dialogue if ever attention seemed to be drawn to overtly sexual gestures.) And if it be asked why, in that case, we need the sexual action of the play at all, it is because the play, though in words like all important drama, is not a discussion of sex (like, say, Shaw's *Getting Married*) but a dramatic presentation of it. The interaction between the copulations and the conversations is the source alike of dramatic tension and of meaning.

The formal formula of the play is: complicate the *pas de deux*, the dance of boy and girl, with the *change-your-partners*, all the while preserving the simple two-at-a-time presentation. This formula imposes so rigid a pattern upon the chaos that at best a *tour de force* might be expected. Schnitzler avoids mere mechanical symmetry by a further complication—by adding the pattern of *before-and-after*. The purpose of changing the partners is to show us the same person confronting two different lovers and thus revealing two distinct parts of himself. But if we look at the play again we note that Schnitzler has already shown two parts of each performer within each single scene. People are different before and after copulation. Before, a woman may be reluctant and, after, eager, while her man is eager before and reluctant after. The *pas de deux*, the *change-your-partners*, and the *before-and-after* patterns give Schnitzler a large number of possible combinations. They are not, so far as I can see, exploited in any exactly symmetrical way. The only close unity the play has is within each scene. Otherwise, one can simply note that Schnitzler tries to cover the main strata of Viennese society (people, Bohemians, bourgeoisie, nobility), and that, by changing the partners, he makes each scene interact violently with the one preceding and the one following. Thus *Round Dance* is less a drama than a chain of one-actors—"ten dialogues" is Schnitzler's laconic subtitle. The effect is cumulative, and what binding together there is is effected by the linking of the last scene with the first. On the social scale, and perhaps sexually too, all the other characters occupy a place between the two extremes of The Prostitute and The Count.

The Count is the last character to appear and he brings the play to a kind of culmination. (It has no climax.) Since Schnitzler's aim is to render his Action, rather than to have it explained by a *raisonneur*, few of his characters drop obvious hints of the play's meaning. In The Count, though he is no *raisonneur* either, Schnitzler feels entitled to be a little more explicit. So he makes him garrulous and philosophical. The Count is too foolish and inconsistent to be simply the author's mouthpiece. But just for that reason Schnitzler can give him things to say which happen to be true and close to the meaning of the whole criticism of life offered by the play. For instance: "I am sure it is a mistake to believe that the spiritual and the physical are separable." But The Count is effete. He cannot live by his best intuitions. He can only wish afterwards that he had. "It would have been beautiful if I had only kissed her eyes." *It would have been* . . . Sex itself The Count describes as "something which *may* be very beautiful." Meanwhile, "there is no happiness. . . . Pleasure, intoxication—we can have that," and afterwards "sleep is the great leveller like its brother death." Passages like this shed some light back on earlier scenes—the analyst of the play should look again at some of the speeches of The Young Gentleman, for instance.

Human love is always imperfect because no human being can ever be perfectly dovetailed into another. Schnitzler exploits this permanent source of dramatic, and so often comic, tension, and reinforces it with an analysis of the modern ingrown personality (not peculiarly modern, doubtless, yet especially characteristic of modern times). His people are all egotists—that is, split and disastrously incomplete personalities. The first symptom of such limitation is the separation—conscious in some of Schnitzler's characters, unconscious in others—of pleasure and happiness, lust and love. Schnitzler's Vienna is a sort of hell, the same kind of hell portrayed by most good naturalistic drama and fiction: everyday life with a curse on it. And, like most successful naturalists, Schnitzler suggests his passion for the good by the intensity of his vision of the bad.

THE SNOB (1912)

Anyone who knows what a play is can see how this firm and simple structure is built. There are three acts, each consisting of several interviews between two or more of the main characters. The Action is the conquest of Marianne by Christian Maske. In the first act, Christian moves towards his goal by discarding his parents. In the second, he inverts this procedure, deciding that a better method is to bring his parents back. (Cross-currents are created by the death of his mother and the unprepared meeting of The Count and his father.) In the third act, the outward conquest of Marianne —symbolized by marriage—is confirmed by the conquest of her spirit, effected by a lucky series of lies.

The difficulty presented by this play is not in elusiveness of structure but simply in the job of acting it, and this, not because it is "literary," but because it is supremely an actor's play—a play for supreme actors. The modern actor is accustomed to a type of drama which demands realistic acting but which has little or no reference to any real world. How, then, can he tackle Sternheim who is above all concerned with the real world but demands a non-naturalistic mode of presentation? The play got performed, of course, in the heyday of modern German acting and has been successfully revived since the Second World War by Gustaf Gruendgens, but it has never, I think, been done in English. For it requires a style, and our stage today is styleless. Or, if our actors will on occasion master a refined comic manner, it will be that of some school of comedy that is remote enough to be regarded as "artificial," that is, unsatiric, without reference to us. Sternheim demands an artificial style that has not been refined away from all reference to this life, a style whose very artifice, like that of good caricature, is an intensification of the real. What actors today have the craft and the vitality for him?

I hope this question is not rhetorical. Sternheim is one of the very few writers in this century who has achieved critical comedy at all. His hard, clipped prose is the expression of what has become a rarer and rare thing—a strictly comic way of seeing things. So is his severe portraiture. So is his ferociously funny use of device. (Examine for instance the eavesdropping in act three, the soliloquies of Christian that are also comic "turns.") His uncompromising sense of reality drove him, interestingly enough, away from the rounded corners of domestic drama back to the angularity of high comedy. In order to speak the more unerringly of the real world he found himself, like all satirists and comedians, creating also a world of his own. The world of Luise and Theobald, Count Palen and Christian is a fairly astonishing world—another limbo of the same hell depicted in Schnitzler's *Round Dance*. And what is most astonishing of all, I feel, is how serious and how funny, how weighty and how light of touch Sternheim can be at the same time. The ludicrous approaches farce in Act Three when Christian lectures Marianne on philosophy while at the same time undressing her for the wedding night; yet this episode makes a strong point strongly. Similarly, in Act One, an exposition is achieved and a story set in motion while the act is bound together by two bits of silly significant business: the tying of a tie and the formulating of a reply to an invitation. This is comic art as we scarcely see it any more. Perhaps we cannot do it full justice—but shouldn't we try?

SWEENEY AGONISTES (1926)

Mr. Eliot alludes to the play in his *The Use of Poetry and the Use of Criticism*:

> The ideal medium for poetry, to my mind, and the most direct means of social "usefulness" for poetry, is the theatre. In a play of Shakespeare you get several levels of significance. For the simplest auditors there is the plot, for the more thoughtful the character and conflict of character, for the more literary the words and phrasing, for the more musically sensitive the rhythm, and for auditors of greater sensitiveness and understanding a meaning which reveals itself gradually. . . . I once designed, and drafted a couple of scenes, of a verse play. My intention was to have one character whose sensibility and intelligence should be on the plane of the most sensitive and intelligent members of the audience; his speeches should be addressed to them as much as to the other personages of the play—or rather, should be addressed to the latter who were to be material, literal-minded and visionless, with the consciousness of being overheard by the former. There was to be an understanding between this protagonist and a small number of the audience, while the rest of the audience would share the responses of the other characters in the play. Perhaps this is all too deliberate, but one must experiment as one can.

Asked by Mr. Nevill Coghill who Sweeney is, how he saw him, what sort of a man he was, Mr. Eliot replied:

> I think of him as a man who in younger days was perhaps a professional pugilist, mildly successful; who then grew older and retired to keep a pub.

Mr. Coghill's own comments in the same context *(T. S. Eliot, A Symposium compiled by Richard March and Tambimuttu)* are also pertinent. Mr. Coghill is reporting his first acquaintance with the play:

> I was at once moved by the quick, pert, rhymes and rhythms, and the sense of how extremely effective they would be on the stage. And there was that palmary jazz-lyric *Under the Bamboo*. . . . In the end, however, my eye fell on the title-page, and there lay the two little latch-keys left by Mr. Eliot for those who wish to enter his intention: a quotation from Aeschylus, countered by one from St. John of the Cross. . . . I now entered the vision; it appeared to be about a normal man of violence, the natural Orestes, the man who cuts his way out of a problem. His natural motives of horror and disgust have their natural expression in murder. But in an obliquity no less natural, instead of plucking out his own eye

> to enter the Kingdom of Heaven, he tries to pluck out what his eye has seen; and this is murder, the wrong kind of surgery, wrong and useless for (as in the case of Orestes) it brings retribution. KNOCK KNOCK KNOCK. . . . The true solution of Sweeney's predicament, which he neither knew nor took, was not natural but supernatural, namely to divest himself of the love of created beings.

Sweeney Agonistes on the stage. Almost the first thing a director must decide before staging this play is how he is going to interpret the protagonist. I gather that Mr. Rupert Doone, who has produced the play more than once in England, took Sweeney to be the murderer who had put the gallon of lysol in the bath. This interpretation makes for a very clear, concrete, and almost realistic play, a clearer, more concrete and more realistic play, perhaps, than the one Eliot has written.

Sweeney, surely, resembles Harry in *The Family Reunion* in that he has *wished* murder, whether or not he has committed it. To a Christian, wishing a sin is tantamount to committing it; and Eliot's subject, I think, is sin rather than crime, murderousness rather than murder—a subject that is very hard to put across the footlights. A director has simply to acknowledge that the play is somewhat symbolic and abstract.

At least these were my thoughts when I myself produced the play in the library of Schloss Leopoldskron, Salzburg, in the spring of 1949. In addition to naturalistic objects (couch, table, chairs, empty bottles, cigarette smoke), we used a written title slung across the "stage": YOU DON'T SEE THEM, *YOU* DON'T, BUT *I* SEE THEM. It so happened that the last three words of this title were painted on a separate piece of cardboard. Accordingly, until Sweeney's entrance, we displayed only the words: YOU DON'T SEE THEM, *YOU* DON'T, BUT. Sweeney made his entrance from the audience, scanned the incomplete sentence, and with a quick gesture completed it by putting the final board in place: *I* SEE THEM.

In actual use this clumsy-sounding stage-business proved exciting. It also helped the audience to understand what Eliot is trying to say. I might also report that the castle library made an admirable auditorium for the play, perhaps a better one than a real theatre would have. Our not having a stage seemed also no disadvantage. There was a dais for Doris' couch, and enough space in front of it for Sweeney to walk forward —it seems good to have Sweeney walk, as it were, out of the frame of the picture and into (i.e. towards) the audience.

Our production was certainly not the definitive one, but *any* sympathetic production—and this is the important point—will bring out much that the mere reader of the play is likely to miss: for instance, the explosive effect of the various entrances. The most explosive of all the entrances is, of course, that of Snow and Swarts as minstrels in black face. It initiates the last and most brilliant part of Eliot's play. One admires not only the transitions from verse to song and back (twice) but also Eliot's use of that essential feature of theatre: several-things-going-on-at-the-same-time. An essential part of the musical episode is the silent figure of Sweeney. In fact the episode seems to bring to birth, as a sort of protest against its frivolity, Sweeney's long, climactic speech.

One need scarcely dwell on the theatricality of other non-verbal details of the piece: the card game, the intruding telephone, the knocks on the door—repeated in the same pattern till they batter like policemen or doom.

Should a director indicate any sort of connection between the two fragments? Mr. John Finch has suggested reading Mr. Eliot's poem "Sweeney among the Nightingales" between the two scenes. But is one sure that the Sweeney of the poem is also the Sweeney of the play? And, if so, does the sudden introduction of a reader suit the play? Reading something that stands in no relation to the play's narrative? At Schloss Leopoldskron, we simply ran one scene into the next in an effort to make one play out of two fragments. There is a case for regarding *Sweeney Agonistes,* despite its subtitles, as complete. To me at any rate it seems a more fully rounded treatment of the Orestes theme than *The Family Reunion.* The latter has the extra bulk, not of amplitude, but of dilution. It is interesting that Mr. Eliot has its protagonist actually speak the words: "You don't see them, *you* don't, but *I* see them" as part of a long rigmarole about the Eumenides, who this time stand rigid and fleshless in a window, instead of singing and dancing in black face and holding syncopated conversations. It is easy to see—and profitable to ponder—that *The Family Reunion* is a dilution of *Sweeney Agonistes.*

THE THREEPENNY OPERA (1928)

In his *Gesammelte Werke,* Brecht provides the play with the following notes:

THE READING OF PLAYS

For this opera there is no reason to change the motto which John Gay chose for his own *Beggar's Opera*—"*Nos haec novimus esse nihil.*" As far as the printed form of this work is concerned, it presents scarcely more than the prompt-book of a play that has been unreservedly given over to the theatre. It therefore appeals more to the expert than to the "enjoyer." And it should be said that a transformation of as many spectators and readers as possible into experts is highly desirable—it is also under way.

The Threepenny Opera treats of bourgeois conceptions not only in representing them but also in the *way* in which it represents them. The spectator is shown that portion of real life which he wishes to find presented on the stage, but since, at the same time, he is shown some things which he does not wish to see there, and since also he sees his wishes not only carried out but also criticized (he sees himself not as subject but as object), he is thereby enabled to give the theatre a new function. But because the theatre strenuously resists having its function changed, it is a good thing if the potential spectator *reads* plays which are written not only to be presented in the theatre but also to change the theatre: he should read them out of mistrust for the theatre. Today we witness the absolute ascendancy of the theatre over dramatic literature. The ascendancy of the apparatus of the theatre is the ascendancy of the means of production. The apparatus of the theatre resists any change in its functions by immediately assimilating such drama as it comes in contact with, eating away from it everything but the most indigestible elements, which appear in performance to be mere eccentricities. The necessity for playing the new drama properly is lessened by the fact that the theatre can, after its own fashion, play anything: it makes everything "theatrical." Of course, there are economic reasons for this.

TITLES AND BOARDS

The boards and/or screens on which the titles of scenes and songs are projected are a primitive attempt at the *"literarisation of the theatre,"* which, along with the literarisation of all such concerns of public interest, must be developed very much further.* Literarisation means the combination of what is "embodied" with what is "formulated." It enables the theatre to demonstrate its connection with other forms of intellectual activity.

Against these titles there is the objection, from the standpoint of academic dramaturgy, that the author of the play should include all that is to be said in the action itself, that the work itself must express everything: the spectator, so to say, does not think *over* the matter but *out of* the matter. But this way of subjugating everything to one idea, this passion for driving the spectator in one direction so that he can look neither right nor left, up nor down, is, from the standpoint of the new dramaturgy, to be avoided. Drama, too, can use footnotes. One must be able to turn back to an earlier page. Complex seeing must be practiced. "Thinking above the stream" may be more important than "thinking in the stream."

These boards of ours make possible and indeed compel a new style from the actor. This is *the epic style.* On reading the projections of the boards the spectator takes up the attitude of "watching while smoking."

*Readers who wish to know how far the use of projections is carried in performances of *The Threepenny Opera* are referred to German and Austrian stage editions of the play. [E. B.]

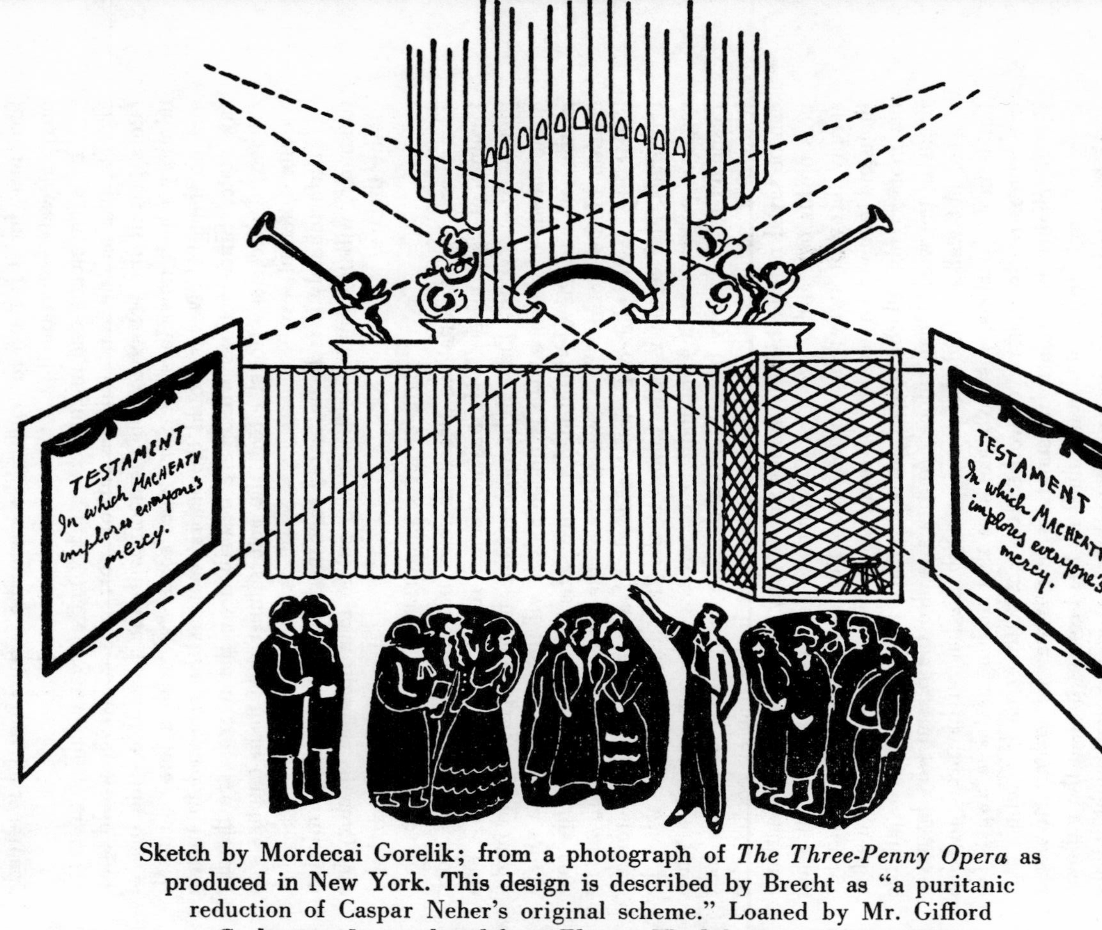

Sketch by Mordecai Gorelik; from a photograph of *The Three-Penny Opera* as produced in New York. This design is described by Brecht as "a puritanic reduction of Caspar Neher's original scheme." Loaned by Mr. Gifford Cochran and reproduced from *Theatre Workshop*, April-July, 1937.

And through this attitude he enforces a better and more intelligent performance, for it is hard to "enthral" a man who is smoking; he is already busy, already entertained.

By such means one might very quickly get a theatre full of dramatic experts, just as one gets stadiums full of sport experts. Never would spectators permit the actors to fob them off with the miserable little bits of mimicry which nowadays they produce "somehow" with a few rehearsals and no thought! Never would the actors' material be accepted in such a raw state. Since actions which are described on the boards are thereby robbed of direct emotional effect, the actors must give them emphasis in a quite different way.

Unfortunately it is to be feared that the boards, and even permission to smoke, will not suffice to bring the public to a more satisfactory use of the theatre.

THE CHIEF CHARACTERS

The character of Jonathan Peachum must not be reduced to the stock formula of "old miser." He has no regard for money. Since he is suspicious of everything that might awaken hope, money seems a quite inadequate means of defence. He is undeniably a villain, and at that a villain in the sense of the old-fashioned theatre. His crime consists in his conception of the world. This conception of the world is worthy, in all its horribility, to be placed beside the deeds of any of the more notorious criminals, and yet he is only following the "trend of the times" when he regards poverty as a commodity. To give a concrete example: when Peachum takes money from Filch in the first scene, he would never lock it up in a cash-box—he would simply stick it in his trouser pocket. He can be saved neither by this money nor by any other. It is conscientiousness on his part and a proof of his complete desperation that he does not simply throw it away; he cannot throw the least thing away. With ten thousand pounds he would not think otherwise. In his opinion neither his money (nor all the money in the world) nor his head (nor all the heads in the world) can suffice. And this is also the reason why he never works, but walks round the premises, with his hat on his head and his hands in his pockets, just to make sure that nothing is taken away. No one who is really afraid ever works. It is not pettiness on Peachum's part that he chains the Bible to its stand for fear it may be stolen. He never gives a thought to his son-in-law until he has brought him to the gallows, since he cannot even conceive of any personal values that might induce him to change his attitude towards a man who has taken his daughter away. The other crimes of Mackie the Knife interest him only in so far as they provide a means for liquidating him. As for Peachum's daughter, she is like his Bible—nothing more than a means of support. The effect of this is not so much repulsive as shattering. When a man is drowning, his worldly goods in general are of little use to him. But he would welcome a lifebelt.

The actress playing Polly will do well to study Mr. Peachum; she is his daughter.

MacHeath should simply be portrayed by the actor as bourgeois. The bourgeois predilection for robbers is explained by the fallacious premise that a robber is not a bourgeois. This error is fathered by another: a bourgeois is not a robber. Is there then no difference between the two?

Yes. A robber isn't always a coward. The attribute "peaceloving," which is attached to the middle class in the theatre, is applicable here when the business-man MacHeath expresses aversion to spilling blood when it is not absolutely necessary—for carrying on the business. The limitation of blood-spilling to a minimum, its rationalization as a business principle. In moments of emergency MacHeath displays extraordinary skill in fencing. He knows what he owes to his reputation. A certain romanticism, *so long as care is taken that it becomes known*, serves the above-mentioned rationalization. He makes very sure that all the daring, or at least fear-inspiring, deeds of his employees are ascribed to him, and tolerates just as little as a university professor that his assistants should ever put *their* signatures to a piece of work. With regard to women, he impresses them less as handsome than as comfortably-situated. The original drawings for Gay's *Beggar's Opera* show a man of about forty, rather undersized but well-built, with a head like a radish, slightly bald, yet not without dignity. He is thoroughly steady, has no humor whatsoever, and his respectability speaks for itself in that his business objective is not so much the robbing of strangers as the exploitation of his own employees. He takes pains to stand in well with the guardians of public security, even when it entails some expense, and all this not merely for his own safety—his practical sense tells him that his own safety and the safety of the present order of society are inextricably bound up together. Any action against the public, such as that with which Peachum threatens the police, would fill Mr. MacHeath with the deepest disgust. In his own eyes, his relations with the ladies of Wapping certainly need an excuse; that excuse, however, is furnished by the peculiar nature of his business. He has taken the opportunity of utilizing a purely business relationship for purpose of pleasure, to which he, as a bachelor, is entitled in moderation; but so far as this intimate side is concerned, he chiefly treasures the regular and pedantically punctual visits to a certain coffee-house in Wapping because they are a *habit*, and the cultivation and multiplication of habits are the chief aim of his bourgeois existence.

In any case the actor must on no account take these visits to an unruly house as the basis for his characterization of MacHeath. This habit is simply one of the far from rare, though inexplicable, cases of bourgeois daemonism.

MacHeath naturally prefers to meet the sexual requirements of his nature by combining them when he can with certain homely amenities—by sleeping, for example, with women who are not without means. In his marriage he sees an insurance of his business. The nature of his business makes unavoidable his temporary absence from the metropolis, trivial as he may regard it, and his employees are extremely unreliable. In dreaming of his future, he sees himself, not hanging from the gallows, but standing by the side of a peaceful trout-stream which he can call his own.

The Commissioner of Police, Brown, is a very modern phenomenon. He conceals within himself two very different people: the private citizen and the official. And this is not a schism *in spite of* which he lives, but one *by* which he lives. And in company with him the whole of society. In private he would never lend himself to that which as an official he considers his duty. In private he cannot hurt a fly (and wouldn't need to). Hence his affection for MacHeath is completely genuine. Not even certain monetary advantages deriving therefrom can make it suspect: after all, everything in this life is tainted. . . .

HINTS FOR THE ACTORS

As far as putting the material across is concerned, the spectator should not experience "empathy"; rather there should be a two-way traffic between actor and spectator, for in spite of all strangeness and separateness the actor addresses himself, ultimately, to the spectator. Also the actor should tell the spectator more about the character he represents than is to be found "in his part." He must naturally behave in such a way as facilitates the action, but he must also be able to take into consideration his relationship to events other than those in the plot; he must not serve the plot alone. For example, when Polly is in a love scene with MacHeath, she is not only MacHeath's beloved but also Peachum's daughter, and not only Peachum's daughter but also her father's employee. Her relationship with the spectator must contain her criticism of the spectator's own popular conception of robbers' wives and merchants' daughters.

[1]The actors should avoid portraying the gang as a collection of gloomy individuals with red handkerchiefs round their necks, who frequent low haunts and with whom no respectable man would drink a glass of beer. They are naturally steady, sedate men, some of them inclined to obesity and they are all quite affable outside their profession.

[2]The actors can here show the usefulness of the bourgeois virtues and the intimate connection between the tender emotions and knavery.

[3]Here should be emphasized the brutal energy a man needs in order to create a state of affairs in which it is possible to display the dignity proper to a human being (in this case, a bridegroom).

[4]Here should be represented the "exhibition" of the bride and all her physical attractions at the final moment of reservation. For at the moment when the supply is withdrawn, the demand is driven up to its zenith. The bride is generally desired, and the bridegroom then "makes the running." A thoroughly theatrical proceeding. It should also be shown that the bride eats very little. One often sees the most delicate creatures devour huge meals—but brides? Never.

[5]In the presentation of such things as Peachum's business, the actors need not worry unduly about the progress of the action in the ordinary sense. However, they must depict not a milieu but a series of events. The impersonator of one of these beggars must so enact the process of choosing an effective and suitable wooden leg (trying one, laying it aside, trying another and then returning to the first) that the audience will decide to make another visit to the theatre at just the time when this particular action comes on; and nothing prevents the theatre from announcing such a feature on a "board" upstage.

[6]It is highly desirable that Polly Peachum be regarded by the audience as a pleasant and virtuous girl. Just as she showed in the second scene her entirely unselfish love, now she must display a practical frame of mind without which the former would have been mere frivolity.

[7]These ladies are in undisturbed possession of their means of production. Hence they must not give the impression of being free. To them democracy cannot offer the freedom which it offers to those whose means of production can be taken away.

[8]Actors playing MacHeath, who show no qualms at portraying the death struggle, usually object to singing this third verse: they would naturally not reject a *tragic* presentation of sex. But sex in our time undoubtedly belongs to the realm of comedy, for our sexual life is a direct contradiction of our social life, and this contradiction is comic because it can be historically superseded—by another order of society. Hence the actor must present such a ballad humorously. The representation of sex on the stage is very important—partly because it always brings in a primitive materialism. The artificial and transitory nature of all social superstructures also becomes plainly visible.

[9]This ballad contains, as do others in this work, some lines from François Villon. See also the *Second Finale*, the *Epistle to His Friends*, and *Ballade in Which MacHeath Begs Forgiveness of All. (Ballade de Villon et de la Grosse Margot, Ballade intitulée Les Contrediz de Franc-Gontier, Epistre à ses amis, L'épitaphe Villon, Ballade par laquelle Villon crye mercy à chascun* are the relevant French texts.)

[10]This scene is inserted for such actresses of Polly's part as have a gift for comedy.

[11]Walking round the cage in a circle, MacHeath can now repeat all

the various gaits he has hitherto displayed to the public: the cock-sure step of the seducer, the despairing slouch of the fugitive, the superior tread of self-confidence, etc. In a short space of time he can once again portray all MacHeath's attitudes of the last few days.

[12]At this point, for example, the actor of the Epic Theatre will not strain to aggravate MacHeath's fear of death and make it the dominating effect of the whole act, or the result will be that the subsequent demonstration of *true* friendship is lost upon the audience. (Friendship is only true when restricted. The moral victory of MacHeath's two truest friends will scarcely be lessened by the moral defeat they suffer when they are *not quick enough* in handing over the means of their existence to rescue their friend.)

[13]Perhaps the actor will here find a chance to indicate the following: MacHeath quite correctly realizes that his case is a horrible miscarriage of justice. Indeed, should justice pounce on bandits less infrequently than it does, it would entirely forfeit its present reputation.

ON THE SINGING OF THE SONGS

When he sings, the actor effects a change of function. Nothing is more appalling than when he behaves as though he hasn't noticed that he has left the ground of sober speech and is singing. The three planes—sober speech, oratorical speech, and singing—must always remain separate one from another, and on no account must oratorical speech indicate an intensification of sober speech, or singing an intensification of oratorical speech. Hence, in no case, where words fail for overabundance of feeling, can song be employed. The actor must not only sing but must also show that he is *meant* to be a singer. He is not so much attempting to bring out the feelings contained in his song (can one offer others food which one has already eaten?) as to reveal those "gestures," which, so to speak, are the habits and usages of the body. To this end it is preferable, when he is studying his part, for him not to use the exact words of the text but current vulgar forms of speech which express the same meaning in slang. As far as melody is concerned, he need not follow it blindly: there is a manner of speaking-against-the-music which can be extremely effective and which comes from an obstinate matter-of-factness, independent of and uninfluenced by music or rhythm. Should he take up the melody, this must be an event, to emphasize which the actor can plainly show his own enjoyment of the melody. It is good for the actor if the musicians are visible. It is also good if the actor makes visible preparations for his song (putting a chair in position, combing his hair, etc.). In singing it is particularly important that the manifestor be manifest.

WHY IS MACHEATH ARRESTED TWICE AND NOT ONCE?

The first prison scene is, from the point of view of the German classic drama, a digression. From our point of view it is an example of primitive epic form. It is indeed a digression if one follows the system of the old dynamic drama, insisting on the primacy of the idea, and making the spectator always wish for one definite end—here, the death of the hero. For thus one, so to speak, creates an ever greater demand for the supply and forces the thought all in one channel to enable the spectator to participate strongly with his feelings; feelings only trust themselves on fully certain ground and cannot tolerate disappointments. Epic dramaturgy, taking its stand on materialism, is less interested in the "investment" of its spectators' feelings. Indeed it knows no goals, only endings. It envisages actions proceeding not only in straight lines but also in curves and even leaps. The "dynamic" drama, taking its stand on idealism, treating of the individual, was, when it began its course (among the Elizabethans), more radical in all decisive points than was, two hundred years later, the classic German drama which substituted the dynamics of the represented individual for the dynamics of representation. (The followers of the followers of the Elizabethans have sunk lower, and now the classic dynamics of representation have fallen before the smart, calculated arrangement of a mass of effects; and the individual, in the process of complete decomposition, with nothing outside himself to feed on, yields on the stage nothing but empty "roles." The late bourgeois novel at least worked out a psychology in order, so it hoped, to analyze the individual—as though he still existed!) The great Elizabethan playwrights were not so self-denying in their choice of material. The sweep of their spade was much wider—in relation, for instance, to events not presented on stage. In their dramas all sorts of external influences play a part. They did not reject such deviations of individuals from their rectilinear course as were caused by "life," but instead used these deviations as dynamic motors. An "irritation" penetrates the individual himself and in him is finally overcome. The whole impress of this drama comes from the accumulation of resistances. The desire for a cheap ideal formula does not yet determine the arrangement of the substance. Something of Baconian materialism is in this drama: the individual himself still has flesh and blood and struggles against all formula. Now, wherever there is materialism, there arise epic forms in drama. In comedy, which has always been more materialistic, a "lower" form, they are most frequently apparent. Today, when man must be regarded as "the totality of social relationships," the epic form is the only one which can comprehend those processes that are the dramatist's material for a comprehensive picture of the world. Man, even physical man, can only be understood through the processes in which and by which he exists. He must be considered as the object of one experiment after another conducted by society. The new drama presents these experiments. To this end it must show connections and relationships on all sides.

It needs "static" and has a tension which controls all its individual components. The scenes charge each other with tension. (Epic form is therefore anything but a revue-like stringing together of separate "numbers.")

WHY MUST THE KING'S MESSENGER BE ON HORSEBACK?

This work is a representation of bourgeois society (and not only of the underworld, of the "disreputable"). Bourgeois society has produced a bourgeois world order—and therefore a particular world outlook, without which it could never exist. The arrival of the king's mounted messenger is, as the bourgeois conceives his world, quite indispensable. Mr. Peachum, when he profits financially by the uneasy conscience of society, is using the messenger: what else *could* he use? Theatre people should consider why nothing is more stupid than to do away with the *horse* of the mounted messenger—as nearly all "modernist" directors of this work have done. When a judicial murder is being played it is imperative, in order that the theatre may perform its function in bourgeois society, that the journalist who reveals the innocence of the murdered man should be drawn into court of justice by a swan. For is it not obviously tactless to betray the public into laughing at itself by making the arrival of the mounted messenger an object of merriment? Without the arrival of a mounted messenger in some form or other, bourgeois literature would degenerate into the presentation of actual conditions. The mounted messenger guarantees that one's enjoyment of intolerable conditions shall not be disturbed; he is therefore a *sine qua non* of a literature whose *sine qua non* is non-intervention.

Naturally, the third finale is to be played with absolute seriousness and dignity.

(Kurt Weill's music for *The Threepenny Opera (Die Dreigroschenoper)* is published by Universal-Edition, Vienna. The present English text fits the music. E. B.)

DON PERLIMPLIN (1931)

Poets are often justly accused of writing "literary," non-theatrical plays. But no one in his senses will ever bring that charge against García Lorca. Read the stage directions alone of this play *Don Perlimplin.* In the description of the settings we find a marvelous sense of spatial relations—consider Belisa's window in the prologue, or the five balconies later. We find an equally marvelous sense of movement, not only in the dialogue, but in the use of music and—not to be forgotten—the "black paper birds." Most of all, the author stipulates a scheme of colors that is part and parcel of his drama as well as being lovely in itself. The green of Don Perlimplin's normal clothing, the red of his cloak when he is disguised as the young man: here we have symbols, on the one hand, of life and nature, on the other of death and love—Belisa wears a red velvet cape and later a red dress. The colorless colors, black and white, are just as dramatically used. At the outset the furniture is black while Don Perlimplin's wig is white: thus the organic human figure is highlighted against the inorganic background. Very soon we see Belisa, white in her half-nakedness: and here white is contrasted with white, since Don Perlimplin's is that of age, Belisa's that of youth. The prologue ends with the flight past the balcony of "black paper birds."

It may be that the friends of Lorca's theatre, in their enthusiasm for his use of the non-verbal arts, have done him less than justice as an interpreter of life. For Lorca was a dramatist, and drama is no more pure beauty, like music and abstract painting, than it is pure entertainment, like commercial theatre. The dramatist works in words, and the other arts are for him auxiliary. We should not allow the incredible delicacy of Lorca's workmanship to keep us from seeing that, in *Don Perlimplin,* we have a true drama.

A beautiful young woman is married off to a comic old man. Already on the wedding night she betrays him with representatives of the five races of the earth. Later she loves in particular one young man whose face she has never seen because, in his letters, he pays more attention to her body than to her soul. Now the young man turns out to be her husband in disguise. He wanted to save her by enabling her to love someone more than she loved her own body. If, of course, Belisa is to keep her young man forever, Don Perlimplin must kill him. And thereby the young man kills Don Perlimplin. At this ending, the wires are cleverly crossed. Don Perlimplin speaks in the role of the young man—but Belisa goes on regarding him as Don Perlimplin. In fact she declares she now loves Perlimplin *with body and soul*—but she still anxiously asks after the young man.

A well-defined little action. Lorca's figure of "covering" and "uncovering" as used by the sprites in the play expresses his awareness of form and technique: a special delicacy alike of concealment and revelation is of the essence of the play. The basic dramaturgic pattern is simple. It is the pedagogic pattern again, Don Perlimplin being the teacher, Belisa the pupil; and the teaching proceeds by conflict, experience, and suffering, until the teacher gives his life. Lorca shows his mastery of theatrical beauty, but he also, and fundamentally, is concerned with ugliness and pain, that is, with life. As his American editors put it:

> *Don Perlimplin* is decorous and formal—but that is not to say that it has no verve or sweep of emotion. Always this emotion is focussed, clarified, by an emphasis on form which serves to hold attention on the idea—on Don Perlimplin's neatly worked out intellectualization of the loves and emotions he can no longer participate in. There is an impersonal quality in even the most ardent scenes, even in the language of love. A maintenance of this just balance between form and emotion secures the satiric effect.

And not the satiric effect only, one may add. It is this balance, if I understand aright, that makes the thing a work of art. It secures the *dramatic* effect.

THE INFERNAL MACHINE (1934)

Josephe Péladan, Hugo von Hofmannsthal, and André Gide have all, during the past half century, written interesting plays about Oedipus. As drama, however, none of these can match Cocteau's *Infernal Machine*. The wit and histrionic brilliance of this play need no pointing out. Like Yeats and Lorca, Cocteau indicates his mastery of the stage in marvelously suggestive stage directions. (See, for instance, the initial suggestions for the 4 scenes.) But there are subtleties of form and theme which may escape the casual reader and which the director should try to make clear in the theatre.

As to form, Cocteau clearly belongs to the same phase of dramatic history as Yeats, Eliot, Obey, Lorca, and Brecht. He breaks open the closed form of Sophocles and starts the narrative at a much earlier stage. The action is further "cooled off" by the use of a choric Voice which announces ahead of time the events and their meaning. This cooling off is a liberation of the spectator, whose attention can now dwell, unbothered, on each scene, the urge to know what comes next being minimized. Eschewing Sophoclean concentration, the dramatist writes four acts which in tempo and mood are as distinct as four different plays. Unity is nevertheless achieved, I think, by many small repetitions and by a genuine oneness of theme.

The theme is that the gods constitute an infernal machine* which destroys Oedipus, but that he, though originally a commonplace fellow, outdoes the gods in the end by accepting his fate and entering the glory of myth. It might be asked why the play is needed if the Voice sums all this up. The answer is not only that no summary can ever be the equivalent of a work of art but that the drama in this case elucidates the summary.

> After delusive good fortune, the king is to know true misfortune and supreme consecration, which, in the hands of the cruel gods, makes of this playing-card king, in the end, a man.

Thus the Voice. But the fourth act, which follows, does not obviously endorse this statement. Has Cocteau failed to fulfill his intention? Or does he intend an irony—the Voice's account of things being deliberately contradicted by the facts? Or is the transformation of "playing-card king" into "man" something different from what at first we suppose? The last interpretation seems best to fit the case. One expects, perhaps, that Cocteau's opportunistic and shallow young Oedipus will at last become mighty and profound. One expects, that is to say, a transformation of *character*.

*"*Machine contenant de la poudre et des projectiles et destinée à faire explosion, à répandre la mort*" (*Petit Larousse*).

And partly this is what one gets: one is surprised at the willingness and courage with which Oedipus seeks the truth and accepts his fate. Yet, on the whole, it is not Oedipus' character that changes but his place in the scheme of things, *our* scheme of things. This man who could have had no importance for us had his life continued to be successful becomes, through his misfortunes, legendary, that is, universally significant. A cipher becomes importantly human, thus not only "a man" but "man." Cocteau uses the religious term "consecration." It is but a figure of speech. The apotheosis of Oedipus is purely aesthetic: he enters into the glory of myth where we, the onlookers, the people who know the myths, the backward-lookers, may contemplate him.

Tiresias' declaration that Oedipus has entered into glory sends us back to an earlier speech of Tiresias, addressing Oedipus:

> You are pursuing classic glory (gloire classique). There is another kind: obscure glory (gloire obscure), the last resource of the arrogant person who persists in opposing the stars.

This remark is very close to the centre of Cocteau's play. His vulgar, modern Oedipus is afflicted with a sort of lower *hubris*. He is in great danger of winning for himself obscure—that is, dark, sinister—glory, a legendary *notoriety*. In the end, as I have said, he proves capable of accepting his fate and his glory will indeed be classic. At least in Tiresias' opinion. There will always be plenty of Creons to deny it.

Perhaps a word should be said about other cohesive elements in this play. Look again at the ending. Tiresias tries to explain to Creon that Oedipus and Antigone now no longer come under politicians' authority: they belong "to the people, poets, and unspoiled souls." This conclusion, like Tiresias' remark about glory, takes us back to earlier scenes—to The Son whose child's vision was better than The Matron's, to the first act, in which The Phantom, invisible to chiefs, queens, and high priests, is seen by common soldiers. The end of the first act is in sharp contrast to the end of the last act: Laius, dead, is a private person, Oedipus is "man."

Drama proceeds by revealing and developing relationships between people. Two relationships seem of outstanding importance in this play: that between man and gods, and that between Oedipus and Jocasta. The former nexus is first very clearly described by The Voice, then much more mysteriously depicted in the most difficult of the four acts, the second. Here Anubis and Nemesis-Sphinx stand for the non-human order, the infernal machinery, in all its arbitrariness:

> There are mysteries within mystery, gods above gods. We have our gods and they have theirs. That's what is called infinity.

Nowhere is Cocteau's version of the story more pointedly un-Greek than in having the Sphinx give her secret away.

In most versions, the relationship of Oedipus and Jocasta is entirely overshadowed by the fact of incest. Cocteau brings it into the light. Oedipus is a young fellow ambitious to win a queen, Jocasta a not very young woman who has a penchant for the bodies of nineteen-year-old boys. Strewing his early scenes with premonitions of incest, Cocteau makes Oedipus and Jocasta rather favor the idea of mother-and-son-love. This love remains somewhat sinister, belonging perhaps to the realm of "gloire obscure," until the closing scene of the play. Now that Jocasta is dead and Oedipus mutilated, the marital relation is at an end, and the pair are simply mother and son again. Purified they can pass, with Antigone, into "gloire classique."

A FULL MOON IN MARCH (1935)

W. B. Yeats wrote more plays, and had more to do with the theatre, than either Eliot or Lorca. Although his early plays have too much in common with Victorian closet drama, nearly all of them were performed. What was lacking was not experience in the theatre but a dramatic kind of verse. Between 1910 and 1920 Yeats became a "modern" poet, and this meant, among other things, that he developed a more dramatic mode of utterance that could be used in lyrics and plays alike. The most conspicuous lack in the early Yeatsian drama was made good.

To be sure, the verse of *A Full Moon in March* is not as experimental as that of Eliot's plays. Much of it is in blank verse—a metre which, for theatrical purposes, was pretty much worn out three hundred years ago. In other respects, though, the battle against Shakespeare which Eliot and Yeats (as much as Shaw himself) agree to be necessary for the dramatist today is here continued. No one would dream of calling *A Full Moon* Shakespearean. Insofar as it is derivative, it derives from the Japanese Noh plays. In British drama it is something entirely *sui generis,* a wholely Yeatsian creation, though full of good things for any younger playwright who can take a hint.

Like all the more original playwrights of the 'twenties and 'thirties, Yeats felt the need of breaking down the accepted dramatic forms, of writing with a new freedom, and letting new forms grow. The forms of the nineteenth century, as they culminated in, say, Ibsen and Chekhov, were, so to speak, hermetic. They gave playwrights like Obey and Cocteau and Eliot and Lorca claustrophobia. The new men opened up the drama with choruses and narrators and new materials especially from folktale, myth, and religion.

Sometimes this meant formlessness. But Yeats was on guard. His striving after form and compression is shown in the composition of *A Full*

Moon which exists in an earlier, looser version under the title *The King of the Great Clock Tower*. Yeats found he could do without the king and work with the two main characters and two attendants. The dramaturgic base of *A Full Moon* resembles that of *Don Perlimplin* (and, to a lesser extent, that of *Fantasio*): the subject is the victory of a "good" man, who seems to be fighting a losing battle, over a "good" woman. In both plays the man dies for the woman, and the woman, desolated, is brought closer to self-fulfillment.

The method of the two playwrights also has something in common. Both start with folkish material and employ a fairy-tale atmosphere. Both use very beautifully the non-verbal arts of the stage, visual and auditory. But where Lorca seeks richness, Yeats, whose early plays had staggered beneath their load of decoration, seeks that stabbing violence of emotion which the drama above all other arts can produce. After the excrescences of *The King of the Great Clock Tower* have been cut away, we are left with a small tight structure in four sections:

1. Introduction. A stanzaic poem establishes the theme of love, which is associated with "crown of gold or dung of swine."
2. The main body of the dialogue. In blank verse. Largely a duet of Queen and Swineherd who are identified with "crown of gold" and "dung of swine" respectively. We find that the Swineherd is not interested in winning a kingdom for himself but in introducing the Queen to love, the forest, and the dung of swine. Then we see the violent part of the folktale re-fashioned into a symbol of the sexual act and procreation. That, despite appearances, the Swineherd is the victor is signalized in a gesture: the Queen, contradicting her announced intention, "drops her veil."
3. The dance with the severed head. What the attendants seem to say is that, while in the folktale the Queen defeated the Swineherd and proved it by putting his head on a stake, and while both in folktale and legend it is common enough for a Queen to have a man, our Queen does not quite fit either category. She cuts off his head but then the dead lips sing and the victory at last is with the Swineherd. Literally, she dances to his tune. (Note how the words of both Queen and Swineherd pass imperceptibly on to the lips of the attendants: a triumphant example of Yeats' use of chorus.)
4. The Second Attendant's last two song-poems round off the action. The Swineherd rises, the Queen descends. The Swineherd becomes a "twinkle in the sky." The Queen, we infer, is compared to the statue of a saint descending from its niche. Though saints carry in pitchers "all time's completed treasure" they lack one essential thing: "their desecration and the lover's night." The penultimate

poem—"The moon shone brightly . . . A full moon in March"—sends us back to Section 2 in which the Queen confessed herself "cruel as the winter of virginity." Before the end the winter snow has melted beneath the moon of the spring equinox. Speaking of the story of the severed head in his preface, Yeats says: "it is part of the old ritual of the year: the mother-goddess and the slain god."

In sum, Yeats' dramatic situation is not used to define individual character, or as the starting-point of a plot, but as a gateway to what he called the "deeps of the soul-life." But, at the end, we are not left holding a mere Maeterlinckian mood; we are given a theme, namely, that, if we are to live, our wintry and saintly virginity must descend into the dung of passion.

Perhaps I am making it sound as if Yeats' theme were simply tacked on at the end. Actually, though the theme is stated explicitly enough in the concluding poem, it is also incorporated in the play—not by the logic of event, but by form, by rhythm. One recalls Kenneth Burke's description of the tragic rhythm: from purpose to passion to perception. Is not that exactly the rhythm of *The Full Moon in March*? From the Swineherd's boldly affirmed purpose, to the Queen's climactic passion, to the perception on our part of what it all signifies. A familiar rhythm indeed, though the play seems in most ways an unfamiliar sort of play. Might one not call it a dramatic meditation? For though Yeats disliked the naturalistic drama of thought, he himself called for a theatre that was "masculine and intellectual," a place of "intellectual excitement," of "that unearthly excitement that has wisdom for fruit." *A Full Moon in March* is a general meditation upon life. But I call it a *dramatic* meditation because the generalities, the thoughts, are thoroughly assimilated to the lovely and varied art of the theatre.

N.B. If the reader wants "background" there are nowadays many inexpensive handbooks—such as Freedley & Reeves' *History of the Theatre* and John Gassner's *Masters of the Drama*—where he can find it. My own book *The Playwright as Thinker* was also, in its way, a background book: I was trying to give an historical and sociological account of the modern repertoire or at least a considerable portion of it. The rather fragmentary notes in the present book contribute, if at all, to the understanding of each play as a work of art. I say *if at all* not so much out of modesty as from a feeling that so far dramatic art has not been very consciously understood. There is no book which does for drama even as much as Percy Lubbock did for the novel in *The Craft of Fiction*.

I should like to direct the reader's attention to certain acute analyses of plays in this volume: of *La Parisienne* in Jacques Copeau's *Souvenirs d'un autre temps* and in Louis Jouvet's *Réflexions du Comédien*, and of *The Infernal Machine* in Francis Fergusson's *The Idea of a Theatre*. More detective work has been done on *Sweeney Agonistes* by T. H. Thompson in his essay "The Bloody Wood," reprinted in Leonard Unger's anthology *T. S. Eliot, a Selected Critique*.